Memory Detection

Traditional techniques for detecting deception, such as the "lie-detector test" (or polygraph), are based upon the idea that lying is associated with stress. However, it is possible that people telling the truth will experience stress, whereas not all liars will. Because of this, the validity of such methods is questionable. As an alternative, a knowledge-based approach known as the "Concealed Information Test" has been developed which investigates whether the examinee recognizes secret information – for example a crime suspect recognizing critical crime details that only the culprit could know. The Concealed Information Test has been supported by decades of research, and is used widely in Japan. This is the first book to focus on this exciting approach and will be of interest to law enforcement agencies and academics and professionals in psychology, criminology, policing, and law.

BRUNO VERSCHUERE is an associate professor of forensic psychology at the Psychology Department, University of Amsterdam.

GERSHON BEN-SHAKHAR is a professor emeritus of Psychology at the Hebrew University of Jerusalem, and former President of the Open University of Israel.

EWOUT MEIJER is an assistant professor in the Psychology and Neuroscience Department of Maastricht University.

Memory Detection

Theory and Application of the Concealed Information Test

Edited by

Bruno Verschuere,
Gershon Ben-Shakhar,
Ewout Meijer

CAMBRIDGE
UNIVERSITY PRESS

CAMBRIDGE UNIVERSITY PRESS
Cambridge, New York, Melbourne, Madrid, Cape Town,
Singapore, São Paulo, Delhi, Tokyo, Mexico City

Cambridge University Press
The Edinburgh Building, Cambridge CB2 8RU, UK

Published in the United States of America by Cambridge University Press,
New York

www.cambridge.org
Information on this title: www.cambridge.org/9780521136150

© Cambridge University Press 2011

First published 2011

Printed in the United Kingdom at the University Press, Cambridge

A catalogue record for this publication is available from the British Library

Library of Congress Cataloguing in Publication data
Memory detection : theory and application of the concealed information
test / [edited by] Bruno Verschuere, Gershon Ben-Shakhar, Ewout Meijer.
p. cm.
ISBN 978-0-521-13615-0 (pbk.)
1. Lie detectors and detection. 2. Memory. 3. Deception.
I. Verschuere, Bruno. II. Ben-Shakhar, Gershon.
III. Meijer, Ewout. IV. Title.
HV8078.M46 2011
363.25′4–dc22
2010045954

ISBN 978-0-521-76952-5 Hardback
ISBN 978-0-521-13615-0 Paperback

Dedicated to the memory of David Lykken

Contents

List of figures   *page* x
List of tables   xii
Notes on contributors   xiii
Acknowledgments   xvii

Part I Introduction

Science on the rise: birth and
development of the Concealed Information Test   3
CHRISTOPHER J. PATRICK

1 Encouraging the use of the Guilty Knowledge Test
   (GKT): what the GKT has to offer law enforcement   12
   WILLIAM G. IACONO

**Part II The laboratory: theoretical and
empirical foundations of the Concealed
Information Test**

2 Detecting concealed information using autonomic
   measures   27
   MATTHIAS GAMER

3 Detecting concealed information in less than a
   second: response latency-based measures   46
   BRUNO VERSCHUERE AND JAN DE HOUWER

4 P300 in detecting concealed information   63
   J. PETER ROSENFELD

5 Detecting of deception and concealed information
   using neuroimaging techniques   90
   MATTHIAS GAMER

6   New and old covert measures in the Concealed
     Information Test   114
     EITAN ELAAD

7   Theory of the Concealed Information Test   128
     BRUNO VERSCHUERE AND GERSHON
     BEN-SHAKHAR

**Part III   Field applications of concealed
             information detection: promises and perils**

8   Limitations of the Concealed Information Test in
     criminal cases   151
     DONALD J. KRAPOHL

9   Validity of the Concealed Information Test in
     realistic contexts   171
     EITAN ELAAD

10   Leakage of information to innocent suspects   187
     M. T. BRADLEY, CLAIR A. BAREFOOT, AND
     ANDREA M. ARSENAULT

11   Countermeasures   200
     GERSHON BEN-SHAKHAR

12   Psychopathy and the detection of concealed
     information   215
     BRUNO VERSCHUERE

13   Clinical applications of the Concealed
     Information Test   231
     JOHN J. B. ALLEN

14   Daily application of the Concealed Information
     Test: Japan   253
     AKEMI OSUGI

15   The Concealed Information Test in the courtroom:
     legal aspects   276
     GERSHON BEN-SHAKHAR AND MORDECHAI
     KREMNITZER

Part IV   Conclusions

16   Practical guidelines for developing a CIT   293
     EWOUT MEIJER, BRUNO VERSCHUERE,
     AND GERSHON BEN-SHAKHAR

     Epilogue: current status and future developments in
        CIT research and practice   303
     GERSHON BEN-SHAKHAR, BRUNO
     VERSCHUERE, AND EWOUT MEIJER

     Index   310

Figures

2.1 Typical response pattern of a participant who committed a mock crime and was instructed to conceal knowledge *page* 29

2.2 Phasic heart rate changes of participants who committed a mock crime and subsequently accomplished a CIT 34

4.1 Three ERPs and EOG from the scalp sites Fz, Cz, and Pz 65

4.2 The events in the complex trial protocol 78

4.3 Pz and EOG to probe and irrelevant items in the simple guilty (SG) and countermeasure (CM) conditions 79

5.1 Visualization of the processing stream of functional magnetic resonance imaging (fMRI) data 93

5.2 Results of the ALE meta-analyses of activation peaks in the Differentiation of Deception paradigm and the Concealed Information Test 100

7.1 Conditioned Response Theory 131

13.1 The relationship between ongoing electroencephalographic (EEG) activity (top) and the event-related brain potential (ERP; bottom) 239

13.2 Identity B's ERPs at site Pz for words learned by Identity A and Identity B, and for unlearned words (left column), and comparable data from four college student controls labeled C01–C04 (right column). 240

14.1a An example of responding in the CIT. Examinee A showing inhibition of respiration and larger SCR to the critical item "2" 269

14.1b An example of responding in the CIT. Examinee A showing inhibition of respiration and larger SCR to the critical item "3" 270

14.2a An example of responding in the CIT. Examinee B
       showing larger SCR and HR deceleration to the
       critical item "1"   270
14.2b An example of responding in the CIT. Examinee B
       showing larger SCR and HR deceleration to the
       critical item "4"   271
14.3a An example of responding in the CIT. Examinee C
       showing larger SCR and lower NPV to the
       critical item "4"   271
14.3b An example of responding in the CIT. Examinee C
       showing larger SCR and lower NPV to the critical
       item "2"   272
14.4a An example of responding in the CIT. Examinee D
       showing inhibition of respiration to the critical item "3"   272
14.4b An example of responding in the CIT. Examinee D
       showing inhibition of respiration to the critical item "1"   273

Tables

2.1 Weights and quantification details of physiological measures that were integrated in the logistic regression model for the prediction of the truth status   *page* 39

3.1 The concealed information oddball test   49

3.2 The autobiographical implicit association test   55

4.1 Probe and Iall RTs (ms) in baseline and experimental blocks in SG, CM, and innocent (IC) groups   82

4.2 The number (maximum = 1,000) of bootstrap iterations in which the bootstrapped average (hypothetical) probe was greater than that of the irrelevant items (Iall/Imax)   85

5.1 Included studies in the meta-analysis of activations in the Differentiation of Deception (DoD) and the Concealed Information Test (CIT) paradigm   99

5.2 Significant clusters (p < 0.05, corrected using the false discovery rate) identified in the analyses of activation likelihood estimates (ALE) within the Differentiation of Deception (DoD) and the Concealed Information Test (CIT) paradigm   101

5.3 Individual classifications in neuroimaging studies on deception and information concealment   105

9.1 Frequencies and cumulative relative frequencies of mean standardized scores computed on SRR to critical items in the field studies   173

11.1 A summary of studies designed to examine the effects of countermeasures on the outcomes of the CQT   202

11.2 A summary of studies designed to examine the effects of countermeasures on the outcomes of the CIT   203

12.1 Main findings of psychopathy research on concealed information detection   221

Contributors

JOHN J. B. ALLEN is Distinguished Professor of Psychology, Cognitive Science, and Neuroscience at the University of Arizona. He is a fellow of the Association for Psychological Science, and last year was president of the Society for Psychophysiological Research. His work, published in over 100 journal articles, chapters, and books, has been funded by the National Institutes of Health and the National Alliance for Research in Schizophrenia and Depression (NARSAD). His research interests include: the etiology and treatment of depression, including alternative treatments for depression; the psychophysiological assessment of memory, amnesia, and deception; and the psychophysiological underpinnings of emotion.

ANDREA M. ARSENAULT is a PhD student in the clinical psychology program at the University of New Brunswick. She has a special interest in forensic psychology, primarily in the area of deception detection, especially using physiological recordings. Her current research focuses on the cognitive and emotional factors in deception and detection especially within the Concealed Information Test (CIT) and the Guilty Actions Test. Additionally, she is interested in both the field of memory, specifically encoding and retrieval of eyewitness memory under emotional conditions and in the applicability of psychological research to the legal system.

CLAIR A. BAREFOOT is an MA student at the University of Regina. She has strong interests in the Concealed Information Test and has contributed to developments expanding the use of the test in social settings. The test becomes analogous to a survey technique where individuals are not considered innocent or guilty; rather they are informants who can disclose information without consequence to themselves.

GERSHON BEN-SHAKHAR is a professor emeritus of psychology at the Hebrew University of Jerusalem. His main area of research is cognitive psychophysiology and he has published about 100 articles and book chapters, mostly focusing on the role of stimulus novelty and significance in orienting response elicitation and habituation, and on psychophysiological detection of deception (PDD). His PDD research has dealt with applied issues and with attempts to understand the mechanism underlying differential responding to the significant information in the CIT. Together with John Furedy he authored *Theories and Applications in the Detection of Deception: A Psychophysiological and International Perspective*.

M. T. BRADLEY is a professor of psychology at the University of New Brunswick. His research areas include the studies of deception, and issues in statistics. He conceives of attempts of information concealment and deception as cognitively driven acts that are in definable socially constrained contexts. He has consulted with a wide variety of groups and individuals over issues in the detection of deception.

JAN DE HOUWER is Professor of Psychology at Ghent University. His research concerns the manner in which automatic preferences are learned and can be measured. Regarding the learning of preferences, he focuses on the role of stimulus pairings (associative learning). With regard to the measurement of preferences, he developed new reaction time measures and examined the processes underlying various measures. Jan De Houwer has (co-)authored more than 100 publications in international journals including *Psychological Bulletin*, *Behavioral and Brain Sciences*, and *Journal of Experimental Psychology: General*. He is editor of the journal *Cognition & Emotion*.

EITAN ELAAD is a professor of psychology at the Department of Behavioral Sciences, Ariel University Center, Israel, a post held since 2001. Between 2006 and 2009 he was the chairman of the department. He is the director of the psychophysiological laboratory in which colleagues, doctoral and graduate students are conducting their research. Since 1977 he has been engaged in research and lectures on lying and lie detection. His main fields of interest are psychology and law, decision-making biases, memory, lying behavior, and detection of deception with special emphasis on psychophysiological detection of concealed information.

MATTHIAS GAMER is a postdoctoral researcher at the Department of Systems Neuroscience located at the University Medical Center in Hamburg-Eppendorf, Germany. His research is mainly devoted to forensic psychophysiology with an emphasis on basic as well as applied issues. He conducted several studies utilizing measures of the central (EEG, fMRI) and the autonomic nervous system (SCR, respiration, heart rate, etc.) to characterize psychophysiological mechanisms that are involved in deception and information concealment. He is also working on studies that allow for estimating the validity of the Concealed Information Test in realistic settings.

WILLIAM G. IACONO is Distinguished McKnight University Professor and Director, Clinical Psychology Training Program, University of Minnesota. He has served as a consultant regarding lie detection to the US Congress Office of Technology Assessment, the CIA, and the Joint Security Commission of the Clinton Administration. He served on the Department of Defense Polygraph Institute's Curriculum and Research Guidance Committee and on the Minnesota Department of Corrections Sex Offender Polygraph Task Force. He has testified in state and federal court regarding the scientific status of lie detection, voice stress analysis, and "brain fingerprinting" as well as before the Kansas and Georgia State Legislatures and the US Senate.

DONALD J. KRAPOHL is a former US government polygraph examiner and researcher, and he is assigned to the US Department of Defense National Center for Credibility Assessment (NCCA) at Ft. Jackson, South Carolina. He is a contributor to law enforcement, technical, scientific, government, and general interest publications on the polygraph and related topics. Mr Krapohl is also the Editor-in-Chief of the publications of the American Polygraph Association. His continuing professional interests are the development of best practices for field use of credibility assessment technologies, and engagement between the scientific and practitioner communities in this field.

MORDECHAI KREMNITZER is the Bruce W. Wayne Professor of International Law at the Hebrew University of Jerusalem and was formerly Dean of the Faculty. He teaches criminal law and constitutional law. Since 1994, he has been a senior fellow at the Israel Democracy Institute. Since 2008 has held the post of vice-president of the Israel Democracy Institute. Professor Kremnitzer has published extensively in the fields of criminal, military, public, and international law. He is co-author of the proposal for a new general part of the penal code for Israel (a proposal which has been adopted by the Knesset). In 2009 he received the Humboldt Research Award.

EWOUT MEIJER is an assistant professor at the Psychology and Neuroscience Department of Maastricht University. He has been conducting research on the psychophysiological detection of deception since 2003, and is currently working on the implementation of the Concealed Information Test in collaboration with the Amsterdam police.

AKEMI OSUGI is a polygraph examiner of the Forensic Science Laboratory, Hyogo Prefectural Police Headquarters, in Japan. She has been performing the CIT under the criminal investigation on a daily basis since 2008, and also conducting researches on the mechanisms of the CIT using mainly event-related potentials since 2003.

CHRISTOPHER J. PATRICK is a professor of clinical psychology at Florida State University. His interests include psychopathy, antisocial behavior, substance abuse, emotion, personality, and cognitive neuroscience. He is author of more than 120 articles and book chapters, and Editor of the *Handbook of Psychopathy*. A recipient of Early Career awards from the American Psychological Association and the Society for Psychophysiological Research, Dr Patrick is immediate Past President of the Society for Scientific Study of Psychopathy and serves as a scientific advisor to the DSM-V PPD Work Group.

J. PETER ROSENFELD obtained his PhD at the University of Iowa in 1971, after receiving undergraduate and Masters degrees (English Literature) at Columbia University, and has been full professor at Northwestern University since 1979. He is Past President of the Association for Applied Psychophysiology and Biofeedback (1990–1991), and served on the editorial board of *International Journal of Psychophysiology*, *International Journal of Rehabilitation and Health*, the *Journal of Credibility Assessment and Witness Psychology*, and *Applied Psychophysiology*. Professor Rosenfeld has (co-)authored more than 140 publications. His main research focus since the 1980s has been neuroscientific lie detection.

BRUNO VERSCHUERE is an associate professor of forensic psychology at the Psychology Department, University of Amsterdam. Since 2000 he has conducted research on challenging topics in clinical and forensic psychology, including deception, psychopathy, and the polygraph. His main research focus is to advance deception research using a fundamental analysis in terms of attention and emotion. His research has been published in leading journals in the field, including *Psychological Science*, *Biological Psychology*, and *Psychophysiology*.

Acknowledgments

The editors wish to thank all authors for their contribution and for their willingness to review other chapters. Additionally, we would like to thank John Furedy for his thoughtful comments on previous drafts of this book, and Harald Merckelbach, Peter Van Koppen, and Marko Jelicic for assisting in the review process.

Part I

Introduction

Science on the rise: birth and development of the Concealed Information Test

Christopher J. Patrick

> Intrigued by the polygraphic equipment in my laboratory, my two assistants had asked if I did any lie detector work and I had been forced to admit that I knew nothing about the subject. Equipped as we were with time, facilities, and ignorance, we resolved to do an experiment on lie detection.
>
> (Lykken, 1981)

In 1959, University of Minnesota psychology professor David Lykken reported an experimental study of a new type of lie detector test that he termed the "Guilty Knowledge Test" (GKT). As indicated in the foregoing quote from his 1981 book, Lykken was unfamiliar with established methods of lie detection used by police and other field examiners at the time of this study. As a result, he relied upon basic principles of experimental psychology to devise a test that focused on probing for specific relevant knowledge of the incident under investigation rather than on detection of lying per se.

A cornerstone of Lykken's technique was the fundamental concept of experimental control: to ensure that the observed ("dependent") effect is attributable to the experimental ("independent") manipulation, one must establish a comparison condition that mirrors the experimental condition in all respects aside from the manipulation of interest. With this principle in mind, the GKT was composed of items in multiple-choice format, with alternative choices for each item (one of them crime-relevant, the others extraneous) formulated to appear equally plausible to an innocent examinee. As a function of this, consistently enhanced reactions to crime-relevant alternatives could readily be interpreted as indicating the presence of "guilty knowledge." Another cornerstone of the technique was probability theory: to minimize the likelihood of an innocent examinee exhibiting a guilty pattern of responding by chance, one can simply increase the number of items in the test. With this concept in mind, Lykken designed the GKT to include a series of different items, each referencing a distinct salient detail of the targeted incident – such that a specific probabilistic estimate of "guilt" (i.e., possession of crime-relevant knowledge) could be computed on the basis of an individual's pattern of reactivity to critical items on the test. A further notable feature of Lykken's GKT was the use of a physiological response variable known to be sensitive to the familiarity or meaningfulness of a stimulus event – electrodermal reactivity, or galvanic skin response (GSR) as it was commonly known at the time.

Lykken's inaugural study of the GKT demonstrated the technique to be highly effective in distinguishing between knowledgeable ("guilty") and naïve ("innocent") participants tested regarding their involvement in alternative mock crime scenarios: forty-eight out of forty-eight participants (100 percent) tested regarding a scenario in which they *had not* participated were correctly identified as innocent; forty-four out of fifty (88 percent) tested regarding a scenario in which they *had* participated were correctly identified as guilty. Thus, the mean accuracy of the test across guilty and innocent suspects was 94 percent. In a subsequent study, published the following year, Lykken (1960) demonstrated that individuals pre-instructed in the use of countermeasures (i.e., strategies for defeating the test by inhibiting responses to crime-relevant alternatives, or augmenting reactions to control alternatives; see Chapter 11 of this volume) could nonetheless be successfully detected as guilty on the GKT by systematically comparing their magnitude of reactivity to varying alternatives across items of the test to assess for unexpected non-randomness in response patterns. Examples of non-random response patterns, indicative of deliberate effort to defeat the test, would include instances in which the largest response on most or all items occurred to the second alternative, or in which the crime-relevant alternative reliably yielded the *smallest* response.

Despite the novelty of the approach and the impressive results of these initial studies, the use of physiological measures to detect lies was not a primary investigative focus of Lykken's and his 1960 follow-up report was the last empirical study he conducted in this area. Nonetheless, stimulated by this foray into this domain of applied psychology, Lykken immersed himself in the available literature on the use of polygraph procedures by field examiners and over the years emerged as one of the world's leading scientific experts on lie detection – contributing many influential conceptual and critical review articles along with what would become the authoritative scholarly book on the subject.[1]

---

[1] A 1991 (auto)biography of Lykken, published in the *American Psychologist* on the occasion of his receipt of the association's lifetime career award for contributions to the field of psychology in the public interest, noted that: "From 1970 until recently, Lykken estimates that he has spent 25% of his professional time in advocacy relating to polygraphic interrogation. Although there is no longer much intellectual content in

Through his initial readings in the area, Lykken learned that a procedure akin to the GKT had been used at times by police polygraph examiners with criminal suspects. This procedure, termed the "peak of tension" test, was introduced by early American lie detector guru (and Stanford psychology dropout) Leonarde Keeler in the 1920s. The test entailed presenting the examinee with a series of alternative descriptors pertaining to one salient aspect of a crime (e.g., possible sums of money that could have been taken in a theft) and watching for a pattern of steadily increasing physiological arousal up to the point of the key descriptor (i.e., the actual amount taken), followed by a decline in arousal thereafter. A variant of this technique, the "searching peak of tension test," was used to probe for some key detail of a crime (e.g., the location of a body within a general target area) that was in fact unknown to investigators. Keeler is also credited with developing the "card" or "numbers" test, a GKT-like demonstration used by examiners to this day to persuade test subjects of the polygraph's effectiveness prior to the actual test.[2]

Another thing Lykken learned from his readings was that the type of lie detector test used most commonly by police examiners in real-life criminal investigations was very different from the scientifically oriented GKT. The standard method in use for the testing of criminal suspects was the Control Question Test (CQT), a procedure developed in the 1940s by John Reid, an influential figure in the emerging field of forensic polygraphy. Reid was an attorney and interrogative specialist rather than a researcher, and thus his notion of "control" lacked the precision of an experimentalist's. His control questions consisted of decoy items dealing with acts of general wrongdoing, intended to deflect the "psychological set" of innocent examinees away from the relevant questions targeted at the specific incident under investigation. Skillful interactions between the polygrapher and the examinee – directed at influencing the examinee's perceptions of the relative importance of differing test questions – were viewed as critical to the effectiveness of the CQT. In cases where an examinee's behavior and reactions during the test pointed toward guilt, the examination concluded with a post-test interrogation aimed at extracting a confession. Police examiners who used the CQT argued that it yielded confessions in a high proportion of such cases.

the lie detector controversy, this work has social value, political, psychopathological, and even anthropological interest, and can be adversarial enough to serve as the moral equivalent of war."

[2] Early reports documenting use of the card test procedure included Geldreich (1941), Ruckmick (1938), and Van Buskirk and Marcuse (1954).

As a scientist, Lykken was flatly unimpressed with the CQT – characterizing it as a "bloodless third degree." In particular, Lykken pointed out that inherent dissimilarities between the so-called control questions and the crime-relevant test questions constituted a built-in bias against innocent suspects. His concerns about the procedure intensified as real-life cases came to his attention in which innocent individuals had faced prosecution and imprisonment after failing polygraph tests of this type. In a classic paper published in the *American Psychologist*, Lykken (1974) appealed to psychologists in the academic community to become involved in research and debate on polygraphic lie detection in order to challenge existing techniques developed by non-scientists and establish more credible alternatives. A centerpoint of this paper was an argument for the GKT as an alternative, scientifically based approach to detecting deception in specific-incident criminal investigations: "A polygraphic lie detection method known as the Guilty Knowledge Technique appears to have the potential for very high validity in the restricted number of criminal investigations where it is applicable. But the GKT seems to be unknown to professional polygraphers and there have been no studies either of its range of applicability or of its validity in field situations" (p. 738).

Lykken's article proved effective in getting academic researchers interested in lie detection and in utilizing the GKT as an experimental methodology. During the 1960s, several more published reports using the GKT appeared in the literature. These included a number of studies by two research teams, one led by Martin Orne in the United States (e.g., Gustafson and Orne, 1963; Thackray and Orne, 1968) and the other by Sol Kugelmass in Israel (e.g., Kugelmass and Lieblich, 1966; Kugelmass *et al.*, 1967), along with a small number of studies by other investigators (e.g., Davidson, 1968; Kubis, 1962). By the time the first edition of *Tremor in the Blood* was published in 1981, lie detection had developed into an active area of investigation among psychology researchers and the GKT – nowadays called the Concealed Information Test, or CIT – had emerged as its dominant experimental paradigm. However, the test remained largely ignored by field examiners in the United States and it took several more years for the first published report of the field validity of the CIT – by Israeli investigator Eitan Elaad (1990) – to appear. Even now, well into the twenty-first century – at a time where CIT studies routinely incorporate direct measurement of brain response and advanced quantitative approaches to decision-making – the technique is still not used to any significant extent by field examiners in North America and has achieved standard usage only in the nation of Japan (see Chapter 14 of this volume).

What factors account for this curious persisting gap between scientific progress and practical implementation? While a number of factors could be cited (including the broader implementability of the CQT in field cases), the main one is that field examiners who routinely use the CQT in specific-incident investigations believe – despite conceptual arguments (Lykken, 1974, 1981) and scientific evidence (Iacono and Patrick, 2006; Office of Technology Assessment, 1983) to the contrary – that this procedure is virtually infallible (see also Chapter 8 of this volume). The reason for this persisting belief is that the feedback that field examiners receive regarding the accuracy of decisions they make in polygraph test cases is selective – and systematically biased toward affirming the outcome of the test.

This state of affairs was demonstrated in a field study of the CQT by Patrick and Iacono (1991). These investigators followed up all cases tested by the police polygraph unit in a major Canadian city over a five-year period; file records from referring detachments were reviewed to identify instances in which CQT polygraph subjects were verified as either innocent or guilty based on evidence that emerged after the polygraph examination was conducted. A major finding of the study was that virtually all of the feedback police polygraph examiners received regarding their decisions consisted of information stemming from post-test confessions of test subjects – that is, some portion of examinees were verified as guilty by their own confession (either immediately after the polygraph test, or later in the investigation), and others were cleared as innocent based on the confession of some other suspect in the case.

A further striking finding of the study was that the outcome of the polygraph test itself systematically influenced the nature of feedback that examiners received: suspects identified as "deceptive" on the polygraph test were considered guilty whether they confessed or not, leading case investigators to abandon alternative avenues of investigation – and thus opportunities for the outcome of the polygraph to be refuted; subjects identified as "innocent" on the test were normally dismissed as suspects, leading investigators to shift their efforts toward other suspects – again precluding opportunities for the polygraph to be "proven wrong." As a function of these systematic biases, police polygraph examiners almost never received post-examination feedback that disconfirmed their test decisions – perpetuating their view of the CQT as infallible.

Due to systematic biases of this sort, and the barrier they pose to establishing credible estimates of polygraph accuracy in real-life cases, the validity of the CQT remains a matter of ongoing debate – and the CQT continues to be the most common type of test used in specific-incident investigations by police and other agencies around the world. Nonetheless, alongside the persistant use of the CQT in the field, the CIT has continued to grow and develop as a scientific procedure. During the 1970s and 1980s, substantial research was devoted to examining the impact of various factors on detectability in the CIT, including motivation to appear truthful, innocuous exposure to crime-relevant details, feedback regarding physiological responses to test items, dispositional factors such as anxiousness and extraversion, and drugs of various types including alcohol, anxiolytics, and stimulants. The CIT was well-suited to parametric studies of this kind because of its classic experimental-control format and amenability to standardization. As a function of these attributes, the CIT also gained popularity as an experimental paradigm for studying basic processes contributing to phasic electrodermal response.

An important development in the mid-1980s was the incorporation of brain event-related potential (ERP) measures into the CIT (Farwell and Donchin, 1986; Rosenfeld *et al.*, 1987; see Chapter 4 of this volume). Up to this point, most studies of the CIT had utilized electrodermal response as the main dependent measure, with a smaller number of studies including respiratory or cardiovascular indices. The use of ERP measures to detect guilty knowledge was a natural progression because it had long been known that the P300 component of the ERP in particular is sensitive to the familiarity or meaningfulness of stimulus events. The use of P300-based CIT procedures including multiple iterative stimulus presentations opened the door to sophisticated quantitative approaches to classifying individuals as truthful or deceptive – including use of "bootstrap" resampling (Farwell and Donchin, 1991) and Bayesian statistical methods (Allen *et al.*, 1992). Brain-based CIT procedures have also been used to elucidate specific cognitive processes underlying deception; studies of this sort (e.g., Johnson *et al.*, 2003) have utilized differing ERP components to index putatively distinct operations associated with efforts to deceive. A related exciting development is the recent use of functional neuroimaging methods to investigate deception-related processes in the CIT detection context (see Chapter 5 of this volume). The first published study of this kind was by Spence *et al.* (2001).

Another important development over the past two decades has been the increasing documented use of CIT procedures in field settings (see Chapter 9 of this volume). Although the CIT was used before this time in Japan on a routine basis in police investigations (Fukumoto, 1980; Nakayama, 2002; Yamamura and Miyata, 1990), as noted earlier, the first published study of the field validity of the CIT – by Elaad – did not appear until 1990. A second study of this type was published by Elaad and his colleagues in 1992, and this was followed a year later by a report of the field validity of a P300-based CIT procedure by researchers in Japan (Miyake *et al.*, 1993). Although these reports raised some concerns about the accuracy of the CIT with guilty suspects – perhaps owing to the lesser saliency or certitude of crime-relevant details in real-life cases – they nonetheless encouraged further implementation and evaluation of the procedure as an alternative to the CQT in field settings.

The current volume, the first to be devoted entirely to the CIT, is a testament to the ongoing growth and development of this scientifically oriented approach to detecting deception. The current volume highlights the impressive body of literature that has emerged using this paradigm in the half-century since Lykken's (1959, 1960) classic studies – including experimental research addressing basic topics such as orienting and habituation, memory, factors contributing to physiological reactivity, and processes underlying deception, as well as applied research evaluating the general validity of the technique and various factors affecting detectability. Following an initial chapter (by Iacono) that presents a compelling case for widespread adoption of the CIT by law enforcement agencies, Chapters 2 through 6 address varying response parameters that have been utilized in studies of the CIT (from electrodermal activity to functional brain response), with Chapter 7 providing a detailed theoretical analysis of processes underlying physiological reactivity to items on the test. Chapters 8–12 address issues pertaining to implementation of the CIT in field settings, including limits to its range of applicability, constraints on generalizability of laboratory findings to real-life contexts, the problem of information leakage prior to testing, and potential moderators of test accuracy in real-life cases (use of countermeasures; psychopathic tendencies). Chapters 13–14 focus on applications of the CIT to the assessment of memory function in clinical cases as well as to the evaluation of criminal suspects in police investigations. Chapter 15 addresses legal issues pertaining to field use of the CIT, and Chapter 16 describes recommended procedures for constructing and administering the CIT in field settings.

Victor Hugo (loosely translated) observed that "there is no army so powerful as an idea whose time has come." The CIT is an idea whose time has come. It has proven highly generative as an experimental paradigm, its practical potential has been demonstrated through a growing list of documented uses in real-life settings, and longstanding barriers to its widespread implementation in the field (including allegiance to the CQT and unawareness of or unwillingness to try alternatives) appear to be crumbling. In this regard, the current volume represents an important and welcome addition to the literature – one that seems likely to promote increasing reliance on scientific concepts and methods in efforts to distinguish between truth and deception in practical contexts. This is a book David Lykken would be pleased to see side by side on the shelf with his classic *Tremor in the Blood*.

REFERENCES

Allen, J. J., Iacono, W. G., and Danielson, K. D. (1992). The identification of concealed memories using the event-related potential and implicit behavioral measures: a methodology for prediction in the face of individual differences. *Psychophysiology*, 29, 504–522.

Davidson, P. O. (1968). Validity of the guilty knowledge technique: the effect of motivation. *Journal of Applied Psychology*, 52, 62–65.

Elaad, E. (1990). Detection of guilty knowledge in real-life criminal investigations. *Journal of Applied Psychology*, 75, 521–529.

Farwell, L. A., and Donchin, E. (1986). The "brain detector:" P300 in the detection of deception. *Psychophysiology*, 24, 434.

(1991). The truth will out: interrogative polygraphy ("lie detection") with event related brain potentials. *Psychophysiology*, 28, 531–547.

Fukomoto, J. (1980). A case in which the polygraph was the sole evidence for conviction. *Polygraph*, 9, 42–44.

Geldreich, E. W. (1941). Studies of the galvanic skin response as a deception indicator. *Transactions of the Kansas Academy of Science*, 44, 346–351.

Gustafson, L. A., and Orne, M. T. (1963). Effects of heightened motivation on the detection of deception. *Journal of Applied Psychology*, 47, 408–411.

Iacono, W. G., and Patrick, C. J. (2006). Polygraph ("lie detector") testing: current status and emerging trends. In I. B. Weiner and A. Hess (eds.), *Handbook of Forensic Psychology*, 3rd edn. (pp. 552–588). New York: Wiley.

Johnson, R., Jr., Barnhardt, J., and Zhu, J. (2003). The deceptive response: effects of response conflict and strategic monitoring on the late positive component and episodic memory-related brain activity. *Biological Psychology*, 64, 217–253.

Kubis, J. F. (1962). *Studies in Lie Detection: Computer Feasibility Considerations.* RADC-TR 62–205, Contract AF 30(602)-2270. Air Force Systems Command, U.S. Air Force, Griffiss Air Force Base. New York: Rome Air Development Center.

Kugelmass, S., and Lieblich, I. (1966). The effects of realistic stress and procedural interference in experimental lie detection. *Journal of Applied Psychology*, 50, 211–216.

Kugelmass, S., Lieblich, I., and Bergman, Z. (1967). The role of "lying" in psychophysiological detection. *Psychophysiology*, 3, 312–315.

Lykken, D. T. (1959). The GSR in the detection of guilt. *Journal of Applied Psychology*, 43, 385–388.

(1960). The validity of the guilty knowledge test: the effects of faking. *Journal of Applied Psychology*, 44, 258–262.

(1974). Psychology and the lie detector industry. *American Psychologist*, 29, 725–739.

(1981). *A Tremor in the Blood: Uses and Abuses of the Lie Detector*, 1st edn. (2nd edn., 1998). New York: McGraw-Hill.

Miyake, Y., Mizutani, M., and Yamahura, T. (1993). Event related potentials as an indicator of detecting information in field polygraph examinations. *Polygraph*, 22, 131–149.

Nakayama, M. (2002). Practical use of the concealed information test for criminal investigation in Japan. In M. Kleiner (ed.), *Handbook of Polygraph Testing* (pp. 49–86). San Diego: Academic Press.

Office of Technology Assessment (1983). Scientific validity of polygraph testing: a research review and evaluation. Washington, DC: Office of Technology Assessment.

Patrick, C. J., and Iacono, W. G. (1991). A comparison of field and laboratory polygraphs in the detection of deception. *Psychophysiology*, 28, 632–638.

Rosenfeld, J. P., Nasman, V. T., Whalen, R., Cantwell, B., and Mazzeri, L. (1987). Late vertex positivity in event-related potentials as a guilty knowledge indicator: a new method of lie detection. *Polygraph*, 16, 258–263.

Ruckmick, C. A. (1938). The truth about the lie detector. *Journal of Applied Psychology*, 22, 50–58.

Spence, S. A., Farrow, T. F. D., Herford, A. E., Wilkinson, I. D., Zheng, Y., and Woodruff, P. W. R. (2001). Behavioural and functional anatomical correlates of deception in humans. *Neuroreport*, 12, 2433–2438.

Thackray, R. I., and Orne, M. T. (1968). A comparison of physiological indices in detection of deception. *Psychophysiology*, 4, 329–339.

Van Buskirk, D., and Marcuse, F. L. (1954). The nature of errors in experimental lie detection. *Journal of Experimental Psychology*, 47, 187–190.

Yamamura, T., and Miyata, Y. (1990). Development of the polygraph technique in Japan for detection of deception. *Forensic Science International*, 44, 257–271.

1   Encouraging the use of the Guilty Knowledge Test (GKT): what the GKT has to offer law enforcement

William G. Iacono

Overview: The Guilty Knowledge Test (GKT) has gained favor with academic psychology, but outside of Japan, it is seldom used in the field. Although the low likelihood of false positives constitutes a major advantage of the GKT, this feature has not provided sufficient impetus for the GKT to be adopted in police work due to concerns about false negatives and the possibility that the GKT may not be applicable in many crimes. Largely ignored are the facts that failed GKTs provide strong prima facie evidence of guilt and that steps can be taken to increase the number of cases for which the GKT is applicable. In many respects, GKT results have properties similar to fingerprint evidence, and few would dispute the value of fingerprints in solving crimes. Emphasis on these aspects of the GKT could go a long way toward encouraging its greater use by law enforcement.

It is a fitting tribute to David Lykken that a half century after the initial publication of his two papers that introduced psychology to the Guilty Knowledge Test (Lykken, 1959, 1960; also referred to as the Concealed Information Test, or CIT),[1] this book is capturing GKT history and providing a foundation for the next fifty years of research on applied memory detection. It is not well known that when Lykken undertook these studies, his goal was not to provide an alternative to the lie detection techniques that were in vogue at the time. In fact, he knew nothing about these methods, and was extending work he did as part of his dissertation, developing a sensible approach for detecting liars that he thought was likely to resemble procedures used by law enforcement. It was not until he did the literature reviews for these papers that he discovered how lie detection was actually attempted using the Control

---

[1] Throughout this chapter, the original terminology proposed by David Lykken (the GKT) was used, although the term, CIT, used nowadays by most researchers in this area, was adopted by all other chapters in this book.

12

Question Test (CQT; also referred to as the Comparison Question Test). This in turn gave way to his later well-articulated criticism of the CQT that first emerged as an article in the *American Psychologist* (Lykken, 1974).

As a budding psychophysiologist, David already knew enough to understand that psychophysiological lie detection per se was unlikely to be practical. The classic work of Ax (1953) and Schachter (1957) had shown that while one could identify an individual as aroused by measuring peripheral physiological responses, and that group data could be used to differentiate patterns of arousal across different emotions, one could not discern what emotion any given individual was experiencing by inspecting his or her pattern of physiological reactions. He concluded that whatever emotions were likely to be associated with lying, it would not be possible to determine if any given person was guilty by recording peripheral psychophysiology while denying an accusation. And by that time, the CQT had already been invented, an implicit acknowledgement that there was no unique lie response.

The CQT

Although there are several different types of question on a CQT, lying on a CQT is inferred by the pattern of responses to two different questions. The relevant or "did you do it" question asks whether a suspect committed the crime. For instance, in a rape case, a relevant question might take the form "Did you force Glenda to have sexual intercourse with you?" The response to this question is then compared to that of a control (also called a probable lie or comparison question), e.g., "Have you ever lied to get out of trouble?" The innocent are expected to respond more strongly to the control question because this is the only question that will bother them, and they are likely to be lying when they answer this question "no" because it is believed that lying to get out of trouble is a common practice. By contrast, the guilty are expected to give a stronger response to the relevant question because it elicits a more important lie.

The chief criticism of the theory underlying the CQT is that denying a false accusation is likely to be emotionally disturbing for an innocent person, especially if false detection brings with it serious adverse consequences, such as public humiliation, ostracism, and possible prosecution. The repercussions likely to follow from a failed control question are not likely to be as severe, and there is no way to know in a given case to what extent the control question provides a psychologically adequate counter to the emotional impact of the false accusation covered by the relevant question. The CQT is thus biased against the innocent, a conclusion that has been supported by several field studies of the CQT. For instance, Patrick and Iacono (1991) reported a false positive rate of over 40 percent when highly trained police polygraph examiners blindly rescored confession-verified CQTs.

The GKT

The goal of a properly constructed GKT is to determine whether a suspect possesses knowledge about a crime that could exist only if the suspect was guilty. GKT items are developed by gathering crime facts that only the perpetrator and the police investigating the crime could be expected to know. As typically constructed, a GKT would consist of a series of multiple-choice questions, each with alternatives that would appear equally plausible to the innocent, but one of which would be readily identifiable to the guilty. For instance, if a house was broken into and its resident beaten to death, a series of GKT items might be as follows:

(1) If you are the one who killed Glenda Fisbee, then you would know where in the house her body was found. Was it in (a) the basement, (b) the kitchen, (c) the bathroom, (d) the attic, (e) the bedroom.
(2) If you committed this crime, then you would know how she was killed. Was she bludgeoned with (a) a brick, (b) a crowbar, (c) a baseball bat, (d) a pipe, (e) a hammer.
(3) [More questions that build on this theme, dealing with, for example, the method of entry into the home, a valuable item that was stolen, etc.]

As each question is asked, the suspect's physiological responses are recorded to each multiple-choice alternative. For the innocent, who does not know the answer to the question, chance determines which alternative elicits the strongest physiological response. For the guilty person, the largest response should occur to the correct alternative because it alone is recognized as crime-relevant and has more significance than any of the other alternatives. Consistently larger responses to guilty alternatives across questions provides strong probative evidence of guilt.

For Lykken (1981, 1998) and many others concerned about high false positive error rates likely to accompany use of the CQT, a selling feature of a properly constructed GKT is that it is not biased against the innocent. Lykken noted that for a GKT with ten multiple-choice questions, each with five equally plausible alternatives, the chance that an innocent person would give the largest response to the relevant alternative on just half of the questions is slim, corresponding to a false positive rate of under 1 percent. Laboratory studies of the GKT have also shown that the innocent are unlikely to fail a GKT (Ben-Shakhar and Elaad, 2003). As appealing as this quality of the GKT is to those who are concerned about the implications of falsely implicating an innocent person as guilty, this feature has not compelled widespread adoption of the GKT by law enforcement agencies.

Selling the GKT to law enforcement

Good police work does not lead to indiscriminate arrest or routine casting of suspicion on innocent people. Those suspected of involvement in crimes are typically implicated because there is some evidence pointing to their guilt. Hence, from the perspective of law enforcement, a good deception detection procedure will be one that protects the innocent while not making it easy for the guilty to go free. Unfortunately, it is on this second account that the GKT is perceived by the police to fall short.

There are many reasons why a GKT may yield a false negative outcome. At present, especially from a law enforcement perspective, the greatest weakness of the GKT lies in the likelihood that the guilty may not recognize the crime-relevant information covered by GKT questions. Ideally, the examiner who develops GKT items will uncover information easily recognized by the guilty party, but at present, there is insufficient research supporting either how best to ensure this outcome or how much confidence to place in the validity of any given GKT. What perpetrators attend to during the commission of a crime, what they are likely to remember, and how long they are likely to remember it are all relevant to this issue. In addition, individual difference factors that determine whether a given criminal recalls crime facts and crime characteristics may also be important. For instance, it is not known how being under the influence of a psychoactive substance may affect recall or whether an impulsively committed crime of passion would elicit the same quality of memory as the same crime committed with a well-thought-out plan. Nor is it known how well an individual who commits a crime serially is able to recall facts specific to the one instance the police become aware of. An additional frequently voiced concern about the GKT is that is it not applicable in all crimes – some crimes simply do not generate the quality of privately held information the police need to be able to develop a GKT. And as is the case for the CQT, countermeasures may prove a threat to the GKT (see Chapter 11 of this volume).

But do these concerns justify dismissing the GKT as little more than an academic research tool? Consider the following case. Glenda was sleeping alone in her home when a masked intruder woke her with a knife held to her throat. Under threat of death, she cooperated when the intruder stuffed a rag in her mouth to silence her and blindfolded her by placing duct tape over her eyes. After he subsequently lashed her arms and legs to the bedposts, he placed headphones over her ears. She listened helplessly as classic love poems were played to her from an audio CD. As the intruder marked her naked body with her lipstick, she struggled to decipher the phrases he was writing. Still under the threat of death, she remained still as he shaved her lower body, including her pubis. In desperation, she listened as Viennese waltzes began to play through the headphones and he massaged her body with lavender scented oil. After removing the headphones, he kissed her lightly on the cheek and left. Worried what would happen if he returned, she was relieved when day broke and she managed to free herself from one of the ropes binding her.

A case such as this contains a great deal of information that could be used to develop a GKT. To name but a few, questions could be designed that would cover the weapon used, type of blindfold, nature of the audio recordings, method of confinement, and details related to the various rituals performed by the intruder. Given a properly prepared set of questions based on this information, it is unlikely that an innocent suspect would respond consistently to guilty alternatives dealing with such unusual detail. For reasons given above, it is possible that a guilty person would avoid detection despite the examiner's best efforts to construct a valid GKT. What is important to consider, however, is *what we would make of a suspect who hit on most of the guilty alternatives while also having no explanation for how the guilty alternatives could come to have personal significance.* Under these circumstances, the evidence of guilt would be damning.

The GKT as an analog to fingerprints

GKT outcomes can be interpreted much like fingerprint evidence. Evidence pointing to the possession of guilty knowledge is incriminating, but the absence of such evidence may have ambiguous meaning. Although fingerprints are not available at all crime scenes, few would argue that this provides grounds for dismissing their evidentiary value in those instances when they are available. Just as the case may be for a passed GKT, a crime scene that does not turn up a "hit" in the form of incriminating fingerprints does not necessarily exonerate a suspect.

There are various reasons why fingerprint evidence may not be present, including the application of "countermeasures" like wearing gloves or wiping the scene clean. When incriminating fingerprints are uncovered, they point to guilt only if no plausible explanation for their presence is forthcoming. In the case of our hypothetical GKT, we might expect a man who runs a spa for women that offers lavender-oil massages and unwanted body hair removal to fail his GKT. However, I would argue that knowing this man's vocation, a test that contained items with content that could be construed as relevant to his business would not be appropriate for inclusion in the GKT in the first place.

An argument that has been used to discourage use of the GKT is that the information needed to develop a GKT is often not available. Prior to discovering the value of fingerprints, the same could be said about them. It was not until criminalists were trained regarding what to look for and how to properly collect the evidence that the use of fingerprints became routine. The same could be said about crime scene information usable for a GKT. If the evidentiary value of a failed GKT were recognized, properly trained individuals investigating the crime scene would understand how to gather evidence, including interviewing victims and creating photographs, in a manner that would optimize the development of GKT questions in anticipation of the future identification of suspects. These same individuals could also learn how to protect the confidentiality of GKT-relevant information, thereby decreasing the likelihood that it would become generally known even to the innocent, thus compromising its usefulness. The likely increased yield in cases suitable for a GKT could be substantial if appropriate evidence-gathering procedures were adopted such as those that have been used by the Japanese police. The Japanese, who have been designing proper GKTs for many decades, have considerable expertise in identifying facts that are likely to be remembered and keeping them concealed (for a detailed description of the GKT usage in Japan, see Chapter 14 of this volume).

GKT advantages in administration

Execution of a CQT that satisfies the professional standards of polygraph examiners is a complex affair. Perhaps the most involved part is the pre-test interview, particularly question development. This effort involves defining words and formulating questions that a suspect can readily understand and answer with an unambiguous "yes" or "no" answer, choosing control questions that are appropriate given the case facts and the suspect's background, discouraging the suspect from making too many admissions to the control questions, not letting the suspect catch on to the purpose of control questions, and convincing the suspect that lies will be caught. In the CQT (unlike the GKT) the two types of questions are formulated differently and the distinction between relevant and comparison questions could be made by anyone. Certainly anyone who is familiar with the procedure (there is a vast literature open to the general public that describes the CQT's procedure, rationale and classification rules in great detail) can discern which are the relevant and which are the comparison questions and also know that only the relevant questions are of real concern. The rationale of the CQT is based on deceiving the examinees. A test based on deception cannot be routinely relied upon, particularly in our age of open and easily accessible knowledge.

To convince examinees that the "lie detector" is sensitive to their lying, many CQTs include a "stim" or "acquaintance" test (also called a "card" or "numbers" test). Ironically, these tests, designed to show the suspect that the procedure will work, are a type of single-question GKT. Although stim tests come in many forms, a common procedure is for the examinee to choose a number between one and ten, write it down on a piece of paper, and place the written choice in full view of the examiner. The examiner then asks the suspect if the number was three, eight, five, etc., and the suspect responds "no" to each alternative possibility. In other versions, the examinee may be asked to choose a card from a marked deck. The exercise succeeds if the examiner can convince the suspect that the alternative eliciting the "lie" produces a clear response, thus adding to the suspect's concern about lies being detected. Whether such a test is included at all or when it is introduced during the administration of the CQT is at the discretion of the examiner.

These features of CQT administration serve to undermine any claim that the CQT is a standardized, objective procedure with results that are independent of examiner judgment. This in turn limits confidence in the value of any given CQT since it is impossible to know how the many subjective decisions made by an examiner influenced the outcome.

GKT administration need not be subject to similar concerns. If a trained criminalist prepares the evidentiary file in anticipation of a possible GKT, the difficult work needed to develop relevant question content would already be largely completed. In fact, it is not necessary for the person creating the GKT questions to meet or have any first-hand knowledge of a suspect, and the procedure can be administered (and scored) by a computer. The only need for interaction with the examinee regarding test content involves confirming that the suspect lacks awareness of crime details and that the items on the test do not have personal significance.

Scientists support development of the GKT

A serious problem faced by the polygraph profession is that their methods are largely scorned by scientists, and this undermines the credibility and legitimacy of their work. As the recent report of the National Research Council (NRC) of the National Academies of Sciences (National Research Council, 2003) highlighted, scientific skepticism regarding the CQT is based on the fact that it does not have a sound theoretical basis, the quality of research relied on to justify its use is poor, the field has not accumulated knowledge or strengthened its scientific underpinnings in any significant manner, and the claims of high accuracy are unrealistic. They go on to conclude: "Almost a century of research in scientific psychology and physiology provides little basis for the expectation that a polygraph test could have extremely high accuracy" (p. 212). These criticisms have dogged the CQT for half a century, and there is little reason to believe that this situation will change in the future. As a consequence, applied lie detection goes forward largely divorced from science, with little likelihood of ever capturing the interest or support of scientists.

The same cannot be said of the GKT. The NRC noted that the GKT has consistently drawn on psychological theory (see also Ben-Shakar and Furedy, 1990). As the current volume amply illustrates, dozens of scientists from around the world are actively researching aspects of the GKT, leading to the publication of hundreds of reports on this technique that consistently find their way into the best psychological journals. In a survey of psychologists and psychophysiologists, Iacono and Lykken (1997) found little support for CQT polygraphy, but considerable support for the GKT. For instance, asked if it was reasonable to conclude that a criminal suspect who had failed eight of ten items on a GKT had guilty knowledge about a crime, 72 percent of polled members of the Society for Psychophysiological Research and 77 percent of American Psychological Association respondents answered "yes."

Unlike the CQT, which has not been found to meet standards for what constitutes scientific evidence in legal proceedings, the GKT may be capable of meeting these standards (Ben-Shakhar *et al.*, 2002; see also Chapter 15 of this volume). When CQT results are proffered as evidence, the opinion of the examiner regarding a person's truthfulness is presented as a conclusion. How this opinion might be rightly qualified by examining the process followed to administer the CQT is unknown because the consequences of following certain procedures or deviating from common practices cannot be estimated. Because the GKT is based on a scientific rationale that is easy to grasp, the sensibleness of the process followed in GKT administration can be evaluated by the court and the weight given to the result adjusted accordingly.

Although from the perspective of scientists prospects for the CQT appear bleak, considerable optimism exists regarding the future of the GKT. The potential for scientists and the polygraph profession to work together on the development of the GKT is thus strong. Doing so would have the added benefit of elevating the status of police polygraphy by showing it was ready to use science to the advantage of law enforcement.

Getting started

Most polygraph examiners have little practical experience with the GKT, and techniques for developing good GKT questions do not make up a substantial part of their training. Fortunately, thoughtful people have outlined ideas regarding how to construct a valid GKT, and these leads can be evaluated and developed further, see for example Chapter 16 of the present volume. In addition, there is considerable published research on the GKT, and it covers many important topics related to GKT test construction, quite a few of which are covered in a recent meta-analysis (Ben-Shakhar and Elaad, 2003). Although the GKT has seldom been used in the United States, it is the preferred method of deception detection in Japan. Japanese examiners have gained considerable experience and knowledge over the years in GKT question construction, and this information is detailed in various reports (Hira and Furumitsu, 2002; Nakayama, 2002).

Valid GKTs can be conducted with the same instrumentation used in other polygraph tests. In addition, the GKT can readily be adapted for use with various psychophysiological methods, including recording fMRI and brain event-related potential (ERP) responses. At present it is not clear to what degree these techniques are likely to improve on the accuracy of GKTs carried out with autonomic measures. Nevertheless, there may be distinct advantages to their use. For instance, it may be possible to develop an ERP-GKT that is immune to countermeasures (Meixner and Rosenfeld, 2009; Rosenfeld *et al.*, 2008). The type of "brain fingerprinting" ERP-GKT developed by Farwell and Donchin (1991) includes a procedure that can be used to build confidence that a given test administration is likely to be valid. A standard GKT includes among the multiple-choice alternatives key items involving possible guilty knowledge and irrelevant alternatives. The enhanced procedure includes as well test stimuli that are known to be recognizable to all who take the test. If these stimuli do not show a brain response establishing that these stimuli are in fact recognized, the particular test administration can be discarded as invalid (for further discussion, see Iacono, 2007).

Summary and conclusion

False positive errors are always an important concern. Although it would be unwise to conclude that the GKT is immune to false positives, given that uninformed innocent individuals have no basis for recognizing guilty knowledge, it is likely that GKT guidelines can be put in place that render these errors highly improbable. Included procedures should optimize the likelihood that GKT questions have alternatives that, to an innocent person, appear to have equal plausibility of being crime-connected. Steps can be taken to conceal GKT-relevant crime facts from public awareness, and even to conceal them from those interviewing suspects so that guilty knowledge is not inadvertently planted in those undergoing interrogation. In addition, a failed GKT can be administered to known innocent individuals to develop an estimate of the false positive rate for the specific test.

The low likelihood of false positives constitutes a major advantage the GKT has over the CQT. This feature, however, has not provided sufficient impetus for the GKT to be adopted by law enforcement for several reasons, including uncertainty in how much faith to put in passed GKTs and concern about the extent to which the GKT is broadly applicable. Largely ignored are the facts that failed GKTs provide strong prima facie evidence of guilt when they are failed and steps can be taken to increase the number of cases for which the GKT is applicable. In many respects, GKT results have properties similar to fingerprint evidence, and few would dispute the value of fingerprints in solving crimes. Although the CQT is unstandardized and its administration is dependent on subjective decisions the examiner must make, the GKT can be administered in a manner that largely safeguards against biased test construction and administration. Finally, the field of deception detection is ripe for the formation of an alliance between scientists interested in applied psychophysiology and law enforcement, a partnership that has the potential to enhance the crime-solving success of the police.

In this chapter I have emphasized the value of a failed GKT for identifying guilty parties. This emphasis reflects the fact that although the low likelihood of false positives is a well appreciated feature of the GKT, the inculpatory worth of a failed GKT has been underappreciated, especially by law enforcement. By stressing this point, however, I do not mean to imply that passed GKTs are of no value. Failing to score at above chance on a thoughtfully constructed GKT based on the assault of Glenda (described above) would provide strong evidence that a suspect did not possess guilty knowledge in this case. How an individual could have committed this crime and not recognize carefully chosen guilty knowledge items must be considered. For instance, confidence would be reduced if the crime was carried out many years ago and the suspect was an alcoholic. The possible use of countermeasures would also have to be considered. At present, little research has been devoted to detecting the use of countermeasures during a GKT, but it may be the case that some variants of the procedure, like those based on brain potential recording, can be refined to produce inconclusive outcomes in cases where behavioral and event-related potential data deviate from an expected pattern as might occur when countermeasures are attempted (see Iacono, 2007).

When David Lykken concluded the first edition of his book, *A Tremor in the Blood* (Lykken, 1981), he hoped that law enforcement would develop a healthy skepticism of conventional lie detection methods while also developing an interest in applying the GKT to criminal investigations. Although the extent to which each of these goals has been realized is debatable, it is clear that much more has to happen before the police embrace the use of the GKT. Hopefully this text, which includes chapters that describe successful forensic applications of the GKT in Japan, will provide some of the additional impetus needed to achieve this worthwhile objective.

REFERENCES

Ax, A. F. (1953). The physiological differentiation between fear and anger in humans. *Psychosomatic Medicine*, 15, 433–442.

Ben-Shakhar, G., and Elaad, E. (2003). The validity of psychophysiological detection of information with the Guilty Knowledge Test: a meta-analytic review. *Journal of Applied Psychology*, 88, 131–151.

Ben-Shakar, G., and Furedy, J. J. (1990). *Theories and Applications in the Detection of Deception*. New York: Springer-Verlag.

Ben-Shakhar, G., Bar-Hillel, M., and Kremnitzer, M. (2002). Trial by polygraph: reconsidering the use of the guilty knowledge technique in court. *Law & Human Behavior*, 26, 527–541.

Farwell, L. A., and Donchin, E. (1991). The truth will out: interrogative polygraphy ("lie detection") with event related brain potentials. *Psychophysiology*, 28, 531–547.

Hira, S., and Furumitsu, I. (2002). Polygraphic examinations in Japan: application to the guilty knowledge test in forensic investigations. *International Journal of Police Science & Management*, 4, 16–27.

Iacono, W. G. (2007). Detection of deception. In J. Cacioppo, L. Tassinary, and G. Berntson (eds.), *Handbook of Psychophysiology*, 3rd edn. (pp. 688–703). New York: Cambridge University Press.

Iacono, W. G., and Lykken, D. T. (1997). The validity of the lie detector: two surveys of scientific opinion. *Journal of Applied Psychology*, 82, 426–433.

Lykken, D. T. (1959). The GSR in the detection of guilt. *Journal of Applied Psychology*, 43, 385–388.

(1960). The validity of the guilty knowledge technique: the effects of faking. *Journal of Applied Psychology*, 44, 258–262.

(1974). Psychology and the lie detector industry. *American Psychologist*, 29, 725–739.

(1981). *A Tremor in the Blood: Uses and Abuses of the Lie Detector*. New York: McGraw-Hill.

(1998). *A Tremor in the Blood: Uses and Abuses of the Lie Detector*, 2nd edn. New York: Plenum.

Meixner, J. B., and Rosenfeld, J. P. (2009). Countermeasure mechanisms in a P300-based concealed information test. *Psychophysiology*, 47, 57–65.

Nakayama, M. (2002). Practical use of the concealed information test from criminal investigation is Japan. In M. Kleiner (ed.), *Handbook of Polygraph Testing* (pp. 49–86). San Diego: Academic Press.

National Research Council. (2003). *The Polygraph and Lie Detection*. Washington, DC: National Academies Press.

Patrick, C. J., and Iacono, W. G. (1991). A comparison of field and laboratory polygraphs in the detection of deception. *Psychophysiology*, 28, 632–638.

Rosenfeld, J. P., Labkovsky, E., Winograd, M., Lui, M. A., Vandenboom, C., and Chedid, E. (2008). The Complex Trial Protocol (CTP): a new, countermeasure-resistant, accurate, P300-based method for detection of concealed information. *Psychophysiology*, 45, 906–919.

Schachter, J. (1957). Pain, fear, and anger in hypertensives and normotensives. *Psychosomatic Medicine*, 15, 433–442.

Part II

The laboratory: theoretical and empirical foundations of the Concealed Information Test

2 Detecting concealed information using autonomic measures

Matthias Gamer

Overview: Already in the first empirical demonstration of the Concealed Information Test (CIT), it was shown that electrodermal responses can be used to detect concealed knowledge with high accuracy. This chapter summarizes the huge number of studies on autonomic measures in the CIT that have been conducted in the last decades. Taken together, it is now well established that the recognition of crime-related items results in larger skin conductance responses, respiratory suppression, heart rate deceleration and reductions of pulse volume amplitudes when compared to neutral control items. This response pattern results from a coactivation of the sympathetic and the vagal branch of the autonomic nervous system and it is at least in part related to the orienting response. Recent studies have shown that the validity of the CIT can be further increased by systematically combining electrodermal, respiratory and heart rate responses by means of a logistic classification function. Finally, important questions for future research on autonomic measures in the CIT are outlined.

Introduction

More than fifty years ago, Lykken (1959) demonstrated that phasic skin conductance changes can be used to detect concealed knowledge with high validity. In this influential study, four groups of participants were examined. One group was asked to commit two mock crimes (a murder and a theft), thereby gaining knowledge of several crime-related details. Two more groups carried out only one of these mock crimes while remaining ignorant to the relevant details of the other scenario and a fourth group was exposed to neither of these mock crimes. Subsequently, all participants were tested for both scenarios by asking for knowledge of critical items that resembled details of the mock crime scene (e.g., certain objects and their placement in the room where the crime was committed). These items were presented along with several equally plausible neutral (control) alternatives in a question format that is highly similar to multiple-choice tests. Solely by using the amplitude of galvanic skin responses elicited by each test item as the dependent measure, Lykken was able to correctly identify 100 percent of the innocent participants and he detected concealed knowledge in 88 percent of cases where a mock crime was committed. On the one hand, concealed crime-related knowledge led to larger skin conductance responses to relevant items as compared to neutral alternatives. On the other hand, non-systematic responses to these item types were observed when the examinee was innocent with respect to the scenario tested. One year later Lykken (1960) showed that these differential skin conductance responses to concealed knowledge and neutral items are remarkably stable against the effects of faking. Lykken called this novel approach of testing whether an examinee was involved in a crime the Guilty Knowledge Test (GKT). Recently, it has also been referred to as the Concealed Information Test (CIT).

Until now, most studies on the CIT exclusively focused on electro-dermal measures but already since the late 1960s, other physiological measures reflecting the activity of the autonomic nervous system were utilized (Podlesny and Raskin, 1977, 1978; Thackray and Orne, 1968). After some inconclusive results in the beginning, there seems to be con-sensus nowadays that the concealment of knowledge results in larger skin conductance responses (SCRs), respiratory suppression, heart rate deceleration and reductions of pulse volume amplitudes when com-pared to neutral control items (see Figure 2.1).

The purpose of this chapter is to review the validity of different per-ipheral physiological measures and to discuss psychological mechanisms that may affect these bodily responses. Furthermore, a model is derived on how to combine these different measures in order to enhance the val-idity of the CIT. Finally, I am going to put forward some suggestions for future research on applied and basic research questions in this domain.

Electrodermal measures

Since the very beginning of systematic research on the CIT, it has been shown that the amplitudes of skin resistance (Lykken, 1959, 1960) or skin conductance responses (Horneman and O'Gorman, 1985; Waid *et al.*, 1979) are larger for relevant items than for neutral control items when an examinee is concealing knowledge. This is not only true for mock crime studies resembling realistic field conditions (Davidson, 1968). It was also found when examinees were instructed to conceal knowledge of previously chosen cards (Ben-Shakhar, 1994) or numbers (Horvath, 1978, 1979), memorized code words (Waid *et al.*, 1978; Waid

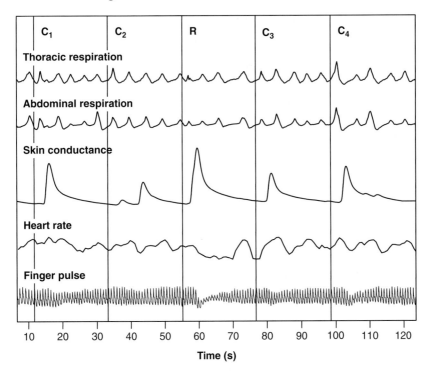

Figure 2.1 Typical response pattern of a participant who committed a mock crime and was instructed to conceal knowledge of all crime-related items in the CIT. R denotes the critical relevant item and C_1 to C_4 represent the neutral control items.

and Orne, 1980), personal details or autobiographic information (Ben-Shakhar *et al.*, 1975; Elaad, 1994). Comparable results were also found in two field studies from Israel that relied on confessions to establish ground truth (Elaad, 1990; Elaad *et al.*, 1992).

With respect to the focus of CIT research on electrodermal measures, it is not surprising that quantitative reviews of CIT validity concentrated on this response system. One extensive review was published by MacLaren (2001).[1] Overall, fifty treatment groups of twenty-two laboratory studies on the CIT were included in this analysis. For the group of $N = 843$ informed subjects, he reported hit rates ranging from 25 percent to 100 percent with a weighted mean of 76 percent (sensitivity). With respect to the specificity, 59 percent to 100 percent of

[1] There was at least one study in the review of MacLaren (2001) that did not solely rely on electrodermal measures (Timm, 1982). However, the validity estimates of most studies were calculated using only skin conductance or skin resistance measures.

N = 404 noninformed participants were correctly classified with a weighted mean of 83 percent. The only moderating variable that could be identified in this analysis was the enactment of a mock crime. Thus, the sensitivity of the CIT was higher (82 percent for N = 666) when guilty subjects carried out a mock crime before undergoing CIT testing compared to those examinees who were otherwise informed about the relevant details.

An extensive meta-analysis on the validity of electrodermal measures in the CIT was carried out by Ben-Shakhar and Elaad (2003). However, instead of reporting hit rates that depend on a single arbitrarily chosen cutoff, these authors used measures from signal detection theory (the effect size d and the area A under the receiver operating characteristic [ROC] curve) to determine the validity of the CIT across all possible cutoff points (cf. Lieblich et al., 1970). Overall, 169 experimental conditions of eighty laboratory studies with N = 5,198 subjects were included in the meta-analysis. Across all studies, CIT detection efficiency was high (d = 1.55, A = 0.82) and considerably larger than the lower limit of "large effect sizes" (d = 0.80; see Cohen, 1988). Replicating the results of MacLaren (2001), it was found that electrodermal measures had higher validity when participants carried out a mock crime. Moreover, a larger number of CIT questions as well as a high level of motivation were associated with larger effect sizes. The mode of responding had a significant effect on CIT validity only when the motivation to pass the test was low. In this case, a deceptive verbal response increased the electrodermal differentiation of relevant and control items in the CIT. When confining the analysis to those ten experimental conditions that were conducted under optimal conditions (N = 222), effect sizes were found to increase to d = 3.12 and A = 0.95.

Taken together, these results confirm the high validity of electrodermal measures for the detection of concealed knowledge. On the neurophysiological level, skin conductance changes strongly correlate with sympathetic nerve activity (Wallin, 1981), thus indicating that the electrodermal responses in the CIT result from a differential sympathetic activation following relevant and neutral control items when the examinee is able to differentiate between these item categories. In a variety of experimental settings, SCR amplitudes exhibit important characteristics of the orienting response (OR; Sokolov, 1963). Namely, SCR amplitudes show response decrement (habituation) to stimulus repetition, recovery to a change stimulus and a dishabituation following the change stimulus (Barry, 1996). Furthermore, SCR amplitudes increase with stimulus intensity and significance (Jackson, 1974; Siddle et al., 1979). This link between SCR amplitudes and the OR led to the assumption that the CIT primarily relies on the OR. According to this notion, relevant items embedded in the CIT questions have a sort of significance or signal value for guilty subjects thereby eliciting stronger orienting responses that are more resistant to habituation than responses to neutral control items (Lykken, 1974). Although recent research has questioned whether the OR concept is sufficient to fully explain the physiological response pattern in the CIT (Gamer et al., 2008b; Verschuere et al., 2007b), this theoretical framework still allows for explaining a variety of different influences on the electrodermal responses in the CIT (cf. Ben-Shakhar and Furedy, 1990, pp. 111ff., and Chapter 7 of this volume).

Respiratory measures

In CIT studies, respiration is typically recorded by measuring changes in the volume of thorax and abdomen. This can be accomplished by attaching pneumatic or piezo-electric transducers around the chest and the abdomen with belts or Velcro straps. The signal of these transducers has an arbitrary unit when the stretch of the transducer is not calibrated, thus direct comparisons between participants are not possible.

Early studies on the validity of respiratory measures reported that neither respiratory rate nor amplitude allow for a valid differentiation of guilty and innocent participants in the CIT (Bradley and Ainsworth, 1984; Podlesny and Raskin, 1978; Thackray and Orne, 1968). However, this situation changed substantially after Timm (1982) proposed a different method of quantifying respiratory responses. Instead of scoring respiratory rate and amplitude separately, he suggested to measure the total length of the respiration tracing in a fixed period of time following stimulus presentation (e.g., 10 or 15 s). Using this method, one gets an integrative estimate of respiratory activity, called respiration line length (RLL). This measure is reduced when breathing gets slower as well as when the respiratory amplitude is reduced. It can therefore account for intra- and inter-individual differences in respiratory responsiveness that might have been responsible for the negative results that were found in earlier CIT studies. It has now been repeatedly demonstrated in laboratory (e.g., Ben-Shakhar et al., 1999; Bradley and Rettinger, 1992; Gamer et al., 2006; Verschuere et al., 2007a) as well as in field studies (Elaad et al., 1992) that RLL is smaller for relevant items as compared to neutral CIT items when the examinee is concealing knowledge. Since the RLL might be disproportionally affected by the start of measurement, it has been suggested to slowly increase the weight that is given to RLL segments at the beginning of the measurement window (typically in the first second) and correspondingly reduce the weights at the end of the scoring interval (Timm, 1982). Although this approach has been routinely adapted in CIT studies (e.g., Elaad, 2009), validity estimates do not seem to differ from a simple RLL scoring using similar weights for the whole measurement period (Gamer *et al.*, 2006).

Until now, it has not been systematically examined whether RLL is similarly affected by variations of the CIT paradigm as are electrodermal measures. A recent analysis of field cases in Japan, however, indicates that the extent of a respiratory apnea following relevant CIT items is larger when the question is directly related to a (serious) crime (Suzuki *et al.*, 2004). A smaller response was found for more peripheral details such as the precise time the crime was committed. By contrast, the electrodermal data only showed a main effect of critical vs. neutral CIT items. These data indicate that respiratory suppression might be more sensitive to emotional factors than electrodermal measures. As a consequence, RLL validity might be higher in the field as compared to laboratory settings (cf. Elaad *et al.*, 1992).

Respiration is regulated by a complex interplay of central and autonomic (mainly parasympathetic) structures as well as by peripheral feedback circuits (Lorig, 2007). In contrast to electrodermal measures, respiration is under voluntary control which might cause a problem for CIT examinations when examinees try to manipulate their breathing pattern. Although it has been shown that respiration might not be as affected by mental countermeasures as electrodermal responses (Ben-Shakhar and Dolev, 1996), conflicting results have been reported for physical countermeasures (Honts *et al.*, 1996; see also Chapter 11 of this volume). In these studies, examinees were not explicitly instructed to alter their breathing pattern. Thus, it is still unclear whether a direct manipulation of respiratory responses can serve as an effective countermeasure to reduce the sensitivity of the CIT.

Although it is still debated whether respiratory responses can be considered as a formal index of the OR (Barry, 1996), it has been reported that respiratory suppression exhibits some important characteristics that are related to the OR framework. For example, a reduction of breathing can be observed following unexpectedly presented stimuli (Stekelenburg and van Boxtel, 2002) and responses tend to habituate with stimulus repetitions (Barry, 1983). These characteristics also play an important role in OR accounts on CIT responding which may thus explain the validity of RLL measures to some degree.

Cardiovascular measures

The validity of several cardiovascular measures has been examined in the CIT setting. One of the most common and important measures in the traditional lie detection approach utilizing the Comparison Question Test (CQT) is the so-called cardio channel (Kircher and Raskin, 1988; Podlesny and Raskin, 1977). This measurement is accomplished by applying a cuff that is typically inflated to a pressure somewhere between systolic and diastolic blood pressure to the upper arm. Changes in pressure are recorded by connecting the inflated cuff with latex tubing to an amplifier. Most likely, cardio recordings reflect changes in relative blood pressure (Posey et al., 1969). In CIT settings, it has been repeatedly demonstrated that this cardio signal has no validity for the differentiation of guilty and innocent subjects (Elaad and Ben-Shakhar, 1989; Gamer et al., 2006; Podlesny and Raskin, 1978). Moreover, it has been shown that the electrodermal differentiation of relevant and neutral CIT items might be reduced because of the discomfort caused by the inflated blood pressure cuff (Horvath, 1978). For these reasons, it can be recommended to abstain from using this device in CIT examinations but future research will show whether continuously measured blood pressure using more sophisticated noninvasive techniques might allow for the detection of concealed knowledge (Podlesny and Kircher, 1999).

A more promising cardiovascular measure in CIT applications at the moment is the phasic heart rate. After some disappointing results in the beginning (Balloun and Holmes, 1979; Podlesny and Raskin, 1978), it is now well established that concealed knowledge results in a relative decrease of heart or pulse rate in comparison to neutral control items (e.g., Ambach et al., 2008; Bradley and Ainsworth, 1984; Bradley and Janisse, 1981; Gamer et al., 2006; Verschuere et al., 2005, 2007a).

When participants are required to verbally respond to each item immediately, a biphasic response can be typically observed before heart rate returns to baseline again (see left panel of Figure 2.2). This response consists of an initial acceleration followed by a subsequent deceleration that is more pronounced for relevant than for neutral CIT items given the examinee is able to differentiate between these item categories. The initial acceleration is typically missing or less pronounced when examinees remain silent (Gamer, et al., 2008b; Verschuere et al., 2004). It has thus been speculated that this heart rate increase is related to the preparation of the answer and the act of answering whereas the subsequent deceleration seems to be more related to the enhanced direction of attention toward the environment or to one's own bodily responses when guilty subjects are confronted with critical details (Gamer et al., 2006; Raskin and Hare, 1978). To directly test the contribution of both processes to the heart rate pattern, one can delay the verbal response to the test items (Willrich et al., 2003). Indeed, when requiring a verbal

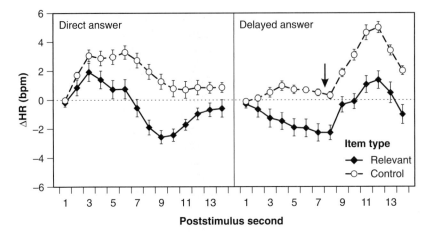

Figure 2.2 Phasic heart rate changes of participants who committed a mock crime and subsequently accomplished a CIT. The left panel shows heart rate responses as a function of item type for a group of $N = 30$ subjects who verbally denied each item immediately (Study 1 of Gamer et al., 2008a). The right panel depicts the heart rate changes for a different group of $N = 36$ subjects who were instructed to deny only after the offset of the visually presented details that were shown for 7 s (Willrich et al., 2003). The onset of the answer period is marked with an arrow.

response only several seconds after stimulus onset, concealed items elicit an immediate heart rate deceleration that differs from a small accelerative response elicited by neutral items. In the subsequent period of the verbal answer, a non-discriminative accelerative response to both item types can be observed (see right panel of Figure 2.2). Thus, the biphasic heart rate response that can be observed when answering directly seems to result from a temporal overlap of verbalization and attentional processes with the former being non-diagnostic and the latter allowing for a valid differentiation of guilty and innocent examinees (cf. Verschuere et al., 2009).

A third cardiovascular measure that has attracted considerable attention in laboratory studies on the CIT is the finger pulse as measured by photoplethysmographic techniques. On the one hand, pulse rate can be derived from these recordings (e.g., Bradley and Ainsworth, 1984; Verschuere et al., 2009); on the other hand, finger pulse amplitudes can be measured that reflect the degree of constriction of peripheral blood vessels. Using a CIT, Podlesny and Raskin (1978) showed that concealed relevant items elicit substantial peripheral vasoconstriction peaking around 8 s after stimulus onset. By contrast, neutral items were only accompanied by a moderate reduction of finger pulse amplitudes. More recently, Elaad and Ben-Shakhar (2006) suggested computing the overall length of the finger pulse signal as a combined estimate of pulse amplitude and rate changes. This can be accomplished similar to the calculation of the respiration line length and has been labeled finger pulse waveform length (FPWL). Several CIT studies showed that FPWL is consistently smaller for concealed as compared to neutral items but across studies, validity estimates seem to be slightly lower than for electrodermal measures (Ambach et al., 2008; Elaad and Ben-Shakhar, 2006, 2008; Verschuere et al., 2009). In contrast to the original claim that FPWL integrates pulse rate and amplitude changes, it was recently shown that FPWL validity seems to largely rely on the latter variable (Vandenbosch et al., 2009).

With respect to the autonomic regulation of cardiovascular responses, one has to differentiate between heart rate changes and peripheral vasoconstriction. The former is under control of both the sympathetic and parasympathetic branch of the autonomic nervous system with the vagal system exerting a much wider range of control over cardiac chronotropy (Berntson et al., 2007). The vascular smooth muscles in the bodily periphery, however, are primarily under control of the sympathetic nervous system. Thus, the heart rate decelerations that were observed for concealed CIT items can in principle result from either a reduction of sympathetic activity or an increase of vagal innervation. As these changes were found to occur very rapidly after stimulus presentation, it seems more likely that they are mediated by the vagal nervous system that was shown to respond much faster to behaviorally relevant events than the sympathic nervous system. Taken together, concealing information results in a relative reduction of the heart rate simultaneously to an increase of skin conductance and peripheral vasoconstriction. This indicates that both branches of the autonomic system are coactivated in the CIT (cf. Berntson et al., 1991).

Similar to the electrodermal responses, it has been suggested that the OR is the critical psychophysiological mechanism that underlies the cardiovascular response and especially the heart rate pattern in the CIT (Verschuere et al., 2004). Two arguments can be put forward against this explanation: first, electrodermal measures that are regarded to be the key index of an OR neither correlate with heart rate responses across individual CIT questions (Gamer et al., 2008b) nor across subjects (Gamer et al., 2008a). Second, skin conductance and heart rate responses show a differential course of habituation across CIT questions. SCRs tend to decrease across the test, whereas heart rate responses remain stable

(Gamer *et al.*, 2008b). Thus, simple OR theories do not fully account for the physiological response pattern and it might be necessary to widen the focus to a broader theory of information processing that incorporates the OR account as well as other psychophysiological mechanisms that have been proposed to explain decelerative heart rate responses to behaviorally relevant stimuli (Wölk *et al.*, 1989).

Other measures

Few studies also examined the diagnostic potential of other physiological measures that are related to the activity of the autonomic nervous system. For example, it was shown that pupil responses allow for a valid detection of concealed knowledge with concealed items eliciting larger pupil dilatation than neutral ones (Bradley and Janisse, 1981; Janisse and Bradley, 1980; Lubow and Fein, 1996). Although pupil responses are modulated by sympathetic as well as vagal influences, post-stimulus dilatation was found to be highly correlated with skin conductance responses (Bradley *et al.*, 2008). Thus, the pupil changes that were found in the CIT seem to reflect the same differential sympathetic activation for concealed and neutral items that was also found with respect to the electrodermal activity.

Based on a brief report of deception-related changes in facial temperature (Pavlidis *et al.*, 2002), a recent study also examined whether concealed knowledge can be detected from subtle changes of facial skin surface temperature (Pollina *et al.*, 2006). By utilizing thermography to measure infrared emission from the human face, it was found that examinees who committed a mock crime showed larger temperature increases to critical CIT items as compared to neutral ones in a region directly below the eyes. Such differential responses could be examined briefly after stimulus onset and were absent in a group of uninformed examinees. Using an individual classification approach, concealed knowledge could be identified in more than 90 percent of participants in this particular study. These small increases in facial temperature can in principle reflect changes in underlying muscle activity or blood microcirculation but face flushing seems to be primarily mediated by the sympathetic nervous system (Drummond and Lance, 1987) and might therefore be strongly correlated to electrodermal responses. However, facial thermography may be interesting for covert measurements of physiological changes in the CIT as it does not require attaching sensors to the examinee.

In principle, other measures of autonomic nervous system activity that have not been discussed so far might be useful for the detection of concealed information. For example, the T-wave amplitude of the electrocardiogram which is related to sympathetic activation (Furedy, 1985; Rashba *et al.*, 2002) or the changes in heart rate variability that reflect sympathetic as well as vagal innervation (Berntson *et al.*, 1997) might serve as physiological indicators of information concealment. However, it seems unlikely that such new autonomic measures will fundamentally change our view of physiological responding in the CIT since electrodermal, respiratory and heart rate measures already allow for indirectly assessing a wide range of autonomic system activity including different aspects of sympathetic and parasympathetic outflow. For the same reason, one should not expect dramatic increases of CIT validity based on new autonomic indices. Thus, it seems more promising to combine physiological measures across different response systems.

Combining autonomic responses

As I outlined above, electrodermal, respiratory and cardiovascular measures have high validity for the detection of concealed information. These measures can be easily recorded simultaneously with standard (computerized) polygraphs but the question emerges of whether such a multimodal approach is really useful in CIT settings. Do diagnoses get better when adding more physiological measures? How should we combine different channels in order to maximize the validity of the final diagnosis?

A simple approach that was adopted by several studies is to average (standardized) response differences between relevant and neutral control items across physiological channels. Given the absolute value of this score is high, one can assume that the examinee was able to differentiate between relevant and neutral CIT items. Values around zero indicate non-systematic responses to these item types which would allow for inferring that the examinee is innocent. Indeed, it was shown that CIT validity can be increased above the best single measure by pooling electrodermal and respiratory responses in laboratory (Ben-Shakhar and Dolev, 1996; Ben-Shakhar and Elaad, 2002; Ben-Shakhar *et al.*, 1999) and field settings (Elaad *et al.*, 1992). Comparable results were obtained for combinations of electrodermal, respiratory and cardiovascular measures (Elaad, 2009; Elaad and Ben-Shakhar, 2006, 2008), but conflicting results were also reported (Verschuere *et al.*, 2007a).

The main shortcoming of such an averaging approach is that differential contributions of several physiological measures are not adequately taken into account. Although field experts disagree about the most valid physiological index with respect to traditional lie detection approaches relying on the CQT, they tend to assign different weights to the physiological channels. For example, some examiners suggested to mainly rely on respiratory measures (Slowik and Buckley, 1975). Other researchers have shown that electrodermal responses have higher validity than respiratory and cardiovascular measures in the CQT and consequently proposed a set of optimal weights for the prediction of the truth status with larger weights being assigned to electrodermal responses (Kircher and Raskin, 1988).

We tested the utility of such a flexible classification approach in CIT settings and found high validity coefficients when assigning larger weights to electrodermal and respiratory measures as compared to heart rate responses (Gamer *et al.*, 2006). This approach relied on a stepwise logistic regression model that has fewer restricted assumptions than comparable statistical methods such as discriminant analysis. In its implementation in CIT settings, the logistic regression function that allows for determining the probability of information concealment $P(Y = 1)$ given a vector of physiological response differences between relevant and neutral items X for each examinee i is:

$$P(Y_i = 1 \mid X_i = x_i) = \frac{e^{\beta_0 + \sum_j \beta_j x_{ij}}}{1 + e^{\beta_0 + \sum_j \beta_j x_{ij}}}$$

The regression constant is β_0 and β_j represent different weights for each of j physiological channels. In the analysis, parameter weights are adjusted to maximize the differentiation of guilty and innocent subjects. The result is a value P for each participant that corresponds to the probability that this examinee is concealing knowledge.

We recently cross-validated the classification model that was originally proposed by Gamer *et al.* (2006) on data from 7 studies with 275 guilty and 53 innocent examinees (Gamer *et al.*, 2008a). It turned out that the weighted combination of SCR amplitudes, respiration line length and heart rate responses yielded slightly (but significantly) larger validity coefficients than the best single measure (for weights of the classification function see Table 2.1). These results were stable across different protocols and various samples. Similar results have been reported for trial-by-trial classifications within each participant (Ambach *et al.*, 2008). From these data, it can be recommended to record multiple physiological measures in CIT examinations and to combine them in a weighted manner. However, it remains to future research to determine whether this classification function also allows for deriving accurate diagnoses in the field context that largely differs from laboratory research especially with respect to motivational and emotional conditions.

Table 2.1 *Weights and quantification details of physiological measures that were integrated in the logistic regression model for the prediction of the truth status*

Measure	Quantification	Time window	β	SE	Wald
SCR	Largest skin conductance increase	0.5 to 10.5 s	4.24	1.38	9.51
Respiration	Respiration line length	0 to 10 s	−6.31	2.18	8.37
Phasic HR	Mean HR change in relation to last prestimulus second	0 to 15 s	−1.97	0.88	5.08
(Constant)			−3.92	1.11	12.52

Note: Limits of the measurement window are relative to stimulus onset; SCR = skin conductance response, HR = heart rate, SE = estimated standard error of regression coefficients. Nagelkerke's R^2 values increased from 0.58 via 0.80 to 0.85, when RLL and mean HR were included into the regression model in addition to the SCR measure (data set from Gamer *et al.*, 2006).

Taken together, the combination of several autonomic measures enhances CIT validity. From the scientific perspective, however, it is not fully clear why this is the case. The simplest explanation is that each physiological response cannot be measured with perfect reliability. Thus, a combined measure would always allow for a better differentiation of guilty and innocent examinees given that measurement errors across physiological channels are not highly correlated. A more plausible explanation, however, is related to psychophysiological mechanisms that are reflected in these measures. As outlined above, electrodermal, respiratory, and cardiovascular measures seem to differentially reflect sympathetic and parasympathetic outflow and they cover slightly different aspects of psychological processes such as the OR. Moreover, some measures seem to be more sensitive to habituation than others (e.g., Gamer *et al.*, 2008b) and physiological responsiveness across data channels might vary between individuals (Foerster, 1985). This can be as extreme as around 5 percent to 10 percent of the normal population do not show any skin conductance response to non-aversive external stimulation (so-called non-responders, Gruzelier *et al.*, 1981). As a consequence, correlations between electrodermal, respiratory, and cardiovascular measures in the CIT rarely exceed values of $r = 0.30$ (Gamer *et al.*, 2008a). It is thus beneficial to combine these measures in order to cover different aspects of information concealment as well as to incorporate individual differences in physiological responsiveness.

Summary and conclusions

Taken together, examinees that are concealing information can be validly differentiated from unaware participants by comparing electrodermal, respiratory, and cardiovascular responses to relevant and neutral items in the CIT. A combination of skin conductance response amplitudes, respiration line length, and heart rate changes by means of a logistic regression model further enhances the validity of the test. Both branches of the autonomic nervous system contribute to these physiological responses that are closely – but not exclusively – related to the orienting response.

Open questions for future research are twofold. From the applied perspective, it would be interesting to test whether other measures that are not directly related to the activity of the autonomic nervous system provide incremental validity. The main problem, however, stems from substantial procedural differences to the standard CIT format when utilizing behavioral measures, event-related brain potentials or neuroimaging techniques. Most importantly, more item repetitions are necessary for these latter applications and the interstimulus interval is typically reduced such that a reliable quantification of autonomic responses is impeded. However, recent research indicates that it might be promising to examine such combinations as it was shown that behavioral measures (Meijer *et al.*, 2007), event-related brain potentials (Gamer and Berti, 2010), and functional magnetic resonance imaging data (Gamer *et al.*, 2007; Gamer *et al.*, in press) may in part reflect different psychological processes than electrodermal responses when examinees are concealing information. They may thus provide incremental validity in the CIT.

A second line of research that has been largely neglected until now is related to the mechanisms and experimental conditions that affect different autonomic measures. Extensive meta-analytic research has only been conducted for electrodermal data so far (Ben-Shakhar and Elaad, 2003) and it remains largely unknown whether the same conditions that affect skin conductance measures also modulate respiratory and cardiovascular responses. At the moment it seems unlikely that different autonomic measures respond uniformly in CIT examinations. For example, there is evidence for certain respiratory patterns in field examinations that rarely occur in the laboratory whereas electrodermal responses do not seem to differ substantially between these conditions (Suzuki *et al.*, 2004). Moreover, skin conductance and heart rate responses show a different habituation pattern in a CIT examination which might indicate that both measures reflect partly different psychological processes (Gamer *et al.*, 2008b). To gain more insight into this research question, it would be necessary to examine very large samples of participants while carefully manipulating experimental conditions that might differentially affect electrodermal, respiratory, and cardiovascular measures.

To sum up, autonomic measures can be easily recorded in the CIT, they can be objectively analyzed and they were shown to be highly valid. Each upcoming technique aiming to detect concealed information on an individual basis should be compared to this standard with respect to practicability and validity.

REFERENCES

Ambach, W., Stark, R., Peper, M., and Vaitl, D. (2008). An interfering Go/ No-go task does not affect accuracy in a Concealed Information Test. *International Journal of Psychophysiology*, 68, 6–16.

Balloun, K. D. and Holmes, D. S. (1979). Effects of repeated examinations on the ability to detect guilt with a polygraph examination: a laboratory experiment with a real crime. *Journal of Applied Psychology*, 64, 316–322.

Barry, R. J. (1983). Primary bradycardia and the evoked cardiac response in the OR context. *Physiological Psychology*, 11, 135–140.

(1996). Preliminary process theory: towards an integrated account of the psychophysiology of cognitive processes. *Acta Neurobiologiae Experimentalis*, 56, 469–484.

Ben-Shakhar, G. (1994). The roles of stimulus novelty and significance in determining the electrodermal orienting response: interactive versus additive approaches. *Psychophysiology*, 31, 402–411.

Ben-Shakhar, G., and Dolev, K. (1996). Psychophysiological detection through the guilty knowledge technique: effects of mental countermeasures. *Journal of Applied Psychology*, 81, 273–281.

Ben-Shakhar, G., and Elaad, E. (2002). Effects of questions' repetition and variation on the efficiency of the guilty knowledge test: a reexamination. *Journal of Applied Psychology*, 87, 972–977.

(2003). The validity of psychophysiological detection of information with the Guilty Knowledge Test: a meta-analytic review. *Journal of Applied Psychology*, 88, 131–151.

Ben-Shakhar, G., and Furedy, J. J. (1990). *Theories and Applications in the Detection of Deception: A Psychophysiological and International Perspective.* New York: Springer.

Ben-Shakhar, G., Gronau, N., and Elaad, E. (1999). Leakage of relevant information to innocent examinees in the GKT: an attempt to reduce false-positive outcomes by introducing target stimuli. *Journal of Applied Psychology*, 84, 651–660.

Ben-Shakhar, G., Lieblich, I., and Kugelmass, S. (1975). Detection of information and GSR habituation: an attempt to derive detection efficiency from two habituation curves. *Psychophysiology*, 12, 283–288.

Berntson, G. G., Cacioppo, J. T., and Quigley, K. S. (1991). Autonomic determinism: the modes of autonomic control, the doctrine of autonomic space, and the laws of autonomic constraint. *Psychological Review*, 98, 459–487.

Berntson, G. G., Quigley, K. S., and Lozano, D. (2007). Cardiovascular psychophysiology. In J. T. Cacioppo , L. G. Tassinary, and G. G. Bernston (eds.), *Handbook of Psychophysiology* (pp. 182–210). Cambridge University Press.

Berntson, G. G., Bigger, J. T. J., Eckberg, D. L., Grossman, P., Kaufmann, P. G., Malik, M., Nagaraja, H. N., Porges, S. W., Saul, J. P., Stone, P. H., and van der Molen, M. W. (1997). Heart rate variability: origins, methods, and interpretive caveats. *Psychophysiology*, 34, 623–648.

Bradley, M. T., and Ainsworth, D. (1984). Alcohol and the psychophysiological detection of deception. *Psychophysiology*, 21, 63–71.

Bradley, M. T., and Janisse, M. P. (1981). Accuracy demonstrations, threat, and the detection of deception: cardiovascular, electrodermal, and pupillary measures. *Psychophysiology*, 18, 307–315.

Bradley, M. T., and Rettinger, J. (1992). Awareness of crime-relevant information and the guilty knowledge test. *Journal of Applied Psychology*, 77, 55–59.

Bradley, M. M., Miccoli, L., Escrig, M. A., and Lang, P. J. (2008). The pupil as a measure of emotional arousal and autonomic activation. *Psychophysiology*, 45, 602–607.

Cohen, J. (1988). *Statistical Power Analysis for the Behavioral Sciences*. Hillsdale, NJ: Erlbaum.

Davidson, P. O. (1968). Validity of the guilty-knowledge technique: the effects of motivation. *Journal of Applied Psychology*, 52, 62–65.

Drummond, P. D., and Lance, J. W. (1987). Facial flushing and sweating mediated by the sympathetic nervous system. *Brain*, 110, 793–803.

Elaad, E. (1990). Detection of guilty knowledge in real-life criminal investigations. *Journal of Applied Psychology*, 75, 521–529.

  (1994). The accuracy of human decisions and objective measurements in psychophysiological detection of knowledge. *Journal of Psychology*, 128, 267–280.

  (2009). Effects of context and state of guilt on the detection of concealed crime information. *International Journal of Psychophysiology*, 71, 225–234.

Elaad, E., and Ben-Shakhar, G. (1989). Effects of motivation and verbal-response type on psychophysiological detection of information. *Psychophysiology*, 26, 442–451.

  (2006). Finger pulse waveform length in the detection of concealed information. *International Journal of Psychophysiology*, 61, 226–234.

  (2008). Covert respiration measures for the detection of concealed information. *Biological Psychology*, 77, 284–291.

Elaad, E., Ginton, A., and Jungman, N. (1992). Detection measures in real-life criminal guilty knowledge tests. *Journal of Applied Psychology*, 77, 757–767.

Foerster, F. (1985). Psychophysiological response specificities: a replication over a 12-month period. *Biological Psychology*, 21, 169–182.

Furedy, J. J. (1985). Joint use of heart-rate and T-wave amplitude as non-invasive cardiac performance measures: a psychophysiological perspective. In J. F.

Orlebeke, G. Mulder, and L. J. P. van Doornen (eds.), *Psychophysiology of Cardiovascular Control* (pp. 237–256). New York: Plenum Press.

Gamer, M., and Berti, S. (2010). Task relevance and recognition of concealed information have different influences on electrodermal activity and event-related brain potentials. *Psychophysiology*, 47, 355–364.

Gamer, M., Bauermann, T., Stoeter, P., and Vossel, G. (2007). Covariations among fMRI, skin conductance, and behavioral data during processing of concealed information. *Human Brain Mapping*, 28, 1287–1301.

Gamer, M., Rill, H.-G., Vossel, G., and Gödert, H. W. (2006). Psychophysiological and vocal measures in the detection of guilty knowledge. *International Journal of Psychophysiology*, 60, 76–87.

Gamer, M., Verschuere, B., Crombez, G., and Vossel, G. (2008a). Combining physiological measures in the detection of concealed information. *Physiology & Behavior*, 95, 333–340.

Gamer, M., Gödert, H. W., Keth, A., Rill, H.-G., and Vossel, G. (2008b). Electrodermal and phasic heart rate responses in the Guilty Actions Test: comparing guilty examinees to informed and uninformed innocents. *International Journal of Psychophysiology*, 69, 61–68.

Gamer, M., Klimecki, O., Bauermann, T., Stoeter, P., and Vossel, G. (in press). fMRI-activation patterns in the detection of concealed information rely on memory-related effects. *Social Cognitive and Affective Neuroscience*.

Gruzelier, J., Eves, F., Connolly, J., and Hirsch, S. (1981). Orienting, habituation, sensitisation, and dishabituation in the electrodermal system of consecutive, drug free, admissions for schizophrenia. *Biological Psychology*, 12, 187–209.

Honts, C. R., Devitt, M. K., Winbush, M., and Kircher, J. C. (1996). Mental and physical countermeasures reduce the accuracy of the concealed knowledge test. *Psychophysiology*, 33, 84–92.

Horneman, C. J., and O'Gorman, J. G. (1985). Detectability in the card test as a function of the subject's verbal response. *Psychophysiology*, 22, 330–333.

Horvath, F. (1978). An experimental comparison of the psychological stress evaluator and the galvanic skin response in detection of deception. *Journal of Applied Psychology*, 63, 338–344.

(1979). Effect of different motivational instructions on detection of deception with the psychological stress evaluator and the galvanic skin response. *Journal of Applied Psychology*, 64, 323–330.

Jackson, J. C. (1974). Amplitude and habituation of the orienting reflex as a function of stimulus intensity. *Psychophysiology*, 11, 647–659.

Janisse, M. P., and Bradley, M. T. (1980). Deception, information and the pupillary response. *Perceptual and Motor Skills*, 50, 748–750.

Kircher, J. C., and Raskin, D. C. (1988). Human versus computerized evaluations of polygraph data in a laboratory setting. *Journal of Applied Psychology*, 73, 291–302.

Lieblich, I., Kugelmass, S., and Ben-Shakhar, G. (1970). Efficiency of GSR detection of information as a function of stimulus set size. *Psychophysiology*, 6, 601–608.

Lorig, T. S. (2007). The respiratory system. In J. T. Cacioppo, L. G. Tassinary, and G. G. Bernston (eds.), *Handbook of Psychophysiology* (pp. 231–244). Cambridge University Press.

Lubow, R. E., and Fein, O. (1996). Pupillary size in response to a visual guilty knowledge test: new technique for the detection of deception. *Journal of Experimental Psychology: Applied*, 2, 164–177.

Lykken, D. T. (1959). The GSR in the detection of guilt. *Journal of Applied Psychology*, 43, 385–388.

(1960). The validity of the guilty knowledge technique: the effects of faking. *Journal of Applied Psychology*, 44, 258–262.

(1974). Psychology and the lie detector industry. *American Psychologist*, 29, 725–739.

MacLaren, V. V. (2001). A quantitative review of the guilty knowledge test. *Journal of Applied Psychology*, 86, 674–683.

Meijer, E. H., Smulders, F. T., Johnston, J. E., and Merckelbach, H. L. (2007). Combining skin conductance and forced choice in the detection of concealed information. *Psychophysiology*, 44, 814–822.

Pavlidis, I., Eberhardt, N. L., and Levine, J. A. (2002). Seeing through the face of deception. *Nature*, 415, 35.

Podlesny, J. A., and Kircher, J. C. (1999). The finapres (volume clamp) recording method in psychophysiological detection of deception examinations. *Forensic Science Communications*, 1, 1–18.

Podlesny, J. A., and Raskin, D. C. (1977). Physiological measures and the detection of deception. *Psychological Bulletin*, 84, 782–799.

(1978). Effectiveness of techniques and physiological measures in the detection of deception. *Psychophysiology*, 15, 344–359.

Pollina, D. A., Dollins, A. B., Senter, S. M., Brown, T. E., Pavlidis, I., Levine, J. A., and Ryan, A. H. (2006). Facial skin surface temperature changes during a "concealed information" test. *Annals of Biomedical Engineering*, 34, 1182–1189.

Posey, J. A., Geddes, L. A., Williams, H., and Moore, A. G. (1969). The meaning of the point of maximum oscillations in cuff pressure in the indirect measurement of blood pressure. Part I. *Cardiovascular Research Center Bulletin*, 8, 15–25.

Rashba, E. J., Cooklin, M., MacMurdy, K., Kavesh, N., Kirk, M., Sarang, S., Peters, R. W., Shorofsky, S. R., and Gold, M. R. (2002). Effects of selective autonomic blockade on T-wave alternans in humans. *Circulation*, 105, 837–842.

Raskin, D. C., and Hare, R. D. (1978). Psychopathy and detection of deception in a prison population. *Psychophysiology*, 15, 126–136.

Siddle, D. A., O' Gorman, J. G., and Wood, L. (1979). Effects of electrodermal lability and stimulus significance on electrodermal response amplitude to stimulus change. *Psychophysiology*, 16, 520–527.

Slowik, S. M., and Buckley, J. P. (1975). Relative accuracy of polygraph examiner diagnosis of respiration, blood pressure, and GSR recordings. *Journal of Police Science and Administration*, 3, 305–309.

Sokolov, E. N. (1963). *Perception and the Conditioned Reflex*. Oxford: Pergamon Press.

Stekelenburg, J. J., and van Boxtel, A. (2002). Pericranial muscular, respiratory, and heart rate components of the orienting response. *Psychophysiology*, 39, 707–722.

Suzuki, R., Nakayama, M., and Furedy, J. J. (2004). Specific and reactive sensitivities of skin resistance response and respiratory apnea in a Japanese concealed information test (CIT) of criminal guilt. *Canadian Journal of Behavioral Science*, 36, 202–219.

Thackray, R. I., and Orne, M. T. (1968). A comparison of physiological indices in detection of deception. *Psychophysiology*, 4, 329–339.

Timm, H. W. (1982). Analyzing deception from respiratory patterns. *Journal of Police Science and Administration*, 10, 47–51.

Vandenbosch, K., Verschuere, B., Crombez, G., and De Clercq, A. (2009). The validity of finger pulse line length for the detection of concealed information. *International Journal of Psychophysiology*, 71, 118–123.

Verschuere, B., Crombez, G., De Clercq, A., and Koster, E. H. W. (2004). Autonomic and behavioral responding to concealed information: differentiating orienting and defensive responses. *Psychophysiology*, 41, 461–466.

(2005). Psychopathic traits and autonomic responding to concealed information in a prison sample. *Psychophysiology*, 42, 239–245.

Verschuere, B., Crombez, G., Smolders, L., and De Clercq, A. (2009). Differentiating orienting and defensive responses to concealed information: the role of verbalization. *Applied Psychophysiology and Biofeedback*, 34, 237–244.

Verschuere, B., Crombez, G., Koster, E. H. W., and De Clercq, A. (2007a). Antisociality, underarousal and the validity of the Concealed Information Polygraph Test. *Biological Psychology*, 74, 309–318.

Verschuere, B., Crombez, G., Koster, E. H. W., Van Bockstaele, B., and De Clercq, A. (2007b). Startling secrets: startle eye blink modulation by concealed crime information. *Biological Psychology*, 76, 52–60.

Waid, W. M., and Orne, M. T. (1980). Individual differences in electrodermal lability and the detection of information and deception. *Journal of Applied Psychology*, 65, 1–8.

Waid, W. M., Orne, M. T., and Wilson, S. K. (1979). Effects of level of socialization on electrodermal detection of deception. *Psychophysiology*, 16, 15–22.

Waid, W. M., Orne, E. C., Cook, M. R., and Orne, M. T. (1978). Effects of attention, as indexed by subsequent memory, on electrodermal detection of information. *Journal of Applied Psychology*, 63, 728–733.

Wallin, B. G. (1981). Sympathetic nerve activity underlying electrodermal and cardiovascular reactions in man. *Psychophysiology*, 18, 470–476.

Willrich, A. T., Adler, I., Rill, H., Gödert, H.-G., and Vossel, G. (2003). Detection of concealed knowledge: the effects of written versus pictorial stimulus presentation on skin conductance responses and phasic heart rate. *Journal of Psychophysiology*, 16, 252.

Wölk, C., Velden, M., Zimmermann, U., and Krug, S. (1989). The interrelation between phasic blood pressure and heart rate changes in the context of the "baroreceptor hypothesis". *Journal of Psychophysiology*, 3, 397–402.

3   Detecting concealed information in less than a second: response latency-based measures

Bruno Verschuere and Jan De Houwer

Overview: Concealed information is typically assessed with physiological measures. To overcome the limitations of physiological measures, an assessment using response latencies has been proposed. At first sight, research findings on response latency-based concealed information tests seem inconsistent. Our procedural analysis of the various latency-based tests indicates that tests based on a manipulation of relevant stimulus-response compatibility, such as the oddball task (Farwell and Donchin, 1991; Seymour *et al.*, 2000), have typically produced robust results. These results are promising, but need to be extended with research examining vulnerability to faking and performance under more realistic circumstances.

A wide range of physiological indices have been registered in order to detect concealed information: skin conductance, heart rate, respiration, pulse volume, facial temperature, event-related potentials, and cerebral blood oxygenation. Laboratory studies have typically produced large effect sizes, confirming the validity of concealed information measures that are based on these indices (Ben-Shakhar and Elaad, 2003; Gamer *et al.*, 2008; Langleben *et al.*, 2002; Rosenfeld, 2002). However, physiological measures have their limitations. First, none of these measures allows for perfect detection, leaving room for improvement. Second, certain functional characteristics of physiological indices (e.g., habituation, non-responding) can undermine the validity of concealed information tests, based on these indices. Third, all physiological measures require sophisticated and often expensive machinery. From this perspective, there may be merit in measures that are based on other types of indices.

In psychology, one of the most extensively studied behavioral indices is response latency. Response latencies can be registered with cheap, unsophisticated, and universally available equipment: a single computer. We will argue that there are paradigms that allow to accurately detect concealed information using response latency. Specifically, we suggest that paradigms based on a manipulation of relevant stimulus-response compatibility result in the large effect sizes needed for individual classification purposes.

The Association Reaction Method

The idea to use response latency for deception detection is hardly new. From the very beginning of scientific psychology, researchers have investigated how long it takes people to lie vs. to tell the truth. This early research modified the Association Reaction Method (Jung, 1910) for deception detection. Using this method, the examinee is provided with a cue word and asked to give an association. It was reasoned that the nature of the given association may reveal deception. Take the example of someone trying to conceal having entered a room with red ink on the desk. The association "red" to the cue word "ink" may indicate concealed knowledge. The examinee may also give an association that does not reveal concealed knowledge (e.g., ink – "black"), but it was assumed that this would require more time for the deceptive examinee than for the truthful examinee (Henke and Eddy, 1909).

One of the main developers of the polygraph test, Marston (1927) used a variant of the method in ten psychology students. They were presented with cards that had ten words, aligned in two columns of five words. Participants were instructed to start either from bottom left, bottom right, upper left or upper right, and to give an association with each word. For half of the cards, however, participants needed to "lie," and start at a different location. As expected, four participants ("the positive type") responded slower when lying. However, three others were faster when lying ("the negative type"), and four ("the mixed type") did not show consistent differences in reaction time between lying and truth telling. These results were not very encouraging. It was concluded that response latency is under voluntary control, and the association reaction method was abandoned.

Deceptive communication

From the 1970s, researchers started to focus on deceptive interpersonal communication. A large number of communication characteristics have been investigated. To illustrate, an extensive meta-analysis examined 158 different aspects (DePaulo et al., 2003). These can be broadly classified into verbal (e.g., unusual details, immediacy, inconsistency), nonverbal (e.g., head, leg, or hand movement), and paraverbal (e.g., pitch). Response latency, defined as the time between the end of a question and the start of the answer, is among the paraverbal cues that was often examined. As in the Association Reaction Method, the common prediction is that people need more time to initiate deceptive communication compared to truthful communication. In a prototypical study, Harrison et al. (1978) set up an interview situation. One hundred and forty-four undergraduate students were assigned the role of either interviewer or interviewee. The interviewer asked questions such as "What would you like to do next summer?" and "What would you like to do after graduating from Davis?" The interviewee was prompted by one of two lights – not visible to the interviewer – to give a deceptive or truthful answer of about 20–30 s. The average time needed to initiate lies vs. truths was calculated. The meta-analysis of DePaulo et al. included thirty-two such estimates, covering data from 1,330 subjects. Standardized mean difference, Cohen's d, was calculated as a measure of effect size. The effect size was 0.02 [95 percent confidence interval -0.06, 0.10], again indicating that lying and truth telling did not differ reliably in response latency.

Neuroscientific (dis-)interest in response latency

There are some disadvantages to the measurement of response latency in the Association Reaction Method and in interview situations. Participants are not always encouraged to respond as fast as possible. Absent such instructions, there will be great variability in response latencies, and participants may easily control performance. Moreover, the main task is often very simple, and focused directly upon the subject under investigation, for example asking participants directly to lie or tell the truth. Response latency tasks may be more valid when they are speeded, less direct, or more difficult. From the 1960s, cognitive psychologists have examined human information processing and introduced a number of such response latency-based measures. From the late 1980s, neuroscientists started applying those paradigms to deception research. The most commonly used paradigm is the oddball task (see Table 3.1). In this task, participants are instructed to detect briefly (e.g., 300 ms) presented rare *target* items among frequent *irrelevant* items. Because of their infrequent presentation and task relevance, the target items typically result in larger response latencies and larger P300- evoked potentials compared to the irrelevant items. To adopt this basic paradigm to detect concealed information a number of *probe* items are embedded among the irrelevant items. Farwell and Donchin (1991, Experiment 1) used probe items related to a mock espionage that participants had or had not executed. When tested on the crime

Table 3.1 *The concealed information oddball test*

Stimulus type	Example	Frequency of presentation	Instructions	Predicted outcome
Target	BRAM	Rare (1/6)	Press "Yes"	Slow and inaccurate
Probe	JAN	Rare (1/6)	Press "No"	Slow and inaccurate
Irrelevant	ADRIAAN, GEERT, RUDI, GILLES	Frequent (4/6)	Press "No"	Fast and accurate

they were innocent of, the probe items were indistinguishable from the irrelevant items and produced similar responses in P300 amplitudes and response latencies. When tested on the crime they had committed, however, the probe items resulted in larger P300 amplitude and larger response latencies than the irrelevant items. In fact, this response latency lengthening was seen in all knowledgeable individuals (M = 79 ms, SD = 53 ms, *Range* = 11–206 ms).

With their main interest in central nervous activity, ERP/fMRI researchers have not always statistically analyzed (Rosenfeld et al., 2007) or even reported (e.g., Farwell and Smith, 2001; Rosenfeld et al., 1988) findings for response latencies in the oddball task. Nonetheless, several ERP studies have reported that response latencies successfully reveal concealed information (Allen et al., 1992; Allen and Movius, 2000; Farwell and Donchin, 1991; Gamer et al., 2007; Meijer et al., 2007; Nittono and Kubo, 2008; Rosenfeld et al., 2008; Rosenfeld et al., 2004; Verschuere et al., 2009c).[1]

In the study by Allen et al. (1992), a list of words was memorized to perfection, and served as targets in a first oddball task. After a thirty-minute break, participants learned a new set of words that served as targets in the second oddball task. The twenty participants were explicitly instructed to hide recognition from the old targets words, which now served as probes. P300 amplitude and response latencies (77 ms difference) allowed to discriminate the probes from the irrelevant items with near perfect accuracy. Two additional experiments were conducted in

[1] Most, but not all ERP studies resulted in the typically observed robust effects. The Mertens and Allen (2008) study found the expected response latency lengthening to mock crime-related items (97 ms) compared to control items in guilty participants. Surprisingly, however, a significant effect (44 ms) was also seen in innocent participants. It is not clear why these results deviate from the other studies.

which deception was emphasized in the instructions (Experiment2; $n =$ 20) and a small financial reward (Experiment3; $n = 20$) was provided for successfully concealing brainwave signs of probe recognition. In both experiments, response latencies could discriminate probes from irrelevant items with near perfect accuracy. The chance of erroneously identifying one of the irrelevant items as one of the probes with response latencies (i.e., false positive rate) was very low in all three experiments (5 percent or lower). This procedure may be useful for the assessment of (feigned) memory deficits, and has been successfully applied by Allen and Movius (2000) in the study of inter-identity amnesia in dissociative disorder.

The advantage of a response latency measure for concealed information detection is in its ease of application. The studies reviewed so far (Allen *et al.*, 1992; Allen and Movius, 2000; Farwell and Donchin, 1991) all involved relatively complex ERP recordings. The high validity of the response latency measure does not necessarily hold without the concurrent ERP recording. Because the saliency of the ERP recording (wearing an electrode cap etc.), and the instructions sometimes explicitly ask participants to focus upon the ERP recordings, participants may have not tried to control their reaction time performance. In three experiments, Seymour *et al.* (2000) examined whether the reaction time effects hold without the concurrent measurement of event-related potentials. The study design in their first experiment was a replication of the mock espionage scenario by Farwell and Donchin (1991) except that ERPs were not recorded and that a response deadline of 1,000 ms was added. The data ($n = 35$) confirmed that probes resulted in higher error rates and a marked increase in response latencies of about 300 ms compared to the irrelevant items. Using a 1,500 ms response deadline, Seymour and Kerlin (2008) replicated this finding in thirty-two undergraduates. The latter study included an additional condition ($n = 32$) in which facial stimuli were used, which resulted in a similarly large effect.

An important question is whether response latencies allow concealed information detection with the same accuracy as physiological measures. The most extensively investigated and best validated physiological measure is skin conductance responding (see Chapter 2). A direct comparison of response latencies and skin conductance on a single test is not that straightforward. Skin conductance recording is typically based upon a small number of trials (e.g., twenty) to avoid habituation, and a lengthy inter-stimulus interval (e.g., 20–25 s) to avoid overlapping responses. Response latency measures typically use much more trials and a much shorter inter-stimulus interval. A test that balances between these requirements to measure both responses may be sub-optimal for one or both measures. A recent study conducted in our lab took an alternative approach and tested subjects with both tests, one after the other (Verschuere *et al.*, 2009b). This way, each measure can be obtained under ideal conditions. Thirty-two undergraduates first filled in an autobiographical questionnaire and were then asked to feign complete amnesia and hide recognition of their autobiographical information. If successful, participants gained a monetary reward. Physiological responses to five questions concerning their identity were recorded with the polygraph (e.g., "Is your name ADRIAAN GEERT? JAN? RUDI? GILLES?"). In the oddball task, participants were required to press one button for a set of previously memorized target items (e.g., BRAM) and another for all other items – including the autobiographical items – within 800 ms. The order of the two tests was counterbalanced across participants. Both tests discriminated successfully between concealed autobiographical and control information, and resulted in similarly high effect sizes (RTs: $d = 1.97$ vs. SCR: $d = 1.46$).

Taken together, these studies indicate that response latencies obtained in the oddball task can reliably differentiate between probe and irrelevant items, also without concurrent physiological measure, to an accuracy level similar to that achieved with the best autonomic nervous system measures, and when participants are warned not to respond differentially to probe items.

On the hypothesized role of stimulus-response compatibility in response latency-based tests

Our conclusion that response latencies obtained in the oddball task provide a valid measure for concealed information detection may seem provocative in the light of the conclusion of researchers such as Gronau *et al.* (2005, p. 147) who stated that the practical utility of latency-based tests of concealed information is questionable. We do not think that response latency per se provides a valid means for concealed information detection. The paradigm in which response latencies are obtained is crucial. The conclusion made by Gronau *et al.* was based upon findings from several different paradigms. Although there are many differences between these paradigms, the crucial difference may be that only the oddball task relies upon a manipulation of stimulus-response compatibility.

Stimulus-response compatibility refers to the compatibility between features of the stimuli that are presented and the required response.

The classic Stroop task (Stroop, 1935) is a well known example of a task in which stimulus-response compatibility is manipulated. Participants are presented with words presented in different colors and asked to name the color of the word. Although word content is irrelevant, it varies across trials such that there is a match with the required response on compatible trials (e.g., blue written in blue), but not on incompatible trials (e.g., blue written in yellow). On incompatible trials, there is a conflict between the response elicited by the stimulus and the required response. Blue written in yellow, for example, will elicit a stimulus-driven tendency to answer to blue, which the participant needs to override in order to give the correct yellow answer. As a result, people are typically slower and less accurate on incompatible trials than on compatible trials.

Gronau *et al.* (2005) modified the Stroop task for concealed information detection. Participants were presented with critical and control words presented in one of four colors, and instructed to name the color of the words within a 1,500 ms response deadline. The critical words were mock crime-related in a first experiment, and autobiographical in a second experiment. Response latencies between the critical and the control words differed significantly only in the second experiment. Engelhard *et al.* (2003) also failed to find response latency differences between mock crime-related and control words in a modified Stroop. These findings do not necessarily contradict our hypothesis. Word content in this task is not related to the required response. There is no stimulus-response incompatibility in this task, and therefore, it is not really a Stroop (Algom *et al.*, 2004; De Houwer, 2003b). This is not to say that one cannot find differences between concealed and control words in this task. There may be other processes producing such effects, for example concealed information demanding attention (Verschuere *et al.*, 2004b). The point here is that this effect is not related to stimulus-response incompatibility, and therefore it is much smaller than that observed in stimulus-response incompatibility tasks.

Let us consider another response latency paradigm that has been applied to concealed information detection. In a series of experiments in our lab, participants were instructed to conceal recognition of a set of pictures they had just memorized (Verschuere *et al.*, 2004a; Verschuere *et al.*, 2005). These pictures were paired with a control picture and presented in a dot probe task. Immediately after the pictures disappeared from the screen, a pair of dots (.. or :) replaced one of the two pictures. Participants had to indicate as fast as possible whether the dots were positioned horizontally or vertically. The prediction that the attention-demanding nature of concealed information would be evident in response latency and error rates was confirmed. The effects (4–11 ms) were, however, much smaller than those typically obtained with the oddball task. Like the modified Stroop, the probe stimuli were not incompatible with the required response in the dot probe.

The same lack of incompatibility holds for two other response latency paradigms that also failed to produce strong effects of concealed information. The lexical decision task requires participants to indicate as fast as possible whether the presented stimulus is a word or a non-word. The tone detection task presents participants with a secondary task (i.e., to detect auditory beeps as fast as possible) during a primary task (i.e., autonomic nervous system based concealed information test). These tasks do not impose a conflict between probe stimuli and the required response. Both tasks failed to produce response latency difference between concealed and control information (Locker and Pratarelli, 1997; Verschuere *et al.*, 2004b).

In sum, tasks that do not manipulate stimulus-response compatibility such as the modified Stroop, the dot probe, the lexical decision, and the tone detection task have not produced robust response latency differences between concealed and control information. The findings with the oddball task are consistently better, possibly because of the built-in stimulus-response incompatibility for probe items. Recall that there are three stimulus types in the oddball task (see Table 3.1): targets, irrelevant items, and probes. Innocent participants can perform the task accurately based upon stimulus familiarity. For them, it is a binary task: familiar (targets) vs. unfamiliar (probes and irrelevant items).[2] Knowledgeable participants cannot base their judgment upon familiarity alone. Stimulus familiarity leads to the correct response for targets and irrelevant items. Probes, however, involve a stimulus-response incompatibility with stimulus familiarity leading to the incorrect response. Knowledgeable participants have to override the familiarity-based response, and base their judgment upon recognition. Because determining familiarity is a fast and automated process (Yonelinas, 2002), knowledgeable participants will typically be slower and less accurate in classifying probes compared to the irrelevant items.

So far, only the oddball task has produced robust response latency effects in the detection of concealed information. Our procedural analysis, however, suggests that there is nothing special about the oddball task that cannot be accomplished in other tasks. Thus, we predict that other response latency paradigms can also produce the robust effects

---

[2] The unique response to the targets has been labelled the "yes," "old," "target," or "recognition" response.

observed in the oddball task if the task creates a stimulus-response conflict. In fact, we should be more specific and state that this will hold for *relevant* stimulus-response compatibility tasks, and not necessarily for *irrelevant* stimulus-response compatibility tasks (see De Houwer, 2003b). This distinction refers to the question whether the incompatibility is related to stimulus features that are immediately relevant for the task or not. In the classic Stroop, for example, word content does not need to be processed in order to perform the task and is thus an example of irrelevant stimulus-response compatibility. The oddball is an example of a relevant stimulus-response compatibility task, because a stimulus feature that allows participants to distinguish target items from irrelevant items (i.e., the fact that target but not irrelevant items are familiar) is also a feature of the probe items (i.e., probes are also familiar).

We believe that for concealed information detection purposes, relevant stimulus-response compatibility tasks are most likely to produce big effects. The main reason is that it is easier to ignore irrelevant stimulus features than relevant stimulus features (De Houwer, 2009). This reasoning is supported by the fact that the modified Extrinsic Affective Simon Task (EAST; De Houwer, 2003a), an irrelevant stimulus-response compatibility task, failed to produce significant effects in our laboratory. In this modification of the EAST, participants reacted to the color of words using responses that were related to the concept "familiar" or to the concept "unfamiliar." The task-irrelevant content of the colored words was manipulated with half of the words related to concealed autobiographical information and half to control information items. The expectation was that participants would find it more difficult to classify the colored words when their content is incompatible with the required response (e.g., give the "unfamiliar" response to concealed information). This expectation was not confirmed. We think this may be due to word content being task-irrelevant, and therefore easy to ignore.

The Implicit Association Test (IAT; Greenwald *et al.*, 1998), for example, is a better candidate because it is a relevant stimulus-response compatibility task.[3] Sartori *et al.* modified the IAT for deception detection purposes (aIAT; Sartori *et al.*, 2008). In the aIAT, participants are asked to classify attribute sentences which are known to be true (e.g., "I am taking part in an experiment") or false (e.g., "I'm in the city library"). The experimenter tries to find which of two categories of target sentences is true; e.g., confession sentences (e.g., "I stole the CD-ROM") vs. denial sentences (e.g., "I did not steal the CD-ROM").

---

[3] It would take us too much space to explain why it is a relevant stimulus-response compatibility paradigm, and thus we refer to interested reader to De Houwer (2003b) for a detailed explanation.

Table 3.2 *The autobiographical implicit association test*

	Required response	
Task	Press left key for	Press right key for
Confession-true	"I have stolen the CD-ROM" or true sentences	"I did not steal the CD-ROM" or false sentences
Denial-true	"I have stolen the CD-ROM" or false sentences	"I did not steal the CD-ROM" or true sentences

All sentences are randomly presented one by one on the computer screen, and participants classify them as fast as possible. The aIAT consists of two blocks, see Table 3.2.

In the compatible block, the true attribute sentences and denial target sentences are mapped to one key, and the false attribute sentences and the confession target sentences are mapped to the second key. In the incompatible block, the assignments are reversed. The innocent examinee is expected to be faster in the compatible block that maps denial with truth and confession with false than in the incompatible block that maps denial with false and confession with truth. The opposite pattern is expected in guilty examinees. As would be predicted from our procedural analysis, the aIAT produced large effects sizes in naïve subjects (Sartori *et al.*, 2008; Verschuere *et al.*, 2009a). The aIAT remains to be adapted for concealed information detection.

Evidence for the role of stimulus-response compatibility

The fact that only the oddball task produced robust effects for concealed information detection provides indirect support for the idea that relevant stimulus-response compatibility may be crucial. The oddball, however, differs in several other aspects from the other tasks that have been used so far (e.g., proportion of probes and irrelevant stimuli, interstimulus interval, central vs. peripheral stimulus presentation). More direct support comes from oddball studies that found that diminishing the stimulus-response incompatibility reduces the probe-irrelevant differentiation. Using a card test procedure, Matsuda *et al.* (2009), omitted the target items, and simply asked participants to press a response button for all stimuli (probes and irrelevant items). With the omission of the target items, the stimulus-response compatibility disappeared, as did the probe-irrelevant response latency difference. Participants in the fMRI study by Gamer and colleagues (2007) memorized two target items (a king of spades and a €100 bank note), and were asked to conceal recognition of two probe items (jack of spades and a €20 bank note). Because of fMRI recording, a longer inter-stimulus interval (5–19 s) was used. Apart from that, the task resembled the Farwell and Donchin (1991) oddball task. Participants pressed one key for recognizing target items, and another key indicating non-recognition for probes and irrelevant items (other playing cards and bank notes). For bank notes, but not playing cards, response latencies were larger for probes compared to irrelevant items. In a follow-up study (Gamer *et al.*, in press), the task instructions were modified such that participants were now simply required to press a response button each time they saw a stimulus (cf. Matsuda *et al.*, 2009). As expected, response latencies no longer differed between probes and irrelevant items. Similar findings were observed in two additional studies (Meijer *et al.*, 2007; Verschuere *et al.*, 2009c).

Recently, Rosenfeld *et al.* (2008) introduced a modification of the oddball task (see also Chapter 4 of this volume). In this "Complex Trial Protocol," the targets have been omitted. Participants are presented with white-colored probes or irrelevant items and requested to press the same left button to indicate perception of all stimuli ("I saw it"). About 1.1 to 1.55 s after stimulus offset, the stimulus reappears, this time in one of five colors. Participants are instructed to press the right button for one predefined (target) color, and the left button for the other four (non-target) colors. Rosenfeld *et al.* observed larger response latencies to the probes compared to the irrelevant items for the first "I saw it" response in guilty participants. This seems at odds with the findings above and with our hypothesis that stimulus-response compatibility is crucial to produce robust response latency differences in the oddball task. However, the Complex Trial Protocol may also involve stimulus-response compatibility. Note that assignment for response buttons was not counterbalanced and participants always first pressed the left "I saw it" button for probes and irrelevant items, and then pressed right or left for target or non-target colors, respectively. Thus the "I saw it" button is also the "non-target" button. As response buttons can acquire a certain meaning through instructions or experience (Eder and Rothermund, 2008), it is possible that the probe-irrelevant response latency difference results from pressing the non-target button to the probes. Clearly, this reasoning needs empirical testing, which can be done easily by counterbalancing response buttons. We predict that the response latency probe-irrelevant difference will be smaller in a condition where the right button or an unrelated third button is used for the "I saw it" response.

Response latency-based tests as an alternative to physiological measures?

Overall, the data support the high accuracy of the oddball task for concealed information detection. Seymour *et al.* (2000) concluded that the response latency-based test is a viable alternative to physiological measures. The only study that has directly compared the ANS-based CIT with the oddball task indicates that the validity of the response latency-based test is comparable to that of the polygraph (Verschuere *et al.*, 2009b). Given the practical advantages of the response latency-based test it seems worthwhile to further examine its potential as an alternative to physiology-based tests.[4]

Certainly, further research is required. There is, for instance, no research available on how the test performs under real-life circumstances. The National Research Council (2003) warned that research from several fields has consistently shown that diagnostic tests perform worse under field circumstances compared to controlled laboratory conditions. Research on the polygraph-based concealed information test supports this reasoning (Carmel *et al.*, 2003; Elaad *et al.*, 1992). Real-life circumstances differ in important aspects related to the examinees (e.g., undergraduates versus crime suspects), motivation (e.g., winning $5 vs. prison sentence), test items (e.g., a list of perfectly memorized words vs. briefly encountered crime-related details), time of test (e.g., immediate vs. years after the crime), and other variables. Researchers are only starting to explore these variables in the response latency-based test. Seymour and Fraynt (2009), for example, examined whether the extent of encoding and the time between encoding and test affected the validity of the oddball test. The test involved 109 undergraduate participants in a mock espionage. All participants first memorized the target items. Participants in the shallow encoding condition went on to read a story that contained the probe items and paraphrased it. Participants in the deep encoding condition engaged in four tasks that required them to analyze the probe items extensively in different modes. Participants were tested either ten minutes, twenty-four hours or one week after probe encoding, and promised $10 to beat the test.

---

[4] The response latency-based test could also be used in combination with a physiology-based test, and combining methods may increase validity. A downside of this approach is that the ease of application advantage that characterizes the response latency-based test is lost.

The probe-irrelevant differentiation was worse in the shallow encoding condition than in the elaborate condition, and deteriorated over time. The response latency difference was about 120 ms in the immediate deep encoding condition, and about 70 ms in the one-week delay shallow encoding condition. These data indicate that the validity of the response latencies based under real-life circumstances will be lower than the estimates obtained under controlled laboratory conditions. Research under more realistic circumstances is needed to establish real-life performance.

Probably the greatest criticism of the response latency-based CIT is that it would be highly vulnerable to faking (e.g., Farwell and Donchin, 1991). A few studies examined this issue. In their 2000 paper, Seymour *et al.* (Experiment 2) set up a replication study that included a warning not to respond differentially to probe and irrelevant items. This warning did not diminish the high accuracy of the response latency-based test. A third experiment went one step further. Participants were informed about the expected pattern of results, instructed to memorize the target items very well, and warned not to respond based upon familiarity alone. The reasoning behind these instructions was that it might help participants to reject probes as non-target items. Again, probe responses were substantially less accurate and slower compared to the irrelevant items, resulting in high accuracy. These results indicate that response latencies may not be as easily controlled as some have suggested. However, the previous studies do not allow for the conclusion that a response latency-based test such as the oddball task is resistant to faking. Rosenfeld *et al.* (2004; Experiment 1) assigned thirty-three undergraduate participants to either an innocent condition, a guilty control condition or a guilty countermeasure condition. Participants in the guilty conditions acquired probe knowledge through the execution of a mock crime. Participants in the innocent conditions did not execute the mock crime and had no probe knowledge. Participants in the guilty countermeasure condition received detailed instructions on how to beat the test. The main strategy was to make irrelevant items relevant. Specific instructions were assigned to five of the six irrelevant items, such as pressing a finger, wiggling a toe or imagining a slap in the face from the experimenter. As expected, high accuracy for both P300 amplitude (54–82 percent depending on the scoring algorithm) and response latency (91 percent) was found in the guilty control condition. False positive rates were low for both measures (0–9 percent). The countermeasures appeared very effective, as accuracy dropped to 45 percent for response latency and 18–54 percent for P300 amplitude. It seems that specific countermeasure instructions allow participants to alter test outcome (Gronau *et al.*, 2005; see also Chapter 11 of this volume; Rosenfeld *et al.*, 2008). A notable difference between these studies and the one by Seymour (2000) *et al.* is that only Seymour uses a response deadline. Degner (2009) showed that a response deadline prevented faking in the response latency-based affective priming task. Imposing a response deadline, however, does not always prevent faking (Verschuere *et al.*, 2009a). Faking thus continues to provide a challenge to the validity of any response latency-based concealed information test.

REFERENCES

Algom, D., Chajut, E., and Shlomo, L. (2004). A rational look at the emotional Stroop phenomenon: a generic slowdown, not a Stroop effect. *Journal of Experimental Psychology: General*, 133, 323–338.

Allen, J., and Movius, H. L. (2000). The objective assessment of amnesia in dissociative identity disorder using event-related potentials. *International Journal of Psychophysiology*, 38(1), 21–41.

Allen, J., Iacono, W. G., and Danielson, K. D. (1992). The identification of concealed memories using the event-related potential and implicit behavioral measures – a methodology for prediction in the face of individual-differences. *Psychophysiology*, 29(5), 504–522.

Ben-Shakhar, G., and Elaad, E. (2003). The validity of psychophysiological detection of information with the Guilty Knowledge Test: a meta-analytic review. *Journal of Applied Psychology*, 88, 131–151.

Carmel, D., Dayan, E., Naveh, A., Raveh, O., and Ben-Shakhar, G. (2003). Estimating the validity of the guilty knowledge test from simulated experiments: the external validity of mock crime studies. *Journal of Experimental Psychology-Applied*, 9, 261–269.

De Houwer, J. (2003a). The extrinsic affective Simon task. *Experimental Psychology*, 50(2), 77–85.

   (2003b). A structural analysis of indirect measures of attitudes. In J. Musch and K. C. Klauer (eds.), *The Psychology of Evaluation: Affective Processes in Cognition and Emotion* (pp. 219–244). Mahwah: Lawrence Erlbaum.

   (2009). Comparing measures of attitudes at the procedural and functional level. In R. Petty, R. H. Fazio, and P. Brinol (eds.), *Attitudes: Insights from the New Implicit Measures*. Hillsdale, NJ: Erlbaum.

Degner, J. (2009). On the (un-)controllability of affective priming: strategic manipulation is feasible but can possibly be prevented. *Cognition & Emotion*, 23, 327–354.

DePaulo, B. M., Lindsay, J. J., Malone, B. E., Muhlenbruck, L., Charlton, K., and Cooper, H. (2003). Cues to deception. *Psychological Bulletin*, 129(1), 74–118.

Eder, A. B., and Rothermund, K. (2008). When do motor behaviors (mis)match affective stimuli? An evaluative coding view of approach and avoidance reactions. *Journal of Experimental Psychology-General*, 137(2), 262–281.

Elaad, E., Ginton, A., and Jungman, N. (1992). Detection measures in real-life criminal guilty knowledge tests. *Journal of Applied Psychology*, 77(5), 757–767.

Engelhard, I. M., Merckelbach, H., and van den Hout, M. A. (2003). The guilty knowledge test and the modified Stroop task in detection of deception: an exploratory study. *Psychological Reports*, 92(2), 683–691.

Farwell, L. A., and Donchin, E. (1991). The truth will out – interrogative polygraphy (lie detection) with event-related brain potentials. *Psychophysiology*, 28(5), 531–547.

Farwell, L. A., and Smith, S. S. (2001). Using brain MERMER testing to detect knowledge despite efforts to conceal. *Journal of Forensic Sciences*, 46(1), 135–143.

Gamer, M., Bauermann, T., Stoeter, P., and Vossel, G. (2007). Covariations among fMRI, skin conductance and behavioral data during processing of concealed information. *Human Brain Mapping*, 28, 1287–1301.

Gamer, M., Verschuere, B., Crombez, G., and Vossel, G. (2008). Combining physiological measures in the detection of concealed information. *Physiology & Behavior*, 95, 333–340.

Gamer, M., Klimecki, O., Bauermann, T., Stoeter, P., and Vossel, G. (in press). fMRI-activation patterns in the detection of concealed information rely on memory-related effects. *Social Cognitive and Affective Neuroscience*.

Greenwald, A. G., McGhee, D. E., and Schwartz, J. L. K. (1998). Measuring individual differences in implicit cognition: the implicit association test. *Journal of Personality and Social Psychology*, 74(6), 1464–1480.

Gronau, N., Ben-Shakhar, G., and Cohen, A. (2005). Behavioral and physiological measures in the detection of concealed information. *Journal of Applied Psychology*, 90(1), 147–158.

Harrison, A. A., Hwalek, M., Raney, D. F., and Fritz, J. G. (1978). Cues to deception in an interview situation. *Social Psychology*, 41(2), 156–161.

Henke, F., and Eddy, M. W. (1909). Mental diagnosis by the association reaction method. *Psychological Review*, 16, 399–409.

Jung, C. G. (1910). The association reaction method. *American Journal of Psychology*, 21 (219–2240).

Langleben, D. D., Schroeder, L., Maldjian, J. A., Gur, R. C., McDonald, S., Ragland, J. D., et al. (2002). Brain activity during simulated deception: an event-related functional magnetic resonance study. *Neuroimage*, 15, 727–732.

Locker, L., and Pratarelli, M. E. (1997). Lexical decision and the detection of concealed information. *The Journal of Credibility Assessment and Witness Psychology*, 1, 33–43.

Marston, W. M. (1927). Reaction-time symptoms of deception. *Journal of Experimental Psychology*, 3, 72–87.

Matsuda, I., Nittono, H., Hirota, A., Ogawa, T., and Takasawa, N. (2009). Event-related potentials during the standard autonomic-based concealed infomation test. *International Journal of Psychophysiology*, 74, 58–68.

Meijer, E. H., Smulders, F. T. Y., Merckelbach, H. L. G. J., and Wolf, A. G. (2007). The P300 is sensitive to concealed face recognition. *International Journal of Psychophysiology*, 66, 231–237.

Mertens, R., and Allen, J. (2008). The role of psychophysiology in forensic assessments: deception detection, ERPS, and virtual reality mock crime scenarios. *Psychophysiology*, 45, 286–298.

National Research Council (2003). *The Polygraph and Lie Detection.* Committee to Review the Scientific Evidence on the Polygraph. Washington, DC: The National Academies Press.

Nittono, H., and Kubo, K. (2008). The effect of intentional concealment on the event-related potentials in a concealed information test. *International Journal of Psychophysiology*, 69(3), 149–150.

Rosenfeld, J. P. (2002). Event-related potentials in the detection of deception, malignering, and false memories. In K. Murray (ed.), *Handbook of Polygrah Testing* (pp. 265–286). San Diego: Academic Press.

Rosenfeld, J. P., Shue, E., and Singer, E. (2007). Single versus multiple probe blocks of P300-based concealed information tests for self-referring versus incidentally obtained information. *Biological Psychology*, 74(3), 396–404.

Rosenfeld, J. P., Soskins, M., Bosh, G., and Ryan, A. (2004). Simple, effective countermeasures to P300-based tests of detection of concealed information. *Psychophysiology*, 41, 205–219.

Rosenfeld, J. P., Cantwell, B., Nasman, V. T., Wojdac, V., Ivanov, S., and Mazzeri, L. (1988). A modified, event-related potential-based guilty knowledge test. *International Journal of Neuroscience*, 42(1–2), 157–161.

Rosenfeld, J. P., Labkovsky, E., Winograd, M., Lui, M. A., Vandenboom, C., and Chedid, E. (2008). The Complex Trial Protocol (CTP): a new, countermeasure-resistant, accurate P300-based method for detection of concealed information. *Psychophysiology*, 45, 906–919.

Sartori, G., Agosta, S., Zogmaister, C., Ferrara, S. D., and Castiello, U. (2008). How to accurately assess autobiographical events. *Psychological Science*, 19, 772–780.

Seymour, T. L., and Fraynt, B. R. (2009). Time and encoding effects in the concealed knowledge test. *Applied Psychophysiology and Biofeedback*, 34, 177–187.

Seymour, T. L., and Kerlin, J. R. (2008). Successful detection of verbal and visual concealed knowledge using an RT-based paradigm. *Applied Cognitive Psychology*, 22(4), 475–490.

Seymour, T. L., Seifert, C. M., Shafto, M. G., and Mosmann, A. L. (2000). Using response time measures to assess "guilty knowledge." *Journal of Applied Psychology*, 85(1), 30–37.

Stroop, J. R. (1935). Studies of interference in serial-verbal reaction. *Journal of Experimental Psychology*, 18, 643–662.

Verschuere, B., Crombez, G., and Koster, E. (2004a). Orienting to guilty knowledge. *Cognition & Emotion*, 18, 265–279.

Verschuere, B., Prati, V., and De Houwer, J. (2009a). Cheating the lie detector: faking in the autobiographical IAT. *Psychological Science*, 20, 410–413.

Verschuere, B., Crombez, G., De Clercq, A., and Koster, E. H. W. (2004b). Autonomic and behavioral responding to concealed information: differentiating orienting and defensive responses. *Psychophysiology*, 41, 461–466.

Verschuere, B., Crombez, G., Degrootte, T., and Rosseel, Y. (2009b). Detecting concealed information with reaction times: validity and comparison with the polygraph. *Applied Cognitive Psychology*, 23, 1–11.

Verschuere, B., Crombez, G., Koster, E. H. W., and Van Baelen, P. (2005). Behavioural responding to concealed information: examining the role of relevance orienting. *Psychologica Belgica*, 45, 207–216.

Verschuere, B., Rosenfeld, J. P., Winograd, M., Labkovsky, E., and Wiersema, J. R. (2009c). The role of deception in the P300 memory detection. *Legal and Criminological Psychology*, 14, 253–262.

Yonelinas, A. P. (2002). The nature of recollection and familiarity: a review of 30 years of research. *Journal of Memory and Language*, 46, 441–517.

4   P300 in detecting concealed information

J. Peter Rosenfeld

Overview: This chapter reviews the use of the P300 ERP in the detection of concealed information since the first published papers in the late 1980s. First, there is a description of P300 as a cortical signal of the recognition of meaningful information. This attribute was applied directly to concealed information detection in the first P300-based CIT protocol called the "three stimulus protocol." There follows a detailed discussion and review of the methods of analysis used to determine guilt or innocence with the P300, as well as the major papers using and extending the three stimulus protocol in areas beyond those reported in the first publications. This discussion closes with the problematic findings showing that the P300-based, three stimulus protocol is vulnerable to countermeasures. The author's theoretical efforts to understand countermeasure vulnerability with this protocol are then described, followed by an introduction of the theoretically based novel protocol (called the Complex Trial Protocol or CTP) developed to resist countermeasures to P300-based CITs. The use of the CTP in detecting self-referring as well as incidentally acquired information (e.g., in a mock crime scenario) are described, as well as its recent use in detection of details of planned acts of terror prior to actual criminal acts. The use of reaction time as well as a novel ERP component called P900 for detecting countermeasures is also described. The chapter concludes with some caveats about remaining research issues.

The P300 event-related potential

Between an electrode placed on the scalp surface directly over the brain and another electrode connected to an electrically neutral part of the

Acknowledgment: I would like to thank John J. B. Allen and Gershon Ben-Shakhar for good reviews (containing several helpful edits) of this chapter.

head (i.e., remote from brain cells, such as the earlobe), an electrical voltage, varying as a function of time, exists. These voltages comprise the spontaneously ongoing electroencephalogram (EEG), and are commonly known as brain waves. If during the recording of EEG, a discrete stimulus such as a light flash occurs, the EEG will break into a series of larger peaks and valleys lasting up to two seconds after the stimulus onset. These waves, signaling the arrival in the cortex of neural activity elicited by the stimulus, comprise the wave series called the event-related potential or ERP.

The ERP is of a small magnitude compared to the ongoing EEG, so it is often obscured in single trials. Thus, one typically averages the EEG samples of many repeated presentations of either the same stimulus or several stimuli of one particular category (e.g., female names, weapon types, etc.). The resulting averaged stimulus-related activity is revealed as the ERP, while the non-stimulus-related features of the EEG average out, approaching a straight line. The P300 is a special ERP component that results whenever a *meaningful* piece of information is *rarely* presented among a random series of more frequently presented, non-meaningful stimuli often of the same category as the meaningful stimulus. For example, Figure 4.1 shows a set of three pairs of superimposed ERP averages from three scalp sites (called Fz, Cz, and Pz overlaying the midline frontal, central, and parietal areas of the scalp, respectively) of one subject, who was viewing a series of test items on a display (from Rosenfeld *et al.*, 2004). On 17 percent of the trials, a meaningful item (e.g., the subject's birth date) was presented, and on the remaining 83 percent of the randomly occurring trials, other items with no special meaning to the subject (e.g., other dates) were presented. The two superimposed waveforms at each scalp site represent averages of ERPs to (1) meaningful items and to (2) other items. In response to only the meaningful items, a large down-going P300, indicated with thick vertical lines, is seen, which is absent in the superimposed waveforms evoked by non-meaningful stimuli. The wave labeled "EOG" is a simultaneous recording of eye-movement activity. As required for sound EEG recording technique, EOG is flat during the segment of time when P300 occurs, indicating that no artifacts due to eye movements are occurring. Clearly, the *rare, recognized, meaningful* items elicit P300, the other items do not. (Note that electrically positive brain activity is plotted down.) It should be evident that the ability of P300 to signal the involuntary recognition of meaningful information suggests that the wave could be used to signal recognized "guilty knowledge" known only to those familiar with the crime details, such as a guilty perpetrators, accomplices, witnesses, and police investigators.

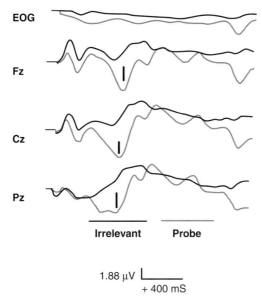

EOG

Fz

Cz

Pz

Irrelevant   Probe

1.88 μV └────
        + 400 mS

Figure 4.1 Three ERPs and EOG, based on Rosenfeld *et al.* (2004), from the scalp sites Fz (frontal), Cz (central), and Pz (parietal). The sweeps are 2,048 ms long. P300 peaks are down-going and indicated with thick vertical lines. They are in response to personally meaningful items (gray lines). They are superimposed on responses to personally non-meaningful items (black lines). Given that the sweeps are about 2 s long, the P300s begin around 400 ms and end around 900 ms. Positive is plotted down.

History of P300 used as a concealed information detector

Fabiani *et al.* (1983) showed that if a list of words, consisting of rare, previously learned (i.e., *meaningful*) and frequent novel words were presented one at a time to a subject, the familiar, previously learned words but not the others elicited a P300. Rosenfeld *et al.* (1987) recognized that the Fabiani *et al.* (1983) study suggested that P300 could be used to detect concealed guilty knowledge. Therefore, P300 could index recognition of familiar items even if subjects denied recognizing them. From this fact, one could infer deception. The P300 would not represent a lie per se but only a recognition of a familiar item of information, the verbal denial of which would then imply deception.

Soon after seeing Fabiani *et al.* (1983), we executed a study (Rosenfeld *et al.*, 1988) in which subjects pretended to steal one of ten items from a box. Later, the items' names were repeatedly presented to the subject, one at a time on a display. Based on visual inspection of the P300s, we found that the items the subjects pretended to steal (the *probes*), but not the other, *irrelevant* items, evoked P300 in nine of ten cases. In that study, there was also one special, unpredictably presented stimulus item, the *target*, to which the subjects were required to respond by saying "yes," so as to assure us they were paying attention to the screen at all times and would thus not miss probe presentations. They said "no" to all the other items, signaling non-recognition, and thus lying on trials containing the pretended stolen items. The special target items also evoked P300, as one might expect, since they too were rare and meaningful (task-relevant). This paradigm had many features of the guilty knowledge test (GKT) paradigm (developed by Lykken in 1959; see Lykken, 1998), except that P300s rather than autonomic variables were used as the indices of recognition.

Donchin and Farwell also saw the potential for detecting concealed information with P300 as a recognition index in the later 1980s, and they presented a preliminary report of their work (in poster format) at the 1986 Society for Psychophysiological Research (SPR) meeting (Farwell and Donchin, 1986), just after our 1987 paper was submitted. This conference abstract summarized Experiment 2 of the paper later published as Farwell and Donchin (1991). This study reported two experiments, the first of which was a full-length study using twenty paid volunteers in a mock crime scenario. The second experiment contained only four subjects admittedly guilty of minor transgressions. In both experiments, subjects saw three kinds of stimuli, quite comparable to those used in our Rosenfeld *et al.* (1988) study, noted above: (1) *probe* stimuli which were items of guilty knowledge that only "perpetrators" and others familiar with the crime (experimenters) would have; (2) *irrelevant* items which were unrelated to the "crime" but were of the same category as the probe; (3) *target* items which were unrelated to the "crime," but to which the subject was instructed to execute a unique response. Thus, subjects were instructed to press a yes-button to the targets, and a no-button to all other stimuli.

The subjects in this first experiment had participated in a mock crime espionage scenario in which briefcases were passed to confederates in operations that had particular names. The details of these activities generated six categories of stimuli, one example of which would be the name of the mock espionage operation. For each such category, the actual probe operation name might be operation "donkey." Various other animal names – tiger, cow, etc. – would comprise the rest of the set of six stimuli including the probe, four irrelevants and one target name. The six (categories) with six stimuli per category yielded thirty-six items that were randomly shuffled and presented twice per block. After each block, the stimuli were re-shuffled into a new random order and re-presented for a total of four blocks. The mock crime was committed one day before the P300 GKT. It is very important to note that prior to the P300 GKT and prior to performance of the mock crime scenario, each subject was trained and tested on the details of the mock crime in which he/she participated. The training was to a 100 percent correct criterion. Therefore the experimenters could be quite certain that these details would be remembered. Subjects were also trained to know the targets. Subjects were also run as their own innocent controls by being tested on scenarios of which they had no knowledge.

Farwell and Donchin (1991) reported that in the twenty guilty cases, correct decisions were possible in all but two cases which could not be unambiguously classified (as either guilty or innocent) and so were put in an "indeterminate" category. Indeed, this would be impressive except that, as just noted, the subjects were pre-trained to remember the details of their crimes, a procedure having limited ecological validity in field circumstances – in which training of a suspect on details of a crime he was denying is clearly impossible. In the innocent condition, only seventeen of twenty subjects were correctly classified yielding an overall detection rate of 87.5 percent with 12.5 percent "indeterminate" outcomes. Thus although the procedure of Farwell and Donchin (1991) did not have traditional false positive nor false negative outcomes, with accurate verdicts for all the classified cases, their procedure left 12.5% of the cases unclassified.

The second experiment of Farwell and Donchin (1991) had only four subjects. These four volunteering subjects were all previously admitted wrongdoers on the college campus. Their crime details were well-detected with P300, but these previously admitted wrongdoers probably had much rehearsal of their crimes at the hands of campus investigators, teachers, parents, etc. Thus – was the P300 test detecting incidentally acquired information or previously admitted, well-rehearsed information?

A very important contribution of the Farwell and Donchin (1991) paper was the introduction of *bootstrapping* in P300-based deception detection. This was a technique that allowed an accurate diagnosis within each individual. In the earlier Rosenfeld *et al.* (1987, 1988) papers, t-tests comparing individual probe and irrelevant averages were performed. That is, the t-test examined the significance of the difference between probe and irrelevant P300 means. We did not report the results of these t-tests, which afforded low diagnostic rates (<80 percent correct), and did not correspond with what our visual inspection of the waveforms showed. Now one realizes that since the database for such t-tests consists of *single trial* ERPs – which are typically very noisy – the t-tests may miss all but the largest intra-individual effects. Farwell and Donchin (1991) had appreciated that most analyses in ERP psycho-physiology were based on group effects in which the grand average of the individual *averages* were compared between conditions. Thus, the database for these tests were *average* ERPs, rather than single sweeps. Farwell and Donchin appreciated also that to do such a test within an individual required multiple probe and irrelevant averages within that individual. These were not usually available since obtaining them would have required running an individual through multiple runs which would have doubtless led to confounding habituation effects, as well as loss of irrelevance of originally irrelevant stimuli which would become relevant via repetition. Bootstrapping was the answer: a *bootstrapped* distribution of *probe* averages could be obtained by repeatedly sampling *with replacement* from the original set of, say, N1 *probe* single sweeps. After each sample is drawn, it can be averaged, so that if one iterated the process 100 times, one would have a set of 100 bootstrapped average probe ERPs. The same procedure could be done with N2 *irrelevant* single sweeps. Then one would have distributions of 100 irrelevant and 100 probe *averages*. A t-test on these cleaner averages would be much more sensitive than such a test on single sweeps. (One usually doesn't need more than 100 iterations, and fifty might do well. N1 and N2 should usually be not much less than twenty-five in my experience, and as suggested by Polich, 1999; Fabiani *et al.*, 2000.)

In fact, once one has distributions of bootstrapped probe and irrelevant averages (which approach the respective actual average ERPs in the limit as developed by Efron, 1979), there are many possibilities for analysis: Farwell and Donchin (1991) reasoned that one ought to statistically compare two cross-correlation coefficients; the cross-correlation of (a) probe and irrelevant P300s with the cross-correlation of (b) probe and target P300s. The idea was that if the subject was guilty, there would be a large P300 in both target and probe ERPs, but not in irrelevant ERPs, so that correlation (b) would be greater than correlation (a). On the other hand, if the subject was innocent, then there would be no P300 in the probe ERP, so that the greater correlation would be (a). If results of ninety of 100 correlation subtractions (b-a) were > 0, then guilt could be inferred.

This method, however, has problems as pointed out by Rosenfeld *et al.* (1991, 2004, 2008) and demonstrated in Rosenfeld *et al.* (2004), even though the method had great success in the Farwell and Donchin

(1991) paper, noted above as having low external validity. One issue that poses a problem for this approach is that although probes and targets may both have P300s in guilty subjects, these waveforms may be out of phase and/or show other latency/morphology differences (as we illustrated in Figure 2 of Rosenfeld *et al.*, 2004). After all, although target P300s were treated as benchmark P300 waveforms by Farwell and Donchin (1991), in fact the psychological reactions to personally meaningful and concealed guilty knowledge probes vs. explicitly task-relevant but inherently neutral targets should differ for many reasons which could account for various morphology differences in the respective P300s. Our view of target stimuli, in summary, is that they are useful attention holders, but not good benchmark waveform producers for probe P300s.

Another problem with the cross-correlation comparison concerns the expectation (Farwell and Donchin, 1991) that the probe-irrelevant correlation will be lower than the probe-target correlation in a guilty party. Actually, in a guilty subject, irrelevant ERPs may contain small P300s as can be seen in Farwell and Donchin (1991), Allen *et al.* (1992) or Rosenfeld *et al.* (1991, 2004). The probe and irrelevant P300 *amplitudes* will differ, but the *shapes* may not, meaning that the Pearson correlation coefficient will scale away the probe and irrelevant amplitude differences, leaving two waveforms that have a *high* correlation. Farwell and Donchin applied a method (called "double centering") designed to correct this problem. The correction computes the grand average waveform (of all probes, irrelevants, and targets) and subtracts it from each probe, irrelevant, and target waveform prior to computation of cross-correlations. The method will be effective in making the probe-irrelevant correlation negative and the probe-target correlation positive if the probe and target P300 amplitudes are about the same size, with both larger than the irrelevant P300, and *if all three waveforms are in phase*. Obviously, this will make the probe-target correlation greater than the probe-irrelevant correlation. However, in cases in which probe and target are more than about 45 degrees out of phase (implying a P300 peak latency difference of 65 or more ms), then this double-centering correction begins to fail. (This observation is based on informal, unpublished simulations by John Allen, and the present author.) Thus I recommend the analysis method described next.

In our studies with bootstrap analysis (Rosenfeld *et al.*, 1991; Johnson and Rosenfeld, 1992; Rosenfeld *et al.* 2004, 2008), in order to avoid the problems associated with correlation comparison just noted, we utilized the simple probe-irrelevant *P300 amplitude differences*, rather than comparative cross-correlations. Thus our approach was to simply develop a distribution of difference values for bootstrapped average probe minus average irrelevant P300s (see Rosenfeld *et al.*, 2004, 2008). Each iterated computation of a bootstrapped probe and irrelevant average lead to a bootstrapped P300 difference calculation. If these bootstrapped differences were > 0 in 90 of 100 iterations, guilt was inferred. (Although this 0.9 criterion has been traditional, it is somewhat arbitrary.) I will re-visit the criterion issue below in the discussion of Meixner and Rosenfeld (2009d). Note that in computing the P300 value for each iterated average, the P300 maximum value is sought within a search window of about 300–700 ms post stimulus. Thus peak latency or phase differences cannot become problematic, as we compute the peak values wherever they fall within the search window. Most recently (Lui and Rosenfeld, 2008; Meixner and Rosenfeld, 2009b), instead of performing the difference computation iterations, we simply applied a t-test to the probe-irrelevant P300 bootstrapped average values.

I briefly cited Rosenfeld *et al.* (1991) above to make a point about bootstrapping. It is worth describing this paper in a bit more detail as part of the early history of P300-based deception detection, inasmuch as it was the first attempt to use P300 methods in diagnosing deception in a scenario that partly modeled the *employee screening Control Question Test*. This is a test that used to be the major application (in terms of number of tests given per year) of all protocols in field detection of deception in the US – until employee screening tests were banned by the US Congress in the federal Employee Polygraph Protection Act of 1988. (There were exceptions to this ban, and security agencies – CIA, NSA, FBI, etc. – still use these tests.)

By way of background, there are two protocols in use in psychophysiological detection of deception (PDD): the *Comparison Question Test* (CQT, formerly known as the *Control* Question Test) and the *Concealed Information Test* (CIT, formerly known as the *Guilty Knowledge Test* or GKT). The two protocols have been the subject of much bitter contention in academic and professional arenas of deception detection. The CQT, preferred by professional "polygraphers" in North America and elsewhere, involves "Did you do it?" type questions, e.g., "Did you take that $5000?" or "Did you kill your wife?" etc. This test is preferred by polygraph professionals because it is relatively easy to compose and apply in various situations, and because it tends to elicit confessions. On the other hand, this procedure is largely rejected by the PDD scientific research community as being unscientific (see Ben-Shakhar, 2002).

Actually our 1991 P300-based procedure contained elements of both CIT and CQT protocols. It was like a CQT in that it probed not about specific crime details, as in the usual CIT, but about past antisocial and illegal *acts* in which a test subject may have been involved. However the structure of the test was clearly that of a CIT: a subject entered the lab and was shown a list of thirteen antisocial or illegal acts aimed at our student-subject population (e.g., plagiarizing a paper, using a false ID for bar service, cheating on a test, smoking pot monthly, etc.). In a situation of perceived privacy (but in fact in a room whose ceiling contained a concealed video camera that relayed subject responses to the experimenter in an adjoining room), the subject checked boxes next to each act of which (s)he had been guilty within the past five years. This made it possible to construct a test containing just one probe item of which the subject was guilty, plus eight other items (including a target and seven irrelevants). We needed this tight control (that would not likely be possible in real field situations) for this first "proof of concept" study of a P300-based CQT-CIT hybrid screening analog. Before testing subjects for P300 responsiveness to probes vs. other stimuli, we ran a bogus recording session and then chose four items to accuse the subjects of having done: "Based on the previous [bogus] run, we think you did A, but you might also have done B, C, or D." The probe item was always either in the B or C position in that quotation, with an innocent, other item in the remaining (of B or C) position. A, B, C, and D were all items perceived by our subject pool to have an equal probability of occurrence in that subject pool. In each subject, we always compared P300s to items B and C in a bootstrap test, referring to these probes and irrelevants, respectively, as "relevants" and "controls" in the language of the CQT. We accurately identified about 87 percent of the thirteen guilty (12/13) and fifteen innocent (13/15) subjects in the study. However, it should be noted that there was a confound in this study: the subjects may have produced P300s to the items they checked "yes" to prior to the recording session because they checked "yes," rather than because these were the remembered guilty items. Clearly, one couldn't run the list checking manipulation prior to testing in the field. Thus, in a near replication study one year later (Johnson and Rosenfeld, 1992), we used one item for all subjects as the probe *prior* to the recording session. This was an item we knew from previous study would yield us about 50 percent guilty and 50 percent innocent subjects. Our diagnostic rate replicated. (We confirmed the "ground truth" by running the list checking session *after* the recording session.) Recently we (Lui and Rosenfeld, 2008) utilized these methods – enhanced with spatial-temporal principal component analysis – with subjects guilty of two and three probes (in two groups), detecting 86 percent and 71 percent of guilty subjects, respectively, although with about 30 percent false positives, yielding Grier (1971) A' AUC values of 0.87 and 0.76 for two and three probe groups, respectively.

Among the early P300 studies, one must also note the study by Allen *et al.*, (1992). This study was somewhat different than those reviewed previously in that it examined detection of newly acquired information, learned to perfection, which is often not as well detected as well rehearsed (self-referring) information (Rosenfeld *et al.*, 2006), but which was well detected in Allen *et al.* (1992), possibly because of the highly original Bayesian analysis they developed to detect concealed information within individuals. Thus, over three subject samples, 94 percent of the learned material was correctly classified, and 4 percent of the unlearned material was incorrectly classified.

It should be added here that various methods of individual diagnosis have been compared by Allen and Iacono (1997), Rosenfeld *et al.* (2004), Abootalebi *et al.* (2006) who also introduced an original wavelet classifier method, and by Mertens and Allen (2008). Allen and Iacono (1997) compared Bayesian analysis, bootstrapped cross-correlations, and bootstrapped amplitude differences applied to the data of Allen *et al.* (1992). They found no difference in the effectiveness of the first two methods but found both to be superior to the bootstrapped amplitude difference method. However Allen and Iacono (reporting an overall accuracy of 87 percent) utilized the *baseline-to-peak* index of P300 amplitude (in their amplitude difference computations) which we never use since we and others (such as Meijer *et al.*, 2007) found it to be at least 25 percent less accurate than our *peak-to-peak* method. In the Abootalebi *et al.* (2006) paper, the ROC curves displayed for the wavelet classifier, bootstrapped cross-correlation, and bootstrapped *peak-to-peak* amplitude methods show considerable overlap, although small differences can be seen favoring either the bootstrapped amplitude difference method (e.g., Rosenfeld *et al.*, 2008) or the wavelet classifier method depending upon the location in the curve in ROC space. The bootstrapped cross-correlation method of Farwell and Donchin (1991) performed consistently worst, although the differences among the three methods were small. (The three methods correctly detected 74 percent to 80 percent of the subjects in a mock crime protocol. However it is difficult to compare accuracy levels obtained in different studies since protocols and thresholds of classification differ.) Rosenfeld *et al.* (2004) *consistently* found that the peak-to-peak amplitude difference method outperformed the cross-correlation method. This study was the only one in which comparisons were made on two stimulus sets, one involving autobiographical data, and the other involving mock crime details, neither stimulus set being pre-learned to perfection. By contrast, Mertens and Allen (2008) found that the bootstrapped peak-to-peak amplitudes performed worse than either the cross-correlation or Bayesian approaches. However this was demonstrated in *only* some comparisons involving countermeasure groups, and when innocent subjects were considered, the bootstrapped peak-to-peak amplitude difference method performed better than the cross-correlation method. All these results from the four comparative studies reviewed together suggest that no one method is ubiquitously superior. However, comparisons were indeed difficult within the Mertens and Allen (2008) study because their correlation approach uniquely used an indeterminate category, and bootstrap criteria differed between their two bootstrap methods. Moreover, only the Mertens and Allen (2008) study reported poor rates of accuracy overall (48 percent at *best*) in the virtual reality environment which only they used. They also used the highest number of irrelevant stimuli (ten) deployed by any of these studies, which no doubt made for a uniquely demanding task, possibly accounting for their low accuracy. More systematic work of this type is certainly in order. Although it appears presently that when the tested material is learned to perfection prior to testing, all methods work equally well, other situations that lead to greater P300 latency variation, perhaps related to uncertainty of stimulus recognition, favor the peak-to peak amplitude difference method. This tentative conclusion needs further verification.

All the protocols used in previous sections may be denoted as *3-stimulus protocols* (3SPs), in that they all present subjects on a given trial with either a probe, an irrelevant stimulus, or a target stimulus (requiring a unique response) in the same temporal position on each trial. During the past two decades, there were multiple applications of the original 3SPs in which the type of information to be detected varied according to the anticipated needs of various agencies. There were also various technical questions addressed that concerned P300 measurement and analysis in the CIT context. Our lab became interested in detecting simulated malingering in modeled head injury populations. We were concerned also with utilizing a different dependent measure related to P300, namely the distribution of amplitudes across the scalp. This foray was reviewed previously (Rosenfeld, 2002) so I will say no more about it now beyond the fact that although P300 *scalp distribution* seemed to distinguish malingering and non-malingering as a robust group effect, the individual detection rates never exceeded 75 percent, which is not very impressive. Our work indicated, however, that P300 *amplitude* did consistently well in identifying memory malingerers (Rosenfeld *et al.*, 2002). Moreover, in an extensive series of related papers of high quality,

Van Hooff and colleagues have pursued the use of P300 in memory assessment with very positive results (e.g., Van Hooff *et al.*, 1996; Van Hooff and Golden, 2002; Van Hooff *et al.*, 2009).

In a different line of original research, Lefebvre *et al.* (2007) applied the 3SP to the measurement of eyewitness identification accuracy in a clever model of identification of culprits in a simulated police lineup. Subjects observed a mock crime on a videotape and then were tested on their abilities to identify culprits as opposed to bystanders and/or other lineup members after varying time delays between crime and test up to a week. The P300s elicited by probe (culprit) faces confirmed recognition of correct faces. The authors concluded, "P300 provided a reliable index of recognition of the culprit relative to the other lineup members across all time delay conditions. Although participants' accuracy decreased at the 1-week time delay compared to no delay and the 1-h time delay, the P300 effect remained strong for participants that made correct identifications irrespective of the time delay." This novel fact that face stimuli could be used to elicit P300 as an index of concealed *pictorial* information was replicated by Meijer *et al.* (2007).

Regarding the technical developments in measuring and analyzing P300 from 1992–2004, the papers by Allen and Iacono (1997), as well as by Abootalebi *et al.* (2006), in which various analytic methods were compared, have already been discussed. It remains to detail that in my experience, the best method of measuring P300 *solely for purposes of detecting concealed information* is to measure it from its positive peak to its subsequent negative peak using filter settings of 0.3Hz to 30Hz. We discussed why this is so in Soskins *et al.* (2001). One major reason is that we always detect at least 25 percent more guilty subjects with no additional false positives using this peak-peak (p-p) method than we do using the standard baseline-to-peak method. This is based on at least ten of our studies. We have had independent confirmation recently from Meijer *et al.* (2007). I want to make clear that *I am not advocating this p-p method for any other uses of P300, especially regarding theoretical questions*, since the p-p method may measure more than pure P300 as noted in Soskins *et al.* (2001).

Other technical issues came up recently regarding approaches to P300 bootstrap analysis, and regarding the confidence interval criteria used in these tests. They arose in the context of our later described, novel protocol for P300-based detection of concealed information (Rosenfeld *et al.*, 2008). This protocol was devised to deal with the serious issue of countermeasures (CMs) to P300-based detection of concealed information in the 3SP. It is best to delay this discussion until the CM issue is covered next.

Countermeasures to P300 as a concealed recognition index

Many eminent people assumed for many years that the P300 CIT (in its original 3SP format) would be unbeatable because the stimuli were presented so rapidly (every 2–4 s) and responded to by the brain so quickly (300–700 ms) that subjects would have no way to utilize CMs. Lykken (1998, p. 293) put it this way, "Because such potentials are derived from brain signals that occur only a few hundred milliseconds after the GKT alternatives are presented ... it is unlikely that counter-measures could be used successfully to defeat a GKT derived from the recording of cerebral signals." Ben-Shakhar and Elaad (2002) similarly wrote, "ERP measures seem to be immune against countermeasures because they are based on a repeated rapid presentation of the items (e.g., one item per second). When items are presented at such a rapid pace, it is virtually impossible to execute countermeasures to the control items." Our eminent colleague, Donchin, has repeatedly expressed this view to me in email correspondence even after publication of Rosenfeld *et al.* (2004), to be reviewed below, and after its approximate replication and extension by Mertens and Allen (2008). Our original 2004 demonstration of CMs to the 3SP arose from some simple reflections about that 3SP.

The instructions to subjects in the 3SP are to press a target button when targets are presented, and an alternative, non-target button on all other trials, both irrelevant and probe. (Verbal responses such as "Yes" for target or "No" for non-target may be substituted.) It is expected that rare probes will evoke a P300 because even though they are not explicitly task-relevant, their crime-related or personal significance makes them meaningful and salient only to guilty subjects. Targets will also evoke a P300 because they *are* explicitly task-relevant. This is why Farwell and Donchin (1991) expected probe and target P300s to look alike and, therefore, cross-correlate in guilty subjects.

It occurred to us that if simply making a unique, *overt* response to an irrelevant, *experimenter-designated* target stimulus could endow it with P300-eliciting properties, it also ought to be possible for subjects to learn to instruct themselves to make unique *covert* responses to *self-designated* irrelevant stimuli. When these formerly irrelevant stimuli become covert, relevant targets, they too should evoke P300s, making their averages indistinguishable from probe P300 averages. Once the probe-irrelevant difference is lost, the 3SP should no longer work, since now the probe-irrelevant correlation should be not appreciably different than the probe-target correlation.

All this is what we showed in Rosenfeld *et al.* (2004), utilizing either a *multiple probe protocol* (as in Farwell and Donchin, 1991, and as described in Rosenfeld *et al.*, 2007) or one of our own one-probe protocols, and utilizing either bootstrapped cross-correlation differences (an 82 percent hit rate was reduced to an 18 percent hit rate with CMs) or bootstrapped simple amplitude differences (a 92 percent hit rate was reduced to 50 percent with CMs). Mertens and Allen (2008) used a somewhat different scenario involving simulated mock crimes represented in virtual reality software, but showed that similarly conceived CMs dramatically reduce hit rates obtained without CMs.

The Rosenfeld *et al.* (2004) report was critically reviewed by Iacono in an archival volume (Iacono, 2007), but some of the critical points were inaccurate and/or misleading. For example, "the classification hit rate difference between guilty and countermeasure subjects was not statistically significant." The large numerical differences were actually given above, and in fact varied in significance from $p < 0.05$ to $p < 0.08$ across two studies. It would have been more accurate to state that the significance varied from marginally to *actually statistically significant*.

Iacono continued his critique by emphasizing that "*no test should be accepted as valid if the irrelevant and target stimuli cannot be easily differentiated.*" In fact, a glance at Figure 1 of Rosenfeld *et al.* (2004) makes it clear that this italicized phrase, *does not actually apply to our 2004 study* since that figure shows in the CM group that *the target P300s tower over the irrelevant (and probe) P300s* [my italics]. Indeed, the superimposed P300s for the three stimuli in the CM group greatly resemble the neighboring comparable superimpositions from the innocent group in the same figure and that is precisely the idea of the CM strategy – to make the CM-using guilty subject look innocent!

Iacono also casts doubt about the "salience of [our] probes" because they "did not elicit responses as large as the targets." In fact in the Farwell and Donchin (1991) first experiment, the task-relevant target P300s are clearly larger than probe P300s – as expected – in eighteen of twenty cases. The data of Rosenfeld *et al.* (1991) are similar. It appears to be an individual matter as to which stimulus, probe, or target will be more salient for a particular subject. It is also worth noting that although the Rosenfeld *et al.* (2004) paper contained two studies, all Iacono's criticisms refer only to the first. There were other matters, but overall we appreciated that Iacono did conclude positively about our "important" CM study that it was "the first to explore how countermeasures might affect this type of GKT."

Thus, it became apparent to us that the next major and long overdue challenge for P300-based information detection was to come up with a CM-resistant protocol. As similarly stated in Rosenfeld *et al.* (2008), to

increase CM resistance of the P300-based CIT, we attempted to identify factors in the older P300 protocols that potentially compromised
the test's sensitivity. The most obvious factor seemed to be the combination of the explicit target–nontarget decision with the implicit probe-
irrelevant discrimination, both of which occur in response to the sole
stimulus presented in each trial of the original 3ST protocol. That is,
the subject's explicit task in each trial of the 3ST is to decide whether or
not the stimulus is a target. However, it is also expected that the inherent salience of a probe stimulus (due to its personal or crime relevance)
would nevertheless lead to an enhanced P300 as the target–nontarget
discrimination was made. This meant that processing resources would
have to be divided between the explicit target task and the implicit
probe recognition. We reasoned that, because diversion of resources
away from an oddball task by a second task reduces the oddball evoked
P300 (Donchin *et al.*, 1986), likewise the probe P300 may be reduced
by a concurrent target discrimination task. Thus we developed a novel
protocol in which the probe-irrelevant discrimination would be separated from a time-delayed target–nontarget discrimination. We referred
to the new protocol accordingly developed as the *complex trial protocol*
or CTP.

A novel CM-resistant protocol

In the CTP, each trial begins with the presentation of either a rare (p =
0.2) probe or a frequent (p = 0.8) irrelevant (stimulus 1 or S1) and the
subject is instructed to respond as soon as possible on a single response
box with a single button press (Response 1 or R1) no matter whether
probe or irrelevant is presented. This is called the "I saw it" response
because the response simply signals the operator that the stimulus was
perceived regardless of its type. Then, after a random quiet interval of
about 1.2 to 1.8 s, a second stimulus (S2), either a target or non-target,
appears and the subject must give a specific differential response (R2)
to signal target or non-target. (Recently, we have used number strings
for target and non-targets.) The protocol is called complex because
there are two separated tasks (S1/R1 and S2/R2) on each trial. The
S1/R1 task allows us to compare probe to irrelevant P300s. The target task, though delayed, maintains attention and helps us enforce task
compliance. (See Figure 4.2.)

The protocol was the most accurate we have ever reported for the
detection of self-referring (birth date) stimuli. With no CMs (a "simple
guilty" or SG condition) we detected 12/12 subjects with a flexible P300
search window; or 11/12 with one fixed search window for all subjects.
Using the same kind of CMs as in Rosenfeld *et al.* (2004), in which

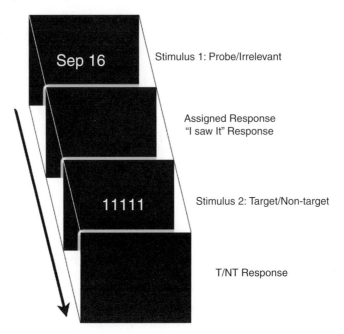

Figure 4.2 The events in the complex trial protocol using a date for S1 and a number string for S2.

subjects made a unique, assigned CM to each of the four irrelevants, we detected 11/12 subjects (flexible search window) or 10/12 (fixed search window). In a replication study in the same report, we detected 12/12 subjects in both SG and CM conditions with fixed search windows.

The diagnoses are based on bootstrap tests in which the probe P300 (peak-to-peak) was compared against the average of all irrelevant P300s (P vs. Iall test) with a p = 0.9 confidence interval. We reported further that (1) the CM condition caused increased probe and irrelevant (see Figure 4.3) P300 waves in each subject in both replications (an effect which we also saw in Winograd and Rosenfeld, 2008, who extended the CTP protocol for use in the detection of incidental details of a mock crime), and (2) reaction time (RT) was dramatically increased to probes and more so to irrelevants when CMs were used, so much that just within the CM run, irrelevant RTs were larger than probe RTs.

Regarding the CM condition's increasing effect on probe P300s, we suggested that the CM task forced greater attention to S1 as subjects needed to decide on each trial whether or not to execute a CM. This increased attention, we suggested, led to enhanced probe P300s. This effect may have been occurring but we also saw possibilities for still

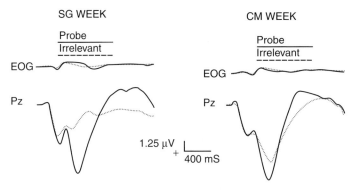

Figure 4.3 These are the Pz and EOG superimposed probe and irrelevant ERPs from the no countermeasure or simple guilty (SG) and countermeasure (CM) conditions of Rosenfeld *et al.* (2008) which were run over two successive weeks with the same subjects. The large down-going deflections are P300s. The enhanced irrelevant P300 in the CM week results from CM efforts (positive is plotted down).

another effect: we had reasoned in Rosenfeld *et al.* (2008) that since subjects made unique CM responses to each of four irrelevant stimuli, but of course, not to the probe, the latter could become the sole stimulus not requiring the added CM response, which would add salience to the probe beyond its inherent personal meaningfulness, thereby increasing its P300 amplitude. Meixner and Rosenfeld (2009b) demonstrated this *omit effect* rather unequivocally by showing that when a particular irrelevant stimulus, "IO," is presented in a series among four other irrelevant stimuli, each of which requires a specific assigned CM-like response, but not IO (Omitted Irrelevant), IO alone evokes a P300. If a meaningful probe-like item is substituted for IO, then the P300 virtually doubles in size. If CM-like responses are assigned to *all* five stimuli (omit effect removed), then the probe-like item elicits a P300 of about the same size as that evoked by IO.

It seemed to us at the time of the 2008 paper that having subjects generate a unique CM to each irrelevant stimulus was the best way to beat the test, since all irrelevants would become P300-eliciting covert targets, as in Rosenfeld *et al.* (2004). After finding the *omit effect*, we appreciated that from the guilty perpetrator's perspective, the best CM strategy might be to attempt to counter only a subset of irrelevant stimuli. Thus, Rosenfeld and Labkovsky (in press) conducted a new experiment with a modified version of the CTP in which only two of four irrelevants were countered. We also decided in this study to make the CMs purely mental, in an attempt to beat our recently observed RT effect of CM use (which were observed mostly with physical CMs in Rosenfeld *et al.* 2004, 2008). Subjects said silently to themselves either their first or last names upon seeing specifically one or the other irrelevant stimuli to be countered. The CTP was modified in such a way that a random five-button response box was used for R1. That is, the subjects said "I saw it" by pressing one of five randomly chosen buttons. The reasons for this novel R1 are given in Rosenfeld and Labkovsky (in press).

The results of this study were that the enormous increase in probe P300 associated with CM use seen in Rosenfeld *et al.* (2008) evaporated, a finding further supporting the *omit* hypothesis. Nevertheless we still detected 100 percent of SG subjects and CM users using the P vs. Iall test at p = 0.9 confidence. We have now run a total of five new studies in which one, two, three, four, and five CMs (the last included CMs against probe also) were used against four irrelevants in five groups of twelve subjects each. Hit rates in these groups were always 11/12 (92 percent) or 12/12 (100 percent) in P vs. Iall bootstraps at p = 0.9 (Labkovsky and Rosenfeld, 2009).

A promising alternative approach to a CM-resistant protocol was introduced by Lui and Rosenfeld (2009). We simply presented the key stimuli subliminally, the conceptualization being that stimuli not consciously perceived cannot be countered. The method accurately classified guilty and innocent subjects at 86 percent overall, with ROC-based discrimination of 0.88. This protocol was ERP-based, but could be tried with other dependent measures.

Recent developments in bootstrap tests about probe size

It was noted earlier that one robust finding in both Rosenfeld *et al.* (2008) and Rosenfeld *et al.* (2004) was that the use of CMs to irrelevants led to increased RTs. This proved to be a useful though not unsurprising finding, since it seems obvious in retrospect that if a subject needs to stop and reflect on which assigned CM response is to be used when a given irrelevant is presented, time will pass. Actually, the probe-irrelevant discrimination appears to take longer also as RT for probes is also elevated by CM use, though not as much as for irrelevants, in which case the extra cognitive step of CM response selection must occur.

The test we and others have mostly used in making decisions about a subject's guilt asked if the probe P300 was greater than an average of P300s to all irrelevant stimuli, the P vs. Iall test. The result of this test establishes that that probe P300 is greater than the irrelevant P300 average, but does not establish that the probe P300 is larger than each and every irrelevant P300, which one may want to know in some situations (e.g., in the "search CIT," when examiners are unaware of the critical items). Such a test requires that the probe P300 be greater than the largest irrelevant P300 at some level of confidence. This is the P vs. Imax test, and is obviously extremely rigorous, and could acceptably require use of a confidence level below 0.9. The confidence level for any test is acceptable so long as it is not lowered to a point at which one begins to see appreciable numbers of false positives in innocent control subjects. Thus the ROC curve from signal detection theory becomes useful as it relates the hit rate to the false positive rate, and it becomes possible to specify a confidence level for bootstrap testing in a manner such that the area under the ROC curve must exceed a certain amount, say, 0.9. This issue will be reconsidered when we discuss situations in which one does not know the identity of the probe in advance, such as in cases of suspected terrorist arrests, *prior to* commission of an act of terror (Meixner and Rosenfeld, 2009a).

The extreme rigor and sometimes concomitant loss of sensitivity of the P vs. Imax test can be somewhat tempered if one utilizes the elevated RT effect of CM use as a screen: that is, in both Rosenfeld *et al.* (2008) and Rosenfeld and Labkovsky (in press), we utilized the elevating CM effect on RTs as follows: if the test of P vs. Imax was significant, the subject was simply diagnosed as guilty. (If additionally, the RT for Imax was significantly greater than the probe RT, we noted also the probable use of CMs.) If the test of P vs. Imax failed, but the RT for Imax was greater than the probe RT, CM use was assumed, and the bootstrap test was performed on the probe vs. the *second largest* irrelevant – assuming its RT was not greater than the probe RT – and the result was referred to as an *RT-screened* P vs. Imax test result. If the RT for the second largest irrelevant was greater than that to the probe, one could proceed to the next largest irrelevant, and so on. The rationale for this screening procedure is the assumption (now backed by much data) that if the RT to an irrelevant stimulus is significantly elevated relative to the probe, one can assume a CM was used for that irrelevant, and there is no point testing a probe P300 against an irrelevant P300 likely to have been enlarged by a covert CM response. In both Rosenfeld *et al.* (2008) and Rosenfeld and Labkovsky (in press), the screened P vs. Imax tests yielded 92 percent (11/12) detection of CM-users.

In the RT screening procedure, we have described a comparison of the probe RT with irrelevant RTs, *all collected within one block*. It

Table 4.1 *Probe and Iall RTs (ms) in baseline and experimental blocks in SG, CM, and innocent (IC) groups.*

Group	Base-P	Base-Iall	Exp-P	Exp-Iall
SG	401.8	390.8	392.8	393.4
CM	483.9	460.3	806.5	1196.9
IC	469.1	442.2	393.7	397.3

is often the case that this procedure reveals CM use, particularly if a subject executes even a purely mental CM response *discretely, prior to* the "I saw it" response. Very recently, we have trained a novel batch of special CM users who execute CMs (two for four irrelevants) *simultaneously* with their "I saw it" responses, (Sokolovsky *et al.*, 2009). This "lumping" strategy reduces the within-session RT differences between probes and countered irrelevants (although guilt is detected in 83 percent of the CM-users with P300 amplitude anyway). However no matter what type of CM strategies subjects use, the RT average in a CM session is always at least 150 ms larger than in non-CM sessions. Much larger SG vs. CM differences in RT were found in Rosenfeld *et al.* (2008) and in Winograd and Rosenfeld (2008) in which all four irrelevants were countered. This suggests that the irrelevant RTs in a test session could be compared to RT data from some kind of baseline/control session so as to index CM use. This is what we did in Winograd and Rosenfeld (2008). In this study, prior to the mock crime execution, subjects were given a baseline RT task in the same format as the CTP except they were tested on knowledge of selected playing cards. In Table 4.1 are the RTs in the baseline and post-mock crime experimental sessions for probe (P) and irrelevant stimuli (all averaged together = Iall).

It is evident that in the CM experimental session, probe RTs are elevated by about 400 ms and Iall RTs by 800 ms in comparison to all other RTs. These dramatic increases can obviously be used as CM indexes.

It is appreciated that there is the possibility that a subject planning to use CMs will simply intentionally delay RTs in the *baseline* test. However, using upper limits for RTs will prevent such efforts from being successful (Ratcliff and McKoon, 1981; Seymour *et al.*, 2000). Moreover, there is no reason why a normative distribution of RTs in a situation with no motivation for CMs cannot be collected. Such "norms" could be used to test suspected CM-inflated RTs.

What if you lack advance knowledge of "ground truth"? Are there attendant analytic questions?

Since September 11, 2001, interest in deception detection in general increased, and in particular, interest especially developed in situations in which suspected terrorists might be captured and questioned prior to commission of a specific terrorist act. Such a situation poses new challenges to P300-based detection, even using the putatively powerful new CTP protocol. For example, one may arrest a suspected terrorist, but one doesn't necessarily know where, when, or how he plans to strike. However, intelligence may provide a few ideas about reasonable and probable answers to these questions, so that one can construct lists of plausible item sets for each category of information in which one is interested, for example, a set of US cities likely to be attacked. This is not necessarily a simple matter, and would likely be based on extensive prior investigation, including analysis of the "chatter" monitored in terrorist networks by authorities, as well as on results of interrogation of other suspects in custody, and so on. However one then is faced with the question of identifying which is the probe item to be used in tests of whether or not it elicits the largest P300 among a set of such stimuli.

John Meixner in our lab recently (the data are still being analyzed) undertook to model this situation (Meixner and Rosenfeld, 2009a). A subject in a guilty (SG) group (n = 12) was given a briefing document we prepared explaining that he was to play the role of a terrorist agent and plan a mock terrorist attack on the United States. The document detailed several different possible options he could choose regarding how to carry out the attack. The subject then read detailed descriptions of four types of bombs that could be used, four locations in the city of Houston that could be attacked, and four dates in July when the attack could take place. The descriptions contained pros and cons of each potential choice and instructed subjects to choose one type of bomb, one location in Houston, and one date on which to attack. After reading the briefing document, the subject was instructed to compose a letter to the fictitious superior in the terrorist organization describing the choices made. Subjects in the innocent (IN) group (n = 12) completed a similar task, but planned a vacation instead of a terrorist attack. Then after electrode attachment, a subject completed three separate blocks of the CTP task, with each block testing for a separate concealed information item. Subjects were shown potential cities where the terrorist attack could occur (Houston was the correct item), potential types of terrorist attacks (with Bomb as the correct item) and potential months the attack could occur in (with July as the correct item).

The data for each block were analyzed in three ways: in one way the correct item was considered the probe and its P300 was tested against the average P300 of five other irrelevant items in each block for this study (the P vs. Iall test). The second analysis (P vs. Imax) tested the known probe P300 against the maximum irrelevant (without RT screening, as we have not yet analyzed RT data). *Finally, we did an analysis for situations in which ground truth was lacking* (Allen et al., 1992, did something similar as demanded by their Bayesian approach to the question determining the probability that a word was from a learned list, given its evocation of a P300). We simply assumed that if the subject was concealing information concerning one item of the six tested in each block, it would evoke the largest P300, so we tested the largest P300 (the hypothesized probe P300) against the next largest P300 (the "Blind" Imax test; we assumed this second largest P300 to be the largest evoked by an irrelevant item). This was actually a conservative test since we might have tested the largest P300 against the average of *all* the remaining P300s for the other stimuli. Such a test, however, might have had a cost in specificity. We used 1,000 bootstrapped iterations for each block, then combined data from three blocks and averaged across blocks to yield the following table of results (see Table 4.2).

The numbers under the guilty and innocent designations show the three-block average number (maximum = 1,000) of bootstrap iterations in which the bootstrapped average probe or hypothetical probe (for blind Imax) tested as greater than the average of other P300s as designated. Each of the twelve rows represents a subject in each column for guilty and innocent groups. Means are shown in third row from bottom. Guilty diagnostic fractions are shown in second row from bottom, and the respective areas under ROC curves (AUC) are shown in the bottom row. It is apparent that we obtained perfect guilty-innocent discrimination in P vs. Iall and P vs. Imax tests, and excellent discrimination (AUC = 0.979) in the blind tests.

It should be added that in the above experiment, we were again using the CTP approach with incidentally acquired, newly learned information, which we have previously shown (Rosenfeld et al., 2006, 2007) to be not well detected with the 3SP. It is furthermore to be emphasized that in this study, subjects studied their newly acquired information for only thirty minutes, whereas it is likely that a real terrorist would have repeatedly rehearsed the details of a planned terrorist act to greater levels of processing depth. Thus it is quite possible that the signal to noise ratio in probe vs. irrelevant stimulus comparisons was probably less than in other situations we have worked with, and likely less than in field situations. In this connection, we note that although for the first P

Table 4.2 *The number (maximum = 1,000) of bootstrap iterations in which the bootstrapped average (hypothetical) probe was greater than that of the irrelevant items (Iall/Imax)*

P vs. Iall		P vs. Imax		Blind Imax	
Guilty	Innocent	Guilty	Innocent	Guilty	Innocent
1,000	648	985	287	985	603
1,000	610	999	416	998	602
955	598	889	476	892	649
996	611	898	430	893	605
994	150	946	17	943	689
909	475	698	284	761	547
945	600	677	365	702	536
997	555	959	250	961	569
999	586	908	217	907	565
985	690	888	382	886	706
912	390	667	129	698	650
903	644	837	215	842	702
966	**546**	**863**	**289**	872	**619**
12/12	0/12	12/12	0/12	10/12	0/12
AUC = 1.0		**AUC = 1.0**		**AUC = 0.979**	

vs. Iall test, we were able to use a bootstrap confidence interval of 0.9, as in previous studies, for the unscreened and rigorous P vs. Imax test, we had to drop our confidence interval to any value from 0.5 to 0.65 in order to achieve an AUC = 1.0. There is nothing inherently wrong with this adjustment since it is seen by examining the means of the third and fourth columns of the above table, that the numbers of positive iterations for *both* probe and Imax values are well below those seen under the P vs. Iall columns. Similarly, for the blind Imax test, we used a 0.75 confidence interval to get the best discrimination.

A guilty decision in the above study was based on totals for three blocks of data. It is certainly also of interest to know how many (of three possible in each subject) details of the planned terrorist act could be discerned. For that datum, one needs to know how many *individual blocks* led to positive outcomes on bootstrap tests. Using a confidence interval of 0.9, with no a priori specification of the probe, we were able to correctly identify twenty-one of thirty possible terrorist act details in the ten of twelve subjects correctly identified in blind Imax tests. The CTP appears to hold promise for the anti-terrorist challenge. (Other CIT-based attempts to deal with this challenge in very different ways were reported by Lui and Rosenfeld, 2009, reviewed briefly above, and Meijer *et al.*, in press.)

Conclusions

It is clear that whatever promise any of the P300-based protocols hold for real-world application, there are problems yet to be solved, despite the progress of the past two decades. The CTP is a new method that appears to show more CM resistance than any of its predecessors, but it too needs further research. Rosenfeld and Labkovsky (in press) observed for the first time a possibly novel ERP component called "P900" (with a latency of about 900 ms) that is maximal at Fz and Cz. It is seen only in countermeasure users in probe ERPs and sometimes in non-countered irrelevant ERPs, but not in countered irrelevant ERPs. This may prove a useful CM index in situations that may yet be seen in which RT is not a useful CM index. For example, the new "lumping" CM noted above (in which subjects make CM and "I saw it" responses simultaneously; Sokolovsky *et al.*, 2009) seems to pose problems for use of a probe-irrelevant, within-session RT difference to detect CM use. Clearly we need to fully document the phenomenology of and better understand P900 before its profitable application. Obviously, the application of the CTP to anti-terror situations needs much more work; in particular, the effect of CMs needs documentation in the anti-terror protocol described above. Finally, and this is true for all deception detection protocols, certainly not excepting the CTP, the effect of time passage between crime (or crime planning) and testing is not well known, but is clearly critical. There have been some preliminary efforts which are promising (e.g., Hamamoto *et al.*, 2009; Lefebvre *et al.*, 2007) but there is much work needing to be done on this crucial variable.

REFERENCES

Abootalebi, V., Moradi, M. H., and Khalilzadeh, M. A. (2006). A comparison of methods for ERP assessment in a P300-based GKT. *International Journal of Psychophysiology*, 62, 309–320.

Allen, J. J. B., and Iacono, W. G. (1997). A comparison of methods for the analysis of event-related potentials in deception detection. *Psychophysiology*, 34, 234–240.

Allen, J. J. B., Iacono, W. G., and Danielson, K. D. (1992). The identification of concealed memories using the event-related potential and implicit behavioral measures: a methodology for prediction in the face of individual differences. *Psychophysiology*, 29, 504–522.

Ben-Shakhar, G. (2002). A critical review of the Control Questions Test (CQT). In M. Kleiner (ed.), *Handbook of Polygraph Testing* (pp. 103–126). San Diego: Academic Press.

Ben-Shakhar, G., and Elaad, E. (2002). The Guilty Knowledge Test (GKT) as an application of psychophysiology: future prospects and obstacles.

In M. Kleiner (ed.), *Handbook of Polygraph Testing* (pp. 87–102). San Diego: Academic Press.

Donchin, E., Kramer, A., and Wickens, C. (1986). Applications of brain event related potentials to problems in engineering psychology. In M. Coles, S. Porges, and E. Donchin (eds.), *Psychophysiology: Systems, Processes and Applications* (pp. 702–710). New York: Guilford.

Efron, B. (1979). Bootstrap methods: another look at the jackknife. *The Annals of Statistics*, 7(1), 1–26.

Fabiani, M., Gratton, G., and Coles, M. G. H. (2000). Event-related brain potentials: methods, theory, and applications. In J. T. Cacioppo, L. G. Tassinary, and G. Berntsen (eds.), *Handbook of Psychophysiology* (pp. 85–119). New York: Cambridge University Press.

Fabiani, M., Karis, D., and Donchin, E., (1983). P300 and memory: individual differences in the von Restorff effect. *Psychophysiology*, 558 (abstract).

Farwell, L. A., and Donchin, E. (1986) The brain detector: P300 in the detection of deception. *Psychophysiology*, 24, S34 (abstract).

Farwell, L. A ., and Donchin, E. (1991). The truth will out: interrogative polygraphy ("lie detection") with event-related potentials. *Psychophysiology*, 28, 531–547.

Hamamoto, Y., Hira, S., and Furumitsu, I. (2009) Effects of refreshing memory on P300-based GKT administered one month after a mock crime for repeated offenders. Poster presented at 49th Ann. Meeting, Society for Psychophysiolological Research. Berlin.

Iacono, W. G. (2007). Detection of deception. In J. T. Cacioppo, L. G. Tassinary, and G. Berntsen (eds.), *Handbook of Psychophysiology* (pp. 668–703). New York: Cambridge University Press.

Johnson, M. M., and Rosenfeld, J. P. (1992). Oddball-evoked P300-based method of deception detection in the laboratory II: utilization of nonselective activation of relevant knowledge. *International Journal of Psychophysiology*, 12, 289–306.

Labkovsky, E. B., and Rosenfeld, J. P. (2009) Accuracy of the P300-based complex trial protocol for detection of deception as a function of number of countered irrelevant stimuli. Poster presented at 49th Ann. Meeting, Society for Psychophysiolological Research. Berlin.

Lefebvre, C. D., Marchand, Y., Smith, S. M., and Connolly, J. F. (2007) Determining eyewitness identification accuracy using event-related brain potentials (ERPs). *Psychophysiology*, 44, 894–904.

Lui, M. and Rosenfeld, J. P. (2008). Detection of deception about multiple, concealed, mock crime items, based on a spatial-temporal analysis of ERP amplitude and scalp distribution. *Psychophysiology*, 45, 721–730.

Lui, M. and Rosenfeld, J. P. (2009). The application of subliminal priming in lie detection: scenario for identification of members of a terrorist ring. *Psychophysiology*, 46, 889–903.

Lykken, D. T. (1998). *A Tremor in the Blood: Uses and Abuses of the Lie Detector*, 2nd edn. New York: Plenum Press.

Meijer, E. H., Smulders, F. T., and Merckelbach, H. L. (in press). Extracting concealed information from groups. *Journal of Forensic Sciences*.

Meijer, E. H., Smulders, F. T., Merckelbach, H. L., and Wolf, A. G. (2007). The P300 is sensitive to concealed face recognition. *International Journal of Psychophysiology*, 66, 231–237.

Meixner, J. B., and Rosenfeld, J. P. (2009a). Identifying terrorist information using the P300 ERP component. Poster presented at 49th Ann. Meeting, Society for Psychophysiolological Research. Berlin.

Meixner, J. B., and Rosenfeld, J. P. (2009b). Countermeasure mechanisms in a P300-based concealed information test. *Psychophysiology*, 47, 57–65.

Mertens, R., and Allen, J. J. (2008). The role of psychophysiology in forensic assessments: deception detection, ERPs, and virtual reality mock crime scenarios. *Psychophysiology*, 45, 286–298.

Polich, J. (1999). P300 in clinical applications. In E. Niedermeyer and F. Lopes da Silva (eds.), *Electroencephalography: Basic Principles, Clinical Applications and Related Fields*, 4th edn. (pp. 1073–1091). Baltimore and Munich: Urban & Schwarzenberg.

Ratcliff, R., and McKoon, G. (1981). Automatic and strategic priming in recognition. *Journal of Verbal Learning and Verbal Behavior*, 20, 204–215.

Rosenfeld, J. P. (2002). Event-related potentials in the detection of deception, malingering, and false memories. In M. Kleiner (ed.), *Handbook of Polygraph Testing* (pp. 265–286). New York: Academic Press.

Rosenfeld, J. P., and Labkovsky, E. (in press) New P300-based protocol to detect concealed information: resistance to mental countermeasures against only half the irrelevant stimuli and a possible ERP indicator of countermeasures. *Psychophysiology*.

Rosenfeld, J. P., Biroschak, J. R., and Furedy, J. J. (2006). P300-based detection of concealed autobiographical versus incidentally acquired information in target and non-target paradigms. *International Journal of Psychophysiology*, 60, 251–259.

Rosenfeld, J. P., Shue, E., and Singer, E. (2007). Single versus multiple probe blocks of P300-based concealed information tests for autobiographical versus incidentally learned information. *Biological Psychology*, 74, 396–404.

Rosenfeld, J. P., Angell, A., Johnson, M., and Qian, J. H. (1991). An ERP based, control-question lie detector analog: algorithms for discriminating effects within individuals' average wave forms. *Psychophysiology*, 32, 319–335.

Rosenfeld, J. P., Rao, A., Soskins, M., and Miller, A. R. (2002). P300 scalp distribution as an index of deception: control for task demand. *Journal of Credibility Assessment and Witness Psychology*, 3(1), 1–22.

Rosenfeld, J. P., Soskins, M., Bosh, G., and Ryan, A. (2004). Simple effective countermeasures to P300-based tests of detection of concealed information. *Psychophysiology*, 41, 205–219.

Rosenfeld, J. P., Nasman, V. T., Whalen, I., Cantwell, B., and Mazzeri, L. (1987). Late vertex positivity in event-related potentials as a guilty knowledge indicator: a new method of lie detection. *International Journal of Neuroscience*, 34, 125–129.

Rosenfeld, J. P., Cantwell, G., Nasman, V. T., Wojdac, V., Ivanov, S., and Mazzeri, L. (1988). A modified, event-related potential-based guilty knowledge test. *International Journal of Neuroscience*, 24, 157–161.

Rosenfeld, J. P., Labkovsky, E., Winograd, M., Lui, M. A., Vandenboom, C., and Chedid, E. (2008). The Complex Trial Protocol (CTP): a new, countermeasure-resistant, accurate P300-based method for detection of concealed information. *Psychophysiology*, 45, 906–919.

Seymour, T. L., Seifert, C. M., Mosmann, A. M., and Shafto, M. G. (2000). Using response time measures to assess "guilty knowledge." *Journal of Applied Psychology*, 85, 30–37.

Sokolovsky, A. W., Rothenberg, J., Meixner, J. B., and Rosenfeld, J. P . (2009). Sequential versus simultaneous stimulus acknowledgement and countermeasure responses in P300-based detection of deception. Poster presented at 49th Ann. Meeting, Society for Psychophysiolological Research. Berlin.

Soskins, M., Rosenfeld, J. P., and Niendam, T. (2001). The case for peak-to-peak measurement of P300 recorded at .3 Hz high pass filter settings in detection of deception. *International Journal of Psychophysiology*, 40, 173–180.

Van Hooff, J. C., and Golden, S. (2002). Validation of an event-related potential memory assessment procedure: intentional learning as opposed to simple repletion. *International Journal of Psychophysiology*, 16, 12–22.

Van Hooff, J. C., Brunia, C. H. M., and Allen, J. J. B. (1996). Event-related potentials as indirect measures of recognition memory. *International Journal of Psychophysiology*, 21, 15–31.

Van Hooff, J. C., Sargeant, E., Foster, J. K., and Schmand, B. A. (2009). Identifying deliberate attempts to fake memory impairment through the combined use of reaction time and event-related potential measures. *International Journal of Psychophysiology*. Online April 15.

Winograd, M. R., and Rosenfeld, J. P. (2008). Mock crime application of the complex trial protocol P300-based concealed information test. *Psychophysiology*, 45, S62 (abstract).

5 Detecting of deception and concealed information using neuroimaging techniques

Matthias Gamer

Overview: In the last decade, neuroimaging techniques became increasingly popular to study the neural underpinnings of psychological processes and consequently these methods were also applied in deception research. After giving a brief overview on neuroimaging methods, this chapter summarizes studies using functional magnetic resonance imaging or positron emission tomography to examine the neural underpinnings of deception and information concealment. A meta-analysis was carried out to determine the clustering of brain activation peaks across studies when contrasting deceptive with truthful answers in the Differentiation of Deception (DoD) paradigm or critical details with neutral items in the Concealed Information Test (CIT). A ventral frontoparietal network that is involved in detecting behaviorally relevant stimuli by matching them with previously acquired memory representations was recruited in both experimental paradigms. On this basis, first attempts to derive individual diagnoses from neuroimaging data will be described and the application of the DoD paradigm to forensic questions will be critically discussed. With respect to the CIT, neuroimaging techniques can be highly useful to shed light on the neural processes underlying information concealment and this knowledge can ultimately help to improve CIT validity.

Introduction

Traditionally, autonomic measures have been used to detect deception and there is a long tradition of utilizing these recordings for detecting concealed information as well (Lykken, 1959, 1998). However, new techniques emerged in the last decades that allow for examining brain activity with high temporal (e.g., techniques relying on electroencephalography) or spatial resolution (e.g., functional magnetic resonance imaging [fMRI]). The former techniques are especially useful for differentiating neurocognitive processes that occur within a few hundred milliseconds whereas the latter methods allow for precisely determining the anatomical location of brain activation in a certain task. With the advent of these modern techniques, the question emerged whether it would be more promising to use such direct measures of information processing in the brain instead of relying on peripheral manifestations of these processes in the activity of the autonomic nervous system. Pioneering researchers that applied neuroimaging techniques to the field of deception research even argued that "a primary problem with the polygraph is that it measures peripheral arousal, not deception itself" (Kozel *et al.*, 2004a, p. 852). Langleben and colleagues also emphasized that the specificity of the polygraph "is limited because it relies on the correlates of peripheral nervous system activity, while deception is a cognition event with top-down control by the central nervous system" (Langleben *et al.*, 2005, p. 262).

Based on such reasoning, the first neuroimaging studies examining deceptive behavior were published at the beginning of the twenty-first century (Ganis *et al.*, 2003; Langleben *et al.*, 2002; Spence *et al.*, 2001). A variety of questioning techniques has been adapted for these studies and despite substantial discrepancies in the brain regions that were found to be related to deceptive responding (Spence, 2008), there are now two companies in the United States which are promoting commercial lie detection tests based on neuroimaging (Cephos Corp: www. cephoscorp.com; No Lie MRI: www.noliemri.com).

The purpose of this chapter is to review the neuroimaging studies in the field of deception research that have been conducted so far. In contrast to earlier reviews (e.g., Christ *et al.*, 2009), a special emphasis will be given to the experimental paradigms that have been applied because activated brain regions cannot be reasonably interpreted without taking into account the specific questioning technique that was used in the respective study. As most studies in this domain relied on variations of the differentiation of deception paradigm (Furedy *et al.*, 1988) or the Concealed Information Test (CIT, Lykken, 1959), these techniques will be described in more detail and a meta-analysis of the currently available data for these paradigms will be presented. Finally, I am going describe first attempts to derive individual classifications from neuroimaging data and I am going to outline some suggestions for future research in this domain.

Neuroimaging methods

First of all, a brief introduction in neuroimaging methods will be presented to allow for a deeper understanding of the advantages as well as the drawbacks of this technology. A focus will be given to the analysis of fMRI data since this method is becoming the leading technique in the field (Friston, 2009). With some exceptions, however, the basic principles of such data analysis also apply to positron emission tomography (PET).

Strictly speaking, fMRI does not allow for a direct measurement of neural activity. Instead, standard fMRI procedures are sensitive to the ratio of desoxygenated and oxygenated haemoglobin (so-called blood oxygen level dependent [BOLD] contrast) and therefore measure vascular (haemodynamic) responses as a proxy for the underlying neural activity (Logothetis, 2002). Stimulus-related responses as measured by fMRI are typically weak and therefore such experiments require a large number of stimulus repetitions to increase signal-to-noise ratio. Furthermore, fMRI studies typically rely on the principle of cognitive subtraction. Thus, to identify brain regions that are recruited by a certain (psychological) process, conditions are realized that solely differ with respect to whether this process is involved or not. A very simple experiment in the domain of deception research would therefore require at least two experimental conditions: the examinee is instructed to lie to all questions in one condition and answer truthfully in the other. By contrasting the pattern of brain activity in the lie condition with the corresponding pattern in the truth condition, the brain regions critically involved in deception can be derived. It is important to bear in mind that such results are always based on the difference in brain activity between two experimental conditions. Thus, all conclusions that can be drawn from the observed pattern of neural activity critically depend on whether the underlying experimental conditions only differed with respect to the psychological function that was supposed to be examined. This principle is especially important when comparing the different experimental paradigms that were used in the domain of deception research.

In a simple experiment as outlined above, the examinee would be positioned in an MR scanner while answering questions either deceptively or truthfully. During this task, the whole brain of the participants can be scanned with a typical temporal resolution of 2–3 s per volume and an anatomical resolution of 2–3 mm in each spatial direction. The whole experiment typically results in a number of several hundreds of brain volumes that were acquired during the task. Each volume can be divided into a large number of volume elements (so-called voxels) which represent a measured value on a specific location in three dimensional space. These data cannot be analyzed directly, as it is first necessary to preprocess the fMRI volumes (see Figure 5.1).

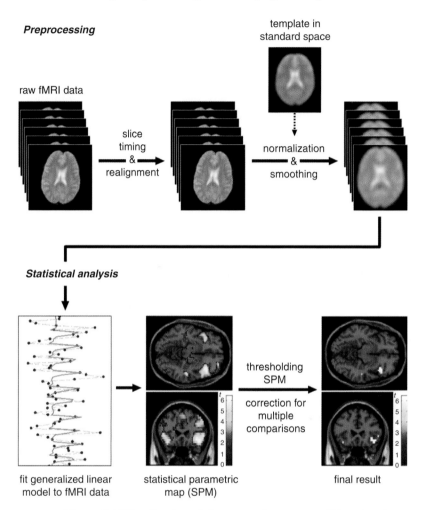

Figure 5.1 Visualization of the processing stream of functional magnetic resonance imaging (fMRI) data.

Typical preprocessing steps include (1) slice timing that corrects for the temporal delay between the sampling of activity in different brain regions; (2) realignment which is necessary to reduce influences of head movements that occurred during the experiment; (3) normalization of the acquired volumes into a standard anatomical space to allow for comparisons between participants; (4) smoothing of the brain volumes to take into account spatial dependencies in the fMRI signal and to optimize conditions for the application of special statistical techniques that require a certain amount of smoothness within each volume. After these preprocessing steps have been accomplished, one can examine the influence of the experimentally manipulated conditions on the fMRI data.

Statistical analyses in this domain typically rely on a mass univariate approach. This means that each voxel of the brain is analyzed independently by applying a generalized linear model to the acquired time series. Thus, not only one statistical test is performed as in the analysis of skin conductance data, for example. Instead, typically 50,000 to 200,000 tests are performed simultaneously. Thinking about issues of multiple testing, it becomes clear that special techniques are necessary to control against Type I errors. Otherwise, assuming uncorrelated data, one would find between 2,000 and 10,000 significantly activated voxels on a typical a priori significance level of $\alpha = 0.05$ even when the null hypothesis (i.e., no voxel is activated) holds for the entire brain. The most important methods to control for multiple testing in the field of neuroimaging are the family wise error rate (Worsley *et al.*, 1996) and the false discovery rate (Genovese *et al.*, 2002).[1] Moreover, such techniques can either be applied to the whole brain or – when specific anatomical hypotheses have been established – to a reduced search space. Having accomplished these processing steps, one gets to the final result of an fMRI analysis which is a statistical parametric map that can be depicted as a figure highlighting brain regions that were more active in one condition as compared to the other (see Figure 5.1). Furthermore, it is useful to report a table of these clusters along with the coordinates of their peak voxels in a standard anatomical space to allow for comparisons between studies.

---

[1] To keep the expected rate of false positive results constant across the application of multiple statistical tests, it is necessary to adjust the a priori significance level α according to the number of calculated tests. The Bonferroni correction that requires dividing α by the number of tests is a simple solution for this problem. However, this procedure turns out to be too conservative in the field of neuroimaging because maps of brain activation are typically smooth and thus spatially correlated. The family wise error rate (Worsley *et al.*, 1996) that is based on Gaussian random field theory takes into account this smoothness of the statistical parametric map and provides a less conservative threshold. Another frequently applied method in neuroimaging is the so-called false discovery rate (Genovese *et al.*, 2002). Instead of controlling for the probability of *ever* reporting false positives across a number of tests, this procedure controls for the occurrence of false-positive results *amongst voxels declared positive* (the discoveries). Thus, the application of the family wise error rate on an a priori significance level of $\alpha = 0.05$ guarantees that there is a confidence of 95 percent that there are no false positives in the neuroimaging results at all. By contrast, one would expect that there are on average 5 percent of voxels spuriously identified as being activated when the false discovery rate is used for thresholding the statistical parametric maps.

As outlined above, the analysis of neuroimaging data requires substantial processing and therefore a number of specific choices about preprocessing and analysis options. Several software packages implementing various algorithms were developed for these purposes. For that reason, results of neuroimaging studies may vary substantially because different preprocessing options were chosen, statistical maps were differentially thresholded to control for multiple comparisons or the search space was restricted to a set of predefined anatomical regions instead of controlling for the whole brain.

Experimental paradigms in neuroimaging studies on deception

Although a variety of different experimental paradigms have been used in neuroimaging studies on deception, these paradigms can be roughly classified into research designs relying on the differentiation of deception (DoD) paradigm or the CIT. The key feature of the DoD paradigm is the comparison of two conditions where participants are required to answer a set of questions either deceptively or truthfully. Thus, both conditions only differ with respect to whether the examinee is lying or telling the truth (Furedy et al., 1988). This paradigm was originally developed to examine the autonomic correlates of deceptive responding in isolation while controlling for other potentially confounding factors such as significance, frequency of occurrence, or emotional associations (e.g., Furedy et al., 1994; Gödert et al., 2001). Neuroimaging studies also implemented variations of this paradigm using questions on daily activities (Spence et al., 2001), autobiographical or nonautobiographical knowledge (Nuñez et al., 2005), or on experienced vs. unexperienced instructed events (Abe et al., 2006). In such studies it has also been varied whether examinees responded manually using key presses or verbally (e.g., Kozel et al., 2004a vs. Abe et al., 2006), whether the answer was predetermined or freely chosen (e.g., Fullam et al., 2009 vs. Spence et al., 2008b) or whether deceptive answers were given according to a previously memorized scenario or had to be spontaneously generated during the examination itself (Ganis et al., 2003).

A series of studies utilizing a variation of the DoD paradigm to examine deception within a mock crime context has been conducted by Kozel and colleagues (Kozel et al., 2005, 2009a, 2009b). In these studies, participants were instructed to either steal a ring or a watch from a drawer. During fMRI scanning, questions focusing on the theft of the ring (e.g., "Did you steal the ring?") or the watch (e.g., "Did you take the watch from the drawer?") were presented and examinees were instructed to deny stealing anything. As both objects were familiar to them and could be recognized as being part of the experiment, these questions only differ with respect to truthful or deceptive responding. Additionally, several neutral (e.g., "Are you a student?") and control questions (e.g., "Have you ever done something illegal?") were shown that had to be answered truthfully. On the level of group analyses, these studies specifically focused on the difference in brain activity between the lie (deceptively denying the theft of the stolen item) and the truth condition (truthful denial of stealing the other item) thereby accomplishing the critical comparison of the DoD paradigm.

In contrast to the DoD paradigm, the CIT focuses on the recognition of critical details instead of deceptive responding (Lykken, 1974). Therefore, physiological responses elicited by a critical detail (e.g., a feature of a crime under investigation) are compared to the responses elicited by equally plausible neutral items. Although deception is no necessary condition for the CIT (Ben-Shakhar and Elaad, 2003), deceptive responding is often required in these studies, too, because examinees are typically instructed to deny knowledge of critical (crime-related) items. The first neuroimaging study utilizing a modification of the CIT was conducted by Langleben et al. (2002). In this study, participants were required to conceal knowledge of a specific playing card that was memorized before fMRI scanning. Brain activity that was elicited by this concealed knowledge was then compared to the response accompanying the (truthful) denial of having hidden another playing card that was not presented before. Thus, in principle this design resembled a CIT with one probe and one neutral control item. This equal frequency of critical and neutral items is considered to be suboptimal within a CIT (Ben-Shakhar, 1977) because when focusing on only one dependent variable (e.g., skin conductance responses), even people without knowledge of critical items would have a risk of 50 percent of showing larger responses to them. In the long tradition of using autonomic measures in the CIT it has thus been recommended to use at least about three to five times more neutral items than critical ones (Lykken, 1998). To the best of our knowledge, we were the first group that directly transferred such a CIT paradigm to a neuroimaging study (Gamer et al., 2007). In this study, participants drew one of three envelopes and were required to memorize the content (a jack of spades playing card and a €20 banknote). During fMRI scanning, pictures of these critical items were presented along with a number of neutral items (other playing cards and banknotes). To ensure that participants paid attention to the stimulus presentation they were instructed to press a different response button whenever a predefined target item (a king of spades playing card and a €100 banknote) was shown. This experimental design closely resembled a modification of the CIT that was used for the measurement of event-related brain potentials (e.g., Farwell and Donchin, 1991; Rosenfeld *et al.*, 1988) and a similar approach was taken by a recent study from Japan (Nose *et al.*, 2009).

Not all neuroimaging studies in this domain either used a DoD or a CIT paradigm, some also mixed both designs within one experiment. For example, Langleben *et al.* (2005) presented two playing cards to their participants but during fMRI scanning, examinees were instructed to truthfully acknowledge familiarity with one card while denying knowledge of the other. Additionally, a recurrent distractor (another playing card) and a variant distractor (a number of different playing cards) were presented in a randomized sequence. In this design, the comparison of deceptive and truthful answers regarding questions on previously presented playing cards resembles a DoD approach whereas the contrast of deceptive answers (concealed knowledge) to responses elicited by the recurrent or the variable distractors resembles a CIT paradigm.

Relevant brain regions for deception and information concealment

Across neuroimaging studies on deception and information concealment, results on the involved brain regions vary. Even studies using similar experimental procedures failed to fully replicate their findings (cf. Spence, 2008). However, all studies found regions in the prefrontal cortex being more activated when deceiving or concealing knowledge. Moreover, most studies reported larger increases of brain activity in deceptive as compared to truthful conditions than vice versa, indicating that truthful responding is easier and represents a basic mode of brain functioning (exceptions are Fullam *et al.*, 2009, and Langleben *et al.*, 2005, for example). To systematically examine which brain regions were consistently shown to be involved in deceptive responding or information concealment, meta-analytic techniques seem to be a useful statistical tool. In the domain of neuroimaging, analyses of activation likelihood estimates (ALE) have been suggested as an adequate method for the formal analysis of the clustering of peak activations across studies (Turkeltaub *et al.*, 2002).

This ALE analysis is based on the idea that the locations of reported peak activations may vary across studies but still show a consistent pattern of activation clustering within a relatively small region. To determine such consistency across studies, peak activations are not viewed as a single point, but rather as probability distributions centered on peaks at the reported coordinates. The union of such activation probabilities across studies (so-called ALE map) can then be used to assess the differential likelihood of activation across the whole brain. To determine the statistical significance of such clustering, it is then necessary to differentiate between voxels within the map that represent signal (i.e., nonrandom clustering of foci) from those that represent noise (i.e., random clustering). This can be achieved by using permutation tests that compare the observed clustering of activation with a random set of foci that are ideally determined by taking into account anatomical constraints (i.e., activations are located in the brain's gray matter, Eickhoff *et al.*, 2009). This ALE analysis thus allows for quantitatively evaluating the convergence of neuroimaging findings. Such an approach was also adopted here for the analysis of brain activations during deception and information concealment.

First of all, relevant studies were searched in PubMed in November 2009 using keywords such as "deception," "concealed information", "fmri," "pet". Publications by known researchers in the field were searched for additional reports. Studies that implemented variations of the DoD paradigm and reported the comparison of deceptive and truthful responding were included in the ALE analysis as well as studies in the CIT paradigm reporting the contrast of critical items vs. neutral alternatives. For our own studies, such contrasts were specified in a reanalysis of the original data (Gamer *et al.*, 2007, in press). This study selection might be incomplete since some studies are not referenced in PubMed or were not found using the respective keywords. Moreover, some studies could not be included because exact coordinates of activation foci were not reported (e.g., Lee *et al.*, 2005; Kozel *et al.*, 2009a) or it remained unclear which conditions were exactly contrasted to obtain the reported differences in brain activation (e.g., Lee *et al.*, 2002; Mohamed *et al.*, 2006). However, the purpose of the current ALE analysis is to give an overview of activation patterns in neuroimaging studies on deception instead of making a claim of exhaustively summarizing all relevant studies in this domain.

After study selection, activation foci reported for the interesting differences in brain activation were collected. For all studies, only the peak activation within each cluster was used for the ALE analysis. When necessary, coordinates were transformed from the Talairach to the MNI space within the software that was also used for calculating the ALE maps (GingerALE 2.0, www.brainmap.org/ale). The final study selection is summarized in Table 5.1. Overall, data from 289 participants were available for the DoD paradigm and from 119 examinees for CIT examinations. It is important to note that the number of

Table 5.1 *Included studies in the meta-analysis of activations in the Differentiation of Deception (DoD) and the Concealed Information Test (CIT) paradigm*

Study	Modality	n	Foci
DoD paradigm: Lie > Truth			
Abe *et al.* (2006)	PET	14	4
Abe *et al.* (2007)	PET	16	5
Abe *et al.* (2008)	fMRI	20	20
Fullam *et al.* (2009)	fMRI	24	2
Ganis *et al.* (2003)	fMRI	10	12
Kozel *et al.* (2004a)	fMRI	10	8
Kozel *et al.* (2004b)	fMRI	8	10
Kozel *et al.* (2005), Model-building group	fMRI	30	7
Kozel *et al.* (2005), Model-testing group	fMRI	31	7
Kozel *et al.* (2009c), Quality mock crime group	fMRI	14	13
Kozel *et al.* (2009b)	fMRI	29	13
Langleben *et al.* (2005)	fMRI	22	4
Nuñez *et al.* (2005)	fMRI	20	8
Phan *et al.* (2005)	fMRI	14	11
Spence *et al.* (2001)	fMRI	10	6
Spence *et al.* (2008b)	fMRI	17	7
Total:		289	137
CIT: Critical item > Neutral alternative(s)			
Bhatt *et al.* (2009)	fMRI	18	9
Gamer *et al.* (2007), Reanalysis	fMRI	14	8
Gamer *et al.* (in press), Reanalysis	fMRI	23	13
Langleben *et al.* (2002)	fMRI	23	2
Langleben *et al.* (2005)	fMRI	22	4
Nose *et al.* (2009), Concealed-information group	fMRI	19	5
Total:		119	41

Note: PET = positron emission tomography, fMRI = functional magnetic resonance imaging.

included experimental conditions (sixteen for the DoD and six for the CIT paradigm) is relatively small. Meta-analyses typically require a larger number of studies to draw firm conclusions about the consistency of findings. Moreover, such a small set of studies does not allow for identifying possible moderator variables that affect the pattern of brain activity. However, the current ALE analysis might still reveal interesting insights into the processing of deception and information concealment by determining those brain regions that are highly consistently activated across a number of studies.

The collected activation foci were submitted to separate ALE analyses for the DoD and the CIT paradigm. A random-effects approach was

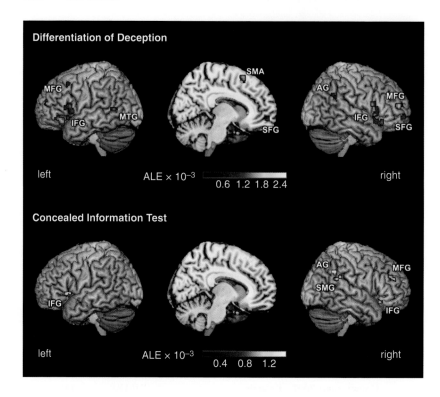

Figure 5.2 Results of the ALE meta-analyses of activation peaks
in the Differentiation of Deception paradigm and the Concealed
Information Test. In both analyses, maps were thresholded at
the ALE value corresponding to $p < 0.05$ corrected for multiple
comparisons using the false discovery rate (FDR). Activation clusters
are labeled according to their anatomical location: AG = angular
gyrus, IFG = inferior frontal gyrus, MFG = middle frontal gyrus,
MTG = middle temporal gyrus, SFG = superior frontal gyrus, SMA
= supplementary motor area, SMG = supramarginal gyrus.

chosen and estimates of spatial uncertainty were empirically determined
(Eickhoff *et al.*, 2009). After calculation of ALE and *p*-values for the
whole brain, statistical maps were thresholded at a level of $p < 0.05$ corrected for multiple comparisons using the false discovery rate (Genovese
et al., 2002). Furthermore, clusters were required to reach a spatial
extent of at least 200 mm³. Results are depicted in Table 5.2 and activation clusters are overlaid on a structural MRI template in Figure 5.2
using MRIcron (Rorden, www.cabiatl.com/mricro/mricron).

Table 5.2 *Significant clusters (p < 0.05, corrected using the false discovery rate) identified in the analyses of activation likelihood estimates (ALE) within the Differentiation of Deception (DoD) and the Concealed Information Test (CIT) paradigm*

		MNI coordinates				
Region	Location	x	y	z	Volume (cm³)	ALE value × 10–3
DoD paradigm: Lie > Truth						
1	Right inferior frontal gyrus, orbital part	55	19	−5	1.58	1.59
2	Right inferior frontal gyrus, opercular part	60	11	17	0.36	1.65
3	Right middle frontal gyrus	38	53	14	0.66	1.93
4		35	60	−3	0.27	1.37
5	Right superior frontal gyrus, medial orbital	13	57	−7	0.34	1.57
6	Right angular gyrus	62	−53	30	0.21	1.22
7	Right supplementary motor area	4	17	59	1.14	2.59
8	Left inferior frontal gyrus, orbital part	−43	30	−10	1.14	1.76
9		−50	17	−6	0.28	1.39
10	Left inferior frontal gyrus, opercular part	−53	14	9	0.98	1.48
11	Left inferior frontal gyrus, triangular part	−33	33	8	0.46	1.92
12	Left middle frontal gyrus	−27	52	18	0.70	1.90
13		−38	18	46	0.25	1.34
14	Left middle temporal gyrus	−59	−58	8	0.29	1.50
15	Left caudate nucleus	−11	12	3	0.22	1.23
16	Left supplementary motor area	−2	22	48	0.24	1.34
CIT paradigm: Critical item > Neutral alternative(s)						
1	Right inferior frontal gyrus, orbital part	39	23	−10	0.68	1.55
2	Right middle frontal gyrus	35	44	23	0.39	1.19
3	Right angular gyrus	59	−51	35	0.44	1.40
4	Right supramarginal gyrus	60	−45	26	0.27	1.14
5	Left inferior frontal gyrus, triangular part	−44	19	−1	0.54	1.29

Note: Clusters were required to reach a spatial extent of at least 200 mm³. The cluster center is reported in MNI coordinates along with the maximum ALE value within each cluster.

Across studies, robustly larger activations were observed bilaterally in the dorsolateral and anterior prefrontal cortex (middle and superior frontal gyrus) as well as in inferior frontal regions when deceiving as compared to truthful responding in the DoD paradigm. Moreover, differential responses were found in the supplementary motor area as well as the angular gyrus. With respect to the CIT paradigm, fewer regions were found to be activated when contrasting critical details with neutral items. However, these results have to be treated with caution because much fewer data were available for the CIT design (see Table 5.1). Interestingly, there is an overlap between the regions that were found in the ALE analyses of the DoD and the CIT paradigm. The inferior frontal gyrus as well as the temporoparietal junction (angular and supramarginal gyrus) were sensitive to deception and concealed knowledge. Moreover, the right middle frontal gyrus was found to be differentially activated in both paradigms although the exact anatomical location seems to differ slightly. Interestingly, the anterior cingulate cortex was neither reliably activated in the DoD nor in the CIT paradigm although several studies explicitly focused their discussion on the relevance of this region for deceptive responding (e.g., Langleben et al., 2002; Nuñez et al., 2005).

With respect to the functional relevance of the involved brain regions, the dorsolateral prefrontal cortex has been consistently implicated in a variety of experimental tasks including response monitoring, novelty detection or conflict resolution (Duncan and Owen, 2000). Furthermore, such lateral prefrontal activations were observed in a number of different memory tests such as working memory tasks, episodic retrieval and semantic memory tests (D'Esposito et al., 2000; Konishi et al., 2000; Nyberg et al., 2003; Ranganath et al., 2003). Thus, these activations do not seem to be specific for deceptive responding, instead they reflect a prefrontal network that is "recruited in solution of diverse cognitive problems" (Duncan and Owen, 2000, p. 481). This reasoning is well in line with another meta-analysis on neural correlates of deception that mainly focused on studies using variations of the DoD paradigm (Christ et al., 2009). In this study, brain activation during deception was compared to activation maps from working memory, inhibitory control and task-switching experiments. It turned out that deception recruited similar – mainly prefrontal – brain regions as the other tasks and it was thus reasoned that "executive control processes, particularly working memory, and their associated neural substrates play an integral role in deception" (p. 1565).

Previous research has also closely linked the inferior frontal gyrus (especially on the right hemisphere) to inhibitory functions (Aron et al.,

2004) and consequently, its activation in the DoD as well as in the CIT paradigm has been interpreted as reflecting response conflicts between lying and truth telling (e.g., Nuñez *et al.*, 2005) or between revealing concealed knowledge as compared to hiding it (e.g., Gamer *et al.*, 2007). However, this interpretation is challenged by one of our recent studies where we removed explicit response conflicts from the experimental design by asking participants to press the same response button for each stimulus (Gamer *et al.*, in press). Even in this case we found larger bilateral activity in the inferior frontal gyrus for critical as compared to neutral CIT items. These results indicate that the inferior frontal gyrus subserves a more general function such as detecting potentially relevant stimuli in a train of irrelevant ones (Kiehl *et al.*, 2001) or facilitating the retrieval of relevant details from memory (Iidaka *et al.*, 2006). The significant cluster in the temporoparietal junction also fits to the former interpretation as this region has been consistently found to be activated by infrequent changes in the environment (Downar *et al.*, 2000, 2002). Thus, activity in a ventral frontoparietal network consisting of the inferior frontal gyrus and the temporoparietal junction is modulated by detecting unexpected or rare events, independent of sensory modality or response demands (Corbetta and Shulman, 2002). These conditions are also capable of eliciting an orienting response (Sokolov, 1963) which in turn is one major psychophysiological concept that underlies differential physiological responding in the CIT (Lykken, 1974). The current brain activation data thus support that the idea that physiological responses in the CIT and potentially also in the DoD are closely related to the theoretical construct of the orienting response (Verschuere *et al.*, 2004).

Taken together, the ALE analyses revealed a bilateral clustering of brain activity in the dorsolateral and anterior prefrontal cortex in the DoD as well as in the CIT paradigm. Moreover, consistent results were obtained for the temporoparietal junction of the right hemisphere. This pattern of activation does not seem to be specific for deception or information concealment but rather reflects the recruitment of brain regions that are necessary for (cognitive) processes such as working memory, relevance detection, or response monitoring which seem to be crucial for deceptive responding (cf. Christ *et al.*, 2009).

Individual classifications

The above-mentioned meta-analysis of brain activation patterns was conducted on group statistics. In the domain of forensic psychophysiology, however, it is especially interesting whether a given method also allows for deriving individual diagnoses. The first studies taking a closer look at individual neuroimaging data in the DoD paradigm were published by Kozel and colleagues. As a first step, these studies tested whether the contrast between deceptive and truthful responding on an individual level reveals an involvement of similar brain regions across examinees. Although a high degree of variability across participants was found in the first study (Kozel et al., 2004b), a relatively consistent activation of the right prefrontal cortex was reported in the second experiment (Kozel et al., 2004a).

In a subsequent extensive study, more than sixty participants were examined in the so-called ring-watch paradigm (a variant of the DoD design) to test the possibility of obtaining individual diagnoses from neuroimaging data (Kozel et al., 2005). Participants were instructed to either steal a ring or a watch in a mock crime setting and they subsequently denied stealing anything. From half of the data ($n = 30$), a model was derived to examine how deceptive and truthful answers differ with respect to the accompanying pattern of brain activation (model-building group). In this step, three clusters were identified that showed the largest difference between both conditions (anterior cingulate cortex, right orbitofrontal/inferior frontal cortex, and right middle frontal gyrus). These clusters were used as functionally defined regions of interest (ROI) and for these areas the number of activated voxels in the deceptive as compared to the truthful condition was calculated for each examinee on a predefined statistical threshold. This metric was then used to determine whether a given examinee was found to be deceptive or truthful depending on whether the difference turned out to be positive or negative. Using such procedure, 93 percent of participants in the model-building group could be correctly classified and replications of this procedure resulted in hit rates between 71 percent and 93 percent in independent samples (see Table 5.3).

Instead of classifying individuals (Kozel et al., 2005), it is also possible to detect deception on the level of single trials (i.e., responses to single questions). Such an approach was adopted by Langleben et al. (2005) using a logistic regression analysis on signal changes in functionally defined ROIs from a preceding group analysis. This approach allowed for a correct classification of 76 percent of deceptive (sensitivity) and 80 percent of truthful responses (specificity) within each participant on average. In a cross validation of this classification function on data of four new examinees, these values slightly changed to 69 percent and 84 percent, respectively. The same data were also analyzed using a computationally extensive multivariate high-dimensionality pattern classification technique (non-linear support vector machine, Davatzikos et al.,

Table 5.3 *Individual classifications in neuroimaging studies on deception and information concealment*

| | | Correct classifications | |
| | | Guilty | Innocent |
Study	Paradigm	(Sensitivity)	(Specificity)
Davatzikos *et al.* (2005)	DoD	21/22 (95%)	
Kozel *et al.* (2005), Model-building group	DoD	28/30 (93%)	
Kozel *et al.* (2005), Model-testing group	DoD	28/31 (90%)	
Kozel *et al.* (2009c), Quality group (ring vs. watch theft)	DoD	25/35 (71%)	
Kozel *et al.* (2009c), Quality group (guilt vs. innocence in committing a mock crime)	DoD	13/14 (93%)	8/21 (38%)
Kozel *et al.* (2009b)	DoD	25/29 (86%)	
Monteleone *et al.* (2009)	DoD	10/14 (71%)	
Nose *et al.* (2009)	CIT	16/19 (84%)	16/19 (84%)

Note: Group labels "Guilty" and "Innocent" refer to participants who were lying or concealing information during the experiment in contrast to examinees who did not commit a mock crime or were unaware of critical probe items.

2005). On the level of single trials that were not included in building the model, a sensitivity of 90 percent and a specificity of 86 percent were achieved. On the level of individual examinees, 95 percent could be correctly identified as answering deceptively (see Table 5.3).

Taken together, these estimates of the test's sensitivity are satisfactory. However, one study also examined whether this technique can be used to correctly identify innocent participants who were not involved in any misdeed (Kozel *et al.*, 2009c). In this mock crime study, specificity was very low (38 percent). A possible reason for this discrepancy between sensitivity and specificity can be found in the questioning technique itself. As this experiment relied on the DoD paradigm, it was necessary to construct a situation that required innocents to lie to specific questions whereas they could truthfully answer questions related to the mock crime. However, physiological responses to these questions can only be reasonably compared when they only differ with respect to deceptive vs. truthful responding (cf. Horowitz *et al.*, 1997). In the respective study, this was not the case as innocents had to answer questions deceptively to create an alibi which differed substantially from relevant question that were related to the mock crime. This dilemma is typical for the DoD design and therefore, Furedy even noted that this paradigm can only be used for basic research and "does not have any direct applied significance" (Furedy *et al.*, 1994, p. 15). A possible solution for the problem of improper comparison questions problem has been proposed by Spence and colleagues (2001). Instead of trying to set up parallel questions, they suggested to use the same questions in two experimental conditions where examinees are once required to answer deceptively and once truthfully. In such situation, each stimulus provides its own control, and one avoids the difficulty of matching lie and truth stimuli. Until now, such an experimental DoD design has only been rarely used in neuroimaging studies but it might be a promising approach even for forensic situations (Spence *et al.*, 2008a).

A paradigm that does not face the issue of improper comparison questions is the CIT whose items are equally plausible and indistinguishable for innocent examinees (Lykken, 1974). Unfortunately, there is only one fMRI study that reported individual classifications in a CIT paradigm (Nose *et al.*, 2009). In this study, signal changes following the critical detail were analyzed in functionally defined ROIs and these values were then compared between participants who knew this item or were unaware of it. To determine an empirical threshold for differentiating between groups and to identify brain regions contributing to this prediction, a stepwise discriminant analysis was used. It turned out that only activity in the right ventrolateral prefrontal cortex contributed to the discrimination and in both groups 84 percent of the participants could be correctly identified. Compared to the costs and complexity of an fMRI study, this validity coefficient is not particularly high because similar hit rates can be achieved using only electrodermal data (e.g., Beijk, 1980).

Summary and conclusions

This chapter provided an overview of the application of modern neuroimaging techniques to the study of deception and information concealment. Although a variety of experimental paradigms have been used in these studies, most relied on variations of the DoD or the CIT design. Using meta-analytic techniques to determine the clustering of activation peaks across studies, it turned out that deception as well as information concealment elicited enhanced activity in a ventral frontoparietal network that is involved in detecting behaviorally relevant stimuli in the environment by matching them with previously acquired memory representations. Deception also recruited a larger dorsolateral and anterior prefrontal network that was associated with cognitive control processes. These results are especially interesting when comparing them to the original motivation for neuroimaging studies on deception. For example, Kozel and colleagues (2005) argued that "a fundamental limitation of ... polygraph testing is that [it measures] nonspecific peripheral emotional/autonomic arousal that might or might not be associated with lying" (p. 605). On the basis of the currently available data, it seems that brain activation patterns are essentially non-specific too, as the observed brain regions are also recruited by a number of tasks that are unrelated to deceptive responding. Thus, these regions seem to be more related to basic processes underlying deception (e.g., working memory, response planning, and monitoring) instead of specifically reflecting the generation of deceit.

It remains an open question for future research to clarify the functional relevance of these prefrontal and parietal brain regions for deception and information concealment (Abe, 2009). This can be achieved by factorially varying experimental conditions that might selectively contribute to the activation of this brain network. Such studies on the CIT have been conducted in the last decades to characterize the influence of motivation, deceptive answering, or type of concealed knowledge on autonomic responding (for a review see Ben-Shakhar and Elaad, 2003) and comparable studies are also desirable with respect to neuroimaging data. Following this line of research, it is also interesting to correlate brain activity with autonomic measures (Gamer *et al.*, 2007; Kozel *et al.*, 2009a) to further isolate brain regions driving sympathetic and parasympathetic outflow which are typically measured in such examinations (Gamer *et al.*, 2008). A second strategy to unravel the neurodynamics of deception is to examine such processes during disruption of involved brain regions. This can either be achieved by investigating patients with abnormal activity or lesions in this network (Abe *et al.*, 2009) or by temporarily modulating neural excitability of these regions using non-invasive techniques such as transcranial direct current stimulation (Karim *et al.*, 2010; Priori *et al.*, 2008).

Regarding the validity of neuroimaging techniques on an individual basis, most studies focused on the DoD paradigm. Although interesting from the perspective of basic research, this questioning technique can hardly be applied to the forensic domain because it requires parallel questions that only differ with respect to deceptive vs. truthful responding. Although it is possible to solve this problem by requiring examinees to answer the same questions once truthfully and once deceptively (Spence *et al.*, 2001, 2008a), it is currently unknown whether such a procedure allows for deriving valid individual diagnoses. Furthermore, as the DoD paradigm explicitly focuses on deception, results that were obtained in the laboratory might not generalize to field settings (Sip *et al.*, 2008). Despite all these problems, such DoD based techniques seem to be commercially available in the United States nowadays. This premature application has been severely criticized by the scientific community (see editorial "Deceiving the law", 2008; Greely and Illes, 2007; Wolpe *et al.*, 2005) and these applications are heavily debated with reference to legal and ethical issues (see Simpson, 2008, and commentaries by Langleben and Dattilio, 2008, and Merikangas, 2008). However, in this discussion the various questioning techniques were rarely differentiated which is especially unfortunate as most of the above-mentioned points of criticism do not apply to memory-based tests such as the CIT. Until now, only one fMRI study detecting concealed knowledge in individual examinees has been published. The reported hit rates did not exceed validity estimates of autonomic measures but applying more sophisticated techniques such as multivariate pattern classification to fMRI data (Haynes and Rees, 2006) might be an interesting approach for future research to enhance CIT validity (Bles and Haynes, 2008).

To close this chapter with a cautious note, more emphasis should be given to the questioning technique in the field of neuroimaging research on deception in the future. This issue was also mentioned by Iacono (2007) who criticized that "these investigations did little to take advantage of the accumulated knowledge regarding the methodological pitfalls associated with the last 50 years of deception detection research" (p. 700). However, using established questioning techniques such as the CIT with modern neuroimaging methods can substantially enhance our understanding of the psychological processes that are involved in such examinations and this knowledge can ultimately help to improve existing methods for detecting deception and concealed knowledge in forensic applications.

REFERENCES

Abe, N. (2009). The neurobiology of deception: evidence from neuroimaging and loss-of-function studies. *Current Opinion in Neurology*, 22, 594–600.

Abe, N., Suzuki, M., Mori, E., Itoh, M., and Fujii, T. (2007). Deceiving others: distinct neural responses of the prefrontal cortex and amygdala in simple fabrication and deception with social interactions. *Journal of Cognitive Neuroscience*, 19, 287–295.

Abe, N., Suzuki, M., Tsukiura, T., Mori, E., Yamaguchi, K., Itoh, M., and Fujii, T. (2006). Dissociable roles of prefrontal and anterior cingulate cortices in deception. *Cerebral Cortex*, 16, 192–199.

Abe, N., Okuda, J., Suzuki, M., Sasaki, H., Matsuda, T., Mori, E., Tsukada, M., and Fujii, T. (2008). Neural correlates of true memory, false memory, and deception. *Cerebral Cortex*, 18, 2811–2819.

Abe, N., Fujii, T., Hirayama, K., Takeda, A., Hosokai, Y., Ishioka, T., Nishio, Y., Suzuki, K., Itoyama, Y., Takahashi, S., Fukuda, H., and Mori, E. (2009). Do parkinsonian patients have trouble telling lies? The neurobiological basis of deceptive behaviour. *Brain*, 132, 1386–1395.

Aron, A. R., Robbins, T. W., and Poldrack, R. A. (2004). Inhibition and the right inferior frontal cortex. *Trends in Cognitive Sciences*, 8, 170–177.

Beijk, J. (1980). Experimental and procedural influences on differential electrodermal activity. *Psychophysiology*, 17, 274–278.

Ben-Shakhar, G. (1977). A further study of the dichotomization theory in detection of information. *Psychophysiology*, 14, 408–413.

Ben-Shakhar, G., and Elaad, E. (2003). The validity of psychophysiological detection of information with the Guilty Knowledge Test: a meta-analytic review. *Journal of Applied Psychology*, 88, 131–151.

Bhatt, S., Mbwana, J., Adeyemo, A., Sawyer, A., Hailu, A., and Vanmeter, J. (2009). Lying about facial recognition: an fMRI study. *Brain and Cognition*, 69, 382–390.

Bles, M., and Haynes, J. (2008). Detecting concealed information using brain-imaging technology. *Neurocase*, 14, 82–92.

Christ, S. E., Van Essen, D. C., Watson, J. M., Brubaker, L. E., and McDermott, K. B. (2009). The contributions of prefrontal cortex and executive control to deception: evidence from activation likelihood estimate meta-analyses. *Cerebral Cortex*, 19, 1557–1566.

Corbetta, M., and Shulman, G. L. (2002). Control of goal-directed and stimulus-driven attention in the brain. *Nature Reviews Neuroscience*, 3, 201–215.

D'Esposito, M., Postle, B. R., and Rypma, B. (2000). Prefrontal cortical contributions to working memory: evidence from event-related fMRI studies. *Experimental Brain Research*, 133, 3–11.

Davatzikos, C., Ruparel, K., Fan, Y., Shen, D. G., Acharyya, M., Loughead, J. W., Gur, R. C., and Langleben, D. D. (2005). Classifying spatial patterns of brain activity with machine learning methods: application to lie detection. *Neuroimage*, 28, 663–668.

"Deceiving the law" (2008). *Nature Neuroscience*, 11, 1231.

Downar, J., Crawley, A. P., Mikulis, D. J., and Davis, K. D. (2000). A multimodal cortical network for the detection of changes in the sensory environment. *Nature Neuroscience*, 3, 277–283.

(2002). A cortical network sensitive to stimulus salience in a neutral behavioral context across multiple sensory modalities. *Journal of Neurophysiology*, 87, 615–620.

Duncan, J., and Owen, A. M. (2000). Common regions of the human frontal lobe recruited by diverse cognitive demands. *Trends in Neurosciences*, 23, 475–483.

Eickhoff, S. B., Laird, A. R., Grefkes, C., Wang, L. E., Zilles, K., and Fox, P. T. (2009). Coordinate-based activation likelihood estimation meta-analysis of neuroimaging data: a random-effects approach based on empirical estimates of spatial uncertainty. *Human Brain Mapping*, 30, 2907–2926.

Farwell, L. A., and Donchin, E. (1991). The truth will out: interrogative polygraphy (lie detection) with event-related brain potentials. *Psychophysiology*, 28, 531–547.

Friston, K. J. (2009). Modalities, modes, and models in functional neuroimaging. *Science*, 326, 399–403.

Fullam, R. S., McKie, S., and Dolan, M. C. (2009). Psychopathic traits and deception: functional magnetic resonance imaging study. *British Journal of Psychiatry*, 194, 229–235.

Furedy, J. J., Davis, C., and Gurevich, M. (1988). Differentiation of deception as a psychological process: a psychophysiological approach. *Psychophysiology*, 25, 683–688.

Furedy, J. J., Gigliotti, F., and Ben-Shakhar, G. (1994). Electrodermal differentiation of deception: the effect of choice versus no choice of deceptive items. *International Journal of Psychophysiology*, 18, 13–22.

Gamer, M., Bauermann, T., Stoeter, P., and Vossel, G. (2007). Covariations among fMRI, skin conductance, and behavioral data during processing of concealed information. *Human Brain Mapping*, 28, 1287–1301.

Gamer, M., Verschuere, B., Crombez, G., and Vossel, G. (2008). Combining physiological measures in the detection of concealed information. *Physiology & Behavior*, 95, 333–340.

Gamer, M., Klimecki, O., Bauermann, T., Stoeter, P., and Vossel, G. (in press). fMRI-activation patterns in the detection of concealed information rely on memory-related effects. *Social Cognitive and Affective Neuroscience*.

Ganis, G., Kosslyn, S. M., Stose, S., Thompson, W. L., and Yurgelun-Todd, D. A. (2003). Neural correlates of different types of deception: an fMRI investigation. *Cerebral Cortex*, 13, 830–836.

Genovese, C.R., Lazar, N.A., and Nichols, T. (2002). Thresholding of statistical maps in functional neuroimaging using the false discovery rate. *Neuroimage*, 15, 870–878.

Gödert, H. W., Rill, H.-G., and Vossel, G. (2001). Psychophysiological differentiation of deception: the effects of electrodermal lability and mode of responding on skin conductance and heart rate. *International Journal of Psychophysiology*, 40, 61–75.

Greely, H. T., and Illes, J. (2007). Neuroscience-based lie detection: the urgent need for regulation. *American Journal of Law & Medicine*, 33, 377–431.

Haynes, J., and Rees, G. (2006). Decoding mental states from brain activity in humans. *Nature Reviews Neuroscience*, 7, 523–534.

Horowitz, S. W., Kircher, J. C., Honts, C. R., and Raskin, D. C. (1997). The role of comparison questions in physiological detection of deception. *Psychophysiology*, 34, 108–115.

Iacono, W. G. (2007). Detection of deception. In J. T. Cacioppo, L. G. Tassinary, and G. G. Bernston (eds.), *Handbook of Psychophysiology* (pp. 688–703). Cambridge University Press.

Iidaka, T., Matsumoto, A., Nogawa, J., Yamamoto, Y., and Sadato, N. (2006). Frontoparietal network involved in successful retrieval from episodic memory. Spatial and temporal analyses using fMRI and ERP. *Cerebral Cortex*, 16, 1349–1360.

Karim, A. A., Schneider, M., Lotze, M., Veit, R., Sauseng, P., Braun, C., and Birbaumer, N. (2010). The truth about lying: Inhibition of the anterior prefrontal cortex improves deceptive behavior. *Cerebral Cortex*, 20, 205–213.

Kiehl, K. A., Laurens, K. R., Duty, T. L., Forster, B. B., and Liddle, P. F. (2001). Neural sources involved in auditory target detection and novelty processing: an event-related fMRI study. *Psychophysiology*, 38, 133–142.

Konishi, S., Wheeler, M. E., Donaldson, D. I., and Buckner, R. L. (2000). Neural correlates of episodic retrieval success. *Neuroimage*, 12, 276–286.

Kozel, F. A., Padgett, T. M., and George, M. S. (2004a). A replication study of the neural correlates of deception. *Behavioral Neuroscience*, 118, 852–856.

Kozel, F. A., Johnson, K. A., Mu, Q., Grenesko, E. L., Laken, S. J., and George, M. S. (2005). Detecting deception using functional magnetic resonance imaging. *Biological Psychiatry*, 58, 605–613.

Kozel, F. A., Johnson, K. A., Laken, S. J., Grenesko, E. L., Smith, J. A., Walker, J., and George, M. S. (2009a). Can simultaneously acquired electrodermal activity improve accuracy of fMRI detection of deception? *Social Neuroscience*, 4, 510–517.

Kozel, F. A., Laken, S. J., Johnson, K. A., Boren, B., Mapes, K. S., Morgan, P. S., and George, M. S. (2009b). Replication of functional MRI detection of deception. *Open Forensic Science Journal*, 2, 6–11.

Kozel, F. A., Johnson, K. A., Grenesko, E. L., Laken, S. J., Kose, S., Lu, X., Pollina, D., Ryan, A., and George, M. S. (2009c). Functional MRI detection of deception after committing a mock sabotage crime. *Journal of Forensic Sciences*, 54, 220–231.

Kozel, F. A., Revell, L. J., Lorberbaum, J. P., Shastri, A., Elhai, J. D., Horner, M. D., Smith, A., Nahas, Z., Bohning, D. E., and George, M. S. (2004b). A pilot study of functional magnetic resonance imaging brain correlates of deception in healthy young men. *Journal of Neuropsychiatry and Clinical Neurosciences*, 16, 295–305.

Langleben, D. D., and Dattilio, F. M. (2008). Commentary: the future of forensic functional brain imaging. *Journal of the American Academy of Psychiatry and the Law*, 36, 502–504.

Langleben, D. D., Loughead, J. W., Bilker, W. B., Ruparel, K., Childress, A. R., Busch, S. I., and Gur, R. C. (2005). Telling truth from lie in individual subjects with fast event-related fMRI. *Human Brain Mapping*, 26, 262–272.

Langleben, D. D., Schroeder, L., Maldjian, J. A., Gur, R. C., McDonald, S., Ragland, J. D., O' Brien, C. P., and Childress, A. R. (2002). Brain activity during simulated deception: an event-related functional magnetic resonance study. *Neuroimage*, 15, 727–732.

Lee, T. M. C., Liu, H., Chan, C. C. H., Ng, Y., Fox, P. T., and Gao, J. (2005). Neural correlates of feigned memory impairment. *Neuroimage*, 28, 305–313.

Lee, T. M. C., Liu, H., Tan, L., Chan, C. C. H., Mahankali, S., Feng, C., Hou, J., Fox, P. T., and Gao, J. (2002). Lie detection by functional magnetic resonance imaging. *Human Brain Mapping*, 15, 157–164.

Logothetis, N. K. (2002). The neural basis of the blood-oxygen-level-dependent functional magnetic resonance imaging signal. *Philosophical Transactions of the Royal Society of London. Series B, Biological Sciences*, 357, 1003–1037.

Lykken, D. T. (1959). The GSR in the detection of guilt. *Journal of Applied Psychology*, 43, 385–388.

(1974). Psychology and the lie detector industry. *American Psychologist*, 29, 725–739.

(1998). *A Tremor in the Blood: Uses and Abuses of the Lie Detector*, 2nd edn. New York: Plenum Press.

Merikangas, J. R. (2008). Commentary: functional MRI lie detection. *Journal of the American Academy of Psychiatry and the Law*, 36, 499–501.

Mohamed, F. B., Faro, S. H., Gordon, N. J., Platek, S. M., Ahmad, H., and Williams, J. M. (2006). Brain mapping of deception and truth telling about an ecologically valid situation: functional MR imaging and polygraph investigation – initial experience. *Radiology*, 238, 679–688.

Monteleone, G. T., Phan, K. L., Nusbaum, H. C., Fitzgerald, D., and Irick, J. (2009). Detection of deception using fMRI: better than chance, but well below perfection. *Social Neuroscience*, 4, 528–538.

Nose, I., Murai, J., and Taira, M. (2009). Disclosing concealed information on the basis of cortical activations. *Neuroimage*, 44, 1380–1386.

Nuñez, J. M., Casey, B. J., Egner, T., Hare, T., and Hirsch, J. (2005). Intentional false responding shares neural substrates with response conflict and cognitive control. *Neuroimage*, 25, 267–277.

Nyberg, L., Marklund, P., Persson, J., Cabeza, R., Forkstam, C., Petersson, K. M., and Ingvar, M. (2003). Common prefrontal activations during working memory, episodic memory, and semantic memory. *Neuropsychologia*, 41, 371–377.

Phan, K. L., Magalhaes, A., Ziemlewicz, T. J., Fitzgerald, D. A., Green, C., and Smith, W. (2005). Neural correlates of telling lies: a functional magnetic resonance imaging study at 4 Tesla. *Academic Radiology*, 12, 164–172.

Priori, A., Mameli, F., Cogiamanian, F., Marceglia, S., Tiriticco, M., Mrakic-Sposta, S., Ferrucci, R., Zago, S., Polezzi, D., and Sartori, G. (2008). Lie-specific involvement of dorsolateral prefrontal cortex in deception. *Cerebral Cortex*, 18, 451–455.

Ranganath, C., Johnson, M. K., and D'Esposito, M. (2003). Prefrontal activity associated with working memory and episodic long-term memory. *Neuropsychologia*, 41, 378–389.

Rosenfeld, J. P., Cantwell, B., Nasman, V. T., Wojdac, V., Ivanov, S., and Mazzeri, L. (1988). A modified, event-related potential-based guilty knowledge test. *International Journal of Neuroscience*, 42, 157–161.

Simpson, J. R. (2008). Functional MRI lie detection: too good to be true? *Journal of the American Academy of Psychiatry and the Law*, 36, 491–498.

Sip, K. E., Roepstorff, A., McGregor, W., and Frith, C. D. (2008). Detecting deception: the scope and limits. *Trends in Cognitive Sciences*, 12, 48–53.

Sokolov, E. N. (1963). *Perception and the Conditioned Reflex*. Oxford: Pergamon Press.

Spence, S. A. (2008). Playing Devil's advocate: the case against fMRI lie detection. *Legal and Criminological Psychology*, 13, 11–25.

Spence, S. A., Kaylor-Hughes, C. J., Farrow, T. F. D., and Wilkinson, I. D. (2008b). Speaking of secrets and lies: the contribution of ventrolateral prefrontal cortex to vocal deception. *Neuroimage*, 40, 1411–1418.

Spence, S. A., Kaylor-Hughes, C. J., Brook, M. L., Lankappa, S. T., and Wilkinson, I. D. (2008a). "Munchausen's syndrome by proxy" or a "miscarriage of justice"? An initial application of functional neuroimaging to the question of guilt versus innocence. *European Psychiatry*, 23, 309–314.

Spence, S. A., Farrow, T. F., Herford, A. E., Wilkinson, I. D., Zheng, Y., and Woodruff, P. W. (2001). Behavioural and functional anatomical correlates of deception in humans. *Neuroreport*, 12, 2849–2853.

Turkeltaub, P. E., Eden, G. F., Jones, K. M., and Zeffiro, T. A. (2002). Meta-analysis of the functional neuroanatomy of single-word reading: method and validation. *Neuroimage*, 16, 765–780.

Verschuere, B., Crombez, G., De Clercq, A., and Koster, E. H. W. (2004). Autonomic and behavioral responding to concealed information: differentiating orienting and defensive responses. *Psychophysiology*, 41, 461–466.

Wolpe, P. R., Foster, K. R., and Langleben, D. D. (2005). Emerging neurotechnologies for lie-detection: promises and perils. *American Journal of Bioethics*, 5, 39–49.

Worsley, K. J., Marrett, S., Neelin, P., Vandal, A. C., Friston, K. J., and Evans A. C. (1996). A unified statistical approach for determining significant signals in images of cerebral activation. *Human Brain Mapping*, 4, 58–73.

6 New and old covert measures in the Concealed Information Test

Eitan Elaad

Overview: In the concealed information polygraph test, suspects are well aware that they are being interrogated and that their physiological responses are being monitored. Such awareness may result in countermeasure attempts by guilty suspects while trying to escape detection. To combat countermeasures, it is possible to remove the standard polygraph sensors and replace them with covert respiration measures. The rationale is that guilty suspects would shift attention from their physiological reaction to the more familiar verbal and facial expressions. The present chapter introduces covert respiration measures and describes how they can be used to reduce countermeasures. Another question is whether covert respiration measures may serve to reduce excitement of overexcited examinees. The issue is further discussed. Attention is also given to early attempts to apply covert voice analysis and to more recent attempts to measure thermal imaging from a distance. Finally, ethical and moral considerations involved in using covert measures are discussed.

A well studied polygraph interrogation format, the Concealed Information Test (CIT) is designed to detect information that an individual tries to conceal (Lykken, 1974, 1998). Normally, suspects are presented with a series of multiple-choice questions, each having one correct alternative (e.g., a feature of the crime under investigation) and several incorrect (control) alternatives, chosen so that an innocent person would not be able to discriminate them from the correct alternative (Lykken, 1998). It is assumed that a guilty person knows the details of the crime, and will therefore show enhanced physiological responses to the correct alternative than to the incorrect alternatives. An innocent suspect, for whom all stimuli are neutral, is expected to respond similarly to all stimuli.

The CIT is usually conducted using standard obtrusive physiological measures (e.g., skin conductance, respiration changes, and cardiovascular activity). Suspects are well aware that they are undergoing an

interrogation and that their physiological responses are being monitored. Guilty examinees who are attached to the polygraph sensors may
attempt to distort their physiological responses. Previous results show
that the CIT is vulnerable to such countermeasures attempts (e.g., Ben-
Shakhar and Dolev, 1996; Elaad and Ben-Shakhar, 1991; Honts *et al.*,
1996; Chapter 11 of this volume). In addition, such awareness might
impair the detection of overexcited guilty examinees due to the extra
stress involved in testing these examinees and the additional noise in
the physiological recordings.

The use of covert measures (i.e., methods of measuring physiological
responses without the awareness of the examinee) may provide a partial solution for these difficulties. Guilty suspects may shift their attention from unfamiliar physiological reactions to the more familiar verbal
responses and facial expressions (Ekman, 2001) and therefore avoid
attempting countermeasures. Nevertheless they are still under interrogation and they are still concerned that their lies might be detected.
This may contribute to larger physiological responses to the correct
than to the incorrect alternatives. Detachment from the transducers
may also serve to reduce excitement of anxious guilty examinees who
might experience the stress of the test. This may enhance detection
accuracy of overexcited examinees. These two possible applications of
covert measures in the CIT are discussed in this chapter.

Using covert measures for detecting concealed information in the
interrogation is very appealing. Even more appealing is the use of covert measures without the awareness of the suspects that they are being
interrogated. There is no need to hook the suspect to a machine, and
information may be gathered from a distance (e.g., telephone, micro-
phone). Collecting information about suspects without their awareness may be welcomed by security personnel, law enforcement officers,
politicians, private investigators, lawyers, and many others as they can
be useful in a variety of anti-terrorism, law enforcement, intelligence,
commercial, and other applications that are based on information
gathering. The use of covert measures may also enrich the interrogation tactics and replace questionable methods that are being used to
force individuals to admit to actions or knowledge of information (e.g.,
intimidating suspects, tricking them into revealing information, criti-
cizing and assaulting the suspects, see Kalbfleisch [1994] for a review).
On the other hand, the use of covert measures may raise ethical and
legal questions. The question of privacy may be raised as well as the
issue of pre-examination consent that is currently required from polygraph examinees. Therefore, one should think of ways to limit and control the use of covert measures. I will describe several covert measures

developed for detecting concealed information, discuss their accuracy and limitations, and conclude with a discussion of the ethical concerns about their use.

Voice stress analyzers

A first attempt to introduce covert measures for the detection of deception took place in the early 1970s when a commercial lie detector employing voice analysis, the Psychological Stress Evaluator (PSE), was distributed. The PSE was welcomed by users from law enforcement agencies as well as from the private sector, was treated as a reliable instrument and was employed in actual criminal interrogations. The PSE is based on the notion that the human voice produces inaudible frequency changes or microtremors that disappear under stress. It was claimed that the pattern of these changes provide a measure of psychophysiological arousal which can be detected from voice recordings. This rationale was never systematically examined and it is not clear if indeed the PSE measures these alleged changes.

As to the validity of the PSE, research did not support it in the CIT context. The few attempts to study the PSE using the CIT format failed to demonstrate any significant accuracy rates beyond chance level (e.g., Brenner *et al.*, 1979; Horvath, 1978, 1979). In the 1990s, a computerized version of the voice analyzer was developed (Computer Voice Stress Analyzer – CVSA). The underlying theory for the computer analyzer remained the same, namely it was promised that the CVSA detects physiological microtremors in the voice path. This version of the PSE was examined with the CIT by the US Department of Defense Polygraph Institute (DoDPI; Cestaro and Dollins, 1994). These authors reported that the CVSA detection rate did not differ from chance level. A more recent attempt to examine the validity of the CVSA (Hollien *et al.*, 2008) was equally disappointing. Note that Hollien *et al.*'s study did not use the CIT but their results are still relevant to the detection of concealed information. Another wave of marketing of voice stress analyzers appeared after September 11, 2001 with the increasing concern about terrorism and the search to enhance security. The analyzers were offered under new names (e.g., TrusterPro, Vericator, Layered Voice Analysis – LVA) but still were proved invalid (e.g., Harnsberger *et al.*, 2009; Sommers *et al.*, 2002).

The question about the use of voice stress analyzers was brought before the National Research Council (NRC) which was preparing a report on the polygraph and lie detection. The NRC is a principle operating agency of the US National Academy of Sciences and the US

National Academy of Engineering in providing services to the US government, the public, and the scientific and engineering communities. The Council is also administered by the US Institute of Medicine. The council's report summarized that: "there is little or no scientific basis for the use of the computer voice stress analyzer or similar voice measurement instruments as an alternative to the polygraph for the detection of deception" (National Research Council, 2003, p. 168).

Covert respiration measures

Recently, an attempt was made to introduce two covert respiration measures which used respiratory effort transducers hidden in the seat and in the back support of a polygraph examination chair (Elaad and Ben-Shakhar, 2008). The transducers recorded changes in the pressure that inhaling and exhaling put on the seat and back support. Responses were defined on the basis of the total respiration line length (RLL) during the 15 s interval following stimulus onset (for a detailed description of RLL definition and measurement see Elaad *et al.*, 1992).

Elaad and Ben-Shakhar (2008) assessed the efficiency of the two covert respiration measures in detecting concealed information and compared them with three standard measures typically used for the detection of concealed information (skin conductance response, respiration, and finger pulse volume). For this end, participants were randomly allocated into "guilty" and "innocent" roles. Participants simulating the guilty conducted a mock crime while those simulating the innocent were ignorant of the critical information. Both guilty and innocent participants were examined in two sessions. In each, either an "unobtrusive" or a "standard polygraph" test was employed. In the unobtrusive condition the participants were told that their task was to cope with a professional lie catcher who will detect their lies from their behavior and therefore they will not be attached to the polygraph. However, during this condition participants' respiration traces were monitored with the two covert measures. In the standard condition, participants were attached, in addition to the two covert respiration sensors, to three non-covert, standard polygraph sensors: respiration, skin conductance response, and finger pulse volume.

Results revealed that under the unobtrusive condition the covert respiration measures produced better than chance discrimination between "guilty" and "innocent" participants. To make detection rates easier to understand, an arbitrary false positive error rate (4.2 percent) was selected. Given this error rate, the covert seat measure was able to detect 44 percent of the guilty participants and the covert back measure

30 percent. Finally, a combined measure of the two covert measures was created. It was defined as the average Z score of the two measures and it displayed 49% detection of guilty participants. Results indicate that the covert respiration measures can be useful in detecting concealed information.

Under the standard condition, results showed once again that the covert measures' detection efficiency was significantly better than chance. Given the 4.2 percent false positive error rate, it was observed that the covert back measure was successful in detecting 44 percent of the guilty suspects. However the seat measure produced much lower detection (18 percent). The standard polygraph condition allows a comparison of the covert measures with the standard polygraph measures. The detection rates computed for the standard respiration measure, finger pulse volume, and skin conductance response, were 27 percent, 51 percent, and 62 percent, respectively. Finally, the combined measure of the two covert respiration measures displayed a 51 percent detection rate of guilty participants. In comparison, the measure that combined the three standard measures displayed 67 percent correct detection. To conclude, the two covert respiration measures and their combination can be used as additional measures in the standard CIT.

Although respiration is the key element in the two covert measures, they seem to record different aspects of respiration. The respiration patterns show that the tracings of the covert back measure and those of the standard respiration measure in the polygraph condition are very similar for guilty participants. In contrast, the covert seat measure looks different. For about half of the participants the pressure that inhaling put on the respiration belt and the back support increases whereas the pressure on the seat decreases and vice versa; exhaling produces pressure on the seat while the pressure on both the respiration belt and the back support decreases.

Under unobtrusive conditions the covert respiration measures are promising. However, a covert version of other standard CIT measures such as heart rate or skin conductance can also be used to detect concealed information in the CIT.

Would covert respiration measures protect against countermeasure attempts?

Studies conducted in laboratory settings have indicated that the CIT is a highly valid method for differentiating between guilty and innocent participants (see Ben-Shakhar and Elaad, 2003 for a review). However, several studies (e.g, Ben-Shakhar and Dolev, 1996; Elaad and Ben-Shakhar, 1991; Honts *et al.*, 1996) demonstrated that the CIT is vulnerable to physical (e.g., biting the tongue), as well as mental countermeasures (e.g., silently counting numbers each time a control item is presented). Such countermeasures may increase false negative outcomes and impair the validity of the CIT. However, it may be expected that only guilty examinees who are aware of being tested with the polygraph would deliberately attempt to distort the results, whereas examinees who are not connected to the polygraph have no reason to make such attempts. Therefore, the use of covert respiration measures may, at least partially, solve the countermeasure problem.

A first attempt to examine the covert measures when participants actually exercised countermeasures was recently made by Elaad and Ben-Shakhar (2009). More specifically, Elaad and Ben-Shakhar examined whether the covert respiration measures can circumvent the use of physical and mental countermeasures. Similar to the study discussed above, participants were tested in two sessions. In the first (the standard phase), a standard CIT polygraph test was employed in which participants were attached to the standard polygraph sensors measuring skin conductance, respiration, and finger pulse volume. In addition, the two covert respiration measures were used. In the second session (the unobtrusive phase) participants were detached from the polygraph sensors and told that their task was to cope with a professional lie catcher who would detect their lies from their behavior recorded on video. To deal with the moral and legal concerns all participants in this study were informed in advance that their physiological responses would be monitored throughout the entire test and participants were required to give a statement that they understood the instructions and agreed to be examined with the polygraph under these conditions. It was hypothesized that when the participants are not connected to the polygraph they would stop using countermeasures and consequently no increase in false negative outcomes will be observed.

To examine this hypothesis, sixty-four college students were randomly allocated either into two "guilty" countermeasure conditions (physical – press their toes against the floor; mental – count silently backward by sevens from a number larger than 200), a "guilty" no countermeasure condition, or an "innocent" condition. Participants in the three guilty conditions were instructed to commit a mock theft. Participants in the innocent condition were instructed to wait outside the office for five minutes. Guilty examinees were instructed to apply their countermeasures selectively to two of the six items in each series. They were cautioned not to use countermeasures in response to critical items or to the first item.

Countermeasure examinees were instructed to begin their countermeasure attempts as soon as they recognized a selected item, to stop for a while to answer "no," and then continue the countermeasure until the next item is presented. Then, a training session began during which participants were asked to practice their countermeasures. The participants were further cautioned to perform the countermeasures unobtrusively in such a way that the polygraph operator will not detect them.

Results for the standard phase revealed that both the seat and the back covert respiration measures performed much like the standard respiration measure in the two countermeasure conditions and in the no-countermeasures condition. Results further showed that the two covert respiration measures were resistant to physical but not to the mental countermeasures. It is possible that pressing the toes against the floor activates muscles that press the seat (and to a lower extent the back) which results in an enlarged rather than reduced waveform length. Hence, physical countermeasures create larger line lengths for the selected incorrect items thereby enhancing the responses to the other items, including the critical item. In that case, the likelihood for a correct detection of the guilty participants increases. In summary, it was demonstrated that the covert measures can be useful when participants are connected to the polygraph and apply physical countermeasures.

It was assumed that in the unobtrusive phase participants would consider deliberate countermeasures aimed to distort physiological responses unnecessary. During this phase the covert seat respiration measure discriminated between guilty and innocent participants under the no-countermeasure and the mental countermeasure conditions but not under the physical countermeasure condition. It seems that when participants stopped pressing the toes against the floor, the increased respiration line lengths for the two selected items disappeared with the advantage of the seat measure. The question is: why the seat measure does not perform just as well as it does under the no-countermeasure condition? A carry over effect may answer this question. It is possible that participants who were engaged in active physical countermeasure attempts in the standard phase, adopted a rather passive attitude in the unobtrusive phase which interfered with the attention they paid to the critical items. The covert back measure was entirely ineffective in the unobtrusive phase.

To conclude, the use of countermeasures is a major obstacle to a successful application of the CIT and therefore it is essential to provide solutions to the problem. It was demonstrated that using covert respiration measures may be part of a solution as both covert measures were resistant to physical countermeasures in the standard phase and the covert seat measure was resistant to mental countermeasures when the transducers were removed.

Are covert respiration measures effective in testing anxious CIT examinees?

The standard and unobtrusive conditions were used again to examine whether the two covert respiration measures, hidden in the seat and back of the examination chair, were effective in detecting concealed information held by anxious and less anxious examinees (Elaad and Cohenca, 2010). It was assumed that the polygraph examination is a stressful and unpleasant experience and some examinees are unable to calm down during the test. It was hypothesized that the stress created by the test interferes with the detection of physiological responses to critical information and impairs the CIT results.

Giesen and Rollison (1980) were the first to examine the relationship between trait anxiety and detection in the CIT when only electrodermal measures were used. They divided their participants into high and low anxiety groups and reported that the more anxious guilty participants were better detected than the less anxious guilty participants. Iacono et al. (1984) examined the relationship between state and trait anxiety and electrodermal detection in the CIT and found no significant correlation. Gudjonsson (1982) found positive relations between reported tension during a card test experiment and interference with the electrodermal detection. Thus, results are mixed and additional research is needed to answer the question as to whether or not electrodermal measures are vulnerable to anxiety effects.

The notion that anxiety interferes with respiration responses is well known and early attempts to study how anxiety affects breathing (Cristie, 1935) were followed by more recent ones (e.g., Barlow, 1988; Bass and Gardner, 1985). Cristie (1935) observed that anxious patients complained of "inability to get enough air into the lungs" and "a sense of oppression or suffocation." These subjective experiences were accompanied by respiration response patterns such as hyperventilation (Bass and Gardner, 1985). Hyperventilation is a physiological state and refers to increased breathing that is in excess of metabolic requirements. Furthermore, variations in stress-related respiratory responses are associated with stress-related cardiovascular responses (Grossman, 1983). For example, it was observed that high trait worry people exposed to stress exhibited increased heart rate following certain stressors (Knepp and Friedman, 2008). Since CIT detection is based on respiratory and cardiovascular inhibition rather than activation, the arousal involved in the examination of anxious examinees may impair detection of guilty examinees that would show no consistent responses to both critical and neutral items. In that case, anxious guilty examinees might escape detection and consequently false negative outcomes would increase.

The use of covert respiration measures may be part of a solution if the detachment of anxious examinees from the polygraph would result in more distinctive responses to critical items by informed guilty examinees.

To examine this question, seventy-four Israeli college students were asked to answer a questionnaire designed to examine state anxiety – the A-state scale of the STAI (Spielberger, 1975). According to their scores participants were divided into high (N = 24), intermediate (N = 25), and low (N = 25) state anxiety groups. Then, participants were instructed to commit a mock theft and were invited to the examination room for a polygraph test. Participants were informed that their task in the experiment was to evade detection of their knowledge of any crime-related information and were promised a monetary reward for successful performance on the task. At this stage the examinees were attached to the standard polygraph transducers and eight CIT questions were presented to them. Participants knew the correct answer to four of them and were not aware of the correct answers to the remaining four. After the completion of the test, examinees were detached from the transducers, a video camera was turned on in front of their face and they were told that an expert lie-catcher will watch the film and will base his decision on their verbal and nonverbal behavior. The eight CIT questions were presented to the examinees again while only the covert sensors monitored respiration. It was assumed that at the unobtrusive phase, participants act in a familiar domain and therefore will feel more secure.

The manipulation check revealed that participants were motivated to conceal information in the standard phase more than in the unobtrusive phase, and were more concerned about the outcome of the test than in the unobtrusive phase. While low and intermediate state anxiety scorers felt more involved in the standard phase than in the unobtrusive phase, high state anxiety scorers felt no difference in involvement. Skin conductance response emerged as the most effective measure in discriminating between known and unknown critical items in the standard phase. However, skin conductance is also more sensitive to anxiety effects than the other two measures – finger pulse volume and respiration. As to covert respiration measures, whereas they tended to be more accurate in the unobtrusive phase than in the standard phase for the less anxious participants (low and intermediate groups), they were not at all effective in detecting concealed information in the unobtrusive phase for the more anxious participants.

It seems that stress interferes with the inhibition of respiration responses. Such inhibition corresponds to enhanced attention to critical stimuli and stronger responses to the more significant than to less significant items. It may be suggested that less stressful conditions are necessary for respiration measures to be effective in the CIT. Unfortunately the unobtrusive phase was unable to provide the optimal conditions for the examination of high state anxiety participants. It should be remembered that the present participants were all guilty and were aware of being interrogated. Under true covert conditions where examinees are unaware of the interrogation, the detachment of the polygraph transducers may be more effective in discriminating between actual knowledge and unknown information. Additional research is needed to clarify this point.

Thermal imaging

Another measure that can be carried out unobtrusively is thermal imaging or thermography. Thermal imaging is based on facial temperature changes which are related to the blood flow. These peripheral measures may be promising. An experimental attempt to determine thermal imaging validity in a CIT format was made by Pollina *et al.* (2006). In this study a radiometer was placed directly in front of the participants at a distance of 1.5 m. Thus, participants were not attached to the measuring device but they were perfectly aware of the physiological measurements. Pollina *et al.* (2006) suggested that thermal image analysis may be used to effectively discriminate between guilty and innocent individuals during the CIT. However, the many dropouts in both experiments (e.g., fifteen of thirty-nine in the second experiment) and the obtrusive nature of the study make it difficult to reach conclusions about the value of thermal imaging as a covert measure in the CIT.

The National Research Council (2003) referred in its report to an earlier paper by the same group of authors (Pavlidis *et al.*, 2002). Pavlidis and his colleagues (2002) claimed that thermal imaging is a valid method for detecting both guilty and innocent participants in a comparison question format, and that blood flow in the face and more specifically around the eyes may be a valid cue for deception.

The National Research Council's conclusion was that the Pavlidis *et al.* (2002) report is a flawed evaluation of the thermal imaging procedure because it used a subset of examinees tested in another study (Pollina and Ryan, 2002) without indicating the selection criteria. According to the National Research Council the study does not provide scientific based evidence to support the use of facial thermography in detecting deception (p. 157). It seems that much additional work is needed to determine whether facial temperature changes may be used to detect concealed information, obtrusively and unobtrusively.

Ethical considerations

The use of covert measures may raise moral, legal, and ethical concerns. One major concern relates to pre-examination consent that is currently required from polygraph examinees. Another concern corresponds to the question of privacy that may be violated by the unobtrusive measures. One way to deal with these concerns is to apply the unobtrusive measurement within the context of a polygraph test. In this case, it is important to receive a written consent of the examinee to be examined with the polygraph. Furthermore, examinees are entitled to be warned in advance that their responses, physiological and/or vocal, would be monitored throughout the entire test. In that case, examinees should sign a statement that they received and understood the warning and that they agree to be examined under these conditions. Such a pre-test warning may satisfy the ethical considerations of properly informing the examinee about the test and at the same time make it possible to use covert measures. Obviously, this limits the applicability of the covert measures and stands in contrast to the wishes of some law enforcement and security personnel to be able to use these measures without informing the suspect of the procedure.

Concluding remarks

The CIT procedure is the only psychological detection technique that enjoys a wide acceptance as a scientifically based technique and has the potential for aiding criminal and investigative procedures. However, the use of countermeasures is a major threat to the efficacy of the CIT and successful implementation of countermeasures can increase false-negative error rate. A study that showed how covert respiration measures confront the countermeasure problem was described. Of the two covert respiration measures only the covert seat measure was resistant to mental countermeasures when the polygraph transducers were removed.

Covert measures may also serve to examine anxious and overexcited examinees. Testing anxious examinees may introduce noise, which may impair the detection of information that guilty examinees possess. By removing the polygraph transducers it was thought that anxious guilty examinees may calm down and be better detected. However, results showed that this was true only for the less anxious guilty examinees. For the more anxious examinees the detachment from the transducers proved to be ineffective.

To enable anxious guilty examinees to calm down, the CIT examiner may tell them about the hidden measures and conduct the entire examination while the standard polygraph sensors are detached (similar to the procedure employed for thermal imaging testing). It is also possible to conduct the CIT without informing the examinees of the hidden measures. Additional research is needed to consolidate the conditions in which anxiety can be reduced by covert measurements.

The described studies used voice measures, thermal imaging, or covert respiration measures in the CIT context. Other measures that have been shown to be successful in a standard CIT may also be measured unobtrusively. Heart rate may be recorded from a distance using laser doppler vibrometry, eye blinks can be monitored from simple video footage, and pupil size can be measures using covertly positioned eye-tracking devices. Even skin conductance can potentially be monitored covertly, e.g., by building the sensors into a computer mouse or joystick the participants have to operate during item presentation. Yet, additional work is needed to determine whether these measures can be effective covert measures of deception or concealment. Although in most of the experiments described in this chapter examinees were aware that they were being interrogated, in principle it is possible to use these measures with suspects who are entirely unaware of the interrogation. Finally, there must be additional thinking of how to use covert measures in correspondence with basic ethical requirements.

REFERENCES

Barlow, D. H. (1988). *Anxiety and its Disorders*. New York: Guilford
Bass, C., and Gardner, W. N. (1985). Respiratory and psychiatric abnormalities in chronic symptomatic hyperventilation. *British Medical Journal*, 290, 1387–1390.
Ben-Shakhar, G., and Dolev, K. (1996). Psychophysiological detection through the guilty knowledge technique: effects of mental countermeasures. *Journal of Applied Psychology*, 81, 273–281.
Ben-Shakhar G., and Elaad, E. (2003). The validity of psychophysiological detection of information with the Guilty Knowledge Test: a meta-analytic review. *Journal of Applied Psychology*, 88, 131–151.
Brenner, M., Branscomb, H. H., and Schwartz, G. E. (1979). Psychological stress evaluator – two tests of a vocal measure. *Psychophysiology*, 16, 351–357.
Cestaro, V. L., and Dollins, A. B. (1994). An analysis of voice responses for the detection of deception. Report No. DoDPI94-R-0001. Ft. McClellan, AL: Department of Defense Polygraph Institute.

Cristie, R. V. (1935). Some types of respiration in the neuroses. *Quarterly Journal of Medicine*, 28, 427–432.

Ekman, P. (2001). *Telling Lies. Clues to Deceit in the Marketplace, Politics, and Marriage.* New York: Norton.

Elaad, E., and Ben-Shakhar, G. (1991). Effects of mental countermeasures on psychophysiological detection in the Guilty Knowledge Test. *International Journal of Psychophysiology*, 11(2), 99–108.

   (2008). Covert respiration measures for the detection of concealed information. *Biological Psychology*, 77, 284–291.

Elaad, E., and Ben-Shakhar, G. (2009). Countering countermeasures in the concealed information test using covert respiration measures. *Applied Psychophysiology and Biofeedback*, 34, 197–208.

Elaad, E., and Cohenca, D. (2010). Reducing anxiety of anxious examinees in the concealed information test using unobtrusive respiration measures. Unpublished manuscript.

Elaad, E., Ginton, A., and Jungman, N., 1992. Detection measures in real-life criminal guilty knowledge tests. *Journal of Applied Psychology*, 77, 757–767.

Giesen, M., and Rollison, M. A. (1980). Guilty knowledge versus innocent associations: effects of trait anxiety and stimulus context on skin conductance. *Journal of Research in Personality*, 14, 1–11.

Grossman, P. (1983). Respiration, stress and cardiovascular function. *Psychophysiology*, 20, 284–300.

Gudjonsson, G. H. (1982). Some psychological determinants of electrodermal responses to deception. *Personality and Individual Differences*, 3, 381–391.

Harnsberger, J. D., Hollien, H., Martin, C. A., and Hollien, K. A. (2009). Stress and deception in speech: evaluating layered voice analysis. *Journal of Forensic Sciences*, 54, 642–650.

Hollien, H., Harnsberger, J. D., Martin, C. A., and Hollien, K. A. (2008). Evaluation of the NITV CVSA. *Journal of Forensic Sciences*, 53, 183–193.

Honts, C. R., Devitt, M. K., Winbush, M., and Kircher, J. C. (1996). Mental and physical countermeasures reduce the accuracy of the concealed knowledge test. *Psychophysiology*, 33, 84–92.

Horvath, F. (1978). An experimental comparison of the psychological stress evaluator and the galvanic skin response in detection of deception. *Journal of Applied Psychology*, 63, 338–344.

   (1979). Effect of different motivational instructions on detection of deception with the psychological stress evaluator and the galvanic skin response. *Journal of Applied Psychology*, 64, 323–330.

Iacono, W. G., Boisvenu, G. A., and Fleming, J. A. E. (1984). Effects of diazepam and methylphenidate on the electrodermal detection of guilty knowledge. *Journal of Applied Psychology*, 69, 289–299.

Kalbfleisch, P. J. (1994). The language of detecting deceit. *Journal of Language and Social Psychology*, 13, 469–496.

Knepp, M. M., and Friedman, B. H. (2008). Cardiac reactivity in high and low trait worry woman. *Psychophysiogy*, 45, S11 (abstract).

Lykken, D. T. (1974). Psychology and the lie detection industry. *American Psychologist*, 29, 225–239.

(1998). *A Tremor in the Blood. Uses and Abuses of the Lie Detector,* 2nd edn. New York: Plenum Trade.

National Research Council (2003). *The Polygraph and Lie Detection.* Committee to Review the Scientific Evidence on the Polygraph. Division of Behavioral and Social Sciences and Education. Washington, DC: The National Academies Press.

Pavlidis, I., Eberhardt, N. L., and Levin, J. A. (2002). Seeing through the face of deception: thermal imaging offers a promising hands-off approach to mass security screening. *Nature,* 415, 35.

Pollina, D. A., and Ryan, A. (2002). The relationship between facial skin surface temperature reactivity and traditional polygraph measures used in the psychophysiological detection of deception: a preliminary investigation, U.S. Department of Defense Polygraph Institute, Ft. Jackson, SC.

Pollina, D. A., Dollins, A. B., Senter, S. M., Brown, T. E., Pavlidis, I., Levine, J. A., and Ryan, A. H. (2006). Facial skin surface temperature changes during a "Concealed Information" test. *Annals of Biomedical Engineering,* 34, 1182–1189.

Sommers, M. S., Brown, T. E., Senter, S. M., and Ryan, A. H. Jr. (2002). Evaluating the reliability and validity of Vericator as a voice-based measure of deception. *International Journal of Psychophysiology,* 45, 28 (abstract).

Spielberger, C. S. (1975). The measurement of state and trait anxiety: conceptual and methodological issues. In L. Levi (ed.), *Emotions – their Parameters and Measurement* (pp. 713–725). New York: The Raven Press.

7 Theory of the Concealed Information Test

Bruno Verschuere and Gershon Ben-Shakhar

Overview: It is now well established that physiological measures can be validly used to detect concealed information. An important challenge is to elucidate the underlying mechanisms of concealed information detection. We review theoretical approaches that can be broadly classified in two major categories: theories that emphasize emotional–motivational factors, and those that emphasize cognitive factors. While emotional–motivational factors do not appear to be necessary for the detection of concealed information, they may enhance discriminability. Research with realistic setups is needed to examine whether emotional–motivational factors may exert a more prominent role in real-life concealed information tests compared with those performed under laboratory conditions. Empirical research largely supports the cognitive approaches and particularly Orienting Response (OR) theory, which can explain most of the research findings related to the Concealed Information Test (CIT). Future work needs to test whether OR theory holds under real-life circumstances, and whether OR theory needs to incorporate other processes (e.g., response inhibition) to fully account for the differential physiological responding to the relevant items in the CIT.

Discussions about polygraph tests typically focus on applied issues regarding the validity of various methods and measures. However, physiological detection of concealed information is also challenging from a theoretical perspective. Furthermore, a clear understanding of how a test works has an important practical value as it allows predicting the conditions, measures, and populations with which it will work. For example, how do psychopaths respond to the test? How many items are needed? Will the test work with examinees that are highly anxious about the upcoming examination? Will the results of laboratory

The authors contributed equally to this chapter.

research generalize to the field? Is brain imaging more reliable than skin conductance? In other words, there is nothing more practical than a good theory. Indeed, modern views of test-validity regard the theoretical understanding of what the test attempts to measure as an integral part of its validity (Messick, 1995). This issue was highlighted in the report of the committee appointed to review the scientific evidence on the polygraph (National Research Council, 2003). A major critique of the committee was related to the lack of theory and theory-driven research focusing on the underlying factors that produce the observed responses in polygraph tests. Unfortunately, the committee did not clearly differentiate between different polygraph techniques. Whereas there is virtually no theoretical work on the Comparison Question Test (CQT), substantial work of this kind does exist on the CIT. Furthermore, as these two methods differ drastically both in what they attempt to achieve (detection of deception in the CQT vs. detection of concealed knowledge in the CIT) and in their choice of relevant and control questions (or items), they may call for different underlying theories. That said, we share the committee's concern, and we hope that our chapter will be an impetus for more research on the mechanisms underlying the CIT.

In this chapter we shall review several theoretical accounts that may explain psychophysiological detection of concealed information. Although several response measures have been implemented, we shall focus upon the oldest and most often applied autonomic nervous system (ANS) based CIT (see Chapter 2 of this volume). One reason is that ANS measures have been mostly investigated. Another and more important reason is that other response measures are obtained in modifications of the ANS-based CIT. RTs, ERPs, and fMRI are most often obtained in the oddball variant of the CIT. This variant differs in important characteristics from the ANS-based CIT, such as stimulus presentation duration, inter stimulus interval (ISI), and the inclusion of target items. These differences can have profound impact on physiological responding. For example, affective pictures elicit greater heart rate deceleration than neutral pictures with 6 s presentation durations but not with a 0.5 s duration (Codispoti et al., 2001). The enhanced P300 to the relevant items that has been repeatedly observed with a short ISI, disappeared when using a longer ISI that is more typical for the ANS-based CIT (Gamer and Berti, 2009). The use of target items requires participants to explicitly reject relevant items, and may increase the demand for response inhibition (see Chapter 3). Findings from the oddball CIT may not generalize to the ANS-based CIT, and different processes may underlie these tests. In addition, only ANS-CIT is actually applied in the field (see Chapter 14 of this volume). We will refer to research on other response measures in footnotes where appropriate.

The different theoretical accounts for the ANS-based CIT can be broadly classified in two major categories (Ben-Shakhar and Furedy, 1990): (1) theories that emphasize motivational and emotional factors (e.g., emotions associated with deception, fear of the consequences of the polygraph test's results, motivation to deceive) and (2) theories that emphasize cognitive factors (e.g., knowledge and awareness of certain information, attentional mechanisms that operate while processing the items).

Emotional–motivational approaches

An early attempt to classify alternative theoretical accounts of psychophysiological detection was made by Davis (1961). He listed three possible mechanisms for the detection phenomenon: the conditional response theory; the punishment theory; and the conflict theory. We add two more emotional–motivational approaches: defensive reflex theory, as a specification of the punishment theory; and motivation impairment theory.

Conditioned response theory

This theory is based upon principles from learning psychology. An important learning principle is that an intrinsically neutral stimulus can impact behavior through association with a stimulus that naturally evokes that behavior. The classic example is Pavlov's dog. Through association with food (Unconditioned Stimulus, UCS), the neutral bell (Conditioned Stimulus, CS) also elicits salivation (Conditioned Response, CR; see Figure 7.1). An example in humans is that cancer patients may dislike the food they ate just before their chemotherapy. Applied to polygraph testing, it is reasoned that the criminal act and the crime scene serve as unconditioned stimuli, and the crime-related items as the conditioned stimuli. Thus, the crime-related items may also evoke arousal (i.e., CR). This theory may seem intuitively plausible in the context of police interrogations about an experience loaded with strong emotions (e.g., a murder suspect shown different pictures of the possible victim). There is, however, no empirical research that has directly tested this theory. Moreover, the theory is unlikely to be generally applicable to all types of concealed information testing. It fails to explain, for example, the results of laboratory studies in which

Figure 7.1 The Unconditioned Stimulus (UCS; e.g., food) naturally elicits the Unconditioned Response (UCR; e.g. salivation). Through contingent pairing with the UCS, the Conditioned Stimulus (CS; e.g., bell) may also evoke salivation.

participants were asked to hide recognition of certain code words or a chosen playing card. Such trivial stimuli don't seem to evoke strong emotions, but they do elicit strong physiological responding (Ben-Shakhar and Elaad, 2003).

Punishment theory and the defensive reflex theory

The punishment theory focuses on the consequences of the polygraph test, rather than on its antecedents. It rests on the assumption that the enhanced responses elicited by the relevant items are due to fear of the consequences of the subject's failure to deceive. The defensive reflex theory can be regarded as a specification of the punishment theory. The defensive reflex (DR; Sokolov, 1963) is elicited by highly aversive stimuli, and is closely linked to fight/flight responding. The reflex serves to protect the organism from aversive stimuli. Applied to the CIT, the theory holds that the CIT test items elicit defensive responding because of their threat value.[1] For the guilty examinees, the relevant items are most threatening, and elicit the strongest defensive responding. For the innocent, the items are of a similar threat value, and thus will elicit similar responding.

Several research findings are relevant to the punishment/DR theory. First, in a direct test of the punishment/DR theory, Kugelmass and Lieblich (1966) manipulated the perceived consequences of a polygraph test. One group of policemen were told that their ability to control their emotions was tested and that only those able to achieve such control and pass the test could qualify to serve in the police force. In the control group, the test was presented as an attempt to examine

---

[1] We use the terms "guilty" vs. "innocent" merely to indicate whether the examinee possesses (mock) crime-related knowledge or not.

whether the apparatus was functioning properly. Despite strongly different consequences, similar CIT detection rates were obtained in the two conditions. Second, the punishment/DR theory predicts that guilty examinees respond fearfully to the relevant CIT items. Fearful responding is characterized by respiratory hyperventilation (Van Diest et al., 2001), heart rate acceleration (Graham and Clifton, 1966), and startle potentiation (Lang et al., 1990). However, hyperventilation is not commonly observed in the CIT. In contrast, knowledgeable individuals typically respond with greater respiratory suppression to the relevant CIT items compared to the control items (e.g., Gamer et al., 2006; Timm, 1982; Verschuere et al., 2004b). In three experiments, Verschuere et al. (2007) delivered mock crime participants with 105 dBA startle probes during relevant and control CIT items. The startle potentiation hypothesis was not supported by the data. Reduced startle modulation was found, both at 300 ms and 3 s after CIT item onset. Particularly problematic for the punishment/DR theory was the reduced startle potentiation to relevant CIT items compared to the control items at the 3 s interval. Several studies have examined heart rate activity in the CIT. These studies often showed an initial heart rate acceleration followed by a secondary deceleration (Gamer et al., 2006; Verschuere et al., 2005). At first, the initial acceleration may seem to support the punishment/DR theory. This initial acceleration, however, is often smaller to relevant than to control items. Moreover, what most differentiates the relevant from the control items is the greater secondary deceleration to the relevant items. Following up on this work, Verschuere et al. (2009) recently showed that the initial acceleration is observed only when subjects respond verbally to the questions, but not when no overt responses are required. The physiological response pattern evoked by relevant items in guilty examinees does not indicate activation of the fear system and the punishment/DR theory fails to explain the high detection rates typically observed in the laboratory in absence of severe consequences (Ben-Shakhar and Elaad, 2003).

Emotional conflict theory

The emotional conflict theory postulates that the enhanced physiological reactions evoked by the relevant items reflect the emotional conflict that results from the urge to tell the truth and the need to lie in order to avoid detection. This idea is related to the early work on human conflict by Luria (1932) who suggested a different type of detection method based on the measurement of hand tremors. Indirect support for the conflict theory comes from a series of studies conducted by John Furedy and his colleagues, using the "differentiation of deception" paradigm (Furedy *et al.*, 1988, 1994, 1991; Vincent and Furedy, 1992). These studies attempted to isolate the deception factor controlling for other factors such as stimulus significance, and relative frequency of the relevant items. It was shown that deception itself can evoke physiological responding. A number of studies have investigated whether deception increased physiological differentiation in the CIT. These studies have compared a deceptive verbal ("no") response to the relevant items with several control conditions, including other verbal responses (e.g., "yes" to all items) or no verbal responding. A number of studies found better differentiation in the overt deceptive condition as compared with control conditions (e.g., Elaad and Ben-Shakhar, 1989; Furedy and Ben-Shakhar, 1991; Horneman and O'Gorman, 1985; Gustafson and Orne, 1965a), but others did not (Kugelmass *et al.*, 1967; Verschuere *et al.*, 2009). A tendency toward better differentiation with overt deception was also found in the meta-analysis by Ben-Shakhar and Elaad (2003), but the effect failed to reach significance. Thus, it seems that overt denial can add to, but is not necessary for, successful concealed information detection. One interpretative difficulty is that the overall aim of the examinee is to conceal the relevant information and thus it can be argued that knowledgeable examinees who remain silent or answer "yes" also experience an emotional conflict. Subjective ratings or post-experimental interviews may shed light on this issue. Such a strategy may also indicate whether the conflict is really "emotional." An alternative possibility is that the enhanced physiological responding to the relevant items results from overt denial being cognitively more demanding than remaining silent or giving a truthful answer (Spence *et al.*, 2004; Vrij *et al.*, 2006).

Motivation impairment

Research on nonverbal cues to deception has shown a "motivation impairment effect," indicating that the more motivated the liar, the more likely the lie to be expressed in nonverbal behavior (Burgoon, 2000; DePaulo and Kirkendol, 1989). The motivation approach is similar to the punishment/DR theory in that both focus upon the consequences of the polygraph test, but it is more general than the punishment/DR theory because punishment is just one instance of motivation.

A series of studies by Martin Orne and his colleagues in the 1960s investigated the relationship between subjects' motivation and the degree of psychophysiological differentiation in the CIT. Gustafson and Orne (1963) motivated their participants by telling them that only people of superior intelligence and emotional control can successfully conceal information and by promising a financial bonus for avoiding detection. This study revealed that motivational instructions enhanced CIT detection efficiency. In a subsequent study, Gustafson and Orne (1965b) manipulated the motivation factor, leading one group of subjects to believe that only highly intelligent individuals with more than the usual amount of control are able to fool the lie detector (i.e., motivation to deceive); whereas a second group was led to believe that it is extremely difficult and even impossible for normal, well-adjusted individuals to prevent themselves from giving certain physiological reactions when they lie (i.e., motivation to be detected). All subjects were tested twice, using a card-test paradigm, and received feedback after the first test. Irrespective of the actual test's outcome, half of the subjects in each group were informed that detection was successful, and the other half that it was unsuccessful. The results showed that motivational instructions interacted with the feedback. Detection efficiency was higher when the feedback contradicted the subject's motivation (e.g., successful detection when motivated to avoid detection) than when it was in line with the subject's motivation (i.e., unsuccessful detection when motivated to avoid detection). The authors concluded that the perceived failure in the first test increased subjects' motivation, resulting in enhanced detection efficiency of the second test. Participants were reasoned to have lost their motivation after perceiving success in the first test. Subsequent studies examining the effects of motivation on CIT detection produced inconsistent results. For example, several studies failed to find enhanced detection efficiency with motivation to avoid detection (Davidson, 1968; Furedy and Ben-Shakhar, 1991; Kugelmass and Lieblich, 1966; Lieblich et al., 1974). On the other hand, the results reported by Elaad and Ben-Shakhar (1989) were consistent with those of Gustafson and Orne (1963). No attempt has been made yet to replicate the more complex manipulation of the motivation factor employed by Gustafson and Orne (1965b). Individual studies may, however, lack sufficient power to detect the motivation effect. The meta-analysis by Ben-Shakhar and Elaad (2003) showed that the motivation to avoid detection significantly improved detection efficiency. This analysis also showed that successful detection was obtained under low motivation conditions. Like overt deception, motivation to avoid detection can enhance CIT detection, but is not a necessary condition for detection.

Evaluation of the emotional–motivational approaches

Research suggests that emotional–motivational factors such as overt deception and motivation to avoid detection may increase CIT detection efficiency. However, significant and often impressive detection rates are obtained under low emotional–motivational conditions: when concealed information concerns neutral stimuli, when there is little or no emotional conflict, when there are no consequences when failing the test, when overt deception is not required, and when subjects are not specifically motivated to avoid detection (Ben-Shakhar and Elaad, 2003). These findings indicate that other processes may be at the heart of the CIT.

Cognitive approaches

Researchers have advanced a number of approaches that have in common their primary focus on cognitive factors associated with processing of the CIT items. Orienting response (OR) theory is the dominant cognitive approach. Two further approaches – dichotomization theory and feature-matching – build upon OR theory.

Orienting response theory

The concept of the orienting reflex was introduced by Pavlov (1927) to describe the reflex which brings about behavioral and physiological responses to a change in the environment. This concept was further developed by Sokolov (1963, 1966) who used the term "orienting response" to describe a complex of reactions evoked by a novel stimulus or a change in stimulation. The definition of the OR as a response to a change in stimulation implies that repeated presentations of the same stimulus would result in a gradual decline in response magnitude, a process which was termed "habituation." Sokolov (1963) formulated a comparator theory that became the dominant OR theory (Siddle, 1991). He postulated that repeated presentations of a given stimulus result in an internal representation of that stimulus input. This representation, termed as the "neuronal model," contains all the parameters of the stimulus. All input information is compared with the existing neuronal models and a mismatch between stimulus input and the models results in an OR. If the input matches with the existing model the OR will be inhibited and habituation will take place. The interesting feature of the OR, which provides this concept with an explanatory power for CIT detection, is that significant stimuli evoke enhanced ORs and are more resistant to habituation (Lynn, 1966; Sokolov, 1963). Lykken (1974) made the connection between OR and the differential responsivity to the relevant items in the CIT. In particular, Lykken (1974) argued that: "for the guilty subject only, the 'correct' alternative will have a special significance, an added 'signal value' which will tend to produce a stronger orienting reflex than that subject will show to other alternatives" (p. 728). For the innocent examinees, the correct items do not possess such significance or signal value and thus all items are equivalent and evoke similar ORs that habituate with stimulus repetition.

There is a wealth of research that speaks to the validity of the OR theory. First, the physiological response pattern elicited by the relevant items in the CIT in knowledgeable individuals is typical for the OR. Specifically, physiological responding to the relevant items is associated with increased skin conductance responding (Lykken, 1959), heart rate deceleration (Verschuere *et al.*, 2004b), respiratory suppression (Timm, 1982), and increased pupil dilation (Lubow and Fein, 1996).[2] Second, it has been investigated whether physiological responding to the relevant CIT items has "OR characteristics." Specifically, it has been examined whether habituation, generalization, and dishabituation are observed in response to the relevant items. Habituation of responding has been observed in several CIT studies (e.g., Balloun and Holmes, 1979; Ben-Shakhar *et al.*, 1975; Verschuere *et al.*, 2005). Generalization was also demonstrated in the CIT by Ben-Shakhar *et al.* (1996) who found that physiological responding to stimuli presented in one modality (e.g., verbal) generalized to other modalities (e.g., pictorial). Ben-Shakhar and Gati (1987) further showed that the strength of responding to a stimulus was positively related to the degree it resembled the critical stimulus. On the other hand, research has failed to demonstrate dishabituation in the CIT (e.g., Ben-Shakhar *et al.*, 2000). Ben-Shakhar and colleagues argued, however, that dishabituation has not been always demonstrated in OR research either (see Siddle and Lipp, 1997). Third, the information processing view of orienting states that the OR serves to allow more elaborate processing of the OR-eliciting stimulus (Kahneman, 1973; Öhman, 1992; Wagner, 1978). OR research that demonstrated positive correlations between OR and later recall of the stimulus material supports this view (e.g., Corteen, 1969). Using a code word paradigm, Waid *et al.* (1978) found that detection was positively correlated with the number of words recalled after the administration of the CIT. Moreover, recalled items were more likely to evoke an electrodermal response than non-recalled items (see also Waid *et al.*, 1981). Other researchers have found a positive association between recall and detection efficiency (e.g., Carmel *et al.*, 2003; Iacono *et al.*, 1984). Using a mock crime procedure, Verschuere *et al.* (2007) presented participants

---

[2] The P300 elicited by the relevant CIT items (Rosenfeld *et al.*, 1988) may also be an index of the OR.

with crime-related and control pictures in a CIT. To assess whether the relevant pictures were processed more deeply, a number of previously unseen details were added to all pictures. The picture of the stolen money (e.g., €10), for example, also included a pen, paper clips, a can of soda, and an envelope. The CIT was followed by a free recall task that required participants to name as many details as possible, and a cued recall task, that required participants to indicate the presented details from a list of possible details. Results from both tasks showed that participants remembered more details from the relevant pictures than from the control pictures. A point of concern is that these studies present correlational data to support the more elaborate processing of the relevant stimuli, preventing to draw causal conclusions regarding psychophysiological responding and memory.[3] Overall, the data provide clear evidence in support of OR theory.

A strict interpretation of OR theory states that emotional–motivational factors are irrelevant. Lykken (1974, p. 728) argued along these lines when he stated that "Whether he is high or low in reactivity, whether he has confidence in the test or not, whether he is frightened and aroused or calm and indifferent, we can still expect that his response to this significant alternative will be stronger than to the other alternatives as long as he recognizes which alternative is correct." The strict OR interpretation has difficulty in explaining the findings that overt deception and motivation to avoid detection can contribute to physiological differentiation in the CIT. However, these findings can be integrated in the OR theory. Rather than a strict view of significance that dichotomizes stimuli as either possessing signal value or not, one can also take a dimensional view that states that stimuli differ in the degree of significance. The emotional–motivational factors described above can increase the significance of the relevant items. Elaad and Ben-Shakhar (1989) made a similar suggestion that motivation and deception can enhance the "noteworthiness" of the relevant items. This reasoning is compatible with at least two more lines of research. First, Bradley and colleagues showed that participants who actually performed a mock crime typically show larger CIT effects than those who were exposed to the relevant information, but did not perform the mock crime (Bradley et al., 1996; Bradley and Rettinger, 1992; Bradley and Warfield, 1984). Actual performance of the mock crime may increase the level of

---

[3] Greater response latencies to the relevant items compared to the control items further supports the idea that the concealed information demands attention (Verschuere *et al.*, 2004b). Recently, Seymour and Fraynt (2009) showed that the more elaborate the relevant items were processed prior to the CIT, the greater the response latency difference between the relevant and the control items.

significance of the relevant items. Second, a number of studies showed that the more salient the relevant items, the better the differentiation in the CIT (e.g., Carmel *et al.*, 2003; Jokinen *et al.*, 2006).

The dichotomization theory

The dichotomization theory, which is closely linked to OR theory, originated from the early work of Lieblich *et al.* (1970), and was later extended by Ben-Shakhar (1977, 1980). The dichotomization theory assumes that knowledgeable examinees differentiate the stimulus set into two distinct categories (relevant vs. irrelevant) and pay attention to just one aspect of the stimuli presented to them during the CIT – whether they belong to the relevant or to the irrelevant stimulus category, while all other aspects of the stimuli (i.e., features distinguishing between different stimuli of the same category) are ignored. In terms of Sokolov's (1963) theoretical formulation, it is postulated that a single neuronal model is formed for each stimulus category. It is further assumed that habituation generalizes within each category, with little or no carry over across categories. Because these are typically more irrelevant than relevant stimuli, they will habituate faster, leading to differential responding in the knowledgeable individual. For the innocent, all stimuli belong to the irrelevant category, and responses will quickly habituate.

Ben-Shakhar and colleagues tested several predictions derived from the dichotomization approach. First, increasing the stimulus frequency of one category should yield more habituation of the stimuli in that category, without affecting the responses to the stimuli in the other category. Thus, the relative overall responsivity to stimuli in a given category should be a decreasing function of the relative frequency of the stimuli in that category. This prediction was examined and confirmed in several studies (Ben-Shakhar, 1977; Ben-Shakhar *et al.*, 1975, 1982; Lieblich *et al.*, 1970). It should be pointed out that the dichotomization theory does not necessarily depend on the assumption that the relevant stimuli in the CIT are signal stimuli that produce enhanced ORs. As long as the relevant stimuli are relatively rare (are presented at a relative frequency of less than 50 percent), they are expected to produce greater physiological responsivity than the irrelevant stimuli. Indeed, Ben-Shakhar (1977) demonstrated that when the irrelevant stimuli are presented with a low relative frequency (between one and eight), they yield a larger average response than the relevant ones, thus demonstrating a "negative detection" (detection of the irrelevant rare stimuli). However, the differential responsivity obtained by Ben-Shakhar (1977) in the two conditions (i.e., a condition of rare relevant stimuli and a condition of rare irrelevant stimuli) was asymmetrical as rare relevant stimuli produced much stronger differential responsivity than rare irrelevant stimuli. Therefore, it was suggested that the relevant items do have a signal value which is an additional factor contributing to the increased physiological responses evoked by these items. Indeed, a subsequent study showed that relevance may be a more potent factor in eliciting orienting than relative novelty (Ben-Shakhar, 1994).

Second, the theory assumes generalization of habituation within each category. This prediction was tested by Ben-Shakhar (1977), who presented a relevant stimulus at a relative frequency of one to eight. In one condition seven different irrelevant stimuli were used, whereas in another condition one irrelevant stimulus was repeated. The results revealed the predicted pattern of essentially identical levels of detection efficiency under the two conditions. That using seven different irrelevant stimuli did not affect electrodermal responding corroborates the notion of within-category generalization of habituation. Third, response magnitude to a given stimulus should be determined by its serial position within its own category. Thus, for example, if the sixth stimulus presented to the subject in a CIT is the second relevant stimulus, it should elicit a response magnitude characteristic of a second stimulus in a habituation function. This prediction was tested and to a large extent corroborated by Ben-Shakhar (1980).

However, several other research findings do not fit with the dichotomization theory. First, CIT detection efficiency should not be affected by the serial position of the relevant item. The physiological responsivity, according to the dichotomization theory, is determined only by the serial position of the stimulus within its own category. In a CIT with a single relevant item, the serial position of this item should not affect differential responding, because it is always the first stimulus in its category. However, Ben-Shakhar and Lieblich (1982) obtained enhanced electrodermal responding with earlier presentations of the relevant stimulus than with late presentations. Second, the dichotomization approach has difficulty explaining the effect of emotional–motivational factors on differential responding to significant stimuli. It was suggested that these factors influence the dichotomization process (e.g., motivation to avoid detection may affect psychophysiological differentiation and detection efficiency through its influence on the process of dichotomizing the stimulus set into clear and distinct categories of relevant vs. neutral stimuli). However, this suggestion seems a bit of a stretch of the theory, and there is no empirical evidence to support it.

The feature-matching approach

The feature matching approach was developed and tested in a research program conducted by Ben-Shakhar and Gati (e.g., Ben-Shakhar and Gati, 1987; Gati and Ben-Shakhar, 1990). This approach was proposed to supplement OR theory, by specifying the nature of the comparator (match/mismatch) mechanism proposed by Sokolov (1963). Specifically, the feature-matching theory rests on the assumption that the process of comparing stimulus inputs with stimulus representations is similar to the process that underlies the comparison of two stimuli in order to make similarity judgments. It dealt with the conditions of OR elicitation by introducing feature-matching definitions of both stimulus significance and stimulus novelty. These definitions are based on the contrast model proposed by Tversky (1977) to account for judgments of similarity. Specifically, it is assumed that both stimulus input and stimulus representation (the neuronal model) can be characterized by sets of features. It was further assumed that OR elicitation is determined by two independent factors – stimulus novelty and stimulus significance. Each factor is assessed with a separate feature-matching process. The degree of *mismatch* between features of the incoming stimulus and the activated neuronal models determines novelty. The degree of *match* between features of the incoming stimulus and the representations of past significant events determines significance. The outcomes of the two matching processes are integrated to produce an OR, which is monotonically related to both significance and novelty. The feature-matching theory of OR elicitation and habituation was examined and generally corroborated in a series of studies (e.g., Ben-Shakhar and Gati, 1987, 2003; Ben-Shakhar *et al.*, 2000; Gati and Ben-Shakhar, 1990). The advantage of this theory over the dichotomization theory lies in viewing stimulus significance as a continuum rather than a dichotomy. In addition, the feature-matching theory implies that OR will generalize to stimuli that share common features with the significant stimulus (Ben-Shakhar *et al.*, 1996). This has important implications for the CIT and in particular for constructing the CIT items. Specifically, it is important to choose irrelevant items that are as distinct as possible from the relevant item. It also means that the CIT may be robust against some changes in the mode of stimulus presentation (e.g., verbal vs. pictorial presentations of the crime-related item).

Summary and conclusions

Clear insight in the underlying mechanisms of a test is an important aspect of test validity. We described several mechanisms that may account for the physiological responses observed in the CIT. These theories can be broadly classified in their emphasis on either emotional–motivational vs. cognitive factors. Theories that have emphasized emotional–motivational factors are the conditioned response theory, punishment/DR theory, emotional conflict theory, and motivation impairment. Conditioned response theory has not been tested empirically, but is unlikely to generally account for the pattern of differential responding to critical stimuli observed in the CIT. Punishment/DR theory has been tested, and is not supported by the available data. There is some support for the emotional conflict and the motivation impairment accounts in that overt deception and motivation to avoid detection can enhance differential responding in the CIT, but the data also indicate that deception and motivation are not necessary for valid detection of concealed information.

The cognitive approaches focus upon the OR theory, which is generally supported by a large body of evidence. According to the OR theory, the relevant items differ between guilty and innocent examinees in stimulus significance. Because all items are equivalent in stimulus significance for innocent examinees, they will elicit ORs of similar magnitude that will gradually habituate. For the guilty examinee, however, the relevant items stand out because of their enhanced significance. As a result, they will elicit enhanced ORs that will habituate more slowly. The dichotomization theory and the feature-matching approach were formulated to supplement OR theory by specifying the comparator mechanism. Research on the dichotomization theory indicates that not only significance, but also novelty affects differential responding to the relevant CIT items. Thus, the lower the relative frequency of the relevant items, the greater the OR it elicits. The feature-matching approach suggests that the greater the match between the presentation of the relevant item in the CIT and the corresponding representation of the crime scene, the greater the OR. Moreover, the greater the mismatch between the relevant and the irrelevant items, the larger the OR elicited by the relevant item. The effects of overt deception and motivation to avoid detection can also be meaningfully integrated in the OR theory. Both factors may exert their influence by increasing the significance of the relevant items.

In sum, OR theory can explain most of the research findings related to the CIT. OR theory has also been successful in generating new predictions. For example, based upon OR theory, Elaad and Ben-Shakhar (2006) proposed and validated a new outcome measure (Finger Pulse Line Length) that combined two OR indicators – heart rate deceleration and peripheral vasoconstriction.

On the other hand, OR theory faces several challenges. First, significance is a very useful concept, but it is also too broad and vague. The positive side is that the significance concept allows integrating a wide variety of findings such as the role of emotional–motivational factors. The downside is that it is not always clear whether a stimulus has "sufficient" significance to elicit OR. Provided intact memory, it seems safe to assume that a rape victim's ethnic background will have sufficient significance to elicit an OR (e.g., "Was the victim Asian? Latin? White? Black?"). But how about the victim's clothes? Again, even with perfect memory, it cannot be ascertained whether such information is sufficiently significant to elicit an enhanced OR. The CIT will benefit from a clear definition of significance, a sharper distinction from related concepts (see, e.g., Dindo and Fowles, 2008), and a better understanding of the conditions necessary for OR elicitation by significant stimuli.

Second, some research findings are hard to reconcile with the OR theory. The heart rate deceleration elicited by relevant items is more extended than one would expect from OR theory. Heart rate typically decelerates 1–5 s after onset of the OR-eliciting stimulus, and then returns to baseline (Richards and Casey, 1992). Yet, the heart rate deceleration to relevant CIT items may last for 15 s. Although OR theory predicts greater startle modulation to the relevant items compared to the irrelevant items, three experiments failed to support this prediction (Verschuere *et al.*, 2007). Verschuere and colleagues (2007) proposed an alternative hypothesis, response inhibition, to explain the startle data.[4] Processes other than orienting may contribute to physiological responding in the CIT, and response inhibition seems a valuable candidate. Trying to suppress the arousal that accompanies the OR may paradoxically increase that arousal. Future work can elucidate whether these findings can be integrated in OR theory.

Third, the bulk of CIT research can be criticized for lacking ecological validity. Laboratory research differs in important aspects from real-life circumstances. Verschuere *et al.* (2004a), for example, found that laboratory participants rated the CIT stimuli as neutral in valence and low in arousal. Stimuli are probably appraised quite differently in real-life situations where the examinee faces severe consequences when failing the test. The difference between the laboratory and the field may be mere quantitative, with the emotional–motivational factors exhibiting a

---

[4] fMRI research further indicates that concealed information is associated with brain regions (e.g., inferior frontal regions; Gamer *et al.*, 2007) that have been related to response inhibition (Aron *et al.*, 2004).

more pronounced role under real-life circumstances than under laboratory conditions. There may also be qualitative differences, and different processes may operate under laboratory and field conditions. This brings to mind the joke of the drunk looking for his wallet under a streetlight. A police officer passes by, and helps to find the wallet, but without success. After a while, the officer asks whether the drunk is sure that his wallet was lost at that location. The drunk answers: "No, it was 50m from here, but at least this spot has a street light."

The controlled but artificial nature of laboratory research may not reveal the mechanisms underlying physiological responding in the CIT under real-life circumstances. Suzuki *et al.* (2004), for example, argued that respiratory apnea is observed only in field examinations, and reflects an "emotional factor." However, these authors did not examine respiratory apnea in the laboratory nor did they argue why the apnea would not fit with OR theory. Respiratory suppression, and respiratory pause in particular has been theorized to be an OR component (Barry, 1977; Stekelenburg and Van Boxtel, 2001). With confessions as the criterion for guilt, field research on the CIT has demonstrated that guilty subjects showed the respiratory suppression to the relevant items that is seen in the laboratory (Elaad *et al.*, 1992). Although relying upon a single outcome measure, these data indicate that also in real life the physiological responding to concealed information may not be determined by the fear system. Verschuere and Meijer (submitted) analyzed the card ("stim") test data from real-life high stake police interrogations and found that the relevant items elicited the typical physiological OR pattern seen in the laboratory: greater skin conductance responding, greater heart rate deceleration, greater respiratory suppression and no increase in cardiac blood pressure. These data suggest that the OR operates not only in the lab, but also in high-stakes, real-life circumstances.

REFERENCES

Aron, A. R., Robbins, T. W., and Poldrack, R. A. (2004). Inhibition and the right inferior frontal cortex. *Trends in Cognitive Sciences*, 8(4), 170–177.

Balloun, K. D., and Holmes, D.S. (1979). Effects of repeated examinations on the ability to detect guilt with a polygraphic examination: a laboratory experiment with a real crime. *Journal of Applied Psychology*, 64, 316–322.

Barry, R. J. (1977). Failure to find evidence of the unitary OR concept with indifferent low-intensity auditory stimuli. *Physiological Psychology*, 5, 89–96.

Ben-Shakhar, G. (1977). A further study of dichotomization theory in detection of information. *Psychophysiology*, 14, 408–413.

(1980). Habituation of the orienting response to complex sequences of stimuli. *Psychophysiology*, 17, 524–534.

(1994). The roles of stimulus novelty and significance in determining the electrodermal orienting response: interactive vs. additive approaches. *Psychophysiology*, 31, 402–411.

Ben-Shakhar, G., and Elaad, E. (2003). The validity of psychophysiological detection of deception with the Guilty Knowledge Test: a meta-analytic review. *Journal of Applied Psychology*, 88, 131–151.

Ben-Shakhar, G., and Furedy, J. J. (1990). *Theories and Applications in the Detection of Deception: A Psychophysiological and International Perspective*. New York: Springer-Verlag.

Ben-Shakhar, G., and Gati, I. (1987). Common and distinctive features of verbal and pictorial stimuli as determinants of psychophysiological responsivity. *Journal of Experimental Psychology: General*, 116, 91–105.

Ben-Shakhar, G., and Lieblich, I. (1982). The dichotomization theory for differential autonomic responsivity reconsidered. *Psychophysiology*, 19, 277–281.

Ben-Shakhar, G., Lieblich, I., and Kugelmass, S. (1975). Detection of information and GSR habituation: an attempt to derive detection efficiency from two habituation curves. *Psychophysiology*, 12, 283–288.

(1982). Interactive effects of stimulus probability and significance on the skin conductance response. *Psychophysiology*, 19, 112–114.

Ben-Shakhar, G., Frost, R., Gati, I., and Kresh, Y. (1996). Is an apple a fruit? Semantic relatedness as reflected by psychophysiological responsivity. *Psychophysiology*, 33, 671–679.

Ben-Shakhar, G., Gati, I., Ben-Bassat, N., and Sniper, G. (2000). Orienting response reinstatement and dishabituation: the effects of substituting, adding and deleting components of nonsignificant stimuli. *Psychophysiology*, 37, 102–110.

Bradley, M. T., and Rettinger, J. (1992). Awareness of crime relevant information and the guilty knowledge test. *Journal of Applied Psychology*, 77, 55–59.

Bradley, M. T., and Warfield, J. F. (1984). Innocence, information, and the guilty knowledge test in the detection of deception. *Psychophysiology*, 21, 683–689.

Bradley, M. T., MacLaren, V. V., and Carle, S. B. (1996). Deception and non-deception in guilty knowledge and guilty actions polygraph tests. *Journal of Applied Psychology*, 81, 153–160.

Burgoon, J. K. (2000). Testing for the motivation impairment effect during deceptive and truthful interaction. *Western Journal of Communication*, 64, 243–267.

Carmel, D., Dayan, E., Naveh, A., Raveh, O., and Ben-Shakhar, G. (2003). Estimating the validity of the guilty knowledge test from simulated experiments: the external validity of mock crime studies. *Journal of Experimental Psychology-Applied*, 9, 261–269.

Codispoti, M., Bradley, M. M., and Lang, P. J. (2001). Affective reactions to briefly presented pictures. *Psychophysiology*, 38, 474–478.

Corteen, R. S. (1969). Skin conductance changes and word recall. *British Journal of Psychology*, 60, 81–84.

Davidson, P. O. (1968). Validity of the guilty knowledge technique: the effects of motivation. *Journal of Applied Psychology*, 52, 62–65.

Davis, R. C. (1961). Physiological responses as a means of evaluating information. In A. D. Biderman and H. Zimmer (eds.), *The Manipulation of Human Behavior* (pp. 142–168). New York: Wiley.

DePaulo, B. M., and Kirkendol, S. E. (1989). The motivational impairment effect in the communication of deception. In J. Yuille (ed.), *Credibility Assessment* (pp. 51–70). Belgium: Kluwer Academic Publishers.

Dindo, L., and Fowles, D. C. (2008). The skin conductance orienting response to semantic stimuli: significance can be independent of arousal. *Psychophysiology*, 45(1), 111–118.

Elaad, E., and Ben-Shakhar, G. (1989). Effects of motivation and verbal response type on psychophysiological detection of information. *Psychophysiology*, 26, 442–451.

(2006). Finger pulse waveform length in the detection of concealed information. *International Journal of Psychophysiology*, 61, 226–234.

Elaad, E., Ginton, A., and Jungman, N. (1992). Detection measures in real-life criminal guilty knowledge tests. *Journal of Applied Psychology*, 77, 757–767.

Furedy, J. J., and Ben-Shakhar, G. (1991). The role of deception, intention to deceive, and motivation to avoid detection in the psychophysiological detection of guilty knowledge. *Psychophysiology*, 28, 163–171.

Furedy, J. J., Davis, C., and Gurevich, M. (1988). Differentiation of deception as a psychological process: a psychophysiological approach. *Psychophysiology*, 25, 683–688.

Furedy, J. J., Gigliotti, F., and Ben-Shakhar, G. (1994). Electrodermal differentiation of deception: the effect of choice vs. no choice of deceptive items. *International Journal of Psychophysiology*, 18, 13–22.

Furedy, J. J., Posner, R., and Vincent, A. (1991). Electrodermal differentiation of deception: memory-difficulty and perceive-accuracy manipulations. *Psychophysiology*, 28, 163–171.

Gamer, M., and Berti, S. (2009). Task relevance and recognition of concealed information have different influences on electrodermal activity and event-related brain potentials. *Psychophysiology*, 47, 355–364.

Gamer, M., Bauermann, T., Stoeter, P., and Vossel, G. (2007). Covariations among fMRI, skin conductance and behavioral data during processing of concealed information. *Human Brain Mapping*, 28, 1287–1301.

Gamer, M., Rill, H. G., Vossel, G., and Godert, H. W. (2006). Psychophysiological and vocal measures in the detection of guilty knowledge. *International Journal of Psychophysiology*, 60, 76–87.

Gati, I., and Ben-Shakhar, G. (1990). Novelty and significance in orientation and habituation: a feature-matching approach. *Journal of Experimental Psychology: General*, 119, 251–263.

Graham, F. K., and Clifton, R. K. (1966). Heart rate change as a component of the orienting response. *Psychological Bulletin*, 65, 305–320.

Gustafson, L. A., and Orne, M. T. (1963). Effects of heightened motivation on the detection of deception. *Journal of Applied Psychology*, 47, 408–411.

(1965a). The effects of verbal responses on the laboratory detection of deception. *Psychophysiology*, 7, 10–14.

(1965b). Effects of perceived role and role success on the detection of deception. *Journal of Applied Psychology*, 49, 412–417.

Horneman, C. J ., and O' Gorman, J. G. (1985). Detectability in the card test as a function of the subject's verbal response. *Psychophysiology*, 22, 330–333.

Iacono, W. G., Boisvenu, G. A., and Fleming, J. A. E. (1984). Effects of diazepam and methylphenidate on the electrodermal detection of guilty knowledge. *Journal of Applied Psychology*, 69, 289–299.

Jokinen, A., Santtila, P., Ravaja, N., and Puttonen, S. (2006). Salience of guilty knowledge test items affects accuracy in realistic mock crimes. *International Journal of Psychophysiology*, 62(1), 175–184.

Kahneman, D. (1973). *Attention and Effort*. Englewood Cliffs, NJ: Prentice Hall.

Kugelmass, S., and Lieblich, I. (1966). Effects of realistic stress and procedural interference in experimental lie detection. *Journal of Applied Psychology*, 50, 211–216.

Kugelmass, S., Lieblich, I., and Bergman, Z. (1967). The role of "lying" in psychophysiological detection. *Psychophysiology*, 3, 312–315.

Lang, P. J., Bradley, M. M., and Cuthbert, B. N. (1990). Emotion, attention, and the startle reflex. *Psychological Review*, 97, 377–395.

Lieblich, I., Kugelmass, S., and Ben-Shakhar, G. (1970). Efficiency of GSR detection of information as a function of stimulus set size. *Psychophysiology*, 6, 601–608.

Lieblich, I., Naftali, G., Shmueli, J., and Kugelmass, S. (1974). Efficiency of GSR detection of information with repeated presentation of series of stimuli in two motivational states. *Journal of Applied Psychology*, 59, 113–115.

Lubow, R. E., and Fein, O. (1996). Pupillary size in response to a visual guilty knowledge test: new technique for the detection of deception. *Journal of Experimental Psychology: Applied*, 2, 164–177.

Luria, A. R. (1932). *The Nature of Human Conflicts*. New York: Liveright.

Lykken, D. T. (1959). The GSR in the detection of guilt. *Journal of Applied Psychology*, 43, 358–388.

    (1974). Psychology and the lie detection industry. *American Psychologist*, 29, 725–739.

Lynn, R. (1966). *Attention, Arousal and the Orienting Reaction*. New York: Pergamon.

Messick, S. (1995). Validity of psychological assessment: validation of inferences from persons' responses and performances as scientific inquiry into score meaning. *American Psychologist*, 50, 741–749.

National Research Council (2003). *The Polygraph and Lie Detection*. Committee to Review the Scientific Evidence on the Polygraph. Washington, DC: The National Academies Press.

Öhman, A. (1992). Orienting and attention: preferred preattentive processing of potentially phobic stimuli. In B. A. Campbell, H. Hayne, and R. Richardson (eds.), *Attention and Information Processing in Infants and Adults* (pp. 263–295). Hillsdale, NJ: Erlbaum.

Pavlov, I. P. (1927). *Condition Reflex*. Oxford: Charandon Press.

Richards, J. E., and Casey, B. J. (1992). Development of sustained visual attention in the human infant. In B. A. Campbell, H. Hayne, and R. Richardson (eds.), *Attention and Information Processing in Infants and Adults: Perspectives from Human and Animal Research* (pp. 30–60). Hillsdale, NJ: Lawrence Erlbaum Associates

Rosenfeld, J. P., Cantwell, B., Nasman, V. T., Wojdac, V., Ivanov, S., and Mazzeiri, L. (1988). A modified event-related potential-based guilty-knowledge test. *International Journal of Neuroscience*, 42, 157–161.

Seymour, T. L., and Fraynt, B. R. (2009). Time and encoding effects in the concealed knowledge test. *Applied Psychophysiology and Biofeedback*, 34, 177–178.

Siddle, D. A. T. (1991). Orienting, habituation, and resource allocation: an associative analysis. *Psychophysiology*, 28, 245–259.

Siddle, D. A. T., and Lipp, O. V. (1997). Orienting, habituation, and information processing: the effects of omission, the role of expectancy, and the problem of dishabituation. In P. J. Lang, R. F. Simons, and M. T. Balaban (eds.), *Attention and Orienting: Sensory and Motivational Processes* (pp. 23–40). Mahwah, NJ: Lawrence, Erlbaum Associates.

Sokolov, E. N. (1963). *Perception and the Conditioned Reflex.* New York: Macmillan.

(1966) Orienting reflex as information regulator. In A. Leontyev, A. Luria, and A. Smirnov (eds.), *Psychological Research in U.S.S.R.* (pp. 334–360). Moscow: Progress Publishers.

Spence, S. A., Hunter, M. D., Farrow, T. F. D., Green, R. D., Leung, D. H., Hughes, C. J., and Ganesan, V. (2004). A cognitive neurobiological account of deception: evidence from functional neuroimaging. *Philosophical Transactions of the Royal Society of London Series B-Biological Sciences*, 359(1451), 1755–1762.

Stekelenburg, J. J., and Van Boxtel, A. (2001). Inhibition of pericranial muscle activity, respiration, and heart rate enhances auditory sensitivity. *Psychophysiology*, 38, 629–641.

Suzuki, R., Nakayama, M., and Furedy, J. (2004). Specific and reactive sensitivities of skin resistance response and repiratory apnea in a Japanse Concealed Information Test (CIT) of criminal guilt. *Canadian Journal of Behavioral Science*, 36, 202–209.

Timm, H. W. (1982). Effect of altered outcome expectancies stemming from placebo and feedback treatments on the validity of the guilty knowledge technique. *Journal of Applied Psychology*, 67, 391–400.

Tversky, A. (1977). Features of similarity. *Psychological Review*, 84, 327–352.

Van Diest, I., Winters, W., Devriese, S., Vercamst, E., Han, J. N., Van de Woestijne, K. P., and Van den Bergh, O. (2001). Hyperventilation beyond fight/flight: respiratory responses during emotional imagery. *Psychophysiology*, 38, 961–968.

Verschuere, B., and Meijer, E. (submitted). Autonomic responding to concealed card recognition in real-life police interrogations.

Verschuere, B., Crombez, G., and Koster, E. (2004a). Orienting to guilty knowledge. *Cognition & Emotion*, 18, 265–279.

Verschuere, B., Crombez, G., Declercq, A., and Koster, E. (2004b). Autonomic and behavioral responding to concealed information: differentiating defensive and orienting responses. *Psychophysiology*, 41, 461–466.

Verschuere, B., Crombez, G., De Clercq, A., and Koster, E. (2005). Psychopathic traits and autonomic responding to concealed information in a prison sample. *Psychophysiology*, 42, 239–245.

Verschuere, B., Crombez, G., Smolders, L., and De Clercq, A. (2009). Differentiating defensive and orienting responses to concealed information: the role of verbalisation. *Applied Psychophysiology & Biofeedback*, 34, 237–244.

Verschuere, B., Crombez, G., Koster, E., Van Bockstaele, B., and De Clercq, A. (2007). Startling Secrets: startle eye blink modification by concealed crime information. *Biological Psychology*, 76, 52–60.

Vincent, A., and Furedy, J. J. (1992). Electrodermal differentiation of deception: potentially confounding and influencing factors. *International Journal of Psychophysiology*, 13, 129–136.

Vrij, A., Fisher, R., Mann, S., and Leal, S. (2006). Detecting deception by manipulating cognitive load. *Trends in Cognitive Sciences*, 10(4), 141–142.

Wagner, A. R. (1978). Expectancies and the priming of STM. In S. H. Hulse, H. Fowler, and W. K. Honig (eds.), *Cognitive Processes in Animal Behavior* (pp. 177–209). Hillsdale, NJ: Lawrence Erlbaum Associates.

Waid, W. M., Orne, E. C., and Orne, M. T. (1981). Selective memory for social information, alertness, and physiological arousal in the detection of deception. *Journal of Applied Psychology*, 66, 224–232.

Waid, W. M., Orne, E. C., Cook, M. R., and Orne, M. T. (1978). Effects of attention, as indexed by subsequent memory, on electrodermal detection of information. *Journal of Applied Psychology*, 63, 728–733.

Part III

Field applications of concealed information detection: promises and perils

8   Limitations of the Concealed Information Test in criminal cases

Donald J. Krapohl

Overview: The Concealed Information Test (CIT) has enjoyed a longer and more energized scientific interest than concern-based methods like the probable-lie Comparison Question Test (CQT). The roots of the CIT and CQT methods in polygraphy can be traced to the United States, and variations of both approaches are taught in virtually all polygraph schools. Despite scientific advocacy for the CIT, polygraph examiners rarely employ it in most countries. In this chapter practical and cultural factors are offered as possible reasons why the CIT did not become the preferred method in the field. The end of the chapter includes suggestions to practitioners, agencies, and scientists on how to expand the use of the CIT.

Since the introduction of the Concealed Information Test (CIT; Lykken, 1959, 1960) this approach has garnered almost universal appeal among scientists who have taken an interest in deception detection. There are about six dozen countries where the polygraph is used for deception detection (Barland, 1999), but the CIT has been adopted by field practitioners to a significant degree in only one of them (Japan). Despite its more firm theoretical foundation and simple elegance over the more popular Comparison Question Techniques (Raskin and Honts, 2002), polygraph examiners have largely ignored the benefits that the CIT offer. The purpose of this chapter is to review the factors that may have limited the CIT's application to real-world criminal investigations.

Before beginning, it may be important to keep in mind a broader truth that underlies the current situation: a divide exists between the scientist

The author is grateful to Dr Gordon Barland, Dr Gershon Ben-Shakhar, Dr Ewout Meijer, and Dr Bruno Verschuere for their thoughtful and helpful suggestions to an earlier draft of this chapter. The opinions expressed are solely those of the author and do necessarily reflect those of the US Defense Intelligence Agency, the US Department of Defense, or the US Government.

and the practitioner in many areas for which there is a field practice, not just in polygraphy (Anderson *et al.*, 2001; Baker *et al.*, 2009; Miretzky, 2007; Munro, 2002; Wilson, 1981). The reasons are many. Divisions may be brought about by dissimilar philosophies, values, experiences, goals, and even language that can frustrate attempts to bridge the two sides. Scientists, for their part, can rightly hold claim to the best knowledge and theories available on which to base field practices. They can demonstrate empirically why certain methods are more valid, are more reliable, and produce more defensible results. Scientists may grow impatient with the intransigence of practitioners for their preferences for less perfect, even parochial and arcane field methods.

On the other side, practitioners in any field are less concerned as to whether scientists have a good theory for their methods: they are only interested in whether they "work."[1] After all, there are many observable phenomena for which scientists don't yet have a good theory, and this is especially true when dealing with characteristics of the human species. The practitioner would lay claim to a closer working understanding of the "real world," of adapting to local conditions, culture, and individual cases. They maintain a degree of indifference toward the recommendations from those they perceive are far removed from daily practice. Honest practitioners would acknowledge that their methods were garnered through collective experience and trial and error, but would characterize this as a refining process. Practitioners purport to know what functions best in the specific setting where they practice. They may resist the advice of the scientist not so much out of arrogance or ignorance (though, admittedly this can be too often the case) but principally from the belief born of successful experience, and an understanding of the needs of those whom they serve.

Turning specifically to polygraphy, there is plenty of evidence to support the conclusion that the CIT method is valid. It exploits a very powerful and universal human tendency to respond differently to stimuli that are contextually salient over those that are not. The CIT would seem to work for everyone who uses it under almost all conditions with virtually every measure that has ever been tried. Though Lykken (1959) proposed the CIT for the electrodermal channel, a CIT-like approach seems to work well with other measures, including electroencephalography (Farwell and Donchin, 1989, 1991; Rosenfeld *et al.*, 1988), reaction time (Crane, 1914–15; Seymour *et al.*, 2000), facial thermal imaging (Pavlidis *et al.*, 2002), respiration line length (Elaad *et al.*, 1992; Timm,

---

[1] That's all very well in practice, but it will never work in theory. French management expression.

1989), plethysmography (Elaad and Ben-Shakhar, 2006; Podlesny and Raskin, 1978), eye movement (Miyake, 1978), fMRI (Langleben *et al.*, 2002), manual grip pressure (Luria, 1932; Runkel, 1936), eye blinks (Fukuda, 2001; Thoneey *et al.*, 2005), pupillary response (Bradley and Janisse, 1981; Lubow and Fein, 1996), heart rate (Verschuere *et al.*, 2004) and others. In 2005, sixteen-year-old high school student Trisha Pasricha received widespread media attention for her science fair project that added stomach muscular contractions to the list of CIT-friendly physiological functions (Brand, 2005). There appears to be few behavioral and physiological signals that cannot be mined for indications of recognition.[2]

In this chapter the Comparison Question Technique[3] (CQT) will be used at times as a point for comparison and contrast with the CIT. The CQT is the preferred approach in most of the world and is used almost exclusively where instrumental lie detection first took hold, the United States. The CQT can take several forms, but most are variations on a theme. It is also at the center of a heated controversy regarding its validity and theoretical foundation (Honts *et al.*, 2002; Iacono and Lykken, 2002), a debate that is not repeated here. The CQT-centric approach preferred in the United States and other countries will provide a useful vantage point from which to examine the reasons the CIT has not been as widely used in countries outside of Japan.

Because the CIT is demonstrably simple, thoroughly studied in the laboratory, scientifically defensible, has a strong theoretical basis, and is a potential solution to the real-world need to verify information, the obvious question is why it has remained at the periphery of field

---

[2] Overt behaviors may also signal concealed information. Consider the following apocryphal courtroom tale: a defendant was being tried for the murder of his wife, though her body was never found. His defense counsel tried to sow the seeds of reasonable doubt in the minds of the jurors, emphatically hammering the point that the prosecution could not demonstrate that the alleged victim was even dead. With a dramatic and sweeping gesture of his arm toward the doors at the back of the courtroom the defense counsel declared in a booming voice, "Why, she could walk right through those doors at any moment." As all eyes followed his gesture toward to the back of the courtroom, the jurors were left to realize that they themselves had reasonable doubt about the woman's death. The defense's display had been powerful, and it clearly made an impression on the jury. The prosecutor was not so impressed. Moving deliberately from his table to stand before the jury, he also gestured toward the courtroom door. Speaking plainly and looking directly into the faces of the jurors he spoke. "I see that everyone in this courtroom turned to look at the courtroom door just now," he said, "everyone, that is, except the defendant. He didn't bother to look because he knows she's not coming through those doors. He knows because he killed her."

[3] Some literature refers to this approach as the Control Question Technique. This expression was replaced in favor of the Comparison Question Technique in 1997 by the US government and two years later by the American Polygraph Association. The latter term will be used in this chapter.

practice in much of the polygraph world. It is here proposed that the relevant factors may be divided into two: the practical and the cultural. Discussion here is organized along these lines. The final section offers recommendations to overcome the marginalization of the CIT in the field.

Practical limitations

It may be instructive to review the conditions that are essential to the CIT approach to criminal investigation so to later compare these with real world conditions. It is important to note that, regardless of technological approach, the following assumptions must be true for any CIT-like test to function as intended.

(1) Those who were not involved in the crime must be naïve as to the details of the crime, and could not surmise those details from what they do know.
(2) Investigators must correctly deduce and exploit the incriminating details a guilty suspect will recognize about the crime.
(3) As with all psychophysiological approaches to deception detection, examinees must cooperate with the testing process.

Naïveté

Beginning with the first assumption, that innocent examinees are ignorant of incriminating details of the crime, this is certainly true in many instances. Crimes committed in private and of which only the perpetrators were privy to the event are ideal circumstances for the CIT. One good example can be found in the sensational 1994 investigation of the murders of Nicole Brown Simpson and Ron Goldman in Los Angeles, California. In that case there were many critical details of the crime that only the murderer would know, and could have been used in a test of the prime suspect, Mr O. J. Simpson (Lykken, 1998). Other criminal investigations where the CIT could have been useful might include these high profile murder cases: Green River Killer, the BTK Strangler, the Soham murders, the Unabomber, the Hillside Strangler, the Yorkshire Ripper, the Boston Strangler, and the Zodiac Killer, to name but a few. In each of these crimes there was plenty of evidence that investigators had available and had not released to the public, which would afford some protection to innocent suspects. In each of these crimes there were multiple suspects, with little to implicate a particular person, and any method that could pare the number of suspects would have served investigators very well.

As sensational as these cases were, it would be an error to conclude that they are representative of the cases police investigate. Indeed, most cases where the polygraph is currently brought into play are not amenable to the CIT. The majority of police investigative cases call for a deception test rather than a recognition test, principally because there are often legitimate reasons that innocent people gain access to the information that might otherwise be used in a CIT. For example, individuals often have justifiable access to details by virtue of living or working in the setting where the crime was committed, and learning those details by witnessing them, finding them, correctly guessing them, or hearing others discuss them (Podlesny, 2003). Similarly, many polygraph cases entail "he said – she said" testimonies, where the real crime details and false statements are generally known to both of the parties that would be tested. Sometimes the crime has no evidence other than the statement of an eyewitness whose credibility is uncertain. The CIT has minimal value in testing self-identified victims and witnesses, and limited utility in missing person cases. There is also the well recognized problem of leakage of crime information by the news media, talkative witnesses and, unfortunately, from the police investigators, all of whom can compromise the assumption of naïveté on the part of potential CIT examinees or at least constrain the availability of testable items. As a general rule, the later the polygraph is applied in the investigative process, the more likely it is that the suspect is to have been exposed to intimate details of the crime.

Selecting stimuli

The second assumption, that investigators can identify and use information for test material that resides undisclosed in the culprit's memory, is perhaps the most difficult problem for CIT users. If the polygraph examiner could know what the examinee attended to during the crime – an easy task in laboratory analogs but much less so in real-world criminal investigations – the CIT would gain far more acceptance and utility among practitioners. Estimating what would be salient to a guilty person about his crime involves leaps of inference ranging from the highly likely to the highly speculative. Indeed, it is generally held in the United States that obtaining a sufficient number of critical items for the CIT is the greatest obstacle to its use. Two separate archival field studies (Podlesny, 1993, 2003) found that the CIT could address perhaps one-sixth to one-twentieth of the criminal cases where CQT polygraphy is currently used by the Federal Bureau of Investigation (FBI). Though not excluded as an adjunct approach, the CIT reportedly did not adequately meet the FBI's investigative requirements.

Part of the success of the Japanese national police with the CIT is their system wherein critical details of the crime are protected from public disclosure, certainly more protected than in US systems. Their investigative procedures increase the number of cases that might be selected for testing. This process allows the Japanese to conduct about 5000 criminal cases per year (Hira and Furumitsu, 2002). It has not been previously reported what percentage of crimes for which the Japanese do not use the polygraph owing to the inability to secure enough critical items. The Japanese police also conduct CQTs under certain circumstances, but only to supplement the CIT (Nakayama, 2002). Whether the Japanese investigative processes offer a lesson to US investigators is a legitimate and important question, especially as regards the shielding of critical information from examinees.

Changes in investigative procedures that better protects the critical information of the crime would no doubt increase the percentage of cases where the CIT could have been employed by the US investigative agencies. To what extent this is true has not been established. There are only data that provide a first glimpse at this possibility, and even then only for the FBI. The original FBI technical report by Podlesny *et al.* (1995), on which the Podlesny (2003) article was based, articulated the reasons why CIT items were not available for the cases in their sample. The data in the technical report permitted a rough estimate of the percentage of cases that might have allowed the CIT had the investigative procedures been altered to protect information better. The reasons for not using the CIT included: the examinee had legitimate access to the crime scene and details; the examinee was the source of the information for which the examination was conducted; the examination was based on unsubstantiated information from a second party or the investigator with no further evidence, and; the examinee acknowledged the behavior, but claimed not to know that it was illegal at the time. Indeed, 85 percent of the criminal investigative polygraph cases conducted by the FBI during the study period fell into one or more of these groups. The sample suggested that only 15 percent of the FBI cases where the CQT had been employed might have permitted the use of the CIT if investigative procedures had managed to protect the crime details. These early data do not support the hypothesis that the CIT could be brought to bear in all or a majority of the FBI's polygraph cases. The issue is not entirely closed, of course. Questions remain as to whether the FBI percentages would be found in other organizations that may use the polygraph differently. Moreover, if the polygraph data were to be submitted as court evidence in the 15 percent of the cases where the CIT was possible, the CIT may have incrementally improved the prosecution of criminals. Also, there may be instances where the polygraph was not used by FBI investigators but the CIT might have contributed to the investigation had it been used. Finally, a replication of the Podlesny (2003) research could offer greater confidence in the findings.

Lykken (1988) suggested that the employment of six critical items in CITs could achieve a high sensitivity and specificity in forensic applications. Most criminal investigators would agree that guilty suspects should recall at least six and probably many more unique facts about their crimes. Recollections of the details of a crime can be reasonably assumed for all perpetrators except a minority with memories seriously impaired by injury, disease, or intoxication. Therefore, the health status of the examinee's memory is probably not a limiting factor for the CIT in most cases. Deciding which in a universe of all possible details about the crime are salient to the culprit, though, is a task that relies not upon scientific rules but on the best guesswork of the polygraph examiner. Currently there are only heuristic and probabilistic approaches available. Will this suspect recognize the house where the burglary took place? Was that suspect paying attention to objects in the room? Will this suspect recall (or even correctly count) how much money was taken during the robbery? Was the room where the crime committed too dark to reveal the type of clothing the victim wore? These questions entail a degree of uncertainty a priori. The Japanese police have found that guilty suspects produce the largest electrodermal response on the critical items the polygraph examiner selects only about two-thirds of the time (Hira and Furumitsu, 2002). The addition of other physiological measures may increase this hit rate, but this would depend on whether the examiner has correctly selected the items the guilty examinee would recognize: adding more sensors or using better algorithms will not improve the examinee's recollection. As noted by Elaad (1998), guilty examinees have the frustrating habit of following their own rules about what is memorable and salient about their crimes, leaving investigators with collective experience and professional acumen to guide their item selection.

The thorny problem of estimating salience of the critical items a priori has so far been the persistent problem for the CIT. It is well recognized that calculating the exact probability of an innocent person's reaction to critical items is algebraically straightforward. In contrast, predicting the guilty person's reaction to a given critical item is largely speculative, especially in field conditions, and relies on factors that resist precise quantification. This is one of the reasons that Lykken (1988) advocated for testing as many potential critical items as possible, so to increase the likelihood of using items that the guilty person would recognize. The proportion of occasions when the CIT could be used, however, is inversely related to the required minimum number of critical items. Though an increasing number of critical items provides more "targets" for the guilty examinee to hit and innocent people to miss, requiring large numbers of critical items works against the more expanded use of the CIT.

Alternatively it has been shown, at least in the laboratory, that repeated testing with fewer critical items may be as accurate as fewer repetitions using a larger number of critical items (Ben-Shakhar and Elaad, 2002; Elaad and Ben-Shakhar, 1997). This is an important finding in that it could invite the use of the CIT to more cases. Field research is necessary to determine whether this wider applicability comes at a cost of diminished sensitivity, however, because it creates a greater dependence on a reduced number of items. If there is no loss of sensitivity with fewer critical items in field studies, it would help overcome one of the key obstacles to CIT usage.

Overall, initial data have not been encouraging regarding the sensitivity of the CIT in field applications. In a thorough evaluation of field and laboratory conditions and the effect on CIT accuracy, Elaad (1998) found that detection of guilty suspects in the field was substantially lower than laboratory data would suggest. Consistent with Elaad's (1998) assessment, work by Carmel *et al.* (2003) found that there was a significant decrement in the detection of critical items when moving from the standard mock crime paradigm toward a more realistic mock crime procedure. The effect may have been attributable to attention and memory factors, where recall of central aspects of the crime by the guilty participants was significantly better than secondary details, both of which had been included in their experimental CITs. Setting aside the data from the secondary critical items did result in significantly better accuracy, an effect that would be consistent with earlier lab research (Ben-Shakhar and Elaad, 2002; Elaad and Ben-Shakhar, 1997). Taken together these data might suggest that fewer, more carefully selected critical items may work better than a shotgun approach of using as many CITs as possible.

Previous writers have commented on the special challenges of testing career criminals (Carmel *et al.*, 2003; Nakayama, 2002). Recall that the CIT is constructed such that there is one critical item and some number of other items that appear to naïve suspects to be potentially relevant but are unrelated to the crime. With career criminals the polygraph examiner runs the risk of crafting irrelevant items that are relevant to another crime committed by the suspect that he wishes to keep concealed. If the suspect finds these items to be salient in the context of the testing, it can reduce or eliminate the contrast in responding between the critical and ostensibly irrelevant items, contributing to a false negative error. Nakayama (2002) also points out that from the CIT experience of the Japanese the career criminal may be unclear about which details belong to which crime he committed. He may not recognize a particular CIT-critical item as being associated with the crime being investigated, reducing the salience of the item. Though not previously reported, a similar problem may also plague the CQT, where career criminals may confuse their crimes and be unsure of their truthfulness to the relevant questions regarding a specific crime, leading to polygraph decision errors.

Finally, a recent field report introduces the possibility that innocent suspects can be fed incriminating details in a covert manner that can contaminate the CIT examination. In his case study Konieczny (2007) reported an incident where an agent acting on behalf of a corrupt police officer was placed in a jail cell with an innocent suspect whom the police officer wanted to fail a polygraph examination. While the police officer's agent and the innocent suspect shared the cell, the agent repeatedly told the suspect an invented story in which the critical elements of that story matched those of a crime being investigated. When the innocent suspect was subsequently tested by the polygraph examiner with three Peak of Tension tests (Keeler, 1930) the results showed that the examinee had reacted to the critical items of the true crime being investigated. The cause of the false positive, posited by the writer, was that the crime details had been implanted in the innocent suspect through the repetition of the invented story by the agent of the corrupt police officer. This conclusion would be consistent with the findings of Bradley and Rettinger (1992) who placed information into the memories of innocent laboratory subjects in a CIT paradigm. In the Konieczny (2007) CIT case, a CQT polygraph test had also been conducted. The CQT exam indicated truthfulness, and the polygraph examiner noted the discrepancy between the two sets of results in his official report. Fortunately, Konieczny (2007) reported that the police officer's scheme was later uncovered and the innocent suspect was exonerated. This was the first published field report revealing a vulnerability of the CIT toward a false positive. The case shows that the CIT is not less susceptible to official mischief than other forensic methods.

Examinee cooperation

The final piece to CIT success is whether the examinee cooperates with the testing process, or in other words, whether the guilty examinee can engage in a countermeasure strategy that will affect the results. This question has been at least partially answered. Beginning first with drugs and alcohol, the current state of the research finds a small or no effect for using these substances during the testing to avoid detection of concealed knowledge (Bradley and Ainsworth, 1984; Iacono *et al.*, 1984, 1992; O'Toole *et al.*, 1994). Likewise, mental strategies appear to have only modest benefit to a potential countermeasurer (Ben-Shakhar and Dolev, 1996; Elaad and Ben-Shakhar, 1991). Physical counter-measures, at least those that are undetectable by movement sensors, do offer real hope to the guilty subjects faced with a CIT (Honts *et al.*, 1996; Honts and Kircher, 1995).

Limitations arising from culture

Even if the practical challenges outlined earlier did not exist, the expanded use of the CIT would still face resistance from some experienced polygraph examiners who, wedded to the methods they learned in polygraph school, find such a radical departure from the CQT protocol unsettling and unnecessary. Polygraph schools in general have not been helpful in that regard. Of the twenty polygraph schools inspected and approved by the American Polygraph Association, only five formally teach the CIT. The Peak of Tension (POT, Keeler, 1930) test remains the standard recognition test in all polygraph schools and its rare use in the field usually involves a single critical item.

Another difficulty arises out of history. Older polygraph examiners can recall when scientist advocates of the CIT worked diligently to bring about legislation that affected their ability to practice. David Lykken, who is credited with the early work on the CIT, repeatedly testified before the US legislature to curtail the use of the polygraph. His efforts culminated with the Employee Polygraph Protection Act (1988) which severely restricted polygraph testing beyond government and law enforcement in the United States. Before and after this legislation he regularly testified against polygraph examiners in court cases, and published articles in national publications that condemned CQT polygraphy. Lykken advocated in favor of the CIT for reasons outlined earlier, and because he saw it as less inclined than the CQT to falsely implicate the innocent. Unfortunately the shadow of Lykken's adversarial relationship with polygraphers fell on the CIT, retarding its acceptance among practitioners for decades.

Unburdened by the US experience, the CIT flourished in Japan where it has been an unchallenged success for criminal testing. Identified errors in the field have been very low (Hira and Furumitsu, 2002), though it is unknown whether the statistics may have been influenced by selection factors that have also cast into question field validity studies of the CQT (see Iacono, 1991). Japanese polygraph examiners are highly educated, well trained, and their results can be admitted as court evidence (Yamamura and Miyata, 1990).

As a point of clarification, the Japanese version of the CIT is modeled on Keeler's Peak of Tension test (Keeler, 1930), a technique taught at virtually all polygraph schools but rarely practiced outside of Japan. Indeed, the older Japanese literature refers to their method as the Peak of Tension test (Hikita and Suzuki, 1965; Imamura *et al.*, 1960; Uruno and Narai, 1956). As with the standard Peak of Tension test, Japanese polygraph examiners administer three presentations of each test using polygraph data channels like those in the United States. They also consider changes in data trends over the course of the test and use global interpretation of the physiological data rather than manual scoring, though automated scoring has been investigated (Yamamura and Miyata, 1990). These testing methods are familiar to polygraph examiners throughout the world.

One essential cultural difference between Japanese polygraph examiners from that of their Western colleagues is the types of errors they are willing to tolerate. The Western preference for the CQT has been associated with an inclination toward false positives, something that the Japanese, with their CIT-centric methods, have managed to avoid (Hira and Furumitsu, 2002). For some scientists the false-positive problem has engendered skepticism toward the CQT regardless of application (Ben-Shakhar and Furedy, 1990).

There appears little disagreement that the CIT is less likely than is the CQT to render false positive decisions. There are two related issues that have not been adequately addressed, however, issues that bear directly on whether polygraph practitioners would readily transition to the CIT. One is the issue of false negatives. First, it should be acknowledged that among scientists there is a widely disseminated view that false positive results from polygraph examinations are a problem that must be strenuously avoided. By implication, false negatives must have a lower cost than false positives. For example, false positives, unlike false negatives, can lead to false confessions, and ultimately to false criminal convictions. This argument has been bolstered by high profile cases identified by advocacy organizations such as the Innocence Project where polygraph testing (real or feigned) prior to intense interrogations by investigators led to false confessions and false convictions (see www.innocenceproject.org for testimonials). The reality of these occurrences is undeniable and unfortunate, but the incidence of this chain of events has not been well documented. It may be helpful to recall in the context of criminal investigations that suspects are routinely questioned and interrogated during the investigation of serious crimes, often intensely, something which would occur even if no polygraph ever existed. Confessions, both true and false, arise in some proportion out of this questioning process. The additive contribution of the polygraph examination toward false confessions of consequential matters may or may not be significant, but any conclusion currently rests on tenuous evidence.

Despite these compelling anecdotes, polygraph testing is viewed among Western investigative agencies to have a net positive effect on criminal investigations. In most of the world the polygraph is used to test suspects for the purpose of focusing investigations. Positive results, both true and false, have the effect of keeping the examinee in the investigative spotlight. False positives may subject an innocent examinee to more investigation, possibly further interviews or interrogations. When confessions result from interrogations, competent interrogators seek information from the suspect that can be independently verified by investigation, providing one level of safeguard against the false confession. Polygraph results themselves are seldom admitted as evidence in the courts of Western nations.

An excessive emphasis on the avoidance of false positives can lead to an underestimate of the cost of false negatives. In the investigative mode, a polygraph false negative may redirect an investigation away from the true culprit, increasing the opportunity for the culprit to flee the area, conceal or destroy evidence, intimidate witnesses, or engage in more crimes. In this context it may be clear why most investigative agencies place a premium on maximizing true positives, with an implicit acceptance of elevated false positives.

The question, then, is a value judgment: what are the concomitant costs of tests of any given sensitivity and specificity? This is an instance of where academics and practitioners (and their agencies) can disagree. In the investigation of crimes, US police and governmental agencies may have a lower tolerance for false negatives than their Japanese counterparts when it comes to polygraph testing as part of the investigative process. Both preferences may be correct, in context. An assessment as to which is superior would be incomplete without a more thorough analysis of the costs and benefits that attend the preferences, how the test results are used, whether there are meaningful checks and balances, and whether the net effect of the preferred method is sufficiently positive to the larger system to justify its inclusion. The context can weigh heavily on which type of error can more easily be borne or remedied.

Another consequential factor within those contexts is whether the method of choice is used as a stand-alone or only as one step in a larger process. For example, if the technique was part of an investigation where the results might influence decisions as to whether the suspect should be scrutinized further by other investigative methods, investigators may place additional value on maximizing true positives. It is helpful to note that false positives can trigger investigations that later exculpate an innocent suspect whereas a false negative that excludes the true culprit, and thereby redirects the investigation away from him, could leave a case unresolved. In other words, a false positive may be more correctible than is a false negative when the testing method is part of a larger process. Conversely, if the technique is used as a stand-alone, such as for legal admissibility, positive results do not typically trigger other investigative methods. In this latter setting there are disadvantages in using methods with reduced specificity, and a more conservative approach may be appropriate.

There are other reasons the Japanese experience may not translate perfectly to all Western settings. One is the difference in crime rates. Consider the following conditions: when matched for population the US has more than 5 times the murder rate, 18 times the rapes, 29 times the robberies, and 119 times the assaults as does Japan (Winslow, 2009). Against this regrettable backdrop are investigative agencies struggling against immense caseloads, and among whom the replacement of an investigative method they consider effective is not seriously contemplated. The central question for US law enforcement organizations is whether a given tool can improve identification and prosecution of offenders. The advantages of the CIT over the CQT are less obvious from this perspective. The US federal government conducts an average of about 6,500 polygraph examinations for criminal investigations per year, almost all with the CQT as the primary method. Restricting polygraphy (or any other credibility assessment technology) to the subset of cases where the CIT can be used would meet resistance among agencies. For this reason, pursuit of a CIT-only approach is likely to be unsuccessful in the near term. A warmer reception would be expected if the CIT were introduced as an adjunct technique, to be used whenever possible but not exclusively. In that context the US government polygraph education program has been giving CIT instruction as a continuing education offering for more than five years.

Another hurdle for the adoption of the CIT across the polygraph profession lies in its decentralization. Consider that the Japanese have assigned all of their polygraph examiners to a single national agency where policy affects all practitioners, in contrast to the United States where there are polygraph programs in twenty-five federal agencies alone, and more than a thousand other polygraph examiners who answer to state and local authorities across hundreds of jurisdictions. This distributed examiner workforce would substantially slow the development of a CIT-centric culture in polygraphy.

Finally, despite whatever differences there may be in validity between the CIT and the CQT, the primacy of the CQT may be difficult to dislodge from agencies simply because the institutional consumers do not perceive the CQT sufficiently flawed to abandon it (though they are most certainly blind to the intricacies of the CIT/CQT controversy). Whatever the CQT validity, it appears to consumers to incrementally improve decision-making by narrowing the list of suspects, verifying the statements of witnesses and informants, and developing useful investigative information across a broad range of investigative circumstances at rates greater than had there been no CQT. The FBI has found that it leads to information of investigative value in about half of the cases that result in decisions of deception (Warner, 2005). The CIT could do this, too, but only in the cases that would permit the CIT. It is easy to understand, therefore, the reluctance of an organization to replace the CQT.

Recommendations for mainstreaming the CIT

All of the barriers to wider field use of the CIT are manageable given sufficient education and time, and in this section are recommendations on how they might be navigated. Some of the recommendations are addressed to the practitioner, others to scientists, and still others to agencies responsible for overseeing polygraph testing. All three sectors will have major parts to play if the CIT is to be more broadly used.

Before beginning, however, a full disclosure is called for regarding the ultimate destination the author proposes for the CIT. It begins with an observation: the CIT/CQT dispute, much like the larger polygraph debate, is notable for its polarization, two hardened camps separated by a metaphorical no-man's land. On one side, many practitioners cling to the unsound position that only deception testing in general, and the CQT in particular, has any value in field examinations. To the other side, some scientists who weigh in on the matter contend that only the

CIT should be used, and if a CIT is not possible the agency should not conduct any type of polygraph test in criminal investigations. Between these two sides are law enforcement agencies who tend to be less informed than either group but who default to the status quo unless there is a tangible value-added with a change in procedures.

A dispassionate assessment, however, would reveal that extreme positions almost always overlook consequential information. Of more real world import, neither the CQT nor CIT approach can truly replace the other approach. Until there is adequate field research to demonstrate the relative limits, merits and accuracy of both (or other) approaches, exclusive use of any one method would be premature. At the present time the ultimate benefit is not found in choosing either the CIT *or* the CQT, but in a judicious inclusion of both CIT *and* the CQT in criminal investigations as circumstances direct, along with the avoidance of over- or under-reliance on the polygraph results. It is from this perspective that the following recommendations are offered.

Practitioners

(1) Include the CIT in the core curriculum of all polygraph schools. The instruction should not only cover the method for conducting the CIT, but also in how to prepare investigators and others to protect information that could be used in a CIT.
(2) Polygraph professional organizations should undertake the task of promoting the CIT in its continuing education offerings.
(3) In cases amenable to both the CIT and CQT, a CIT should always be conducted first. It should be the preferred method for evidentiary applications.
(4) To boost salience of critical items and to reduce confusion, there is reason to believe that CITs may be better administered with images in place of words. Commercial polygraphs are available for presenting images on a screen in tandem with the polygraph operating software, and should be used when possible.

Agencies

(1) Criminal investigators should receive formal instruction on the CIT to sensitize them to the conditions necessary to make that approach successful, and how to collect and control information that would be useful in a CIT.
(2) Whenever possible the CIT should be the first choice in polygraph methods, and always in evidentiary applications.

(3) Agencies should compile a database of photos that can be quickly assembled into CITs for the more common types of crimes.

Scientists

(1) Consider publishing CIT articles in journals to which practitioners and agencies have easier access. If a goal is to change field practices it would seem reasonable that scientists should write to the target audiences. In the same vein, scientists should seek opportunities to address practitioners in their continuing education venues, not just to help educate polygraph examiners on the CIT but also to have a more current and complete appreciation for field conditions and needs.
(2) If false negatives are a problem for the CIT, devise practical remedies. Methods prone to false negatives limit their value to criminal investigations.
(3) Though the CIT is the most scientifically investigated approach to credibility assessment in existence, its external validity remains in question. The field requires ecologically valid research to give confidence in the CIT and to guide its implementation. Both the CIT and CQT appear to work very well in laboratory analogs, but only field studies can provide the evidence for or against field use.
(4) It should be understood that recognition testing, regardless of the technology and its accuracy, can never fill the broader role served by deception testing. If the aim is to improve police capabilities to distinguish the innocent from the guilty, perhaps marginal value could arise from the continuing scientific elucidation of the CIT in exquisite detail, or adding to the already burgeoning list of CIT technologies. The inherent barriers to utility will not be resolved by this line, however. The greater contribution to criminal investigations, from street crime to terrorism, will be the development of a highly accurate deception test that can be brought to bear on the full range of problems facing investigators.

REFERENCES

Anderson, N., Herriot, P., and Hodgkinson, G. P. (2001). The practitioner-researcher divide in industrial, work and organizational (IWO) psychology: where we are now, and where do we go from here? *Journal of Occupational and Organizational Psychology*, 74(4), 391–411.
Baker, T. B., McFall, R. M., and Shoham, V. (2009). Current status and future prospects of clinical psychology. *Psychological Science in the Public Interest*, 9(2), 67–103.

Barland, G. H. (1999). *American Polygraph Association Newsletter*, 32 (3), 16–17.

Ben-Shakhar, G., and Dolev, K. (1996). Psychophysiological detection through the guilty knowledge technique: effects of mental countermeasures. *Journal of Applied Psychology*, 81(3), 273–281.

Ben-Shakhar, G., and Elaad, E. (2002). Effects of questions' repetition and variation on the efficiency of the guilty knowledge test: a reexamination. *Journal of Applied Psychology*, 87(5), 972–977.

Ben-Shakhar, G., and Furedy, J. J. (1990). *Theories and Applications in the Detection of Deception: A Psychophysiological and International Perspective.* New York: Springer-Verlag.

Bradley, M. T., and Ainsworth, D. (1984). Alcohol and the psychophysiological detection of deception. *Psychophysiology*, 21(1), 63–71.

Bradley, M. T., and Janisse, M. P. (1981). Accuracy demonstrations, threat, and the detection of deception: cardiovascular, electrodermal, and pupillary measures. *Psychophysiology*, 18(3), 307–315.

Bradley, M. T., and Rettinger, J. (1992). Awareness of crime relevant information and the guilty knowledge test. *Journal of Applied Psychology*, 77(1), 55–59.

Brand, M. (2005, November 2). A 10th grader's stomach lie detector test. National Public Radio. Retrieved June 2, 2009 at www.npr.org/templates/story/story. php?storyId=4986415.

Carmel, D., Dayan, E., Naveh, A., Raveh, O., and Ben-Shakhar, G. (2003). Estimating the validity of the guilty knowledge test from simulated experiments: the external validity of mock crime studies. *Journal of Experimental Psychology: Applied*, 9(4), 261–269.

Crane, H. W. (1914–15). A study in association reaction and reaction time: with an attempted application of results in determining the presence of guilty knowledge. *Psychological Monographs*, 18(4), 1–73.

Elaad, E. (1998). The challenge of the concealed knowledge polygraph test. *Expert Evidence*, 6(3), 161–187.

Elaad, E., and Ben-Shakhar, G. (1991). Effects of mental countermeasures on psychophysiological detection in the guilty knowledge test. *International Journal of Psychophysiology*, 11(2), 99–108.

(1997). Effects of item repetitions and variations on the efficiency of the guilty knowledge test. *Psychophysiology*, 34(5), 587–596.

(2006). Finger pulse waveform length in the detection of concealed information. *International Journal of Psychophysiology*, 61(2), 226–234.

Elaad, E., Ginton, A., and Jungman, N. (1992). Detection measures in real-life criminal guilty knowledge tests. *Journal of Applied Psychology*, 77(5), 757–767.

Employee Polygraph Protection Act (1988). Public Law 100–347, 100th Congress.

Farwell, L.A., and Donchin, E. (1989). Detection of guilty knowledge with ERPs. *Psychophysiology*, 26(4a), S8.

(1991). The truth will out: interrogative polygraphy ("lie detection") with event-related brain potentials. *Psychophysiology*, 28(5), 531–547.

Fukuda, K. (2001). Eye blinks: new indices for the detection of deception. *International Journal of Psychophysiology*, 40, 239–245.

Hikita, Y., and Suzuki, A. (1965). An experimental study on the reliability of the judgments between CQT technique and POT technique. *National Research Institute of Police Science Bulletin (Polygraph Report)*, 21, 23–64. Text in Japanese.

Hira, S., and Furumitsu, I. (2002). Polygraphic examinations in Japan: application of the guilty knowledge test in forensic investigations. *International Journal of Police Science and Management*, 4(1), 16–27.

Honts, C. R., and Kircher, J. C. (1995). Legends of the concealed knowledge test: Lykken's distributional scoring system fails to detect countermeasures. *Psychophysiology*, 32(S1), S41.

Honts, C. R., Raskin, D. C., and Kircher, J. C. (2002). The scientific status of research on polygraph techniques: the case for polygraph tests. In D. L. Faigman, D. H. Kaye, M. J. Saks, and J. Sanders (eds.), *Modern Scientific Evidence: The Law and Science of Expert Testimony*, Volume 2 (pp. 446–483). St. Paul, MN: West.

Honts, C. R., Devitt, M. K., Winbush, M., and Kircher, J. C. (1996). Mental and physical countermeasures reduce the accuracy of the concealed knowledge test. *Psychophysiology*, 33, 84–92.

Iacono, W. G. (1991). Can we determine the accuracy of polygraph tests? In P. K. Ackles, J. R. Jennings, and M. G. H. Coles (eds.), *Advances in Psychophysiology* (pp. 201–201). Greenwich, CT: JAI Press.

Iacono, W. G., and Lykken, D. T. (2002). The scientific status of research on polygraph techniques: the case against polygraph tests. In D. L. Faigman, D. H. Kaye, M. J. Saks, and J. Sanders (eds.), *Modern Scientific Evidence: The Law and Science of Expert Testimony*, Volume 2 (pp. 483–538). St. Paul, MN: West.

Iacono, W. G., Boisvenu, G. A., and Fleming, J. A. (1984). Effects of diazepam and methylphenidate on the electrodermal detection of guilty knowledge. *Journal of Applied Psychology*, 69(2), 289–299.

Iacono, W. G., Cerri, A. M., Patrick, C. J., and Fleming, J. A. (1992). Use of antianxiety drugs as countermeasures in the detection of guilty knowledge. *Journal of Applied Psychology*, 77(1), 60–64.

Imamura, Y., Yamaoka, K., and Suzuki, A. (1960). An experimental study on the polygraph test: answer and response. *Reports of the National Research Institute of Police Science*, 13, 248–253. Text in Japanese; English abstract.

Keeler, L. (1930). A method for detecting deception. *American Journal of Police Science*, 1(1), 38–52.

Konieczny, J. (2007). An attempt to falsify the results of a polygraph test through the implementation of false memory: a case study. *European Polygraph*, 1(2), 117–121.

Langleben, D. D., Schroeder, L ., Maldjian, J. A., Gur, R. C., McDonald, S., Ragland, J. D., O' Brien, C.P., and Childress, A. R. (2002). Brain activity during simulated deception: an event-related functional magnetic resonance study. *NeuroImage*, 15(3), 727–732.

Lubow, R. E., and Fein, O. (1996). Pupillary size in response to a visual guilty knowledge test: new technique for the detection of deception. *Journal of Experimental Psychology*, 2, 164–177.

Luria, A. R. (1932). *The Nature of Human Conflicts*, translated by W. H. Gantt New York: Liveright, Inc.

Lykken, D. T. (1959). The GSR in the detection of guilt. *Journal of Applied Psychology*, 43(6), 385–388.

(1960). The validity of the guilty knowledge technique: the effects of faking. *Journal of Applied Psychology*, 44(4), 258–262.

(1988). Detection of guilty knowledge: a comment on Forman and McCauley. *Journal of Applied Psychology*, 73(2), 303–304.

(1998). *A Tremor in the Blood: Uses and Abuses of the Lie Detector.* New York: Plenum Trade.

Miretzky, D. (2007). View of research from practice: voices of teachers. *Theory into Practice*, 46(4), 272–280.

Miyake, Y. (1978). A study of skin resistance response, photoplethysmograph vasomotor response and eye movement as indices of lie detection. *Reports of the National Research Institute of Police Science*, 31(2), 18–24.

Munro, E. (2002). The role of theory in social work research: a further contribution to the debate. *Journal of Social Work Education*, 38(3), 461–470.

Nakayama, M. (2002). Practical use of the Concealed Information Test for criminal investigation in Japan. In M. Kleiner (ed.), *Handbook of Polygraph Testing*. San Diego: Academic Press.

O' Toole, D. M., Yuille, J. C., Patrick, C. J. and Iacono, W. G. (1994). Alcohol and the physiological detection of deception: arousal and memory influences. *Psychophysiology*, 31(3), 253–263.

Pavlidis, I., Eberhardt, N. L. and Levine, J. A. (2002). Seeing through the face of deception. *Nature*, 415, 35.

Podlesny, J. A. (1993). Is the guilty knowledge polygraph technique applicable in criminal investigations? A review of FBI case records. *Crime Laboratory Digest*, 20(3), 57–61.

(2003). A paucity of operable case facts restricts applicability of the Guilty Knowledge Technique in FBI criminal polygraph examinations. *Forensic Science Communications*, 5(3). Last accessed on June 2, 2009 at www.fbi. gov/hq/lab/fsc/backissu/july2003/podlesny.htm.

Podlesny, J. A. and Raskin, D. C. (1978). Effectiveness of techniques and physiological measures in the detection of deception. *Psychophysiology*, 15(4), 344–359.

Podlesny, J. A., Nimmich, K. W., and Budowle, B. (1995). A lack of operable case facts restricts applicability of the guilty knowledge deception detection method in FBI criminal investigations: a technical report. U.S. Department of Justice. Quantico, VA.

Raskin, D. C., and Honts, C. R. (2002). The comparison question test. In Kleiner (ed.), *Handbook of Polygraph Testing* (pp. 1–47). San Diego: Academic Press.

Rosenfeld, J. P., Cantwell, B., Nasman, V. T., Wojdac, V., Ivanov, S., and Mazzeri, L. (1988). A modified, event-related potential-based guilty knowledge test. *International Journal of Neuroscience*, 42, 157–161.

Runkel, J. E. (1936). Luria's motor method and word association in the study of deception. *Journal of General Psychology*, 15, 23–27.

Seymour, T. L., Seifert, C. M, Shafto, M. G., and Mosmann, A. L. (2000). Using response time measures to assess "guilty knowledge." *Journal of Applied Psychology*, 85(1), 30–37.

Thoneey J., Kanachi, M., Sasaki, H., and Hatayama, T. (2005). Eye blinking as a lie-detection index in an emotionally arousing context. *Tohoku Psychologica Folia*, 64, 58–67.

Timm, H. W. (1989). Methodological considerations affecting the utility of incorporating innocent subjects into the design of guilty knowledge polygraph experiments. *Polygraph*, 18(3), 143–157.

Uruno, F., and Narai, J. (1956). An experimental study of lie detection. *Reports of the National Institute of Police Science*, 117–129. Text in Japanese, English abstract.

Verschuere, B., Crombez, G., De Clercq, A., and Koster, E. H. W. (2004). Autonomic and behavioral responding to concealed information: differentiating orienting and defensive responses. *Psychophysiology*, 41(3), 461–466.

Warner, W. (2005). Polygraph testing. *FBI Law Enforcement Bulletin*, 74(4), 10–13.

Wilson, G. T. (1981). Relationships between experimental and clinical psychology: the case of behavior therapy. *International Journal of Psychology*, 16(4), 323–341.

Winslow, R. (2009) *A Comparative Criminology Tour of the World*. www-rohan. sdsu.edu/faculty/rwinslow/asia_pacific/japan.html. San Diego State University. Retrieved September 28, 2009.

Yamamura, T. and Miyata, Y. (1990). Development of the polygraph technique in Japan for detection of deception. *Forensic Science International*, 44, 257–271.

9 Validity of the Concealed Information Test in realistic contexts

Eitan Elaad

Overview: Earlier field studies on the Concealed Information Test (CIT) are reviewed from a new perspective. Limitations of the studies as well as factors that account for the relatively large false negative rates are discussed. Two types of CIT practice, the pre-interrogation practice, which is mainly used in Japan, and the interrogation practice are identified and discussed. The advantages of each type of practice are described and suggestions for improvement are made.

The Concealed Information Test, also labeled the Guilty Knowledge Test (Lykken, 1959), is a method of psychophysiological detection that identifies information that knowledgeable (guilty) people do not wish to reveal and ignorant (innocent) people are unable to reveal (see Lykken, 1974, 1998).

Studies conducted in laboratory settings have indicated that the CIT is a highly valid method for differentiating between guilty and innocent participants. For example, Ben-Shakhar and Elaad (2003) conducted a meta-analysis of CIT laboratory studies using electrodermal responses and showed that under optimal conditions (i.e., using a mock crime procedure, motivational instructions, deceptive verbal response to the critical items, and at least five CIT questions) the CIT is highly efficient (i.e., the average effect size estimated under these conditions was 3.12 and the area under the ROC curve was 0.95).

However, field conditions are often less than optimal and typically differ drastically from the experimental conditions. It is therefore absolutely essential to conduct field studies that will provide a more comprehensive picture on the validity of the CIT in its forensic application. Two studies assumed this challenge and made an attempt to estimate CIT validity in real-life situations. The studies were conducted in the early 1990s (Elaad 1990; Elaad *et al.*, 1992) and are reviewed hereafter from a new perspective. This review highlights several concerns regarding the CIT and suggests solutions based on the most recent CIT research.

The efficiency of skin resistance responses in real-life criminal CIT

A first attempt to study the efficiency of electrodermal responses (Skin Resistance Responses – SRR) in real-life criminal interrogations was made by Elaad (1990). For the purpose of the study, a sample of ninety-eight actual CIT criminal records was drawn from the pool of verified polygraph tests of the Israel Police Scientific Interrogation Unit. All records involved CIT examinations conducted between 1979 and 1985. Each record consisted of between one and six CIT questions (M = 2.04, SD = 1.19); each question presented four to eight multiple-choice items (M = 6.89, SD = 0.89), and was repeated two to four times (M = 3.28, SD = 0.62). Forty-eight records (with a total of 100 CIT questions) were drawn from the pool of verified deceptive examinees, and fifty records (with a total of 100 CIT questions) were drawn from a pool of examinees whose innocence was subsequently verified by the confession of another person (for more details see Elaad, 1990).

In a follow-up study (Elaad et al., 1992), a second sample of eighty actual CIT criminal polygraph records, taken from police investigations conducted between 1985 and 1991, was drawn from the pool of verified polygraph tests of the Israel Police Scientific Interrogation Unit. Each record consisted of between one and six CIT questions (M = 1.80, SD = 0.91); each question presented from four to eight multiple-choice items (M = 6.19, SD = 0.66), and was repeated two to four times (M = 3.25, SD = 0.53). The sampling was random with the exception that one-half of the records (with a total of seventy-six CIT questions) were drawn from the pool of polygraph records of verified deceptive examinees and one-half (with a total of sixty-eight CIT questions) were drawn from a similar pool of innocent examinees. Again, verification of guilt or innocence was based on the confession of the perpetrator in each case (a more detailed description of the sample appears in Elaad et al., 1992). Since both studies were in complete agreement concerning the SRR identification rates for both guilty and innocent examinees, both studies are discussed below as a single project.

The largest SRR amplitude within 10 s following the presentation of each CIT item was measured in millimeters on the pattern recorded by the polygraph SRR pen. Scoring was made by a polygraph examiner who was unaware of the correct item. Each scored SRR amplitude was transformed into a standard score relative to the mean and standard deviation of each repetition after the exclusion of the first (buffer) response.

Table 9.1 *Frequencies and cumulative relative
frequencies of mean standardized scores computed on
SRR to critical items in the field studies*

Mean	Guilty		Innocent	
Z scale	Freq.	Cum. %	Freq.	Cum. %
1.00+	19	22	0	0
0.9 to 1.00	4	26	1	1
0.8 to 0.9	2	28	0	1
0.7 to 0.8	10	40	1	2
0.6 to 0.7	6	47	2	4
0.5 to 0.6	8	56	3	8
0.4 to 0.5	6	63	1	9
0.3 to 0.4	1	64	6	16
0.2 to 0.3	8	73	3	19
0.1 to 0.2	5	78	7	27
0.0 to 0.1	5	84	4	31
−0.1 to 0.0	4	89	9	41
−0.2 to −0.1	0	89	12	54
−0.3 to −0.2	4	93	7	62
−0.4 to −0.3	3	97	7	70
−0.5 to −0.4	0	97	7	78
−0.6 to −0.5	1	98	10	89
−0.6-	2	100	10	100
	88		90	

Table 9.1 displays the standardized skin resistance responses to correct items which were averaged for each examinee across questions and
repetitions, yielding one new index for each examinee. The frequency
distributions of the mean Z scores were constructed separately for guilty
and innocent examinees.

A receiver operating characteristic (ROC) curve was generated for
the SRR by comparing the distribution of the mean Z scores computed
for guilty examinees with the distribution of the mean Z scores computed for innocent examinees, across all Zi values. The computed area
was 0.841, with a 95 percent confidence interval of 0.783–0.899 (see
Bamber, 1975 for a description of a method for estimating the variance
of the area statistics). The area under the ROC curve is a statistic that
assumes a value between 0 and 1. An area of 0.5 indicates that the two
distributions are undifferentiated. An area of 1 indicates that there is no
overlap between the two distributions. Ben-Shakhar and Elaad (2003)
reported that the mean area computed across all mock crime studies
in the meta-analysis was 0.872. The ROC analysis indicates that SRR

amplitude is a good indicator of concealed information (the area under the ROC curve is significantly larger than the chance area of 0.50).

To further compare the present field studies with the experimental studies reviewed by Ben-Shakhar and Elaad (2003), the d (a statistic that describes the strength of the effect and reflects the distance in standard deviation units between the centers of the guilty and innocent distributions) and r (a point-biserial correlation between the detection measure and the criterion of guilt vs. innocence) values of the field studies were computed from the published results. Note that these results are based exclusively on the electrodermal measures. Across the two field studies, $d = 1.49$ and r = 0.60. These values are similar to the d and r values obtained for the personal item studies in the meta-analysis but lower than those obtained for the mock-crime studies.

Table 9.1 presents the proportions of cases from the guilty-examinee distribution and from the innocent-examinee distribution that elicited a mean Z score greater than any pre-determined cutoff point (Zi). As indicated in Table 9.1, the 0.7 standard deviation cutoff point produced a hit rate of 40 percent for guilty examinees and a correct detection rate of 98 percent for the innocents. An alternative cutoff point set at 0.4 standard deviations yielded a hit rate of 63 percent (an increase of 23 percent over the hit rate obtained with the previous decision rule) and a correct detection rate of 91 percent for innocent examinees (a 7 percent decrease). It can be seen that as hit rate increases, the rate of false positive decisions also increases.

Efficiency of the Respiration Line Length responses in the criminal CIT

Elaad et al. (1992) used another measure, Respiration Line Length (RLL), to estimate the efficiency of the CIT in real-life situations. The line length of the curvilinear respiration pattern on polygraph paper charts was measured using a video camera and a digital frame store card with which the video image was digitized.

The line length of the curvilinear respiration pattern was measured for each item and was then converted into Z scores relative to the mean and standard deviation of the items in each CIT question (for more details see Elaad et al., 1992).

It appeared that the RLL was an efficient index for the detection of guilt and unlike most experimental findings the RLL and SRR were equally efficient in discriminating between guilty and innocent examinees. The false negative errors computed for the RLL were similar to those computed for the SRR. However, the integration of RLL and

SRR into a combined measure that traded false negative decisions with true negatives, yielded an increase in the rate of correct detections for guilty suspects from either 40 percent (SRR) or 42.5 percent (RLL) to 62.5 percent, and an increase in the rate of false positive decisions from 2.5 percent to 5 percent. Still, in comparison to experimental results, the false negative error rate in real-life CIT application is high.

A Japanese field study

Hira and Furumitsu (2002) reported results of a field study of the Japanese CIT application. Guilt was based on confessions and other physical evidence and innocence was established by the confession of the actual perpetrator. Hira and Furumitsu reported on fifty-two guilty and thirty-two innocent examinees for whom the criterion was available. Using a variety of respiration, SRR, and cardiovascular measures, they conducted a question analysis. According to Hira (personal communication, 2009), between four and nine CIT questions were presented to each examinee with an average of about six questions. Overall, a 74 percent detection rate for guilty examinees (233 of 315 questions presented to guilty examinees) and a perfect detection rate for innocents were observed. Using only SRR, these researchers detected crime-related information in 62 percent of the questions presented to guilty examinees while maintaining the perfect detection rate for innocents.

Elaad and his colleagues (Elaad 1990; Elaad et al., 1992) performed a similar question analysis using the SRR measure on ninety-eight CIT questions administered to guilty suspects as part of their interrogation, and 100 CIT questions presented to innocent examinees. They reported 47 percent correct detection of crime-related items in questions administered to guilty examinees, and 91 percent correct classification of CIT questions presented to innocents.

Limitations of the field studies

In the Israeli field studies, CIT records were drawn *ex post facto*, and the test situation could not have been planned in advance. Thus, factors such as time of administration (the CIT always followed a standard Comparison Questions Test [CQT]; for details see Reid and Inbau, 1977), or the examiner's awareness of the critical information while conducting the test, were inherent in the situation. There is, however, no evidence that examiner's awareness increased response magnitude in the test. On the contrary, Elaad (1997) showed that participants in an experimental setting responded less to the critical information of which the examiner was aware, compared to when the examiner had no knowledge of the critical information.

Inherent in the Israeli field situation was also the small number of CIT questions that were administered (an average of about two). In their review, Ben-Shakhar and Elaad (2003) warned against the use of less than five CIT questions.

Another major problem faced by field validity studies concerns the criterion for guilt or innocence. The described field studies used confessions as an external criterion. The assumption was that a confession confirms the guilt of the confessor and exonerated other examinees from involvement in the investigated crime. The confession criterion has its shortcomings, the most prominent of which is vulnerability to sample selection bias (Iacono, 1991). The probability that a suspect will confess may depend on the CIT results, in that an outcome of guilt may encourage interrogation efforts to induce a confession. On the other hand, an outcome of innocence may convince the police interrogator to dismiss suspicions against the suspect. This may lead to an underestimation of the false negative rate. Furthermore, one cannot exclude the possibility of false confessions. Only the use of a solid criterion for truth, under highly realistic conditions, such as that used by Ginton et al. (1982), can resolve this problem, although their procedure caused a considerable dropout of guilty participants before the test was taken.

What may account for the large false negative rates found in the field studies?

Experimental conditions are often based on simulations (i.e., mock crime experiments) in which participants designated as guilty are required to commit a mock crime (i.e., to steal something from a certain place), whereas participants assigned as innocents do not commit the crime. Then, the CIT is administered and an attempt is made to correctly classify the guilty and innocent participants. In this case, the experimenter often guarantees that all participants learned all the critical items of information and remember them when they take the CIT. Participants are tested immediately afterwards, and therefore failure to notice critical items or loss of memory are not playing a major role in the identification of critical information by guilty participants.

In real life, however, things are entirely different. The crime scene is more complex than the experimental setup, and due to time pressure and stress guilty suspects may fail to notice some crime-related details. Other crime-related details may be noticed but not stored in memory.

Furthermore, real-life CITs may take place weeks or even months after the commission of the criminal act and consequently memory of items that were processed during the crime may decay (Elaad, 1990). Elaad *et al.* (1992) presented an example of a guilty suspect who was tested regarding the color of the scarf he used to strangle his victim. The suspect did not show differential responses to the critical color and it was assumed that the color of the scarf was overlooked or forgotten. However, the same suspect responded differentially to a similar question about the color of the blanket with which the body was covered. This pair of questions is typical of real-life CIT situations, in which perception and retention of information depend on various uncontrolled factors (i.e., mood, time pressure, personal interest in the information, the time elapsed from the crime to the test).

In this respect the study by Carmel *et al.* (2003) is important. Carmel *et al.* conducted an experiment that manipulated the encoding of the critical information and the time of the test. Two types of items were included in this study, central and peripheral. Carmel *et al.* (2003) demonstrated that central items were better recalled after one week and elicited greater SCRs than peripheral items.

The time of testing may also account for the large false negative rates. Many examinees in the Israeli field studies were tested weeks and even months after the crime. Elaad (1997) showed that some Israeli participants, who were tested between two days and one week after committing a mock crime, failed to respond to one or two of four critical items in the CIT.

In the study conducted by Carmel *et al.* (2003) they used a mock crime in which participants were required to steal a CD-ROM. One-half of the participants were assigned to a typical unrealistic mock-crime procedure in which they were informed about all the critical items in advance, were subsequently asked to name all the relevant details, and were prompted of any details they did not recall. The other participants were assigned to a more realistic procedure in which they were not informed about the relevant crime details and were not reminded of the details when they failed to remember them. Furthermore, in the realistic condition participants were given limited time to complete the theft. One-half of the participants were tested immediately after they committed the mock crime and the second half were tested one week later. Carmel *et al.* (2003) reported that the more realistic condition was associated with inferior recall of relevant items and less efficient SCR detection than the standard mock-crime condition. Finally the realistic-delayed condition was associated with lower detection efficiency compared with all other experimental conditions.

In contrast, Hira *et al.* (2001) conducted a mock crime that used P300 event-related potential (ERP) as the detection measure, and reported that all nine guilty participants were correctly identified both immediately after committing a mock crime and one month later. In a following study, Hira *et al.* (2002) re-tested five of the nine original participants one year after the experiment and reported that all five responded to the critical items.

The number of CIT questions that are being used may also account for the large false negative error rates obtained in field studies. The mean number of questions used in the Israeli field studies (2.0 in Elaad, 1990 and 1.8 in Elaad *et al.*, 1992) was rather small. Ben-Shakhar and Elaad (2003) indicated that increasing the number of relevant items (five or more) in experimental conditions is associated with enhanced CIT detection. However, the need to increase the number of CIT items may stand in contrast to the necessity to select only proper CIT items. Proper items are details of the crime that were kept secret from the mass media and unauthorized people, and even from the interrogators who conducted the interrogation, so that completely ignorant (innocent) suspects are unable to identify or even guess these details from segmental information they may have gathered on the crime. Proper items are also details of the crime that are likely to be perceived by knowledgeable (guilty) suspects while committing the crime, and be remembered when the CIT is administered. Therefore, the task of collecting a reasonable number of proper CIT items is not a trivial one.

Nevertheless, Elaad and Ben-Shakhar (1997) showed that even a single CIT question with a sufficient number of repetitions can efficiently discriminate between guilty and innocent examinees. Elaad and Ben-Shakhar (1997) conducted two experiments in which a CIT, based on four different questions, each repeated three times, was compared with a single CIT question repeated twelve times. Both experiments revealed that similar detection efficiencies were obtained in these two conditions. Naturally, this raises the question of habituation with repetitions. Results revealed, however, that the decline of SCR responsiveness to the critical items with repetitions was small and not statistically significant. Furthermore, a considerable differentiation between guilty and innocent examinees was observed even in the final block of questions (the final three questions or repetitions). In a follow-up study (Ben-Shakhar and Elaad, 2002), the effect of question repetition and variation on the efficiency of the CIT based on electrodermal measures was re-examined. This time, personal information items were used instead of details of a mock-crime procedure, and a third experimental condition (twelve different questions, each presented once) was used. In this experiment, a clear advantage for the multiple-questions conditions emerged with the electrodermal measure. The results obtained with twelve different questions were impressive and almost perfect. However, statistically significant differentiation between guilty and innocent participants was observed under all three conditions. It was suggested that efforts should be made to increase the number of CIT questions. However, if only a small number of proper questions are available, increasing the number of repetitions may compensate, to some extent, for the lack of question variation. Further research is required to examine this issue in a real-life context. Similar results would imply that the CIT could be more widely applied.

The CITs reported in the Israeli field studies were administered after a standard CQT which is the most commonly used psychophysiological detection technique in North America and Israel, although it is more controversial than the CIT (e.g., Ben-Shakhar, 2002; Lykken, 1998; National Research Council, 2003; Raskin, 1989; Reid and Inbau, 1977). Thus, it is possible that, due to fatigue and habituation, guilty suspects' responses to the critical items were not as strong as one would have expected or desired.

Another explanation for the weak responses to critical items by guilty suspects is associated with possible countermeasure maneuvers. Studies conducted in experimental settings demonstrated that the CIT is vulnerable to physical countermeasures (e.g., pressing the toes against the floor when control items are presented) as well as mental countermeasures (e.g., counting numbers each time a control item appears). This vulnerability to countermeasures might increase false negative outcomes and impair the validity of the CIT (Ben-Shakhar and Dolev, 1996; Elaad and Ben-Shakhar, 1991; Honts *et al.*, 1996). Although we have no evidence that guilty examinees used countermeasures during the tests that were included in the field studies, it is possible that countermeasure attempts were responsible for some of the false negative outcomes that were obtained.

A recent study (Elaad and Ben-Shakhar, 2009) re-examined the countermeasure issue (for more details see Chapter 6 in this volume). In summary, guilty examinees were trained to apply either physical or mental countermeasures to distort the outcomes of the test. Results indicated that the application of physical countermeasures reduced electrodermal (SCR) accuracy. In contrast, SCR was relatively resistant to mental countermeasures. It was suggested that the two countermeasure types operate through different attentional mechanisms. Physical countermeasures may operate mainly on recognition to which SCR is relatively sensitive. Mental countermeasures may interfere with the slowly developed emotional association of the stimulus, which affects SCR to a lower degree. However more research is needed to corroborate this hypothesis.

Finally, retroactive or proactive misdeeds of some guilty suspects may have interfered with the salience of the crime-related information and with its recognition in the test (killing a man during a robbery should be very salient, whereas the act of stealing a purse may be obliterated in memory by other thefts).

Similarly, the knowledge of guilty suspects may have been blurred by their exposure to inaccurate details of the crime. Guilty suspects' knowledge may be distorted by rumors spread by other people, misinformation provided by the mass media, and segmental information conveyed during the interrogation. Potential distortion of existing knowledge during the interrogation is important and has not been adequately discussed in the context of the CIT (see Allen and Mertens, 2009; Amato-Henderson *et al.*, 1996). Based on the assumption that interrogators possess incomplete information of the crime, they are capable of instilling inaccurate information in guilty suspects. Research results on eyewitness memory support this notion. It has been demonstrated that there is a genuine risk that questioning – especially the way in which questions are worded – may distort eyewitness memory (Baddeley, 1999). For example, eyewitness memory may be manipulated by subtly introducing new and incorrect information during questioning (see Loftus, 1979, for a review). Such memory distortion may also affect guilty suspects' memory. When guilty suspects receive incorrect information of the crime from an authoritative figure (such as the interrogator) they may accept it as fact and revise their memory accordingly. Interrogators may unintentionally impart distorted information, or deliberately deliver false information in an attempt to intimidate a suspect into confessing.

How to improve detection of concealed information in guilty suspects?

The Japanese pre-interrogation practice of the CIT

An interesting attempt to overcome some of the above-mentioned limitations was made by the police in Japan. Hira and Furumitsu (2002, p. 20) noted the enormous amount of time the Japanese police devote to the preparation of CIT items, including a visit to the crime scene. Furthermore, Nakayama (2002, p. 52) indicated that police polygraph examiners meet the victim or witnesses to learn more about the event, if necessary. On average, six CIT questions are prepared for each examinee, which means that a small number of CIT items is not necessarily an integral part of the CIT procedure. Hira and Furumitsu (2002) further indicated that police examiners in Japan administer the CIT before the interrogation begins to prevent leakage of crime-related information during the interrogation. Finally, the standard Comparison Question Test (CQT) is not used in Japan and therefore the CIT is administered as a separate test (for a more elaborate description of the CIT usage in Japan, see Chapter 14 in this volume).

The results of the Japanese field study (Hira and Furumitsu, 2002) highlight the advantage of the pre-interrogation practice over the CIT which is applied during the interrogation. The early administration of the test minimizes inaccurate information delivered to guilty suspects and limits leakage of accurate information to innocents. It also reflects the careful collection of sufficient CIT items and the separate administration of CIT.

The pre-interrogation approach is used primarily for selection purposes where suspicion is not focused on the suspects. Its purpose is to identify suspects for further interrogation by a different interrogator as the Japanese polygraph examiners never interrogate suspects after the CIT (Hira and Furumitsu, 2002, p. 21). In this case, guilty (knowledgeable) suspects have the option to take the test hoping to be successful. Nevertheless, if they fail the test they still have time to think of an explanation for their CIT responses and adopt a proper line of defense (Granhag and Hartwig, 2008). Innocent (ignorant) suspects are confident that the CIT would exonerate them. The strategy of such innocent suspects is "to tell the truth like it happened" (see Granhag and Hartwig, 2008, p. 194).

The pre-interrogation practice is a legitimate CIT procedure that rests on sound theoretical ground. Similar to many experimental studies it follows the "cognitive approach" (Ben-Shakhar and Furedy, 1990) suggested by Lykken (1974). Lykken noted that, "For guilty subjects only, the 'correct' alternative will have a special significance, an added signal value which will tend to produce a stronger orienting reflex than that subject will show to other alternatives" (p. 728). Hence, the main purpose of the pre-interrogation CIT is to look for the individual's knowledge rather than the individual's guilt (see Chapter 14 in this volume).

However, the pre-interrogation practice cannot replace the use of the CIT as part of the interrogation when suspicion is focused on the suspect and additional information about his/her guilt or innocence is necessary to advance the investigation. The interrogation practice of the CIT is more complex than the pre-interrogation practice and has received less attention by researchers. Factors such as the state of mind of suspects who perceive being under focused suspicion, personality features of the suspects, and their emotions during the test may be important. Guilty suspects who undergo the CIT in the more advanced stages of the interrogation have already adopted a line of defense which has not yet convinced the suspicious interrogators (Meissner and Kassin, 2002). They may feel that the CIT is their last opportunity to convince the interrogators of their innocence. This may result in either despair or in enhanced motivation to beat the test. Innocent suspects who experienced disbelief during the interrogation may be concerned that the CIT examiner may not realize that they are innocent and thus may become frustrated (Kassin, 2005). However, assuming that innocent suspects are ignorant of the crime-related information, their prospects to yield truthful outcomes in the CIT are good as demonstrated by the Israeli field studies. Future research should pay more attention to the interrogation practice of the CIT and to its underlying factors.

The formulation of proper CIT questions

Hira and Furumitsu (2002) emphasized the enormous amount of time the Japanese police devote to the preparation of proper CIT items. While the Japanese police make this effort, it is not obvious that law enforcement agencies in other countries are willing or capable to follow the Japanese example. Furthermore, using the CIT-interrogation practice, guilty suspects may receive inaccurate information while being interrogated and may fail to remember some critical information due to the time lag between the event and the test. All this may limit the number of crime-related items that the guilty examinee is aware of. To assist in formulating proper CIT items, the following questions should be asked: (1) Is the examinee interested in the subject raised by the CIT question? (2) Was the critical information actively acquired by the guilty person? (3) Were the critical items prepared by the guilty person in advance of the crime? (4) Is it unlikely that retroactive or proactive misdeeds of the culprit may interfere with the salience of the crime-relevant information? (5) Are the items in the test distinctive enough to be recognized by the guilty examinee? Positive answers to all these questions may indicate that the CIT item is a proper CIT item.

Podlesny (1993) raised the difficulty of gathering a sufficient number of proper CIT items to be used in the test. Podlesny estimated that the CIT could have been used in only 13.1 percent of FBI cases for which polygraph tests were used. This estimate is based on the assumption that at least four different CIT questions are required to construct a proper CIT battery.

Leakage of information

The results of the field studies suggest that leakage of crime-related information did not affect the results of the CIT administered to innocent examinees by the Israeli and the Japanese police. There is, however, another leakage problem that has been neglected: the leakage of incorrect information to guilty participants, which might distort their perception of the crime. Techniques of deception (e.g., good cop/bad cop) are common in police interrogations (Leo, 1992), and are designed to elicit additional information from suspects. In this context, interrogators may subtly introduce new and incorrect information about the crime to intimidate and extract a confession from suspects. This incorrect information may undermine suspects' confidence in the information they possess about the crime, and imply that the interrogator knows a lot more than they actually do. Note that the interrogator is in a position of authority, and some guilty suspects may conform to authority and distort their knowledge accordingly. All the guilty examinees in the Israeli field studies underwent intensive interrogation before they were tested with the polygraph. Although we do not know whether or not incorrect information was conveyed to them during the interrogation, we cannot exclude the possibility that some incorrect information might have been responsible for the large false negative error rate. To limit interrogator's deliberate delivering of false information in an attempt to intimidate a suspect into confessing, interrogators must become aware of the potential damage to the investigation by providing such incorrect information.

Concluding remarks

The CIT procedure is the single psychophysiological detection technique that enjoys wide acceptance as a scientifically based technique. It is grounded in well-established research findings and theory. The advantages and weaknesses of the CIT were discussed and it is suggested that the CIT is a highly valid procedure when properly executed. As such it has the potential to become an important aid in criminal investigations.

This is true for both pre-interrogation and interrogation CIT practices. As to the interrogation CIT, it may be suggested that two important features separate guilty and innocent suspects who experience the burden of suspicion: (1) differential knowledge of crime-related details, and (2) a different state of mind (see Granhag and Hartwig, 2008). Uninformed innocent examinees are truthful concerning all CIT items and therefore are not motivated to deceive or conceal information. Guilt is a state of mind that encourages coping behavior. From the examinee's perspective, the polygraph examiner uses his/her skills to challenge the guilty examinee whose interest is to produce an outcome of innocence. To achieve this aim, guilty examinees must undermine the test and force the examiner to make mistakes in their favor. However, guilty examinees are well aware that they confront a skilled and well-equipped professional and that their odds of "beating" the test are low. The "illusion of transparency" that causes liars to assume that their lies are more easily detected than they actually are, enhances this feeling (Gilovich *et al.*, 1998). To beat the odds, guilty examinees must remain alert and actively cope with the threats (i.e., the critical items). Coping behavior requires increased attention of the examinee to the critical items, which is accompanied with enhanced significance of these items, and increased differential responsiveness to the critical items. As a result, a high level of detection rate is expected. For reasons that have been specified in this chapter, the potential of the CIT conducted during the interrogation was not realized in the field studies and detection efficiency of guilty suspects in the CIT was low. Future research should address the different motivations of guilty and innocent participants and examine the differential effects of these motivation types on the efficiency of the CIT after eliminating all interfering factors. Such new knowledge may contribute to the CIT accuracy.

REFERENCES

Allen, J. B. and Mertens, R. (2009). Limitations to the detection of deception: true and false recollections are poorly distinguished using an event-related potential procedure. *Social Neuroscience*, 4, 473–490.

Amato-Henderson, S. L., Honts, C. R., and Plaud, J. J. (1996). Effects of misinformation on the Concealed Knowledge Test. *Psychophysiology*, 33, S18 (abstract).

Baddeley, A. D. (1999). *Essentials of Human Memory*. Hove: Psychology Press.

Bamber, D. (1975). The area under the ordinal dominance graph and the area below the receiver operating characteristic graph. *Journal of Mathematical Psychology*, 12, 378–415.

Ben-Shakhar, G. (2002). A critical review of the control question test (CQT). In M. Kleiner (ed.), *Handbook of Polygraph Testing* (pp. 103–126). San Diego: Academic Press.

Ben-Shakhar, G., and Dolev, K. (1996). Psychophysiological detection through the guilty knowledge technique: effects of mental countermeasures. *Journal of Applied Psychology*, 81, 273–281.

Ben-Shakhar, G., and Elaad, E. (2002). Effects of questions' repetition and variation on the efficiency of the guilty knowledge test: a reexamination. *Journal of Applied Psychology*, 87, 972–977.

Ben-Shakhar, G., and Elaad, E. (2003). The validity of psychophysiological detection of information with the Guilty Knowledge Test: a meta-analytic review. *Journal of Applied Psychology*, 88, 131–151.

Ben-Shakhar, G., and Furedy, J. J. (1990). *Theories and Applications in the Detection of Deception*. New York: Springer-Verlag.

Carmel, D., Dayan, E., Naveh, A., Raveh, O., and Ben-Shakhar, G. (2003). Estimating the validity of the guilty knowledge test from simulated experiments: the external validity of mock crime studies. *Journal of Experimental Psychology: Applied*, 9, 261–269.

Elaad, E. (1990). Detection of guilty knowledge in real-life criminal investigations. *Journal of Applied Psychology*, 75, 521–529.

(1997). Polygraph examiner awareness of crime-relevant information and the guilty knowledge test. *Law and Human Behavior*, 21, 107–120.

Elaad, E., and Ben-Shakhar, G. (1991). Effects of mental countermeasures on psychophysiological detection in the Guilty Knowledge Test. *International Journal of Psychophysiology*, 11(2), 99–108.

Elaad, E., and Ben-Shakhar G. (1997). Effects of item repetitions and variations on the efficiency of the guilty knowledge test. *Psychophysiology*, 34, 587–596.

Elaad, E., and Ben-Shakhar, G. (2009). Countering countermeasures in the Concealed Information Test using covert respiration measures. *Applied Psychophysiology and Biofeedback*, 34, 197–209.

Elaad, E., Ginton, A., and Jungman, N. (1992). Detection measures in real-life criminal guilty knowledge tests. *Journal of Applied Psychology*, 77, 757–767.

Gilovich, T., Savitsky, K., and Medvec, V. (1998). The illusion of transparency: biased assessments of others' ability to read one's emotional states. *Journal of Personality and Social Psychology*, 75, 332–346.

Ginton, A., Daie, N., Elaad, E., and Ben-Shakhar, G. (1982). A method for evaluating the use of the polygraph in a real-life situation. *Journal of Applied Psychology*, 67, 131–137.

Granhag, P. A., and Hartwig, M. (2008). A new theoretical perspective on deception detection: on the psychology of instrumental mind-reading. *Psychology, Crime & Law*, 14, 189–200.

Hira, S., and Furumitsu, I. (2002). Polygraphic examinations in Japan: application of the guilty knowledge test in forensic investigations. *International Journal of Police Science and Management*, 4, 16–27.

Hira, S., Sasaki, M., Matsuda, T., Furumitsu, I., and Furedy, J. J. (2001). Pz-recorded P300 is highly accurate and sensitive to a memorial manipulation in an objective laboratory guilty knowledge test. *Psychophysiology*, 38, S50.

(2002). A year after the commission of a mock crime, the P300 amplitudes, but not reaction time, are sensitive guilty knowledge test indicators. *Psychophysiology*, 39, S42.

Honts, C. R., Devitt, M. K., Winbush, M., and Kircher, J. C. (1996). Mental and physical countermeasures reduce the accuracy of the concealed knowledge test. *Psychophysiology*, 33, 84–92.

Iacono, W. G. (1991). Can we determine the accuracy of polygraph tests? In J. R. Jennings, P. K. Ackles, and M. G. H. Coles (eds.), *Advances in Psychophysiology*, Volume 4. Greenwich, CT: JAI Press.

Kassin, S. M. (2005). On the psychology of confessions – does innocence put innocents at risk? *American Psychologist*, 60, 215–228.

Leo, R. A. (1992). From coercion to deception: the changing nature of police interrogation in America. *Crime, Law and Social Change*, 18, 35–59.

Loftus, E. F. (1979). *Eyewitness Testimony*. Cambridge, MA: Harvard University Press.

Lykken, D. T. (1959). The GSR in the detection of guilt. *Journal of Applied Psychology*, 43, 385–388.

(1974). Psychology and the lie detection industry. *America Psychologist*, 29, 225–239.

(1998). *A Tremor in the Blood. Uses and Abuses of the Lie Detector*, 2nd edn. New York: Plenum Trade.

Meissner, C. A., and Kassin, S. M. (2002). "He's guilty!": investigator bias in judgments of truth and deception. *Law and Human Behavior*, 26, 469–480.

Nakayama, M. (2002). Practical use of the concealed information test for criminal investigation in Japan. In M. Kleiner (ed.), *Handbook of Polygraph Testing* (pp. 49–86). San Diego: Academic Press.

National Research Council (2003). *The Polygraph and Lie Detection*. Committee to Review the Scientific Evidence on the Polygraph, Division of Behavioral and Social Sciences and Education. Washington, DC: The National Academies Press.

Podlesny, J. A. (1993). Is the guilty knowledge polygraph technique applicable in criminal investigations? A review of FBI case records. *Crime Laboratory Digest*, 20, 59–63.

Raskin, D. C. (1989). Polygraph techniques for the detection of deception. In D. C. Raskin (ed.) *Psychological Methods in Criminal Investigation and Evidence* (pp. 274–296). New York: Springer Publishing Company.

Reid, J. E., and Inbau, F. E. (1977). *Truth and Deception: The Polygraph ("Lie Detector") Technique*, 2nd edn. Baltimore: Williams and Wilkins.

10   Leakage of information to
innocent suspects

*M. T. Bradley, Clair A. Barefoot and Andrea M.
Arsenault*

Overview: A key assumption of the CIT is that the relevant information is known by guilty suspects but not by innocent suspects. Leakage of the relevant information to innocent suspects thereby presents a conundrum for those involved with the development and administration of tests designed to discover concealed information. Leakage is potentially important as it may not be possible to discriminate responding by innocent and guilty suspects to leaked information. This would result in erroneous classification of the innocent suspects. This chapter examines theory and empirical results to better understand: (1) the issues involved in leakage; (2) to ascertain whether situations involving leakage can contribute to a better understanding of information detection; and (3) to explore possible ways of either managing or preventing leakage so that it does not contaminate information detection situations.

The nature of CITs

Behavioral, physiological, emotional, and cognitive reactions to items of information can be used to associate individuals with specific knowledge. A great deal of attention has been paid to make use of these reactions to discover who has knowledge of issues under investigation. In the investigatory and criminal realm, knowledgeable people, however, typically attempt to conceal their knowledge. Unfortunately, most people, including those who routinely engage in deception detection, are not very accurate in discerning if there is hidden information (Bond and DePaulo, 2006; Sato and Nihie, 2009). Physiologically the situation is different: the reactions are less readily under conscious control. They are not necessarily simple but have been well studied and described. Reactions of physiological systems to questions concerning the events under investigation may allow the discernment of knowledge. These are the elements of the CIT.

Challenges for the CIT

CITs are recognition memory tests. Ideally, guilty suspects have been exposed to information, remember it and when later presented with it in a CIT, react to it. On the face of it, CITs are seen in a category of the simplest of discrimination tests but that apparent simplicity is illusionary. When the test is considered more closely issues with perception and memory arise. On the one hand, not all guilty suspects may have seen and remembered all relevant information. Practitioners recognize that particular criminals or the crime situation itself may involve memory issues. Considerable time may have elapsed between the crime under investigation and an interrogation. In that time, a repeat offender may have proactive and retroactive interference with details from other crimes. Drug and/or alcohol use may have been involved to create both perceptual and memory problems (Bradley and Ainsworth, 1984). These issues are discussed in Chapters 8 and 9 of this volume. On the other hand, the police may not be able to control or know what information is available to innocent suspects. This issue is the leakage problem dealt with in this chapter. The problem could result in two effects. In the worst cases: (1) innocent individuals have knowledge of key items of the crime but are not able to explain why they know that information; and (2) guilty suspects may explain their knowledge as a consequence of the leakage of information surrounding the investigation. Just how disruptive is leakage for the CIT?

Early theory on leakage

Lykken (1959, 1974), in his early thinking, assumed that knowledge of key items and their relation to the crime would result in the construction of a simple cognitive model such that the recognition of items in the model would promote an orienting response (OR; Sokolov, 1963) with its attendant physiological responsiveness. The OR is the response to novel (e.g., a surprise) and/or significant stimuli (e.g., "John, this is the police!"). The OR is associated with a number of behavioral and physiological changes: head-turning, increased skin conductance, a decline in heart rate, and respiratory suppression. In theory, critical items in a CIT are special only for the guilty examinee but not for the innocent suspect. Empirical data have generally supported the OR theory of the Concealed Information Test (Verschuere *et al.*, 2004). When items are known by the innocent, whether through leakage, social knowledge, or logic, the innocent may also show enhanced ORs to the critical items. Lykken (1981) suggested that if there was concern that information had been widely circulated, one option was to avoid testing.

A review of research on leakage

Giesen and Rollison (1980) examined whether suspects who had knowledge from another context were less responsive in the CIT than guilty suspects. The "guilty" group was given a scenario in which they committed a murder and actually burned a bloodstained (red-ink) picture. The "informed innocent" group did not enact the mock crime, but was given a story with the same details described in a non-criminal context. Accuracy rates were very high, with 96 percent of the guilty suspects judged guilty. More to the point of leakage, none of the innocent suspects (0 percent) were differentially responsive enough to key items to be judged incorrectly as guilty. This study seems to indicate that information alone does not result in CIT responding. This is in direct contrast to Lykken's assumptions. However, a close examination of this study shows that some factors may have operated in a way to optimize scores for guilty suspects and minimize them for innocent suspects. For both groups, each scenario was read three times. However, for the guilty suspects, the information was direct, integrated, and coherently connected to the subsequent questions. The scenario could be summarized in a sentence or two: "You shot the man with a gun at 6:30 who was using a photo to blackmail you for $10,000 when he grabbed you by the neck. You had to burn the photo because of his bloodstains." The events in the innocent story were not as well integrated. The key details were more or less contained within the following subscripts each of which are their own scenario: the winning of an expensive vacation, the incidental chance purchase of a gun, blood drawn by a thorn on a rose daubed by a Kleenex, the burning of a newspaper ad which was really a coded CIA message, an airplane ride holding the hand of a romantic man. Specifically, in the innocent scenario there was no liquid (blood) stained picture and the burning of a picture never happened. These were critical items in the crime story and represent one-third of the key items in questions. From this perspective, the guilty suspects were questioned on items that were clearly and unambiguously connected to the story, whereas innocent suspects could have been misled on what the key items were. No post-experimental memory test was presented to verify that innocent suspects remembered the key items from their arguably more complex story. Leakage – as defined by exposure of the relevant information – certainly occurred for innocent suspects, but the leaked information may not have been integrated into a retrievable memory model.

Stern *et al.* (1981) replicated the study of Giesen and Rollison (1980). Guilty suspects were detected with 96 percent accuracy, and 11.5 percent of innocent informed suspects were misclassified. Again it seems that Lykken could be wrong with his interpretation that mere knowledge would be sufficient to evoke responding. On the other hand, the study by Stern *et al.* faces the same methodological problems as the one by Giesen and Rollison: there was no memory test, the innocent story was less compelling and inherently more complex, and for the informed innocent suspects the key items were not unambiguously cued by the CIT questions. For example, the key item "snake venom" that was used in the mock murder, was presented as a cure for multiple sclerosis in the story for the informed innocents.

Moreover, both studies had suspects remain silent during questioning. This is a condition that can result in a reduction in detection (Elaad and Ben-Shakhar, 1989; Furedy and Ben-Shakhar, 1991; Horneman and O'Gorman, 1985). Silence apparently did not reduce the successful detection of guilty suspects, but perhaps it did for members of the innocent groups. They may have been minimally involved and may not even have had a reason to pay attention during questioning. Indeed, Ben-Shakhar and Elaad (2003) in their meta-analysis suggested that lack of deceptive verbal responding in non-involving paradigms results in low levels of differential physiological responding. The reason for silence in the above studies was to avoid the problem of innocent suspects having to lie by saying "no" to information coincidentally involved in the crime. Innocent suspects that recognize the key items may feel uncomfortable denying overtly of being aware of them.

Bradley and Warfield (1984) explored a method that allowed informed innocent suspects to be non-deceptive while making overt denials of relevant knowledge. They called this modification of the CIT the Guilty Actions Test (GAT). It retains the key element of the CIT (i.e., association of the perpetrator with relevant knowledge), but now includes action with that information. This was achieved through changing "*Do you know if* (information foils and key item)?" to a form of "*Did you* (engage in some action; i.e., shoot, take) (information foils and key item)?" Informed innocent suspects still have the relevant knowledge, but are no longer lying in their overt denial. This approach was explored in a series of studies (Bradley *et al.*, 1996; Bradley and Rettinger, 1992; Bradley and Warfield, 1984). In contrast to the previous studies, relevant information was related to the crime for both guilty and innocent groups. The guilty, the witness, and the informed innocent groups all had information explicitly related to the crime. Only a "cleaning" group did not; they encountered the relevant information

in an innocent cleaning context. Memory for the relevant information was assured by rewarding participants for each item remembered
in a post-experimental assessment. It was found that guilty suspects
were more detectable (collectively at the 94 percent level with a "no"
response) than informed innocent suspects. Informed innocent suspects may have been less reactive than guilty suspects because (1) they
were not deceptive on key items or (2) they did not connect key items to
the crime. Informed innocent suspects, however, were more responsive
than innocent unaware participants and a false positive rate between
25 percent and 75 percent was found in informed innocent suspects. In
agreement with Lykken's early reasoning, there was a knowledge effect,
and caution seems required if leakage is suspected.

Beyond knowledge alone

The differences in reactivity on the CIT between the guilty and informed
innocent suspects suggest that (1) knowledge is a necessary component and sufficient to evoke responding, but also (2) that other factors
such as guilt or deception may augment responding (Ben-Shakhar and
Elaad, 2003).

Ben-Shakhar et al. (1999) also explored the effectiveness of the GAT.
They examined three groups: guilty participants who had committed
the theft of a small amount of money and a jewel, innocent informed
suspects who were informed of the mock crime information prior to
their interrogation, and uninformed innocent participants. A GAT
was used in which participants had been instructed to answer "no" to
items. This study also featured target tasks with the purpose of drawing the attention of informed innocent suspects. The idea was that their
involvement with the targets would reduce responding to known key
items without affecting detection rates for guilty participants. With 79
percent, guilty suspects were more detectable than innocent informed
participants (42 percent false positive rate) who in turn were more
detectable than uninformed participants (10 percent false positive rate).
This study supports the findings by Bradley and colleagues. Again it
was not simply knowledge that determined responsiveness. Even so,
Lykken's knowledge approach has to be considered important as 42
percent of innocent aware suspects were misclassified as guilty.

Bradley et al. (1996) directly compared the CIT with the GAT. This
comparison allows for differentiation between knowledge and deception and knowledge alone. In this study, guilty and informed innocent
suspects read the material three times and remembered virtually all ten
of the relevant details. Subsequently, guilty participants enacted the

mock crime, whereas innocent participants witnessed the crime. Thus with knowledge being equivalent across guilty and innocent groups, the design manipulated lying: "no" answer vs. repeating the answer. The GAT classified 90 percent of the guilty group correctly, with a false positive rate of 50 percent among innocent witnesses. The CIT with "no" answer correctly detected 80 percent of the guilty group, with a false positive rate of 90 percent. The false positive rate in the repetition CIT was still 70 percent. This is in contrast to the repetition GAT that only had a 30 percent false positive rate. These differences may be related to the different phrasing in the GAT vs. the CIT. The direct questions in the GAT (e.g., "You murdered the victim in a _____?") are clearly untrue for the innocent informed participant, both when repeating the answer and when answering "no." The CIT puts the focus on the information rather than on guilt, which creates a problem for the innocent witness. CIT questions, such as "The killer got the weapon from _____?" promotes the inference that mere knowledge indicates guilt – whether denied or repeated.

Elaad (2009) published a study that offers a complex set of findings that gives both some support to the empirical findings of Bradley *et al.* (1996) with the CIT and some challenges. Elaad used the CIT and had all participants respond with an overt verbal denial. Both guilt (guilt vs. innocence) and context (crime vs. neutral) were manipulated. Guilt was through abetting a confederate and this was operationalized by having participants stand guard outside a room while the confederate committed a crime. In the "crime" context, the confederate emerged from the room and gave a list of information involved in the crime to the guard. In the "neutral" context the abetting guard was directed to a bulletin board and found the crime information in an envelope. Innocent informed participants in the crime context went to an office where they knew a mock crime had been committed, whereas innocent informed participants in the neutral context waited outside a room where an envelope had been lost. Neither of the innocent informed conditions had a guard role to help the confederate criminal. Finally there was an innocent uninformed group. Guilty participants in the crime context recalled 75% of items and were detected at the 55 percent level. Informed innocent participants in the crime context remembered 78 percent of the items and were incorrectly detected at the 55 percent level. Thus, as we would have predicted, innocent participants who have to lie in the CIT are as detectable as guilty suspects. In the neutral context, this effect was even more exaggerated. Guilty suspects had 71 percent memory and were detected at the 55 percent level. Informed innocent suspects had 63 percent of items remembered and a 70 percent false positive level.

The challenge to Bradley *et al.* comes after adjusting for lack of memory and combing skin conductance with respiration and finger pulse volume data. Guilty suspects were detected at the 75 percent and 60 percent level in the "crime" and "neutral" contexts, respectively, but false positives dropped to the 40 percent level for innocent informed participants in both contexts. Thus, despite knowledge and deceit, detection in informed innocent participants can be low. Unfortunately the design was somewhat confounded as incentives differed between the guilt and innocent conditions. Also, involvement may have been low, as reflected in the low recall (62.2 percent to 77.5 percent). Moreover, even though false positives diminished when only remembered items were used, 40 percent remains a high level of false positives, suggesting that the problem with leaked information remains for the CIT.

Finally, Gamer *et al.* (2008) presented results that suggest that innocent aware suspects examined with the GAT are not differentiated from guilty suspects. Guilty suspects learned ten items of information through looking for slips of paper under the items. An informed innocent group was created through the combined the actions of cleaning crime-relevant items in the crime room with the subsequent witnessing of the crime. Thus this innocent group had knowledge through cleaning the items and through seeing the test items as elements in the crime. Recognition memory levels were high at 9.7 for guilty suspects and 9.9 for innocent aware suspects. Guilty and innocent aware participants were not significantly different in responding on the GAT but both differed from an unaware group. A closer examination of the study suggests that their GAT may have been more like a CIT and that informed innocent participants may have considered themselves deceptive in answering the question with a "no." The following sample question helps with the elucidation of the problems: "What color was the carpet in the room you stole the €50 from? Was it ... a) blue?, b) white?, c) yellow?, d) green?, e) red?, f) black?" Saying "no" could be considered deceptive or at least inaccurate if the participant connects the question regarding "the carpet" with the alternatives that are focused on the "carpet color" aspect of the sentence. Under that circumstance the test is a CIT with deception. If, however the innocent participant focuses on the €50 only and treats the list of alternatives as irrelevant then the test can be considered a GAT, but with no relevant alternatives. This example is not singular. The authors point out that the questions targeted ten details that were rather peripheral for the offence, since they mainly represented the room's furniture. The authors tried to emphasize the action by including the accusation (e.g., "you stole") but the results suggest this strategy did not work. In sum, the examination seems a closer replication to the innocent witness overt denial CIT condition in Bradley *et al.* (1996) rather than to the innocent behavior/witness condition with an overtly truthful GAT. Overall, this important study supports two ideas: question wording including the style of test is an important consideration and leakage of information may preclude the use of CITs. Both issues are in need of further investigation.

Theoretical implications

From a theoretical point of view, it is important to examine why informed innocents react less than guilty suspects. To the degree that innocent participants may be less engaged in leaked events, item learning could be influenced, resulting in poorer retrieval and lower detection scores. Some studies found memory levels for informed innocent participants to be at lesser levels than those for guilty participants. Bradley and Warfield (1984) and Bradley and Rettinger (1992) reported higher averages (9.9–10 items) for guilty participants than for informed participants (8.1–9.4 items). This, up to 20 percent memory reduction, cannot, however, account for the up to 75 percent reduction in false positive responding. In other studies, memory may have been responsible for the reduced detection rates. The results reported by Ben-Shakhar *et al.* (1999), for example, may be explained by memory. Guilty participants had perfect memory and were detected at the 79 percent level whereas only 30 percent of innocent aware participants (false positive rates of 42 percent) correctly remembered all items. Presumably better memory amongst the innocent would have resulted in a higher false positive rate.

Remediation for the problem of leakage

Leakage of information is a serious issue for the CIT administration. It presents great but perhaps not insurmountable problems for the test. It is worth considering a variety of potential solutions, some of which we have already examined and some of which are new.

As mentioned earlier, Ben-Shakhar *et al.* (1999) used target tasks with the purpose of drawing the attention of informed innocent suspects. The authors found some support for the idea that involvement with the target task reduced responding to known key items for innocent aware participants. Interestingly the target task did not interfere with responsiveness of guilty suspects. The targets had no influence on memory for guilty participants but may have influenced memory with innocent participants. If innocent informed suspects in real situations would focus on the target tasks to the point of disregarding the relevant information in the CIT, it might help discriminating them from the guilty suspects who presumably would find it more difficult to disregard their more deeply encoded items. Unfortunately, a downside of this study was that informed innocent participants were merely "informed about the relevant details." Thus, it is also possible that the relevant information was not well encoded by the informed innocents. If the target activity was selectively disruptive of memory for innocent informed participants, this could be a very important study.

As a group, the informed innocent react less than the guilty suspects. Thus, there might be something to gain with an inconclusive zone for mid-range scores and concentrating on those with higher scores. If a suspect won't or can't give an explanation for their responsiveness, the items could be re-examined and subcategorized as to how they fit into the crime. For example, further investigation could reveal that for a witness some items would have been hidden from view. A test just based on those potentially obscured items could be more favorable and reveal that the suspect was actually an innocent witness.

Depending on the source, leaked information may be limited and potentially inaccurate. If that is actually the case then a falsely leaked foil for innocent suspects could readily exceed a true item that has not been leaked. This could provide additional protection for innocent suspects. Logic suggests that guilty suspects may not be reactive to such items and would still respond to the real key item in the set. Unfortunately, Honts and Amato (2002) reported that 54.2 percent of guilty suspects, even though they knew the correct item, responded to an incorrect alleged key item.

Verschuere and Crombez (2008) previewed items with suspects before their polygraph test. Such a procedure could be done under conditions that allow the suspects to indicate items that they are aware of. Guilty suspects might indicate some items but presumably would be more circumspect and not admit to knowing all or a large number of items (Bradley *et al.*, 1989). If innocent suspects admitted to knowledge then leakage and sources of leakage could be explored. The questions where no admissions are forthcoming would comprise the core of the test. It might be a smaller test than originally envisioned but it still might be enough and with a GAT as mentioned above for admitted questions the guilty suspects may respond at higher levels than the innocent informed even on those known items. One particularly valuable contribution from this approach is that the review would refresh the memories of guilty suspects such that potential memory confusions mentioned earlier would be avoided.

Uncontrolled information availability

In the typical police investigation with only one offender and a very small number of potential suspects leakage is a problem. From time to time, however, leakage of information may not be problematic. It actually can be an advantage in certain situations. MacLaren (2001) reported an example where the US Customs Service suspected that illegal narcotics were hidden on a ship. They used a searching CIT to interrogate the crew. Similar to a standard CIT, the officials used a multiple-choice question and answer format. The relevant item, however, was unknown but thought to be among the list. Following the interrogation of the crew members, their responses were corroborated and the items to which the crew had collectively responded the greatest were used to locate large amounts of cocaine in the walls of the ship. Thus, combining the responses of the crew, regardless of guilt or innocence, officials were able to gather important information.

Bradley and Barefoot (2010) looked at situations where information is widespread. Under such circumstances it is a matter of pulling together a coherent set of facts to understand a situation. For example, the same single drug dealer could operate amongst a certain set of people. Gang members may have contact with different members behind the scenes. Villagers in a country with peacekeepers may be intimidated by bombers or militants and be reluctant to reveal what they know and confirm what peacekeepers suspect. Bradley and Barefoot (2010) exposed two groups of participants to either bomb-makers or tea-makers. A third, control, group was not exposed to either type of information. They then questioned the participants on a four-item Group CIT (GCIT) and found 80 percent of those exposed to the bomb-makers and 75 percent of those exposed to the tea-makers to be correctly classified. Of the participants in the control condition, 25 percent were misclassified as witnessing tea-making. Part of the impetus for the study was the idea of finding a way that citizens can be engaged in a safe dialogue because (1) having the leaked information is not criminal, (2) citizens can with the GCIT publically say "no" to all items and thereby avoid repercussions from gang members or terrorists, and (3) the group interrogation means a level of anonymity for the those whose physiology was actually informative.

Summary points

Leakage of relevant information to innocent suspects is an important challenge for the CIT, with a false positive rate of 25 percent to

75 percent in informed innocents. This makes it dangerous to conduct CITs if leakage is suspected. There are intriguing aspects of leakage and questioning that need exploration. The GAT approach, the target approach, and the review approach all appear promising.

Lykken was probably correct in suggesting that a psychological model related to the information involved in the crime is constructed. Lykken's surmise suggests that knowledge is at the least necessary and sometimes determinate for responding in a CIT. Lykken's position is challenged through results that show a variety of influences will affect responding such that individuals can have knowledge yet (a) remain undetected or (b) show heightened detection scores when deceptive. The knowledge effect is robust and powerful and the more subtle effects of conditions will have to be understood very well before recommendations can be made with any confidence in a situation involving information leakage. Until this understanding is achieved, Lykken's recommendation of not testing when leakage is suspected has to be considered very seriously. Alternatively, the Japanese technique (Nakayama, 2002) of withholding certain crime information from public consumption could be explored although that may bring up freedom of information issues.

Bradley and his colleagues had expected the GAT would perform at a consistently high level in the identification of guilty suspects. It is directly rather than inferentially accusatory. This has not been the case. CIT and GAT results with guilty suspects are generally comparable. Ben-Shakhar and Elaad (2003) in their meta-analysis show effects of overt deception only in low motivation studies. Perhaps this explains the failure to find an augmentation effect with GATs. Once attention is engaged on enough items little may be gained by more subtle aspects of questioning. The GAT still provides a more affirmative way of denying guilt for innocent people and while still an information test it may be inherently more satisfying to take for innocent suspects.

Conclusions

Our best guess is that in future it may be possible to contend with leakage. With current knowledge, however, there may be too many problems in estimating the effect of leakage. Knowledge in innocent suspects is likely to result in some responding in the CIT that could rival to levels expected from guilty suspects. This could especially be so if the innocent individual learned the details in a logical systematic way through interrogations or detention centre gossip.

REFERENCES

Ben-Shakhar, G., and Elaad, E. (2003). The validity of psychophysiological detection of information with the guilty knowledge test: a meta-analytic review. *Journal of Applied Psychology*, 88(1), 131–151.

Ben-Shakhar, G., Gronau, N., and Elaad, E. (1999). Leakage of relevant information to innocent examinees in the CIT: an attempt to reduce false positive outcomes by introducing target stimuli. *Journal of Applied Psychology*, 84(5), 651–666.

Bond Jr., C. F., and DePaulo, B. M. (2006) Accuracy of deception judgments. *Personality and Social Psychology Review*, 10(3), 214–234

Bradley, M. T., and Ainsworth, D. (1984). Alcohol and the psychophysiological detection of deception. *Psychophysiology*, 21(1), 63–71.

Bradley, M. T., and Barefoot, C. A. (2010). Eliciting information from groups: social information and the guilty knowledge test. *Canadian Journal of Behavioral Science* 42(2), 109–15.

Bradley, M. T., and Rettinger, J. (1992). Awareness of crime relevant information and the guilty knowledge test. *Journal of Applied Psychology*, 77(1), 55–59.

Bradley, M. T., and Warfield, J. F. (1984). Innocence, Information and the CIT in the detection of deception. *Psychophysiology*, 21(6), 683–689.

Bradley, M. T., Fleming, I., and MacDonald, P. (1989). Amnesia, feeling of knowing and the Guilty Knowledge Test. *Canadian Journal of Behavioral Science*, 21(2), 224–231.

Bradley, M. T., MacLaren, V. V., and Carle, S. B. (1996). Deception and non-deception in Guilty Knowledge and Guilty Actions Polygraph Tests. *Journal of Applied Psychology*, 81(2), 153–160.

Elaad, E. (2009). Effects of context and state of guilt on the detection of concealed crime information. *International Journal of Psychophysiology*, 71(3), 225–234.

Elaad, E., and Ben-Shakhar, G. (1989). Stimulus novelty and significance as determinants of electrodermal responsivity: the serial position effect. *Psychophysiology*, 26(1), 29–38.

Furedy, J. J., and Ben-Shakhar, G. (1991). The roles of deception, intention to deceive, and motivation to avoid detection in the psychophysiological detection of guilty knowledge. *Psychophysiology*, 28(2), 163–171.

Gamer, M., Godert, H. W., Keth, A., Rill, H.-G., and Vossel, G. (2008). Electrodermal and phasic heart rate responses in the guilty actions test: comparing guilty examinees to informed and uninformed innocents. *International Journal of Psychophysiology*, 69, 61–68.

Giesen, M., and Rollison, M. A. (1980). Guilty Knowledge vs innocent associations: effects of trait anxiety and stimulus context on skin conductance. *Journal of Research in Personality*, 14, 1–11.

Honts, C. R., and Amato, S. L. (2002). Countermeasures. In M. Kleiner (ed.), *Handbook of Polygraph Testing*. San Diego: Academic Press.

Horneman, C. J., and O'Gorman, J. G. (1985). Detectability in the card test as a function of the subject's verbal response. *Psychophysiology*, 3(2), 330–333.

Lykken, D. T. (1959). The GSR in the detection of guilt. *Journal of Applied Psychology*, 43(6), 385–388.

_____ (1974). Psychology and the lie detector industry. *The American Psychologist*, 9(10), 725–739.

_____ (1981). *A Tremor in the Blood: Uses and Abuses of the Lie Detector*. New York: McGraw-Hill.

MacLaren, V. V. (2001). A quantitative review of the guilty knowledge test. *Journal of Applied Psychology*, 86(4), 674–683.

Nakayama, M. (2002). Practical use of the concealed information test for criminal investigation in Japan. In M. Kleiner (ed.), *Handbook of Polygraph Testing* (pp. 49–86). San Diego: Academic Press.

Sato, T., and Nihie, Y. (2009). Sex differences in beliefs about cues to deception. *Psychological Reports*, 104, 759–769.

Sokolov, E. N. (1963). *Perception and the Conditioned Reflex*. New York: Macmillan.

Stern, R. M., Breen, J. P., Watanabe, T., and Perry, B. S. (1981). Effect of feedback of physiological information on responses to innocent associations and guilty knowledge. *Journal of Applied Psychology*, 66(6), 677–681.

Verschuere, B., and Crombez, G. (2008). Déjà vu! The effect of previewing test items on the validity of the Concealed Information Test. *Psychology, Crime, & Law*, 14, 287–297.

Verschuere, B., Crombez, G., De Clercq, A., and Koster, E. (2004). Autonomic and behavioral responding to concealed information: differentiating defensive and orienting responses. *Psychophysiology*, 41, 461–466.

11   Countermeasures

Gershon Ben-Shakhar

Overview: Countermeasure manipulations performed by guilty suspects pose a major threat to all methods of psychophysiological detection, including the Concealed Information Test (CIT). The present chapter reviews the experimental literature dealing with the effects of various types of countermeasures (physical and mental) on the outcomes of both the Comparison Questions Test (CQT) and the CIT. Most of the studies reviewed demonstrated that it is possible and in fact quite easy to train subjects to produce or enhance their physiological responses to the neutral items in the CIT and the comparison questions in the CQT, and consequently distort the test's outcome. The studies reviewed focused on the effects of both physical and mental countermeasures on various autonomic measures as well as on ERPs. Finally, several means to protect the CIT against the use of countermeasures are raised and discussed.

Introduction

As indicated in previous chapters of this volume as well as in numerous articles, the CIT has great many advantages as a scientifically based method of detecting involvement in criminal or illegal activities (e.g., Ben-Shakhar and Elaad, 2002; 2003; Ben-Shakhar *et al.*, 2002). On the other hand, the CIT is by no means free of obstacles and problems.

One of the most serious deficiencies of the CIT is its vulnerability to the use of countermeasures by guilty or deceptive examinees. Countermeasures are deliberate techniques that might be used by suspects to alter their physiological reactions. Since detection decisions are always based on contrasting the individual's responses to the critical (crime-related) items with his or her responses to the neutral items, countermeasures can be employed in an attempt either to inhibit responses to the relevant items or to create excitation to the neutral items. Since learning to inhibit one's responses to significant

200

stimuli seems to be an extremely difficult task, almost all documented attempts to study countermeasures used various techniques to enhance responses to the neutral items. Fewer attempts have been made to inhibit responses, typically by forming some kind of dissociation from all the test's questions (e.g., the Yoga technique used in Kubis, 1962, counting sheep used by Elaad and Ben-Shakhar, 1991). However, these latter techniques turned out to be less efficient than the former.

In this chapter, I will review studies designed to examine the effects of various types of countermeasures to both the comparison questions in the CQT (for a detailed description of the CQT and the types of questions included in this test, see Raskin, 1986; Raskin and Honts, 2002) and the neutral items in the CIT (see a description in Chapter 1 of this volume by Bill Iacono). Although this volume focuses on the CIT, I will review the effects of countermeasures on both tests because the very same types of countermeasures, designed to create or enhance responses to either the comparison questions in the CQT or to the neutral items in the CIT, are used in both cases. In general, there are two types of countermeasure techniques: physical countermeasures and mental countermeasures. Physical countermeasures are physical activities performed by examinees in order to avoid being detected. For example, examinees may try to inflict pain upon themselves by biting their tongue or breathing heavily each time a CQT comparison question (or a neutral CIT item) is presented. Mental countermeasures refer to any mental activity the examinee performs to create or enhance physiological responding to the comparison questions (or neutral items). Clearly, both types of countermeasures require some sophistication and certain knowledge (e.g., knowing the distinction between the relevant and comparison questions in the CQT or between the relevant and neutral CIT items). However, by now there is an extensive literature in which polygraph procedures including effective countermeasure techniques are described in great detail. Thus, the danger that interested individuals might gain the necessary understanding in order to use countermeasures is a real one.

The effects of countermeasures on psychophysiological detection based on autonomic measures

Several studies that focused on the effects of various countermeasure techniques on the outcomes of both the CIT and the CQT have been reported since the early 1960s. I will first review the CQT studies and then those focusing on the CIT (see Tables 11.1 and 11.2 for brief summaries of CQT and CIT studies, respectively).

Table 11.1 *A summary of studies designed to examine the effects of countermeasures on the outcomes of the CQT*

Study	Measures	Paradigm	Type of countermeasures (CM)	Practice	Main findings
Rovner et al., 1979	All standard field measures	Mock crime	Physical	No practice	No CM effect (88% CDR)
Rovner et al., 1979	All standard field measures	Mock crime	Physical	Practice plus feedback	CM effect (CDR reduced to 62.5%)
Honts et al., 1985	All standard field measures	Mock crime	Single physical	No practice	No CM effect
Honts et al., 1985	All standard field measures	Mock crime	Two physical CMs	Practice	CM effect (47% FNR compared to 0 in control)
Honts et al., 1987	All standard field measures	Mock crime	Two physical CMs	Practice	CM effect (70% FNR compared to 0 in control)
Honts et al., 1994	All standard field measures	Mock crime	One or two physical CMs	Practice	CM effect (45–55% FNR compared to 20% in control)
Honts et al., 1994	All standard field measures	Mock crime	Mental CM	Practice	CM effect (40% FNR compared to 20% in control)

Note: CM – countermeasures; CDR – Correct Detection Rate; FNR – False-Negative Rate.

Studies focusing on the CQT

Dawson (1980) used a mock crime paradigm in an attempt to study the validity of the CQT procedure, using twenty-four student actors trained in the Stanislavsky "method" of utilizing personal memories to

Table 11.2 *A summary of studies designed to examine the effects of countermeasures on the outcomes of the CIT*

Study	Measures	Paradigm	Type of countermeasures (CM)	Practice	Main findings
Lykken, 1960	SCR	Autobiographical information	Multiple	Yes	No CM effect
Kubis, 1962	The three standard field measures	Card test	Modified yoga	Yes	No CM effect
Kubis, 1962	The three standard field measures	Card test	Physical	Yes	CM effect (chance level detection under CM)
Kubis, 1962	The three standard field measures	Card test	Mental	Yes	CM effect (chance level detection under CM)
Elaad and Ben-Shakhar, 1991 EXP1	SCR	Autobiographical information	Mental (dissociation from the entire test)	No	CM effect (44% CDR compared to 78% in control)
Elaad and Ben-Shakhar, 1991 EXP2	SCR	Memorized objects	Mental (dissociation from the entire test)	No	No statistically significant CM effect
Honts et al., 1996	Skin resistance (SRR) and respiration	Videotaped burglary	Physical	Yes	CM effect with SRR, marginally significant effect with respiration
Honts et al., 1996	Skin resistance (SRR) and respiration	Videotaped burglary	Mental	Yes	CM effect with SRR, no effect with respiration
Ben-Shakhar and Dolev, 1996	SCR and respiration (RLL)	Mock crime	Mental	No	CM effect with SCR, no effect with RLL

Table 11.2 (*cont.*)

Study	Measures	Paradigm	Type of countermeasures (CM)	Practice	Main findings
Ben-Shakhar & Dolev, 1996	SCR and respiration (RLL)	Mock crime	Mental	Yes	CM effect with SCR, no effect with RLL
Sasaki *et al.*, 2001	ERP (P300)	Autobiographical information	Mental	No	Reduced P300 under CM, but no significant difference in detection rate
Rosenfeld *et al.*, 2004, Exp1	ERP (P300)	Mock crime	Physical and mental	No	CM effect (18% CDR under CM compared with 82% in control)
Rosenfeld *et al.*, 2004, Exp2	ERP (P300)	Autobiographical information	Physical and mental	No	CM effect (50% CDR under CM compared with 92% in control)
Mertens and Allen, 2008	ERP (P300)	Virtual reality mock crime	Physical and mental	No	CM effect (7–27% CDR under CM compared with 27–47% in control)
Rosenfeld *et al.*, 2008	ERP (P300) with the CTP	Autobiographical information	Physical and mental	No	No CM effect

create emotional states. The subjects were motivated and instructed to use the techniques taught at the Strasberg Theater Institute to appear innocent during the polygraph examination. It was believed that this choice of subjects and procedure would create "an opportunity to determine whether training in a type of mental countermeasure can be used by guilty subjects to successfully appear non-deceptive" (Dawson, 1980, p. 9). However, the results strongly indicated that this type of countermeasure is ineffective because no false-negative decisions were obtained. Honts (2002) raised the possibility that the null effect observed by Dawson (1980) was due to the fact that subjects were not informed about the nature of the CQT and consequently were unable to apply their mental imagery countermeasures effectively.

The effects of physical countermeasures were demonstrated by Raskin and his colleagues in a series of mock crime studies involving the CQT (Honts et al., 1985, 1987, 1994; Rovner et al., 1979). Rovner et al. (1979) demonstrated that providing subjects with detailed information about the CQT and suggesting to them possible countermeasure techniques did not affect the test's outcomes. However, when subjects actually practiced the countermeasures and received feedback on their performance, some effects were observed (false negative outcomes increased from 4 percent to 25 percent and inconclusive outcomes increased from 8 percent to 12.5 percent).

Honts et al. (1985) showed that when subjects simulating the guilty were trained to perform a single physical countermeasure (either to press their toes against the floor as soon as they recognized a comparison question, or to bite their tongues hard enough to produce pain) no countermeasure effects were obtained, and the detection rates in both countermeasure groups did not differ from those obtained in a control group. On the other hand, when subjects simulating the guilty were asked to perform both types of countermeasures, were given a practice examination containing questions similar to those used in the actual examination, and were required to demonstrate their countermeasures before an assistant, a strong effect of the countermeasure manipulation emerged (47 percent false negatives were observed in the countermeasure condition, as compared with 0 percent in the guilty control condition). In fact, the pattern of physiological responses to the relevant and comparison questions in the countermeasure condition was undifferentiated from the pattern observed in a control group simulating innocent suspects. In a subsequent study, Honts et al. (1987) applied once again the multiple physical countermeasures procedure, with stronger incentive to pass the test, and obtained even larger rates of false negative outcomes (out of the ten subjects in the countermeasure condition, seven were classified as innocents, and three as inconclusive).

In an additional study, Honts et al. (1994) demonstrated that even the use of a single physical countermeasure (either pressing the toes against the floor, or biting the tongue) was effective, and between 45 percent and 55 percent of the subjects in the various physical countermeasures conditions were classified as innocents (compared with a false negative rate of 20 percent in a guilty control condition). This series of studies focused primarily on the effects of physical countermeasures on the outcomes of the CQT and clearly demonstrates that these outcomes could be drastically distorted by subjects who are trained in the use of physical countermeasures. Unlike mental countermeasures, physical countermeasures may be detectable. For example, Honts *et al.* (1987) demonstrated that experienced polygraph examiners were unable to detect physical countermeasure users without dedicated equipment. Through the use of electromyographic recordings, however, counter-measures could be detected quite efficient: 90 percent of the counter-measure subjects were correctly detected, with no false-positive errors. This raises the question of whether mental countermeasures could also be effective in distorting the outcomes of polygraph examinations. In addition, it is important to examine whether both types of counter-measures can affect the outcomes of the CIT.

Studies focusing on the CIT

The first attempt to examine the effects of countermeasures on the CIT was reported by Lykken (1960). In this study, subjects were exposed to various techniques designed to produce electrodermal responses to the neutral items and were provided with the opportunity to practice these techniques. However, in spite of the fact that subjects were motivated to avoid detection and were instructed and trained to fake their responses, no false-negative outcomes were reported. It is important to emphasize that Lykken (1960) used a special scoring system designed to overcome the countermeasure attempts. This scoring system was based on the assumption that subjects attempting to fake their responses will try to produce enhanced responses to a fixed number of neutral items in each question. Thus, when a subject is trying to produce artificial responses to two neutral items in each question, then the relevant item will typically produce the third largest response. Lykken's scoring system was therefore based on deviations from a uniform distribution of the ranked responses to the relevant alternatives across questions.

Another early CIT experiment was reported by Kubis (1962) who examined both physical and mental countermeasures. Kubis conducted a card-test experiment and reported that both physical countermeasures (instructing subjects to tense their toe muscles in response to a neutral card number and letting them practice it) and mental ones (instructing the subjects to bring to mind an emotionally exciting situation when presented with an irrelevant number and let them practice it) were effective and reduced detection rates to levels expected by chance. However, Kubis used a complete within-subjects design with four conditions (no CM control condition, modified yoga condition, physical CM and finally mental CM). As the order of these four conditions was fixed, the mental countermeasures always followed the physical countermeasure condition, and therefore the possibility that subjects under the mental countermeasure condition were using the physical measures they had practiced just a few minutes earlier cannot be ruled out. The modified yoga condition designed to detach the subjects from the outside stimuli was ineffective.

Elaad and Ben-Shakhar (1991) examined the effects of mental countermeasures on the outcomes of the CIT using a mental dissociation method. Unlike most countermeasure methods that rely on attempts to create enhanced responses to the neutral items, the mental dissociation method, used by Elaad and Ben-Shakhar (1991), like the modified yoga procedure used by Kubis (1962), was based on distracting attention from all the test questions and thus reducing all the responses. Indeed, when subjects were instructed to count sheep throughout the entire test, some reduction in electrodermal differentiation between relevant and neutral items was obtained. In addition, a significant reduction in correct detection rates under the CM condition, relative to a control no CM condition, was observed only in one out of the two experiments reported by Elaad and Ben-Shakhar (1991).

The Honts et al. (1994) study, mentioned above, included, in addition to the physical countermeasure conditions, a mental countermeasure condition in which subjects were instructed and trained to pick a number larger than 200 and then count backward in units of seven as soon as they heard a comparison question. The results of this condition did not significantly differ from those observed under the physical countermeasure conditions (40 percent of the subjects were mistakenly classified as innocents). In a subsequent study, Honts et al. (1996) examined the effects of both physical and mental countermeasures on the efficiency of the CIT. They applied similar countermeasures as those used by Honts et al. (1994) and obtained significant effects for both types of countermeasures on electrodermal detection (the correct identification rate of guilty subjects was reduced from 80 percent in the control condition to 10 percent and 40 percent in the physical and mental countermeasure conditions, respectively). Smaller effects, with a non-significant mental countermeasure effect, were obtained when the respiration measure was applied. It is important to note that according to Honts et al. (1994) the special scoring method based on deviations from a uniform distribution of the ranked responses to the relevant alternatives across questions proposed by Lykken (1960) was ineffective against the countermeasures employed by Honts *et al.* (1996).

Ben-Shakhar and Dolev (1996) examined the effects of mental countermeasures on the outcomes of the CIT. They used a mock-crime experiment with four groups of subjects:

(1) Innocent subjects who were not involved in the mock crime.
(2) Guilty control subjects who committed the mock crime, but received no countermeasure instructions.
(3) Guilty subjects who received countermeasure instructions.
(4) Guilty subjects who received countermeasure instructions and were allowed to practice the countermeasures.

The countermeasure instructions encouraged subjects to recall emotional situations from their past and imagine themselves in these situations during presentation of neutral items. The results revealed a significant reduction in electrodermal detection efficiency under the two countermeasure conditions, with no differences between them. As in the Honts *et al.* (1996) study, no countermeasures effects were observed with the respiration line length measure.

The effects of countermeasures on psychophysiological detection based on event-related potentials

Since the late 1980s several successful attempts have been made to detect concealed information on the basis of event-related potentials (ERPs) recorded from various brain sites (e.g., Allen *et al.*, 1992; Farwell and Donchin, 1991; Rosenfeld *et al.*, 1988, 1991). These attempts were initially perceived as a possible solution to the problem of countermeasures, as it seems very difficult to perform countermeasures under the rapid stimulus presentation that characterizes the ERP procedure. For example, Ben-Shakhar and Elaad (2002, p. 97) wrote that "ERP measures seem to be immune against countermeasures because they are based on a repeated rapid presentation of the items (e.g., one item per second). When items are presented at such a rapid pace, it is virtually impossible to execute countermeasures to the neutral items." Furthermore, ERPs have a very short latency (they occur within a few hundred milliseconds after stimulus onset), which further makes it difficult to perform effective countermeasures (see Lykken, 1998). Indeed, Sasaki *et al.* (2001) examined the effects of mental countermeasures (counting backwards in units of seven from a number larger than 200) on detection of autobiographical items using the P300 component of the ERP and found that although significantly prolonged reaction time and reduced overall P300 amplitudes to the items were observed under the countermeasure condition, the P300 amplitudes to the relevant items were consistently larger than those to the irrelevant items in both groups. The correct detection rate of the relevant items was 81 percent in the countermeasure condition and 94 percent in the control group, but the difference was not statistically significant.

However, subsequent studies reported by Rosenfeld *et al.* (2004) and by Mertens and Allen (2008) demonstrated that both physical and mental countermeasures were effective. Specifically, Rosenfeld *et al.* (2004) taught their subjects to apply both physical and mental countermeasures to the neutral items and demonstrated that these multiple countermeasure manipulations reduced detection rates of informed subjects from 82 percent in the control-no countermeasure condition to 18 percent in the first experiment and from 92 percent to 50 percent in the second. Mertens and Allen (2008) extended the Rosenfeld *et al.* (2004) study by including both mental and physical countermeasures directed not just at the neutral but also at the target items. In addition, Mertens and Allen (2008) used a virtual reality crime scenario, which seems more realistic than the typical mock-crime procedures traditionally used in CIT studies, and applied several analytical methods for analyzing the data and classify subjects. The results of this study revealed much lower detection rates of "guilty" subjects than those reported in other ERP studies. Even in the guilty-control condition, where no countermeasure instructions were given, detection rates ranged from 27 percent to 47 percent (depending on the classification method used). Countermeasures further reduced detection rates, which ranged from 7 percent to 27 percent in the various conditions and classification methods.

While these two studies demonstrated that countermeasures can be effective even under the rapid stimulus presentation employed in ERP-based CIT, a recent study by Rosenfeld *et al.* (2008) proposed a new protocol (labeled "the complex trial protocol," or CTP), which seems to be resistant to countermeasures. Rosenfeld *et al.* (2008) argued that the traditional protocol that has been used in all P300-based CIT studies is deficient because the explicit target-non-target decision the subjects have to make is combined with the implicit probe vs. irrelevant discrimination, where both must occur in response to a single presentation of each item. This implies that processing resources must be divided between these two tasks at the risk of attenuating P300 to both probe and target. To overcome this difficulty, Rosenfeld and his colleagues developed a new protocol in which the probe vs. irrelevant discrimination is separated from the target-non-target decision, which is delayed by a randomly varying interval ranging from 1.1 to 1.5 seconds. Specifically, each trial in the CTP includes two presentations of each stimulus, separated by 1.1–1.55 s. The first stimulus-S_1 (a probe or an irrelevant item) is presented in white and requires a mere recognition response (pressing a single key). The second presentation-S_2 is in one of five colors, where one particular color is defined as the target. Subjects must make a target-non-target decision in response to S_2. The potential advantage of the CTP is that processing resources are not divided and thus S_1 should elicit large P300 when it a probe. Furthermore, Rosenfeld *et al.* (2008) hypothesized that any attempt to employ countermeasures to S_1 will fail because it will necessarily involve enhanced reaction times.

The results reported by Rosenfeld *et al.* (2008) indicate that the CTP is indeed a highly valid method for detecting concealed knowledge (eleven out of twelve "guilty" subjects were correctly detected under the control-no countermeasure condition and the area under the ROC curve ranged between 0.95 and 0.98). Furthermore, ten out of the twelve "guilty" subjects were correctly detected under the countermeasure condition. In addition, as hypothesized the use of countermeasures was always detected because significantly elevated reaction times to the neutral items were observed in those cases. A replication study (also reported by Rosenfeld *et al.*, 2008) revealed very similar results. Clearly, these results should be replicated in other laboratories before making practical implications.

The effects of countermeasures on psychophysiological detection based on covert respiration measures

A different approach to deal with the threat posed by countermeasures to the outcomes of the CIT was recently adopted by Elaad and Ben-Shakhar (2008, 2009). They examined whether covert respiration measures can be effectively used for the detection of concealed knowledge. The covert measures used in these studies were two respiratory effort transducers hidden in the seat and the back of a standard polygraph armchair. There may be several potential advantages to measuring physiological responses without connecting the examinee to electrodes. One such advantage is related to countermeasures. Elaad and Ben-Shakhar hypothesized that when examinees are not directly connected to the polygraph they will not be motivated to distort their physiological measurements and thus will not perform countermeasures.

In the first study (Elaad and Ben-Shakhar, 2008), a mock-crime experiment was designed to compare the two covert measures with the three standard measures typically used in psychophysiological detection studies (skin conductance response, respiration line length [RLL] and finger pulse waveform length [FPWL]). The results of this study revealed that the two covert measures discriminated between "guilty" and "innocent" subjects at a significantly better than chance levels. Furthermore, one of these measures (the back measure) was as efficient as the standard respiration and cardiovascular measures (the areas under the ROC curve for the covert back measure, the RLL, FPWL and SCR were 0.77, 0.78, 0.80, and 0.86, respectively). In their second study, Elaad and Ben-Shakhar (2009) examined the vulnerability of these two covert measures, together with the three standard measures, to countermeasures. The design of this study included two blocks, such that the first included all five measures and in the second the standard devices were removed. The results revealed that both covert measures were resistant to physical but not to mental countermeasures in the first block. In the second block, only one covert measure (the seat) discriminated between "guilty" and "innocent" subjects under the no-countermeasure and under the mental countermeasure conditions. However, due to ethical considerations, subjects were told that their physiological responses would be monitored throughout the entire test and consequently at least some subjects continued their countermeasure attempts after they were disconnected from the polygraph. Thus, future studies are needed to examine whether the use of covert measures would be effective against countermeasures usage.

Conclusions

The studies reviewed above clearly demonstrate that it is possible and in fact quite easy to train people to produce or enhance their physiological responses to both the CQT comparison questions or the CIT neutral items, and thus distort the outcomes of both the CQT and the CIT. Countermeasures designed to distract examinees from the entire test questions and thus to reduce all responses seem less effective. The question of whether it is sufficient to instruct subjects about the nature of the test, the questions (or items) to which countermeasures should be applied and the nature of the countermeasures, or whether actual practice with the countermeasures is necessary is unclear yet. The results reported by Rovner et al. (1979), with physical countermeasures applied to the CQT, suggest that practice is important. On the other hand, Ben-Shakhar and Dolev (1996) examined the effects of mental countermeasures on the outcomes of the CIT and did not find any differences between a condition of mere instructions and a condition that included a practice session as well.

Several means can be proposed to protect against the use of counter-measures. First, attempts can be made to detect countermeasures usage. For example, Honts *et al.* (1987) demonstrated that specific physical countermeasures were detected by electromyographic recordings (90 percent of the countermeasure subjects were correctly detected, with no false-positive errors). However, it is unclear whether this technique can be applied to all physical countermeasures and it is definitely ineffective against the use of mental countermeasures.

The research on countermeasures indicates that the various physiological measures used for psychophysiological detection are not similarly affected by countermeasures. Particularly, whereas the electrodermal measure, which seems to be the most sensitive measure for the detection of concealed information, is severely affected by both physical and mental countermeasures, the respiration measure is much less affected. Two independent studies (Ben-Shakhar and Dolev, 1996; Honts *et al.*, 1996) showed that detection rates based on the electrodermal measure were considerably reduced when countermeasures were applied, but detection rates based on the respiration measure were much less affected by countermeasures and in both studies the reduction in detection efficiency based on respiration was not statistically significant. This result was recently replicated by Elaad and Ben-Shakhar (2009). Clearly, further research is required to assess the degree to which various physiological measures are affected by countermeasures, but if it turns out that some measures, like the RLL, are relatively resistant to countermeasure manipulations, they should be assigned larger weights when there is a reason to suspect that examinees are trying to fake their physiological responses.

Another direction that can be adopted to avoid the harmful impact of countermeasures is the use of ERPs, with the new protocol (the CTP) developed by Rosenfeld and his colleagues (see Rosenfeld *et al.*, 2008). Clearly, this has to be replicated by independent research, but the studies reported so far indicate that it has a potential. Of course, it is unclear yet whether ERPs can be used in applied settings and, to the best of my knowledge, CIT based on ERP measures has not yet been applied on a large scale.

Finally, the use of covert physiological measures is another possibility. The assumption is that when examinees are unaware that their physiological responses are being monitored, they will not be motivated to use countermeasures. This raises, of course, legal and ethical issues that are beyond the scope of this chapter.

REFERENCES

Allen, J. J., Iacono, W. G., and Danielson, K. D. (1992). The development and validation of an event-related-potential memory assessment procedure: a methodology for prediction in the face of individual differences. *Psychophysiology*, 29, 504–522.

Ben-Shakhar, G., and Dolev, K. (1996). Psychophysiological detection through the guilty knowledge technique: the effects of mental countermeasures. *Journal of Applied Psychology*, 81, 273–281.

Ben-Shakhar, G., and Elaad, E. (2002). The Guilty Knowledge Test (GKT) as an application of psychophysiology: future prospects and obstacles. In M. Kleiner (ed.), *Handbook of Polygraph Testing* (pp. 87–102). San Diego: Academic Press.

(2003). The validity of psychophysiological detection of deception with the Guilty Knowledge Test: a meta-analytic review. *Journal of Applied Psychology*, 88, 131–151.

Ben-Shakhar, G., Bar-Hillel, M., and Kremnitzer, M. (2002). Trial by polygraph: reconsidering the use of the GKT in court. *Law and Human Behavior*, 26, 527–541.

Dawson, M. E. (1980). Physiological detection of deception: measurement of responses to questions and answers during countermeasure maneuvers. *Psychophysiology*, 17, 8–17.

Elaad, E., and Ben-Shakhar, G. (1991). Effects of mental countermeasures on psychophysiological detection in the guilty knowledge test. *International Journal of Psychophysiology*, 11, 99–108.

(2008). Covert respiration measures for the detection of concealed information. *Biological Psychology*, 77, 284–291.

(2009). Countering countermeasures in the concealed information test using covert respiration measures. *Applied Psychophysiology and Biofeedback*, 34, 197–208.

Farwell, L. A., and Donchin, E. (1991). The truth will out: interrogative polygraphy ("lie detection") with event-related brain potentials. *Psychophysiology*, 28, 531–547.

Honts, C. R. (2002). Countermeasures. In M. Kleiner (ed.), *Handbook of Polygraph Testing* (pp. 251–264). San Diego: Academic Press.

Honts, C. R., Hodes, R. L., and Raskin, D. C. (1985). Effects of physical counter-measures on the physiological detection of deception. *Journal of Applied Psychology*, 70, 177–187.

Honts, C. R., Raskin, D. C., and Kircher, J. C. (1987). Effects of physical countermeasures and their electromyographic detection during polygraph tests for deception. *Journal of Psychophysiology*, 1, 241–247.

(1994). Mental and physical countermeasures reduce the accuracy of polygraph tests. *Journal of Applied Psychology*, 79, 252–259.

Honts, C. R., Devitt, M. K, Winbush, M., and Kircher, J. C. (1996). Mental and physical countermeasures reduce the accuracy of the concealed knowledge test. *Psychophysiology*, 33, 84–92.

Kubis, J. F. (1962). *Studies in Lie Detection: Computer Feasibility Considerations*. Technical Report #62–205, prepared for the Air Force Systems

Command. Contract No. AF 30 (602) -2270, project No. 5534, Fordham University.

Lykken, D. T. (1960). The validity of the guilty knowledge technique: the effects of faking. *Journal of Applied Psychology*, 44, 258–262.

(1998). *A Tremor in the Blood: Uses and Abuses of the Lie Detector.* New York: Plenum.

Mertens, R., and Allen, J. J. B. (2008). The role of psychophysiology in forensic assessments: deception detection, ERPs, and virtual reality mock crime scenario. *Psychophysiology*, 45, 286–298.

Raskin, D. C. (1986). The Polygraph in 1986: scientific, professional and legal issues surrounding application and acceptance of polygraph evidence. *Utah Law Review*, 29–74.

Raskin, D. C., and Honts, C. R. (2002). The comparison question test. In M. Kleiner (ed.), *Handbook of Polygraph Testing* (pp. 1–47). San Diego: Academic Press.

Rosenfeld, J. P., Angell, A., Johnson, M., and Qian, J. H. (1991). An ERP based, control-question lie detector analog: algorithms for discriminating effects within individuals' average wave forms. *Psychophysiology*, 32, 319–335.

Rosenfeld, J.P., Soskins, M., Bosh, G., and Rayan, A. (2004). Simple, effective countermeasures to P300-based tests of detection of concealed information. *Psychophysiology*, 41, 205–219.

Rosenfeld, J. P., Cantwell, B., Nasman, V. T., Wojdac, V., Ivanov, S., and Mazzeiri, L. (1988). A modified event-related potential-based guilty-knowledge test. *International Journal of Neuroscience*, 24, 157–161.

Rosenfeld, J.P., Labkovsky, E., Winograd, M., Lui, M.A., Vandenboom, C., and Chedid, E. (2008). The Complex Trial Protocol (CTP): a new countermeasure-resistant, accurate, P300-based method for detection of concealed information. *Psychophysiology*, 45, 906–919.

Rovner, L. I., Raskin, D. C., and Kircher, J. C. (1979). Effects of information and practice on detection of deception. *Psychophysiology*, 16, 197–198.

Sasaki, M., Hira, S., and Matsuda, T. (2001). Effects of mental countermeasure on the physiological detection of deception using the event-related brain potentials. *Japanese Journal of Psychology*, 72, 322–328.

12 Psychopathy and the detection of concealed information

Bruno Verschuere

Overview: The most common application of concealed information detection is crime knowledge assessment in crime suspects. The validity of this application has mainly been investigated in healthy subjects. Criminals may differ in important aspects from healthy subjects. Psychopathy, for example, is quite common among criminal populations. Psychopathy is characterized by affective–interpersonal (e.g., shallow affect) and behavioral–lifestyle (e.g., impulsivity) features. The latter is associated with physiological hyporesponsivity, and could threaten the validity of concealed information detection. I will review empirical research that has examined this possibility. Directions for future research will be discussed.

The most common application of concealed information detection is to assess whether a crime suspect has intimate knowledge about the crime under investigation. A concern with this application is that – particularly under real-life circumstances (Elaad *et al.*, 1992) – guilty suspects may escape detection. Several factors might explain this modest sensitivity. Guilty suspects may not remember certain crime details. Another, less investigated, source of error is individual differences in responsivity. Despite perfect recognition, some individuals do not respond to concealed information. From the very beginning, this was recognized by David Lykken, who stated that college students are "hardly representative of the average run of criminal suspects" and that "perhaps a proportion of the latter would not respond 'normally' in such a test" (p. 387; Lykken, 1959). Lykken did not specify who these non-normal responding individuals might be. We now know that mental disorders are very common in the prison population. A review of 62 studies including more than 20,000 prisoners showed that 65 percent of the prison inmates had a personality disorder, most commonly antisocial personality disorder (47 percent; Fazel and Danesh, 2002). In addition, a sizable percentage of inmates (about 15–30 percent) are

215

estimated to meet clinical criteria for a diagnosis of psychopathy (Hare, 2003). Since antisocial personality and psychopathy are associated with abnormalities in physiological responding (Benning *et al.*, 2005; Fowles and Dindo, 2006; Lorber, 2004; Patrick *et al.*, 2006; Raine *et al.*, 1997), it may be these individuals who are most likely to respond "abnormally" in the Concealed Information Test (CIT).

Criminality, antisocial personality disorder, and psychopathy

Psychopathy is often confounded with related yet distinct concepts such as criminality, psychopathology, and antisocial personality disorder. *Criminality* refers to behavior that legislators in a certain country at a certain point of time consider illegal. *Psychopathology* refers to mental illness. The Diagnostic and Statistical Manual of Mental Disorders (DSM; American Psychological Association, 1994) is one of the most widely used means to organize and describe mental disorders. The DSM describes *Antisocial personality disorder* as a pervasive pattern of disregard for, and violation of, the rights of others that begins in childhood or early adolescence and continues into adulthood. However, an important limitation of the DSM is that it does not differentiate between antisocial personality disorder and *psychopathy*. Yet, there are important clinical, theoretical, and empirical reasons to differentiate the two (Patrick, 2006). Current descriptions of psychopathy go back to the clinical description by Cleckley (1941/1976). His work provided the basis for the Psychopathy Checklist – Revised (PCL-R; Hare, 2003), which is the most often used instrument for the clinical assessment of psychopathy. The twenty items of this checklist were developed to capture Cleckley's clinical description, and include criteria such as superficial charm, grandiose sense of self-worth, pathological lying, impulsivity, juvenile delinquency, and irresponsibility. Factor analytic work has shown that that the Psychopathy Checklist (Cooke and Michie, 2001; Hare, 2003; Harpur *et al.*, 1988) encompasses an affective–interpersonal facet (including charm, grandiosity, and lying) and a behavioral–lifestyle facet (including impulsivity, delinquency, and irresponsibility).[1] Other contemporary

---

[1] There has been discussion of whether a 2-, 3- or 4-factor solution provides the best fit (Hare, 2003). The 3-factor model (Cooke and Michie, 2001) essentially splits Factor 1 into an affective and an interpersonal factor, and restricts Factor 2 to antisocial-impulsive behavior excluding criminality. The 4-factor model (Hare, 2003) retains criminality as a fourth factor. Notwithstanding this debate, there seems to be a consensus that psychopathy is characterized by affective–interpersonal and behavioral-lifestyle characteristics.

psychopathy measures such as the Psychopathic Personality Inventory (PPI; Lilienfeld and Andrews, 1996) and the Levenson Self-Report Psychopathy Scale (Levenson *et al.*, 1995) also have items tapping both the affective–interpersonal and the behavioral–lifestyle facet of psychopathy. The behavioral–lifestyle facet of psychopathy in particular is strongly related to antisocial personality disorder. Reciprocally, it is particularly the affective–interpersonal facet that differentiates psychopathy from antisocial personality disorder.

The psychophysiology of psychopathy

The affective–interpersonal and behavioral–lifestyle components of psychopathy show distinct associations with personality measures, demographic variables, and laboratory task indices of affective and cognitive functioning. The affective–interpersonal facet is related negatively to anxiety, and positively to narcissism and dominance. The behavioral–lifestyle facet is related negatively with socioeconomic status and intelligence, and positively with impulsivity, substance abuse, and diagnoses and symptoms of antisocial personality disorder (Cooke and Michie, 2001; Hare, 2003; Harpur *et al.*, 1988; Patrick, 2006). In addition, recent research indicates that the two psychopathy facets have different psychophysiological correlates.

The affective–interpersonal facet and impaired fear responding

One of the earliest experimental investigations of physiological responding in psychopathy comes from Lykken (1957). Based on clinical judgment, Lykken allocated prisoners to a psychopathic or a non-psychopathic group. All prisoners participated in an aversive conditioning procedure in which a bell sound preceded the occurrence of an electric shock. The results indicated that the psychopathic prisoners showed less skin conductance activity in anticipation of the shock compared to the non-psychopathic prisoners. This finding provided initial support for the idea that a fear deficit underlies psychopathy.

Patrick *et al.* (1993) used the startle eye blink paradigm to test for the presence of a fear deficit in psychopathy. Abrupt intense stimuli such as a loud burst of noise elicit a reflexive startle response. Compared with reactivity under neutral stimulus conditions, the magnitude of this reflex is enhanced during processing of aversive stimuli and inhibited during processing of pleasurable stimuli. Patrick *et al.* (1993) recorded the eye-blink startle response to noise probe stimuli in fifty-four sexual offenders during viewing of neutral (e.g., household objects), pleasurable (e.g., smiling baby), and aversive scenes (e.g., aimed weapons, mutilated bodies) selected from the International Affective Picture System (IAPS). As typically found in healthy controls, low psychopathic prisoners showed startle inhibition during pleasurable pictures, and startle facilitation during aversive pictures. The high psychopathic prisoners displayed the normal startle inhibition for pleasurable pictures, but failed to show startle facilitation for aversive pictures. Further analyses demonstrated that this fear deficit was specifically related to elevations on the affective–interpersonal component of psychopathy (Patrick, 1994).

Benning *et al.* (2005) examined physiological responding to emotional pictures in 355 young adult men from the Minnesota Twin Study. Based upon previous research, they used a broadband inventory of normal personality, the Multidimensional Personality Questionnaire (MPQ; Tellegen, 1982) to estimate scores on the two factors of PPI psychopathy. High Social Potency, low Stress Reaction, and low Harm Avoidance comprised the score for the affective–interpersonal facet. High Aggression along with low Control, low Traditionalism, and low Social Closeness comprised the score for the behavioral–lifestyle facet. Skin conductance and startle eye blink responses to occasionally presented startle probes were measured while participants viewed aversive, neutral, and appetitive IAPS pictures. High scores on the affective–interpersonal factor predicted reduced startle potentiation, and also reduced skin conductance responding to the aversive pictures.

These findings indicate that (1) psychopathy is marked by a fear deficit, and (2) the fear deficit is specifically tied to the affective–interpersonal facet of psychopathy.

The behavioral–lifestyle facet and general hyporesponsivity

In the study described above, Benning *et al.* (2005) also found that high scores on the behavioral–lifestyle factor of PPI psychopathy were related to reduced skin conductance responding to all pictures. This reduced responding was not specific to aversive pictures, but also found for neutral and pleasurable pictures. Rather than a fear deficit, the reduced skin conductance responding points to general autonomic underarousal. Along similar lines, Herpertz *et al.* (2003) examined physiological responding in 8- to 13-year-old normal boys, and boys diagnosed with either conduct disorder (CD), ADHD, or both disorders. In a classic orienting paradigm, the boys were presented with ten presentations of an innocuous 65 dB tone. Compared to both controls and boys with ADHD, the boys with CD alone and with CD-ADHD displayed smaller skin conductance orienting responses to the tones. This finding indicates that electrodermal hyporesponsivity in antisocial individuals is not specific to fearful stimuli, and is not tied to characteristic features of psychopathy. Rather, as shown in a meta-analysis of ninety-five studies by Lorber (2004), an antisocial spectrum of disorders (including, but not limited to the behavioral–lifestyle facet of psychopathy) is associated with reduced skin conductance activity (including to aversive stimuli, but not exclusively). Further research demonstrating reduced executive functioning in neuropsychological tests for individuals with antisocial tendencies (Morgan and Lilienfeld, 2000), and reduced P300 to visual oddball stimuli (Patrick *et al.*, 2006), suggests that the antisocial spectrum is tied to a rather broad "frontal" brain deficit.

Psychopathy and the CIT: predictions

As suggested by the foregoing research findings, there appears to be a "dual deficit" in psychopathy (Fowles and Dindo, 2006). The affective-interpersonal facet is associated with low fear, and the behavior-lifestyle facet is related to general physiological hyporesponsivity that characterizes the antisocial spectrum. This dual deficit model implies that the two facets of psychopathy have diverging predictions for the CIT. Recall that there is no empirical evidence that physiological responding to concealed information is driven specifically by fear (see Chapter 7, this volume). To that extent, the affective–interpersonal facet of psychopathy, associated with fearlessness, may not pose much of a threat to the validity of concealed information detection.

The behavioral–lifestyle facet of psychopathy, on the other hand, may have a detrimental effect on the validity of the CIT due to its association with physiological hyporesponsivity. Reduced orienting, however, does not necessarily lead to reduced detection rates in the CIT. Indeed, to the extent that the differential responding between the concealed and the control information remains clear, the CIT remains valid.

Psychopathy and the CIT: findings

To the best of my knowledge, there are only six peer-reviewed studies published in English that have examined the effect of psychopathy on the ANS-based CIT.[2] Since the analysis above suggests that

---

[2] Several studies that may seem of relevance were not taken in this overview. Block (1957), for example, used a card test, but did not provide a measure of differential responding. Because different processes may underlie the ANS-based CIT and the P300-based CIT, I did not include the P300-based study by Miller and Rosenfeld (2004).

hyporesponsivity is not restricted to psychopathy, I also considered the study by Lieblich et al. (1976) that focused upon criminality. In addition, I included two other studies from doctoral dissertations that have not yet been published in peer-reviewed scientific journals (Dindo, 2008; Meijer, 2008). Table 12.1 summarizes the main design and findings of these studies. Since there are only nine studies, I will discuss each in some detail.

Lieblich et al. (1976) interviewed thirty inmates from a maximum security prison to extract twenty autobiographical items (name, place of birth, favorite cigarette brand, etc.). Each of these critical alternatives was presented amidst four control alternatives in an autobiographical CIT (e.g., "Is your name David? Jacob?" etc.). The prisoners were instructed to sit quietly and listen to all alternatives for each question. The data obtained in this prison sample were compared with those obtained previously in a sample of twenty-seven undergraduates (Ben-Shakhar et al., 1970). Although no demographic information was reported in these papers, it is clear that the samples likely differed in a number of aspects other than criminality. The main analyses showed no difference in hit rate for the two samples. In follow-up analyses, the autobiographical items were divided into five highly relevant (e.g., own name) and fifteen less relevant items (e.g., hobby). Signal detection analyses showed that detection efficiency was highly similar in the two samples for the items of high relevance, but lower in the prisoners' sample than in the undergraduate sample for the less relevant items.

Balloun and Holmes (1979) administered the Psychopathic Deviate (Pd) scale of the Minnesota Multiphasic Personality Inventory (MMPI; Hathaway and McKinley, 1943) to 300 male undergraduates. This MMPI subscale explicitly assesses antisocial behavior and attitudes, including disregard for social conventions, non-conformity, impulsivity, and hostility. The Pd-scale thus measures the behavioral–lifestyle facet of psychopathy. Eighteen high and sixteen low Pd scoring undergraduates participated in the study. The study started with a very difficult intelligence examination involving two other participants, who were actually confederates of the experimenter. The two confederates cheated on the exam and tried to coax the participant into cheating. Eight (45 percent) of the high Pd participants and eight (50 percent) of the low Pd undergraduates cheated. Participants were tested regarding cheating behavior with a CIT, after being warned that cheating constituted grounds for immediate dismissal from the university. The examination consisted of five questions, each having five alternatives, and was administered twice. Since heart rate and pulse volume did not yield significant results, only results for skin conductance were reported. The

Table 12.1 *Main findings of psychopathy research on concealed information detection*

Study	Sample	Psychopathy measure	CIT measure	CIT paradigm	Required response in the CIT	Motivation	Main findings
Lieblich *et al.*, 1976	Thirty prisoners and twenty-seven undergraduates (gender not reported)	None	SCR	Autobiographical	Remain silent	None	Similar detection for central items, but lower detection of peripheral items in prisoners compared to undergraduates
Balloun and Holmes 1979	Eighteen high and fourteen low psychopathic male undergraduates (53% guilty)	Pd-Scale MMPI	SCR	"Real" crime	Repeat answer	Risk of dismissal of university	No group differences
Waid *et al.*, 1979	Thirty unselected male undergraduates (50% guilty)	So-scale of the CPI	SCR	Code words	"no" (deception)	Instructions aimed at self-esteem	Undetected "guilty" less socialized than detected "guilty"
Gudjonsson, 1982	Twenty-four male and twenty-four female healthy controls, twenty-four male and twenty-four female personality disordered patients	So-scale of the CPI	SCR	Chosen card/autobiographical	"no" (deception)	Instructions aimed at self-esteem	No group differences. No correlations with socialization
Verschuere *et al.*, 2005	Twenty-seven (twenty-three female) undergraduates and forty male prisoners	PPI	SCR HR RLL	Autobiographical	Remain silent	None	No group differences. Negative association between PPI-II and differential SCR responding in the prison sample

Table 12.1 (cont.)

Study	Sample	Psychopathy measure	CIT measure	CIT paradigm	Required response in the CIT	Motivation	Main findings
Verschuere et al., 2007	Thirty-one male community volunteers and forty-eight male prisoners	PPI	SCR HR RLL	Autobio-graphical	"no" (deception)	Small monetary reward	Reduced SCR and RLL responding in prisoners vs. community volunteers with raw, but not standardized scores. No correlations with PPI
Meijer et al., 2007	Sixty (eighteen men) community volunteers	PPI	SCR	Autobio-graphical	"no" (deception)	Small financial reward	No association between PPI and SCR
Meijer, 2008	Thirty unselected undergraduates (eleven men)	PPI	SCR	Mock crime	Non-target button press (deception)	Small financial reward	No association between PPI and SCR
Dindo, 2008	132 male undergraduates	PPI	SCR	Autobio-graphical	Remain silent	None	No association between PPI-II and SCR. Negative association between newly created PPI "Irritable Disinhibition" Factor and differential SCR responding, and between MPQ "Hostile Negativity" and differential SCR responding

results showed that the CIT effectively discriminated cheaters from non-cheaters, with discriminative power declining from the first (61 percent sensitivity, 88 percent specificity) to the second administration (17 percent sensitivity, 94 percent specificity). There was no difference in detectability for the high vs. low Pd scoring undergraduates.

In the study by Waid et al. (1979), fifteen "guilty" male undergraduates learned a set of six code words. Fifteen "innocent" undergraduate participants were not aware of the code words. A control question test, a demonstration (card) test, a peak of tension test, and a CIT were administered. To motivate participants to achieve an innocent test outcome, they were told that highly intelligent, mature individuals were able to beat the polygraph. In the CIT, participants were presented with twenty-four words, including the six code words, and asked whether certain words had special meaning to them. The CIT was administered four times, for a total of sixteen code word presentations and seventy-two control word presentations. A code word was considered detected if it elicited a larger skin conductance response than the largest of the three control words for that category. If seven or more of the twenty-four code words were detected, the participant was considered "guilty." Finally, the Socialization (So) scale of the California Psychological Inventory (Gough, 1956) was administered. This questionnaire, like the Psychopathic Deviate Scale of the MMPI, measures the behavioral-lifestyle facet of psychopathy (Kosson et al., 1994). Before discussing the results of this study, some key limitations of the study should be acknowledged. First, we now know that the trivial nature of the stimuli in the code words paradigm limits validity (Ben-Shakhar and Elaad, 2003). Second, the fact that the CIT followed several other polygraph tests is far from optimal. Participants may have been bored, and paid less attention to the stimuli. Moreover, physiological responding is known to decline (habituate) with repeated stimulus presentations, as shown in the study by Balloun and Holmes (1979). Nonetheless, perhaps surprisingly, the CIT effectively discriminated the "guilty" participants from those who were "innocent" at a level significantly above chance (53 percent sensitivity, 93 percent specificity). Further, it was found that the seven undetected guilty participants scored lower on the So scale than the eight guilty participants who were detected. However, the small sample size in this study of unselected undergraduates raises further questions about the robustness of these findings.

Another study by Gudjonsson (1982) included four groups of participants: twenty-four male healthy controls, twenty-four female healthy controls, twenty-four male patients with a personality disorder, and twenty-four female patients with a personality disorder. Most of the patients had a criminal record, and according to Gudjonsson "may be classified as secondary psychopaths." Three CITs were conducted. First, there was a standard card test in which participants chose one out of five cards and were questioned about which number was on the card. The second test was a modified card test in which participants also chose a card and were told not to respond to any number. The examination consisted of five blank and five numbered cards, but only responses to the latter were scored. The third test was an autobiographical CIT consisting of a single question regarding month of birth with one correct and four incorrect alternatives. Each test was administered twice. As in Waid *et al.* (1979) motivational instructions aimed at self-esteem were given. As a measure of differential responsivity, the mean skin conductance response to the control items for each test was subtracted from the response to the critical item. There was no main effect of gender or personality disorder diagnosis on differential responsivity. To assess for effects of socialization, the association between differential responsivity and scores on the CPI So scale was calculated across participants in each group for each test. No significant correlations were found. A point of concern is that these correlations may have been underpowered. On the other hand, given that the correlations varied between -0.39 and +0.23, it seems unlikely that aggregating the data would have produced significant correlations.

None of the studies considered thus far included measurement of both psychopathy factors in the same study, and all studies relied upon a single response measure. Verschuere *et al.* (2005) addressed these shortcomings by investigating the effect of both psychopathy factors on several autonomic measures in the CIT. Thirty-seven male prisoners serving long sentences filled in a questionnaire that asked for autobiographical information. Four relevant autobiographical details (first name, last name, first name of the father, and first name of the mother) were selected from this questionnaire and presented amidst four control alternatives each in the CIT. Prisoners were asked to remain silent and watch the stimuli on a computer screen. To assure they paid attention to the stimuli, participants had to name out loud two digits that were presented during the test. The test was administered twice, with skin conductance, heart rate, and respiration recorded during each administration. It should be pointed out that this design – equal proportion of critical and control items, no motivation to appear innocent, no deception – is far from optimal for individual detection purposes (Ben-Shakhar and Elaad, 2003). Overall, the results for this prisoner sample did not differ significantly from those obtained in a sample of twenty-seven (mostly female) undergraduates. In the prison sample, the PPI was administered. The PPI differs from the Pd-MMPI and the So-CPI used in the previous studies in that it measures both the affective–interpersonal facet (PPI-I) and the behavioral–lifestyle facet of psychopathy (PPI-II). For SCR it was found that PPI-II, but not PPI-I, was negatively associated with differential responding in the CIT ($r = -0.34$). Correlations with heart rate ($r = -0.21$) and respiration ($r = -0.19$) were in the same direction, but were not significant.

Verschuere et al. (2007) conducted an autobiographical CIT in forty-eight male prisoners and thirty-one male community volunteers. The CIT consisted of five questions concerning relevant autobiographical items (first name, last name, first name of the father, first name of the mother, birthday). Each question had one correct and four incorrect items. As in Verschuere et al. (2005), visually presented digit items were included to assure attention to the stimuli. A small monetary reward was offered to participants who succeeded in appearing innocent. Using raw scores, differential responding in the CIT was reduced in the prisoner sample compared to the community sample for skin conductance and respiration measures, but not heart rate. However, this effect was no longer present after within-subject within-block standardization, a data transformation technique that is typically applied in CIT research to diminish individual differences (Ben-Shakhar, 1985). Further, in this study there was no significant relation between the PPI factor scores and physiological responding in the CIT.

Sixty community volunteers (eighteen men) participated in the study by Meijer et al. (2007). Participants were asked to feign complete memory loss and hide their identity, with the promise of a small financial reward for doing so successfully. The CIT consisted of six questions, each having one correct and four incorrect answers. Because three different sets of six autobiographical details were used, the relevance of the autobiographical items was not specified and could have differed between subjects. Using skin conductance, concealed information was detected in 65 percent of the participants. There was no significant association with the PPI factor scores.

Dindo (2008) replicated the autobiographical CIT by Verschuere et al. (2005) in 132 male undergraduates, with SCR as the sole dependent variable. No association between PPI factor scores and the CIT was found. In follow-up analyses, Dindo re-examined this relationship using an alternative four-factor solution of the PPI, consisting of Fearless Nonconformity, Social Potency, Irritable Disinhibition, and Thoughtless Disregard. The Irritable Disinhibition factor consisted of items measuring anger, irritability, and externalizing negative emotionality, and can be viewed as capturing the behavioral–lifestyle facet of psychopathy. This factor correlated negatively ($r = -0.17$) with differential responding in the CIT. In addition, an MPQ factor score related to the behavioral–lifestyle facet of psychopathy (consisting of items measuring external expression of hostility, aggression, blame externalization, stress reaction, and Machiavellian egocentricity), was also negatively associated ($r = -0.17$) with differential responding in the CIT. However, a concern in this study is that the newly proposed factor scores of the PPI and the MPQ were based upon a small data set and have not been replicated yet.

Thirty unselected undergraduates (eleven men) participated in the mock crime study by Meijer (2008). The participants filled in the PPI and then committed a mock theft of €10. They were promised a small financial reward when able to appear innocent in the CIT. There were six questions, each having one correct and five incorrect answers. The CIT included target items that required a unique response: participants were required to press the yes-button to targets and the no-button to all other items. PPI factor scores did not correlate with skin conductance in the CIT. Note that this study may have been underpowered because of the small and unselected sample.

Tentative conclusions

Four studies included a measure of the affective–interpersonal facet of psychopathy (PPI-I). As predicted, no association with the CIT was found for this psychopathy facet. From these studies, we conclude that there is no evidence to date that the affective–interpersonal facet of psychopathy impairs concealed information detection. This conclusion fits with the idea that the CIT does not crucially depend upon strong emotions such as fear. However, it should be kept in mind that none of these studies imposed negative consequences for failing the test. A critical test of the effect of the affective–interpersonal facet of psychopathy on the CIT is one where failing the test has (serious) negative consequences.

Nine studies in this review included measures that captured the behavioral–lifestyle facet of psychopathy (criminality, MMPI-Pd, CPI-So, PPI-II, MPQ-III). None of these studies found a positive association, four found no association (Balloun and Holmes, 1979; Gudjonsson, 1982; Meijer, 2008; Meijer *et al.*, 2007). Five studies found some evidence of a negative association between differential SCR responding in the CIT and behavioral deviancy scores (Dindo, 2008; Lieblich *et al.*, 1976; Verschuere *et al.*, 2005, 2007; Waid *et al.*, 1979). However, three notes of caution are warranted. First, given the methodological weaknesses in these differing studies, the tentative nature of the above-noted conclusion must be stressed. Second, differences in data-analytic strategies may partly explain diverging findings. The data of an individual who shows no measurable SCR to all items of a particular question can be handled in different ways. The "liberal" researcher can decide that there is no differential responding, and hence score that question as 0 (no concealed information indicated). Or, the "conservative" researcher can decide that no meaningful decision can be rendered because there is no assurance of valid measurement for that question, and thus exclude the data for such questions from the analyses. There may be arguments for either approach, but the point here is that the non-responding associated with the behavioral–lifestyle facet of psychopathy is more likely to appear in the data of the "liberal" researcher compared to the "conservative" researcher. From this standpoint, the effect of the behavioral–lifestyle facet of psychopathy may only be present when including non-responding. With this issue in mind, future work should clarify how non-responding was handled.

Recommendations for future research

First, the assessment of psychopathy and psychopathy-related personality traits needs to be extended. All reviewed studies relied exclusively on self-report measures of psychopathy, which may be biased by response tendencies. The validity of the psychopathy assessment could be strengthened by using additional, objective information. Hare's (2003) Psychopathy Checklist-Revised, for example, takes collateral file information into account. Moreover, none of the reviewed studies considered moderating variables that have been identified in the psychopathy literature. Several personality constructs (e.g., aggression, anxiety, and schizotypical traits) have been shown to moderate physiological responding. Raine et al. (1997) have argued that hyporesponsivity in criminal populations is restricted to high schizotypical individuals. The meta-analysis by Lorber (2004) showed that aggression may be related to hyper- instead of hyporesponsivity. It has been further argued that laboratory deficits in psychopathy are restricted to low-anxious psychopathic individuals, and not seen in high-anxious psychopathic individuals (Lorenz and Newman, 2002).

Second, if the negative association between skin conductance responding in the CIT and behavioral deviancy scores would prove to be real, research should seek to clarify why antisocial individuals appear to respond less to concealed information. The dominant position is that reduced orienting reflects a frontal brain deficit. If so, one would expect this deficit to be apparent in independent frontal measures, such as neuropsychological measures of executive functioning (Morgan and Lilienfeld, 2000). Another possibility is that there is no deficit per se, but that antisocial individuals simply do not care as much about the concealed information. This hypothesis seems readily testable, via subjective rating of saliency (Dindo and Fowles, 2008) of the concealed and control items. An alternative explanation is that antisocial individuals are more capable of sabotaging the CIT (Honts and Amato, 2002). Assessment of countermeasure strategies can reveal whether antisocial individuals use different or make more effective use of countermeasure strategies compared to non-antisocial individuals.

Conclusions

As could be predicted from the dual deficit model of psychopathy, there appears (1) no relation between the affective–interpersonal facet of psychopathy, and (2) some evidence for a negative association between the behavioral–lifestyle facet of psychopathy and the CIT. Several studies, however, failed to replicate this latter association. Better empowered studies need to establish the robustness of this relationship. All in all, it seems that psychopathy does not provide a great threat to the validity of the CIT.

REFERENCES

American Psychological Association (1994). *Diagnostic and Statistical Manual*, 4th edn. Washington, DC: American Psychiatric Association.

Balloun, K. D., and Holmes, D. S. (1979). Effects of repeated examinations on the ability to detect guilt with a polygraph examination: a laboratory experiment with a real crime. *Journal of Applied Psychology*, 64, 316–322.

Ben-Shakhar, G. (1985). Standardization within individuals: a simple method to neutralize individual differences in skin conductance. *Psychophysiology*, 22, 292–299.

Ben-Shakhar, G., and Elaad, E. (2003). The validity of psychophysiological detection of information with the Guilty Knowledge Test: a meta-analytic review. *Journal of Applied Psychology*, 88, 131–151.

Ben-Shakhar, G., Lieblich, I., and Kugelmas, S. (1970). Guilty knowledge technique: application of signal detection measures. *Journal of Applied Psychology*, 54, 409–413.

Benning, S. D., Patrick, C. J., and Iacono, W. G. (2005). Psychopathy, startle blink modulation, and electrodermal reactivity in twin men. *Psychophysiology*, 42, 753–762.

Block, J. (1957). A study of affective responsiveness in a lie detection situation. *Journal of Abnormal Social Psychology*, 55, 11–15.

Cleckley, H. (1941/1976). *The Mask of Sanity*. St. Louis, MO: Mosby.

Cooke, D. J., and Michie, C. (2001). Refining the construct of psychopathy: towards a hierarchical model. *Psychological Assessment*, 13, 171–188.

Dindo, L. (2008). *Dual Pathways to Psychopathy: Relations with Skin Conductance Reactivity*. University of Iowa, Iowa.

Dindo, L., and Fowles, D. C. (2008). The skin conductance orienting response to semantic stimuli: significance can be independent of arousal. *Psychophysiology*, 45, 111–118.

Elaad, E., Ginton, A., and Jungman, N. (1992). Detection measures in real-life criminal guilty knowledge tests. *Journal of Applied Psychology*, 77, 757–767.

Fazel, S., and Danesh, J. (2002). Serious mental disorder in 23 000 prisoners: a systematic review of 62 surveys. *Lancet*, 359, 545–550.

Fowles, D. C., and Dindo, L. (2006). A dual-deficit model of psychopathy. In C. J. Patrick (ed.), *Handbook of Psychopathy* (pp. 14–34). New York: Guilford Press.

Gough, H. G. (1956). *California Psychological Inventory*. Palo Alto: Consulting Psychologists Press.

Gudjonsson, G. H. (1982). Some psychological determinants of electrodermal responses to deception. *Personality and Individual Differences*, 3, 381–391.

Hare, R. D. (2003). *The Hare Psychopathy Checklist – Revised*. Toronto: Multi-Health Systems.

Harpur, T. J., Hakstian, A. R., and Hare, R. D. (1988). Factor structure of the Psychopathy Checklist. *Journal of Consulting and Clinical Psychology*, 56, 741–747.

Hathaway, S. R., and McKinley, J. C. (1943). *The Minnesota Multiphasic Personality Inventory*. Minneapolis: University of Minnesota Press.

Herpertz, S. C., Mueller, I. R., Wenning, B., Qunabi, M., Lichterfeld, C., and Herpertz-Dahlman, B. (2003). Autonomic responses in boys with externalizing disorders. *Journal of Neural Transmission*, 110, 1181–1195.

Honts, C. R., and Amato, S. L. (2002). Countermeasures. In M. Kleiner (ed.), *Handbook of Polygraph Testing* (pp. 251–264). London: Academic Press.

Kosson, D. S., Steuerwald, B. L., Newman, J. P., and Widom, C. S. (1994). The relation between socialization and antisocial behavior, substance use, and family conflict in college students. *Journal of Personality Assessment*, 63, 473–488.

Levenson, M. R., Kiehl, K. A., and Fitzpatrick, C. M. (1995). Assessing psychopathic attributes in a noninstitutionalized population. *Journal of Personality and Social Psychology*, 68, 151–158.

Lieblich, I., Shakhar, G. B., and Kugelmass, S. (1976). Validity of guilty knowledge technique in a prisoners sample. *Journal of Applied Psychology*, 61, 89–93.

Lilienfeld, S. O., and Andrews, B. P. (1996). Development and preliminary validation of a self-report measure of psychopathic personality traits in noncriminal populations. *Journal of Personality Assessment*, 66, 488–524.

Lorber, M. F. (2004). Psychophysiology of aggression, psychopathy, and conduct problems: a meta-analysis. *Psychological Bulletin*, 130, 531–552.

Lorenz, A. R., and Newman, J. P. (2002). Do emotion and information processing deficiencies found in Caucasian psychopaths generalize to

African-American psychopaths? *Personality and Individual Differences*, 32, 1077–1086.

Lykken, D. T. (1957). A study of anxiety in the sociopathic personality. *Journal of Abnormal and Clinical Psychology*, 55, 6–10.

(1959). The GSR in the detection of guilt. *Journal of Applied Psychology*, 43, 385–388.

Meijer, E. H. (2008). *Psychophysiology and the Detection of Deception – Promises and Perils*. Maastricht University, Maastricht.

Meijer, E. H., Smulders, F. T. Y., Johnston, J. E., and Merckelbach, H. L. G. J. (2007). Combining psychophysiology and forced choice in the detection of concealed information. *Psychophysiology*, 44, 814–822.

Miller, A. R., and Rosenfeld, J. P. (2004). Response-specific scalp distributions in deception detection and ERP correlates of psychopathic personality traits. *Journal of Psychophysiology*, 18, 13–26.

Morgan, A. B., and Lilienfeld, S. O. (2000). A meta-analytic review of the relation between antisocial behavior and neuropsychological measures of executive function. *Clinical Psychology Review*, 20, 113–136.

Patrick, C. J. (1994). Emotion and psychopathy: startling new insights. *Psychophysiology*, 31, 319–330.

Patrick, C. J. (ed.) (2006). *Handbook of Psychopathy*. New York: Guilford Press.

Patrick, C. J., Bradley, M. M., and Lang, P. J. (1993). Emotion in the criminal psychopath: startle reflex modulation. *Journal of Abnormal Psychology*, 102, 82–92.

Patrick, C. J., Bernat, E. M., Malone, S. M., Iacono, W. G., Krueger, R. F., and McGue, M. (2006). P300 amplitude as an indicator of externalizing in adolescent males. *Psychophysiology*, 43, 84–92.

Raine, A., Benishay, D., Lencz, T., and Scarpa, A. (1997). Abnormal orienting in schizotypal personality disorder. *Schizophrenia Bulletin*, 23, 75–82.

Tellegen, A. (1982). Brief manual of the Multidimensional Personality Questionnaire (MPQ). University of Minnesota.

Verschuere, B., Crombez, G., De Clercq, A., and Koster, E. H. W. (2005). Psychopathic traits and autonomic responding to concealed information in a prison sample. *Psychophysiology*, 42, 239–245.

(2007). Antisociality, underarousal and the validity of the Concealed Information Test. *Biological Psychology*, 74, 309–318.

Waid, W. M., Orne, M. T., and Wilson, S. K. (1979). Effects of level of socialization on electrodermal detection of deception. *Psychophysiology*, 16, 15–22.

13 Clinical applications of the Concealed Information Test

John J. B. Allen

Overview: The Concealed Information Test (CIT) can prove useful in assessing clinical populations where individuals are unable or unwilling to report on their mnemonic experience. Unlike the traditional use of the CIT, where one assumes that individuals are willfully deceiving or concealing information, in clinical settings the CIT is employed to probe whether traces of memory may be present without necessarily assuming deception on the part of the examinee. A small clinical literature has utilized both autonomic and central psychophysiological measures in the CIT paradigm to assess such conditions as prosopagnosia and Dissociative Identity Disorder, and also to assess the possibility of malingering in memory assessment contexts. To date, the key unresolved issue for clinical assessment is whether evidence of recognition with the CIT reflects explicit vs. implicit memory.

Clinical applications of the Concealed Information Test

The Concealed Information Test (CIT) has not been widely used in clinical populations or clinical applications, but illustrative studies suggest that it may provide a useful method for assessing clinical conditions where individuals are unable or unwilling to report on their mnemonic experience. Applications may include a fairly typical implementation of the CIT when assessing memory in cases of claimed amnesia where there is reason to suspect malingering, but they may also involve assessing populations where there is no reason to suspect individuals are willfully misrepresenting their experience.

Other chapters in this volume have covered the basic logic of the CIT, a term that covers a variety of techniques that derive from the original Guilty Knowledge Test devised by David Lykken (Lykken, 1959) as an alternative to the unreliable arousal-based polygraph "lie" detection procedures. In this chapter, the use of the CIT will be highlighted in two clinical conditions (prosopagnosia and Dissociative Identity

231

Disorder), and its use will be discussed for the more general case for assessing memory in clinical settings.

Many studies of clinical disorders follow an experimental or quasi-experimental approach, assessing groups of patients and looking for differences between such patients and matched controls. For such studies, the traditional use of group statistics (e.g., ANOVA) suffices. By contrast, assessment in applied clinical settings focuses on individual cases, and research with rare conditions also often focuses on individual cases, and in these instances decisions must be rendered for each individual examinee. The CIT is well-suited for this type of assessment, as it is typically used in forensic settings where there is also a need to render decisions for individual cases. In the literature involving the CIT in clinical assessment, multiple dependent measures have been used, including the typical skin conductance response (SCR: see Chapter 2 of this volume), but also features of the event-related brain potential (ERP; see Chapter 4 of this volume), and even behavioral measures such as reaction time (RT; see Chapter 3 of this volume). In principle, other measures might also be explored as indices of recognition in the CIT for specific clinical applications (e.g., heart rate change, peripheral vasoconstriction, changes in respiration depth or frequency, alterations of brain hemodynamic signals, etc.).

The validity of the CIT in clinical populations will hinge on many of the factors that would influence the validity of the CIT in traditional forensic settings, but additionally, other factors may be present that might compromise the validity of the results. Many individuals with clinical disorders will take medications, some of which can directly affect the physiological measures of interest (e.g., tricyclic antidepressants have strong anticholinergic properties that will greatly reduce the magnitude of skin conductance responding). Additionally, some individuals with clinical disorders may have cognitive impairments that might limit their ability to participate or that might render the conclusions of a CIT suspect. It is incumbent on the investigator to ensure that specific confounding influences do not interfere with a valid administration of the CIT. One way to ensure that the CIT can appropriately be used in a given clinical group or individual is to conduct a CIT with information that is clearly known to the patient (e.g., basic demographic information such as birth date, name, hometown, etc.), presenting it with similar appearing distractors, in order to validate that the CIT is in fact able to reliably differentiate familiar from unfamiliar material in instances where the patient has clear recollections.

Typically, one would choose to utilize a variant of the CIT in a clinical population or setting to make inferences about the clinical condition;

i.e., the results of the CIT inform the investigator about the condition. It is worth keeping in mind, however, that the use of the CIT in clinical populations also holds the potential to inform the scientific community about the meaning and limits of the CIT, contributing to the construct validity of the CIT. An example of the latter that will be discussed near the end of the chapter is the extent to which the CIT reflects recognition with vs. without phenomenal awareness; i.e., explicit versus implicit memory.

The use of the CIT in clinical conditions

Prosopagnosia

Prosopagnosia is a relatively rare disorder resulting from damage to ventromedial aspects of occipitotemporal cortex that leaves patients with a profound inability to recognize faces (Damasio *et al.*, 1982). A congenital and likely hereditary version of prosopagnosia has also been reported (Kennerknecht *et al.*, 2006, 2007 and 2008), with deficits that generally are not as profound as those in acquired prosopagnosia (Grueter *et al.*, 2007). Although able to recognize familiar individuals via other means (e.g., voice), the task of knowing the identity by looking at the face of another individual (or even of oneself) eludes the patient with prosopagnosia. The disorder thus does not interfere with acquiring and retaining information about other individuals' identities, but interferes specifically with linking that information to the visual percept of the face. Because stored representations concerning identity are clearly preserved, a natural question is whether the CIT might prove sensitive to those representations when the prospagnosic patient is confronted with faces.

In one of the most clever applications of the CIT to date, Bauer (1984) utilized a Guilty Knowledge Test to probe for whether a patient with prosopagnosia would show preserved evidence of discriminating face–name matches and mismatches. In this study, Bauer presented the patient with two sets of faces, one including famous personalities (e.g., Bing Crosby), and the other including family members. As each face was presented for a duration of 90 s, five names were presented auditorily in sequence, only one of which matched the face. The names were presented at 15-s intervals, and all names spoken for a given face were in the same semantic class as the true identity (e.g., for Bing Crosby all names were actors and singers; for the patient's brother, all names were immediate family members). In addition to the patient, two control subjects matched with the patient for age and education were assessed. Three measures were obtained for each subject for both famous and family faces: the naming of the face prior to presentation of the multiple-choice alternatives (spontaneous naming), selecting the correct name following the presentation of all five names, and whether the maximum SCR occurred to the name that matched the face.

Bauer's (1984) results were striking. Although the patient, as expected, was unable to spontaneously name a single famous or family face, and could not select the correct name from among the five alternatives at a rate exceeding chance, the patient had the maximum SCR to the correct identity on 60 percent of the famous face trials and 62.5 percent of the family face trials, significantly exceeding chance in both instances. For the control subjects, they were highly accurate at spontaneously naming (90 percent) and selecting the proper name from among all alternatives (100 percent) for famous faces; for faces of the patient's family, however, they could not accurately identify them (naming 0 percent, selecting 12.5 percent, neither different than chance), since they did not know the patient or the patient's family. The control subjects' SCR was, as expected, sensitive to famous faces, but not the patient's family's faces, with the maximum SCR occurring to the correct name alternative on 80 percent of the famous face trials, but only 37.5 percent of the patient's family face trials, the latter not significantly different than chance.

A follow-up study (Bauer and Verfaellie, 1988) found similar results for famous faces, where electrodermal discrimination of the name that matched the famous face was well above chance and comparable to controls, despite complete lack of the ability to spontaneously name the face, and a severe recognition deficit for these famous faces. Extending this paradigm to unfamiliar faces in a match to sample paradigm, Bauer and Verfaellie (1988) presented an unfamiliar face as a target, followed sequentially by five comparison faces, one of which was the same as the target face. The comparison faces were presented in nonisomorphic viewing condition (e.g., different viewing angle, different lighting). In this task, which did not depend on long-term stored representations of the face or identity, neither overt choice nor electrodermal responding correctly identified the target face at greater than chance levels in the prosopagnosic patient. Control participants significantly exceeded chance levels on both measures.

Bauer (1984) interpreted the findings to suggest that the damage that gives rise to prosopagnosia impairs the overt identification of faces, but preserves what he termed covert recognition, a type of recognition in the absence of phenomenal or explicit awareness. This finding thus suggests that SCR differentiation of familiar and unfamiliar stimuli in the context of the CIT can represent implicit memory; i.e., memory in the absence of awareness. The fact that SCRs can reflect implicit memory phenomena may pose constraints on how results of the CIT are interpreted, a point that will be discussed further near the end of this chapter.

Subsequent work by Tranel and Damasio (1985) with two prosopagnosic patients provides similar results. Unlike the Bauer (1984) study, where the CIT was used to index the match of name with each face, the Tranel and Damasio (1985) study merely indexed facial familiarity, with no way of assessing whether the face could be matched to a name or other identifying information. Using a paradigm developed by Tranel et al. (1985), which involved presenting familiar faces infrequently amidst a sequence of primarily unfamiliar faces, Tranel and Damasio assessed whether prosopagnosic patients showed evidence of familiarity for famous faces, family faces, and (for one patient) faces of individuals that the patient came to know following the onset of prosopagnosia (e.g., clinic doctors, neuropsychologists, nurses, etc.). Both prosopagnosic patients responded electrodermally to a higher percentage of famous faces and of family faces compared to their respective control face stimuli, and they produced significantly larger skin-conductance response amplitudes to these familiar compared to control stimuli. Moreover, in the patient shown faces that would have only been encountered after the onset of prosopagnosia, a similar pattern was observed: the patient responded more frequently and with larger skin-conductance response amplitude to the familiar faces than control faces. This latter finding suggests that the familiarity indexed by the SCR in prosopagnosia is not solely the result of accessing representations formed prior to the lesions, but rather that some degree of familiarity can be obtained after the lesions in prosopagnosia render conscious recognition impossible. But familiarity does not imply that electrodermal differentiation reflects the specific matching of facial features to identity. The findings of Bauer and Verfaellie (1988), in which no electrodermal discrimination was observed in prosopagnosic individuals in the match-to-sample task with previously unfamiliar stimuli, suggests that such matches may only be possible with faces that became familiar prior to the development of prosopagnosia.

Dissociative Identity Disorder

Dissociative Identity Disorder (DID) – formerly named Multiple Personality Disorder (MPD) – is a somewhat controversial diagnosis, and one that witnessed a striking increase in reported prevalence in the United Sates and Canada, but not elsewhere, at the end of the last century (Merskey, 1995). DID, as defined by the *Diagnostic and Statistical Manual*, 4th edition, Text Revision (DSM-IV-TR; American Psychiatric Association, 2000), is characterized by the presence of two or more distinct identities that recurrently take control of the individual's behavior, accompanied by an inability to recall important personal information beyond what might be explained by ordinary forgetfulness. Prior to the publication of the DSM-IV in 1994, amnesia between identities was not required for diagnosis. Multiple Personality Disorder was renamed to Dissociative Identity Disorder in the DSM-IV, and for the first time, the diagnosis required that there be the "inability to recall important personal information that is too extensive to be explained by ordinary forgetfulness" (American Psychiatric Association, 2000). Although amnesia between different identities is not explicitly required, the DSM describes only inter-identity amnesia in the narrative text explaining the diagnostic features (American Psychiatric Association, 2000, pp. 484–485, 526–529).

Assessing amnesia in DID with a test such as the CIT has both pragmatic and scientific value. Pragmatic issues include: (1) providing an objective measure of memory or amnesia that does not rely on self-report in a controversial disorder; and (2) providing objective evidence that may be relevant to legal cases. Legal defenses that hinged on establishing that a defendant had the now outdated diagnosis of MPD (e.g., *State* v. *Badger*, 1988) did not need to conclusively establish the presence of such amnesia to build a defense around the disorder, but contemporary cases wishing to establish the diagnosis of DID would in fact need to do so. Scientific issues include: (1) exploring the nature of amnesia in DID, perhaps leading to refinement of diagnostic criteria; (2) differentiating cases along a continuum of dissociation; and, (3) possibly providing clues to the neural mechanisms of dissociation.

The literature of inter-identity amnesia in cases of DID/MPD is sparse, but the pattern to emerge is one where a typical study will find reports of inter-identity amnesia, yet evidence supporting inter-identity memory transfer (e.g., Allen and Movius, 2000; Dick-Barnes *et al.*, 1987; Eich *et al.*, 1997; Elzinga *et al.*, 2003; Hermans *et al.*, 2006; Huntjens *et al.*, 2002, 2005, 2007; Kong *et al.*, 2008; Ludwig *et al.*, 1972; Nissen *et al.*, 1988; Peters *et al.*, 1998; Silberman *et al.*, 1985). Almost all studies find some evidence consistent with inter-identity amnesia (e.g., patient denies recognition of previously viewed words), and all studies find that there is some degree of transfer of memory across identities. Moreover, despite the self-reports of inter-identity amnesia in DID, there is an absence of objective confirmation of the amnesia reported in DID (Huntjens *et al.*, 2006; Merckelbach *et al.*, 2002) and there is some suggestion that dissociation may lead to a greater alteration of the *perceptions* of one's memories (meta-memory) than an alteration of actual memories (Kindt and van den Hout, 2003).

Thus these findings reveal that reports of amnesia on experimental memory tests produce rather discrepant results from those obtained in clinical interview about symptomatology. Because of the controversial nature of DID (Aldridge-Morris, 1989; Fahy, 1988; Merskey, 1992, 1995; Piper, 1994), and because the potential exists for symptoms to develop in response to situational demands and interpersonal goals (Spanos, 1994, 1996; Spanos *et al.*, 1985), objective, reliable, and valid methods for assessing memory are desirable. The CIT has been used for this purpose in one study of DID (Allen and Movius, 2000).

In the Allen and Movius (2000) study, reviewed below, an event-related brain potential (ERP) version of the CIT was utilized (see Chapter 4 of this volume for an overview of the use of ERPs in the CIT). In principle, an autonomic version of the CIT utilizing skin conductance responding could also be utilized, but no studies to date have done so. In utilizing the CIT to assess inter-identity amnesia in DID, two varieties of assessment protocols could be developed, one to address gaps in memory that presumably reflect the time an alter identity was in control (which to date has not been attempted), and the other to address whether memories from laboratory or clinical tests are shared across different identities (cf. Allen and Iacono, 2001).

To assess the validity of memory gaps, one would require objective documentation of the lost memories and then devise a test that is tailored to the specific incident. This particular use of the CIT is not unlike that used in standard deception detection applications. Moreover, if one identity had recollections of the time that comprises the memory gap for another identity, the specific CIT about this gap could be administered to the identity with that knowledge to confirm that the test generates a positive outcome (i.e., show evidence of memory) and that the CIT is thus adequately constructed before giving it to the identity with the memory gap.

To assess the more general question of whether identities share memories, a clinical or laboratory learning protocol would be administered to one identity, with a corresponding CIT administered to an alter identity that claims to have no knowledge of learning such material. This is the form of the paradigm used by Allen and Movius (2000).

In the study of Allen and Movius (2000), four female participants (age range 36–51) that met DSM-IV criteria for DID were assessed. Each of the four participants was rather typical of cases reported in the literature (Spanos, 1994) in that they were female, they had a history of other psychiatric problems that preceded their diagnosis of DID, and they reported on average about eight identities. On the testing day, participants were examined first as Identity A, and subsequently as Identity B. Identity A learned a list of six unrelated words and then performed a simple computerized recognition task to ensure that she knew those words. After asking her to switch personalities, Identity B then learned a list of six unrelated words other than those learned by Identity A. Once Identity B had learned the list to the criterion of two perfect serial recitations, she was presented with the critical procedure in which words learned by Identity A appeared on one out of seven of the trials, words learned by Identity B appeared on one out of seven of the trials, and words not previously seen by either Identity appeared on five out of seven of the trials. This arrangement made it likely that the learned lists, appearing relatively infrequently against a background of unlearned material, would appear distinct, rare, and significant, conditions that would likely elicit a large P3 amplitude in the event-related potential (ERP; see Figure 13.1) if they were recognized. Identity B's task was to press a "YES" button with one hand if the word on the screen was one of the words she remembered learning, and to press a "NO" button with the other hand for all the other words. It was expected that Identity B would deny knowledge of words learned by Identity A, but acknowledge words learned by Identity B. The CIT could then be used to determine if the ERP provided evidence of recognition of either the list learned by Identity A or Identity B. The test also provides a built-in within-subject control to assess whether the CIT can provide valid results, as Identity B should show the ERP recognition response to words learned by Identity B.

The ERPs obtained in this version of the CIT are displayed in Figure 13.2. Visible in the figure is the considerable variability among individuals. In spite of this variability, any CIT method must be able to render a classification of whether a given list was recognized for each individual. Although beyond the scope of this chapter, there exist a variety of methods for obtaining such classification decisions for individual subjects (see Chapter 4 of this volume for computational details, see Allen, 2002; Allen and Iacono, 1997; Mertens and Allen, 2008).

As can be seen in the figure, among DID participants (left panel), P3 amplitude is larger for words learned by Identity B than for unlearned words, as expected, but the ERP elicited by Identity A's words is not consistently differentiated from the unlearned words. Although P3 amplitude was not uniformly sensitive to the words learned by Identity A, a Bayesian classification procedure that takes into account similarities between conditions across the entire ERP waveform was in fact sensitive

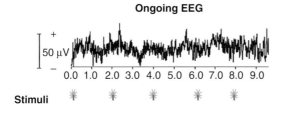

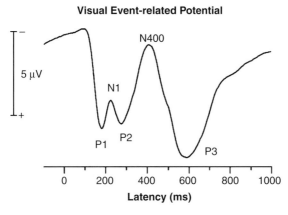

Figure 13.1 The relationship between ongoing electroencephalographic (EEG) activity (top) and the event-related brain potential (ERP; bottom). The top panel depicts voltage changes in the range of 50–100 microvolts that occur across several seconds. Beneath the ongoing EEG is depicted as a series of stimuli that are presented approximately once every 2 s. As can be seen from the figure, no visually discernable changes occur in the EEG as a result of the stimulus presentation. When the EEG activity surrounding multiple presentations is averaged together, however, the ERP in the lower panel emerges. The ERP represents voltage changes on the order of 5–20 microvolts that occur across a 1 s (1,000 msec) interval. Positive is plotted downward, and peaks are labelled for polarity (P = positive, N = negative) and latency (N400 is the negative peak appearing at 400 msec) or for their sequential appearance (P1 is the first major positive peak, P3 is the third positive peak). Relevant to the ERP version of the CIT is P3, whose amplitude is largest when stimuli are perceived as distinct, rare, and significant (cf. Johnson, 1986). If recognizable stimuli occur infrequently, and a patient in fact recognizes them, they should elicit a large P3. Adapted from Allen and Iacono (2001).

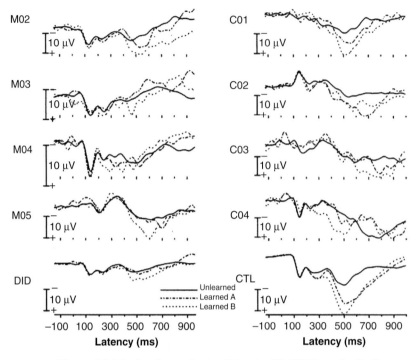

Figure 13.2 Left column depicts Identity B's ERPs at site Pz for words learned by Identity A and Identity B, and for unlearned words. Right column shows comparable data from four college student controls labeled C01–C04, selected from among sixty controls to show variability in individual responses. At the bottom of each column are grand average ERP waveforms at site Pz for DID participants and college-student controls. DID participants were tested as Identity B for recognition of words learned by Identity A, Identity B, and unlearned words. College-student controls were tested for recognition of words for which they denied and concealed knowledge (labeled 'Learned A'), for which they acknowledged learning (labeled 'Learned B'), and for words they had not learned. Only trials where participants responded with recognition of 'Learned B' items and denied recognition of 'Learned A' items and unlearned items are included in the ERP averages. Top panel plots each subject on a different microvolt scale to maximize viewing; Bottom panel plots DID and controls on the same scale. The Bayesian procedure identified both lists A and B as recognized for all eight subjects depicted in the figure, despite considerable inter-subject variability in the appearance of P3. Figure adapted from Allen and Movius (2000).

to words learned by Identity A. This Bayesian procedure utilizes features of the ERP waveform that have proven sensitive to recognized items in previous work (Allen *et al.*, 1992), and computes the posterior probability that an item is familiar to an individual. The Bayesian classification procedure indicated that for all four participants, for lists learned by Identity A as well as those learned by Identity B, there was greater than a 98 percent chance that ERPs signified recognition. It is important to note that these ERP data were based only on trials where Identity B responded "yes" to indicate recognition of Identity B's items, and responded "no" to indicate non-recognition of Identity A's items. Thus, even when Identity B denies knowledge of Identity A's words, her ERP suggests that there is recognition of Identity A's words.

Response latencies told a similar story. Like the pattern of responses seen in college students who deny knowledge of previously learned words, responses for DID participants were slowed for learned words compared to unlearned words. This results from learned words appearing infrequently while a majority of words are unlearned and require a "no" response. Previously learned items that are acknowledged (a "yes" response) require subjects to switch response set and use the other hand for response. Previously learned items for which subjects deny knowledge, but in fact recognize, pose a response conflict whereby subjects are primed to press both the "yes" and the "no" buttons; the responses therefore tend to be slowed, and to be less accurate due to this response competition. The DID patients had a pattern of slowing that was remarkably similar to college students who were instructed to deny knowledge of a previously learned list (Allen and Movius, 2000).

The results of this study using a CIT paradigm suggest that items recently learned by one identity, and denied by a second identity, show electrophysiological and behavioral evidence that is consistent with the interpretation that the items are familiar to the second identity despite self-report to the contrary. A key unresolved issue, and one that is discussed in more detail below, is whether these indices of familiarity – ERPs or reaction time slowing – reflect a conscious recognition (i.e., explicit memory), or whether they might reflect implicit memory, where responses are altered as a result of learning, but this occurs in the absence of phenomenal awareness. The CIT cannot arbitrate between these possibilities, but a follow-up study using measures other than the CIT with DID patients suggests that transfer of memory between identities most likely reflects explicit rather than implicit mechanisms (Kong *et al.*, 2008). In the Kong *et al.* study, words were presented to one identity auditorily, and a different identity was tested for recollection in the visual modality using an exclusion paradigm, showing that memory for previously viewed stimuli transferred between identities. Because of the cross-modal nature of the assessment, it is unlikely that memory transfer was implicit, suggesting that such memory transfer is indeed explicit.

It is also worth noting that the study of Allen and Movius (2000), as well as that of Kong *et al.* (2008), did not, and likely could not, test all possible pairs of identities for any given participant. It may be the case that, even among the participants tested in each study, some pairs of identities may demonstrate a mutual amnesia that would produce dramatically different results than observed. Moreover, it is noteworthy that the type of assessments utilized in these studies do not assess the type of memory impairment that typically characterizes dissociative disorders like DID. The DSM specifies amnesia for "personal information," and typically such information is considered relevant to the experiences of one of the identities. These studies, however, used simple list-learning procedures. As noted previously, it would be possible to develop a CIT test to determine if one identity with a gap in memory shows recognition for personally relevant experiences of another that presumably transpired during such a gap. This approach has not yet been used in DID.

Other clinical conditions

An interesting case study on Pseudologia Fantastica (i.e., pathological lying) utilized an electrodermal CIT to determine whether the facile persistent lies of a patient would be easily detected. Despite the patient's nimble fabrication of being somewhere other than the scene of a mock crime that he'd just committed, the CIT provided clear evidence of guilt (Powell *et al.*, 1983), suggesting that the repeated and persistent lying on the part of this patient was accompanied by a clear recollection of what had transpired.

Assessing memory with the CIT in clinical settings

In clinical memory assessment settings, overt performance on tests of memory constitute the basis for making inferences about the integrity of various memory systems, an approach that is inherently tied to self-report and that depends on individuals accurately representing their experience. In instances where there is reason to doubt the veracity of the self-report, measures of malingering can be used, but some sophisticated subjects are able to discern their purpose and circumvent detection. Thus, an assessment of memory malingering with the CIT could be welcome, providing an objective indicator of memory that is not inherently tied to self-report or intentional performance.

It was this motivation that prompted us (Allen *et al.*, 1992) to utilize a CIT-based ERP memory assessment procedure that assessed memory for recently learned lists of words, a situation that might be comparable to clinical memory testing in the context of a neuropsychological evaluation. (This same paradigm was later adapted for use in the previously described study of DID by Allen and Movius, 2000.) Specifically, the paradigm was designed to assess memory for items retained over a delay, which might be expected to be impaired in individuals with amnesia from any number of etiologies.

In this paradigm, subjects first learned a short list of words to a criterion of perfect serial recitation, and then performed a short recognition task where they responded yes when they saw a recently learned item, and no for anything else. Subjects then learned a second list of words, following a thirty-minute delay, again to a criterion of perfect serial recitation, and then completed the CIT variant where they were to acknowledge having learned words from the recently-presented list, but to deny knowledge of words learned previously on the first list. By including these two categories of learned items, the test provides an assurance that individuals are attending to all stimuli in order to respond affirmatively to the recently learned items, and also provides a built-in control in that all individuals should recognize these recently learned items and thus show a discernable recognition response in the ERP for these items. In a series of three studies, previously-learned items were appropriately detected as recognized 94 percent of the time based on a Bayesian combination of features of the ERP (Allen *et al.*, 1992), and unlearned items were appropriately categorized as non-recognized 96 percent of the time. Importantly, classifying previously learned items as recognized was independent of whether subjects overtly acknowledged learning them (recent list) or denied knowledge of them (first list).

These results suggest the promise of detecting malingering in clinical settings using this CIT-based procedure, as the test is sensitive to memory regardless of whether individuals overtly acknowledge recognition, but missing from the extant database is evidence that truly amnestic individuals would fail to show recognition on this ERP-based CIT. The literature on amnesia has many examples of individuals having no explicit memory, but preserved implicit memory assessed behaviorally (cf. Graf *et al.*, 1984) as well as electrodermally (Verfaellie *et al.*, 1991), thus leaving open the possibility that individuals with bona fide amnesia may indeed still show evidence of recognition using the ERP-based CIT, even in the presence of profound explicit memory deficits, if in fact the CIT can tap implicit memory. Such a finding would limit the clinical utility of such CIT tests. Moreover, under some circumstances, the CIT may be susceptible to erroneous classification of previously unseen or unheard items as recognized by subjects, thus leading to a false-positive outcome. In an ERP-based CIT study that utilized the Deese–Roedeger–McDermott (Deese, 1959; Roediger and McDermott, 1995) paradigm to create false recollections, falsely recognized words were classified as familiar 61–80 percent of the time (Allen and Mertens, 2009), a rate comparable to or exceeding that of actually studied words. A final limitation to this CIT-based procedure is that it is only designed to assess delayed-recognition memory, and many individuals in clinical settings with delayed recall deficits show lesser impairment on tests of recognition, and it is indeed seldom that would they fail to recognize any of the items previously learned.

Addressing this latter concern, van Hooff *et al.* (2009) examined differences between previously presented (old) and new words in a long list of items, reasoning that amnestic patients might recognize some but not all items, and that an old/new effect in the ERP may separate items that are overtly recognized from those that are not (for review, see Friedman and Johnson, 2000). In a sample of nonamnestic college students, some of whom were asked to feign a believable memory impairment, van Hooff *et al.* (2009) found that for both amnesia simulators and non-simulating controls, an old–new ERP difference was observed in both early and later time windows. Importantly, this difference between old and new items in the simulators was independent of their overt classification of the items, suggesting that the ERPs were sensitive to actual mnemonic experience and not the simulated amnestic response. Moreover, van Hooff *et al.* (2009) found that simulators produce longer and more variable RTs. A discriminant function utilizing RT indices as well as an ERP-response discrepancy score was able to correctly classify previously seen words between 87.5 and 91.7 percent of the time across two different studies. As noted by the authors, this study did not test patients with bona fide memory deficits, so the utility of this procedure for clinical purposes must await the results of studies investigating whether the procedure accurately classifies amnestic individuals, or whether instead this procedure may be sensitive to implicit memory effects.

To address a slightly different variant of memory malingering, a series of studies by Rosenfeld and colleagues have also specifically examined the question of whether a CIT-based ERP assessment procedure can detect malingered amnesia for autobiographical material or material learned without a delay before testing (Ellwanger *et al.*, 1996; Rosenfeld *et al.*, 1995, 1998, 1996; for review, see Rosenfeld, 2002). Yet as noted by Rosenfeld (Chapter 4), none have produced sufficiently high rates of detection to warrant clinical use of these CIT-based procedures at present.

For example, volunteers simulating amnesia for autobiographical material (phone number, birth date, and mother's maiden name) were detected 77–93 percent of the time, depending on the nature of the autobiographical material and the extent of coaching the subjects received regarding how real amnesics might perform (Rosenfeld *et al.*, 1995). Volunteers simulating amnesia for autobiographical material (birth date), and also for material in episodic memory (the experimenter's name and a list of 14 words) were detected 43–53 percent of the time (Ellwanger *et al.*, 1996) when assessing recently learned words, and 77–80 percent of the time when assessed for the experimenter's name. For overlearned autobiographical material (birth date), memories were detected 86–100 percent of the time. In all cases, the ability to detect the memories was not influenced by whether a subject was simulating amnesia or responding truthfully.

Malingering of working memory deficits was examined by Rosenfeld *et al.* (1996) by asking subjects to detect whether a three-digit number was the same as or different than a number presented just before a several second interval. Under the most effective of the experimental manipulations, subjects simulating amnesia were detected 70 percent of the time. Rosenfeld *et al.* (1998) obtained similar results using another working memory task (matching to sample procedure) where simulated amnesia was detected 69 percent of the time.

The studies to date that use CIT variants for assessing malingering in clinical memory assessment contexts reveal that familiar material can be detected in simulating individuals at rates ranging from poor to excellent, and that behavioral indices should not be overlooked in the attempt to use a multivariate outcome in the CIT to make such classifications. On the other hand, all work to date has only examined whether the CIT catches simulators, and no studies have examined the key question of whether the CIT would also correctly confirm the reports of amnesia in individuals with genuine memory impairment. Without data to support the latter, the procedure cannot be used in clinical settings, as individuals with memory impairment may show preserved evidence of memory but without phenomenal awareness, and there is reason to suspect that variants of the CIT may be sensitive to such preserved information.

What does the CIT assess: implicit versus explicit memory

An assumption underlying the CIT is that if individuals recognize items on the CIT, they will show evidence of recognition (via SCR, ERP features, RTs, or other measures) on the CIT, and conversely, if they do not recognize items, they will not. In the typical study of the CIT, this is verified by examining whether the CIT appropriately classifies those participants known or thought to be guilty from those that are likely innocent. In such circumstances, the innocent subjects have no recognition whatsoever for the relevant items in the CIT, as they were never exposed to these items in a crime or mock crime, and thus are appropriately protected from being mistakenly classified as guilty. In the clinical contexts reviewed here, however, the situation is markedly different. Individuals who report recognition impairments may in fact retain some level of familiarity with the material being presented, even though they are unable to explicitly recall or recognize that material (e.g., as in prosopagnosia as a clear example). To the extent that certain response channels (e.g., SCR) are sensitive to implicit memory effects, this may indeed limit the utility of the CIT for applied clinical assessment (e.g., assessing amnesia vs. malingering), but at the same time this may also provide a useful probe for research examining implicit recognition in individuals with memory impairment. Because to date the classic CIT has rarely been used in cases of amnesia that may result from brain injury or degenerative disease (see Verfaellie *et al.*, 1991 as the sole exception), it remains unknown whether individuals with amnesia would fail to show recognition on the CIT. Framed differently, it is unclear whether the measures used in the context of a CIT are sensitive to implicit memory.

Only a few studies bear on this issue of whether the kinds of psychophysiological measures used in the CIT may tap explicit vs. implicit memory. Moreover, the extent to which they tap one or the other forms of memory is likely to be paradigm-dependent. The three studies of skin conductance responses in prosopagnosia (e) would support that, at least in these cases, SCRs can index implicit recognition effects. Many other studies that do not employ a CIT approach would also suggest that SCRs can occur in the absence of phenomenal awareness, including, for example, conditioning (Wiens *et al.*, 2003, although see Tabbert *et al.*, 2006), learning (Bechara *et al.*, 1997), perception (Soares and Ohman, 1993), and memory (Newcombe and Fox, 1994; Stormark, 2004).

Similarly, various features of ERPs may be sensitive to familiarity in the absence of overt recognition while others may not. Examining the difference between ERPs to old vs. new words reveals two distinct effects. An earlier mid-frontal scalp topography covaries with the strength of familiarity (Rugg and Curran, 2007) and can represent implicit memory (Paller *et al.*, 2007). A later parietal scalp topography covaries with explicit recollection (Rugg and Curran, 2007). And although patients with demonstrable amnesia have not been assessed with the CIT, an ample literature exists to suggest that this later parietal old–new effect disappears in cases where explicit memory is absent. For example, in Alzheimer's disease, which is characterized by a rapid forgetting of material, ERPs only show evidence of the posterior old–new effect when there is a short lag between the first and second appearance of the item, but not at longer lags (Schnyer *et al.*, 1999).

Jointly, these studies suggest that in cases of demonstrable brain change that may underlie amnesia, some psychophysiological measures that are used in the CIT may reflect some access to intact memories that patients cannot explicitly access. Moreover, the extent to which these measures are sensitive to explicit vs. implicit recollection may vary as a function of instructional set or specific task (e.g., Schnyer *et al.*, 1997). Thus before the CIT can be used in cases of clinical memory assessment, the specific measures of interest (e.g., SCR, ERP, etc.) in the context of the CIT must be examined in both intact subjects as well as those with amnesia due to brain damage or neurodegenerative illness. Without such information, the interpretations of the CIT require caveats. In cases where a properly constructed CIT indicates that individuals have no familiarity with previously learned or known stimulus items, then one can confidently conclude that the individual has no memory for those items, either implicit or explicit. On the other hand, a CIT outcome that would suggest familiarity with such items must at present be regarded as uncertain, as it could represent a case of either explicit memory as in the case of an individual malingering a memory deficit, but it could also represent preserved implicit memory in the absence of subjective awareness as would be seen in many forms of amnesia.

Cognizant of this caveat, however, investigators are encouraged to make greater use of the CIT in the study of clinical conditions and in clinical memory assessment settings. Such work may ultimately help delineate more precisely the specific circumstances (i.e., settings, tasks, populations, autonomic vs. central physiological measures) under which the CIT may reflect implicit or explicit recognition of familiar material.

REFERENCES

Aldridge-Morris, R. (1989). *Multiple Personality: An Exercise in Deception.* Hove: Lawrence Erlbaum Associates, Inc.

Allen, J. J. B. (2002). The role of psychophysiology in clinical assessment: ERPs in the evaluation of memory. *Psychophysiology,* 39, 261–280.

Allen, J. J. B., and Iacono, W. G. (1997). A comparison of methods for the analysis of event-related potentials in deception detection. *Psychophysiology,* 34, 234–240.

(2001). Assessing the validity of amnesia in Dissociative Identity Disorder: a dilemma for the DSM and the courts. *Psychology, Public Policy, and Law,* 7, 311–344.

Allen, J. J. B., and Movius, H. L. (2000). The objective assessment of amnesia in dissociative identity disorder using event-related potentials. *International Journal of Psychophysiology,* 38, 21–41.

Allen, J. J. B., and Mertens, R. (2009). Limitations to the detection of deception: true and false recollections are poorly distinguished using an event-related potential procedure. *Soc Neurosci,* 4, 473–490.

Allen, J. J. B., Iacono, W. G., and Danielson, K. D. (1992). The identification of concealed memories using the event-related potential and implicit behavioral measures: a methodology for prediction in the face of individual differences. *Psychophysiology,* 29, 504–522.

American Psychiatric Association (2000). *Diagnostic and Statistical Manual of Mental Disorders,* 4th edn., Text Revision. Washington, DC: American Psychiatric Association.

Bauer, R. M. (1984). Autonomic recognition of names and faces in prosopagnosia: a neuropsychological application of the Guilty Knowledge Test. *Neuropsychologia,* 22, 457–469.

Bauer, R. M., and Verfaellie, M. (1988). Electrodermal discrimination of familiar but not unfamiliar faces in prosopagnosia. *Brain & Cognition,* 8, 240–252.

Bechara, A., Damasio, H., Tranel, D., and Damasio, A. R. (1997). Deciding advantageously before knowing the advantageous strategy. *Science,* 275, 1293–1295.

Damasio, A. R., Damasio, H., and Van Hoesen, G. W. (1982). Prosopagnosia: anatomic basis and behavioral mechanisms. *Neurology,* 32, 331–341.

Deese, J. (1959). On the prediction of occurrence of particular verbal intrusions in immediate recall. *Journal of Experimental Psychology,* 58, 17–22.

Dick-Barnes, M., Nelson, R. O., and Aine, C. J. (1987). Behavioral measures of multiple personality: the case of Margaret. *Journal of Behavior Therapy & Experimental Psychiatry,* 18, 229–239.

Eich, E., Macaulay, D., Loewenstein, R. J., and Dihle, P. H. (1997). Memory, amnesia, and dissociative identity disorder. *Psychological Science,* 8, 417–422.

Ellwanger, J., Rosenfeld, J. P., Sweet, J. J., and Bhatt, M. (1996). Detecting simulated amnesia for autobiographical and recently learned information using the P300 event-related potential. *International Journal of Psychophysiology*, 23, 9–23.

Elzinga, B. M., Phaf, R. H., Ardon, A. M., and van Dyck, R. (2003). Directed forgetting between, but not within, dissociative personality states. *Journal of Abnormal Psychology*, 112, 237–243.

Fahy, T. A. (1988). The diagnosis of multiple personality disorder: a critical review. *British Journal of Psychiatry*, 153, 597–606.

Friedman, D., and Johnson, R. (2000). Event-related potential (ERP) studies of memory encoding and retrieval: a selective review. *Microscopy Research and Technique*, 51, 6–28.

Graf, P., Squire, L. R., and Mandler, G. (1984). The information that amnesic patients do not forget. *Journal of Experimental Psychology: Learning, Memory, & Cognition*, 10, 164–178.

Grueter, M., Grueter, T., Bell, V., Horst, J., Laskowski, W., Sperling, K., Halligan, P. W., Ellis, H. D., and Kennerknecht, I. (2007). Hereditary prosopagnosia: the first case series. *Cortex*, 43, 734–749.

Hermans, E. J., Nijenhuis, E. R., van Honk, J., Huntjens, R. J., and van der Hart, O. (2006). Identity state-dependent attentional bias for facial threat in dissociative identity disorder. *Psychiatry Research*, 141, 233–236.

Huntjens, R. J., Peters, M. L., Woertman, L., van der Hart, O., and Postma, A. (2007). Memory transfer for emotionally valenced words between identities in dissociative identity disorder. *Behaviour Research & Therapy*, 45, 775–789.

Huntjens, R. J., Peters, M. L., Postma, A., Woertman, L., Effting, M., and van der Hart, O. (2005). Transfer of newly acquired stimulus valence between identities in dissociative identity disorder (DID). *Behaviour Research & Therapy*, 43, 243–255.

Huntjens, R. J., Peters, M. L., Woertman, L., Bovenschen, L. M., Martin, R. C., and Postma, A. (2006). Inter-identity amnesia in dissociative identity disorder: a simulated memory impairment? *Psychological Medicine*, 36, 857–863.

Huntjens, R. J., Postma, A., Hamaker, E. L., Woertman, L., van der Hart, O., and Peters, M. (2002). Perceptual and conceptual priming in patients with dissociative identity disorder. *Memory and Cognition*, 30, 1033–1043.

Johnson, R. (1986). A triarchic model of P300 amplitude. *Psychophysiology*, 23, 367–384.

Kennerknecht, I., Ho, N. Y., and Wong, V. C. (2008). Prevalence of hereditary prosopagnosia (HPA) in Hong Kong Chinese population. *American Journal of Medical Genetics Part A*, 146A, 2863–2870.

Kennerknecht, I., Plumpe, N., Edwards, S., and Raman, R. (2007). Hereditary prosopagnosia (HPA): the first report outside the Caucasian population. *Journal of Human Genetics*, 52, 230–236.

Kennerknecht, I., Grueter, T., Welling, B., Wentzek, S., Horst, J., Edwards, S., and Grueter, M. (2006). First report of prevalence of non-syndromic hereditary prosopagnosia (HPA). *American Journal of Medical Genetics Part A*, 140, 1617–1622.

Kindt, M., and van den Hout, M. (2003). Dissociation and memory fragmentation: experimental effects on meta-memory but not on actual memory performance. *Behaviour Research & Therapy*, 41, 167–178.

Kong, L. L., Allen, J. J., and Glisky, E. L. (2008). Interidentity memory transfer in dissociative identity disorder. *Journal of Abnormal Psychology*, 117, 686–692.

Ludwig, A. M., Brandsma, J. M., Wilbur, C. B., Bendfeldt, F., and Jameson, D. H. (1972). The objective study of a multiple personality. Or, are four heads better than one? *Archives of General Psychiatry*, 26, 298–310.

Lykken, D. T. (1959). The GSR in the detection of guilt. *Journal of Abnormal Psychology*, 43, 385–388.

Merckelbach, H., Devilly, G. J., and Rassin, E. (2002). Alters in dissociative identity disorder. Metaphors or genuine entities? *Clinical Psychology Review*, 22, 481–497.

Merskey, H. (1992). The manufacture of personalities: the production of multiple personality disorder. *British Journal of Psychiatry*, 160, 327–340.

(1995). Multiple personality disorder and false memory syndrome. *British Journal of Psychiatry*, 166, 281–283.

Mertens, R., and Allen, J. J. (2008). The role of psychophysiology in forensic assessments: deception detection, ERPs, and virtual reality mock crime scenarios. *Psychophysiology*, 45, 286–298.

Newcombe, N., and Fox, N. A. (1994). Infantile amnesia: through a glass darkly. *Child Development*, 65, 31–40.

Nissen, M. J., Ross, J. L., Willingham, D. B., Mackenzie, T. B., and Schacter, D. L. (1988). Memory and awareness in a patient with multiple personality disorder. *Brain & Cognition*, 8, 117–134.

Paller, K. A., Voss, J. L., and Boehm, S. G. (2007). Validating neural correlates of familiarity. *Trends in Cognitive Science*, 11, 243–250.

Peters, M. L., Uyterlinde, S. A., Consemulder, J., and van der Hart, O. (1998). Apparent amnesia on experimental memory tests in dissociative identity disorder: an exploratory study. *Consciousness & Cognition: an International Journal*, 7, 27–41.

Piper, A. (1994). Multiple personality disorder. *British Journal of Psychiatry*, 164, 600–612.

Powell, G. E., Gudjonsson, G. H., and Mullen, P. (1983). Application of the Guilty-Knowledge Technique in a case of Pseudologia Fantastica. *Personality & Individual Differences*, 4, 141–146.

Roediger, H. L., and McDermott, K. B. (1995). Creating false memories: remembering words not presented in lists. *Journal of Experimental Psychology: Learning, Memory, & Cognition*, 21, 803–814.

Rosenfeld, J. P. (2002). Event-related potentials in the detection of deception, malingering, and false memories. In M. Kleiner (ed.), *Handbook of Polygraph Testing* (pp. 265–286). New York: Academic Press.

Rosenfeld, J. P., Ellwanger, J., and Sweet, J. (1995). Detecting simulated amnesia with event-related brain potentials. *International Journal of Psychophysiology*, 19, 1–11.

Rosenfeld, J. P., Sweet, J. J., Chuang, J., Ellwanger, J., and Song, L. (1996). Detection of simulated malingering using forced choice recognition enhanced with event-related potential recording. *Clinical Neuropsychologist*, 10, 163–179.

Rosenfeld, J. P., Reinhart, A. M., Bhatt, M., Ellwanger, J., Gora, K., Sekera, M., and Sweet, J. (1998). P300 correlates of simulated malingered amnesia in a matching-to-sample task: topographic analyses of deception versus truthtelling responses. *International Journal of Psychophysiology*, 28, 233–247.

Rugg, M. D., and Curran, T. (2007). Event-related potentials and recognition memory. *Trends in Cognitive Science*, 11, 251–257.

Schnyer, D. M., Allen, J. J. B., and Forster, K. I. (1997). Event-related brain potential examination of implicit memory processes: masked and unmasked repetition priming. *Neuropsychology*, 11, 243–260.

Schnyer, D. M., Allen, J. J. B., Kaszniak, A. W., and Forster, K. I. (1999). An event-related potential examination of masked and unmasked repetition priming in Alzheimer's disease: implications for theories of implicit memory. *Neuropsychology*, 13, 323–337.

Silberman, E. K., Putnam, F. W., Weingartner, H., Braun, B. G., and Post, R. M. (1985). Dissociative states in multiple personality disorder: a quantitative study. *Psychiatry Research*, 15, 253–260.

Soares, J. J., and Ohman, A. (1993). Backward masking and skin conductance responses after conditioning to nonfeared but fear-relevant stimuli in fearful subjects. *Psychophysiology*, 30, 460–466.

Spanos, N. P. (1994). Multiple identity enactments and multiple personality disorder: a sociocognitive perspective. *Psychological Bulletin*, 116, 143–165.

(1996). *Multiple Identities & False Memories: A Sociocognitive Perspective.* Washington, DC: American Psychological Association.

Spanos, N. P., Weekes, J. R., and Bertrand, L. D. (1985). Multiple personality: a social psychological perspective. *Journal of Abnormal Psychology*, 94, 362–376.

State v. *Badger*, 551 207 (Atlantic Reporter 2nd Edition 1988).

Stormark, K. M. (2004). Skin conductance and heart-rate responses as indices of covert face recognition in preschool children. *Infant and Child Development*, 13, 423–433.

Tabbert, K., Stark, R., Kirsch, P., and Vaitl, D. (2006). Dissociation of neural responses and skin conductance reactions during fear conditioning with and without awareness of stimulus contingencies. *Neuroimage*, 32, 761–770.

Tranel, D., and Damasio, A. R. (1985). Knowledge without awareness: an autonomic index of facial recognition by prosopagnosics. *Science*, 228, 1453–1454.

Tranel, D., Fowles, D. C., and Damasio, A. R. (1985). Electrodermal discrimination of familiar and unfamiliar faces: a methodology. *Psychophysiology*, 22, 403–408.

van Hooff, J. C., Sargeant, E., Foster, J. K., and Schmand, B. A. (2009). Identifying deliberate attempts to fake memory impairment through the combined use of reaction time and event-related potential measures. *International Journal of Psychophysiology*, 73, 246–256.

Verfaellie, M., Bauer, R. M., and Bowers, D. (1991). Autonomic and behavioral evidence of "implicit" memory in amnesia. *Brain and Cognition*, 15, 10–25.

Wiens, S., Katkin, E. S., and Ohman, A. (2003). Effects of trial order and differential conditioning on acquisition of differential shock expectancy and skin conductance conditioning to masked stimuli. *Psychophysiology*, 40, 989–997.

14 Daily application of the Concealed Information Test: Japan

Akemi Osugi

Overview: Japan is the only country in the world where the Concealed Information Test (CIT) is applied on a large scale. In Japan, approximately 5,000 examinations are conducted annually by about 100 professional examiners. This chapter provides a detailed description of how those examinations are conducted, from the request for the examination to the report of the result. Procedural aspects such as generating the questions are illustrated with real-life examples. Finally, I discuss the current status of the CIT in Japan and some future prospects of the CIT.

Japan is the only country in the world where the Concealed Information Test (CIT) is applied on a large scale. Furthermore, the CIT is the only polygraph technique used in Japan, as the Control Question Test (CQT) is no longer applied. Polygraph examiners in Japan carry out the CIT on a daily basis. Throughout the country, about 5,000 examinations are conducted annually. These are performed by professional examiners assigned in each prefecture. This chapter provides a detailed description of how the polygraph examination is conducted in Japan, and why the CIT is successfully utilized in Japan.

Examiner

There are about 100 examiners in Japan. All examiners are assigned to a forensic science laboratory of a prefectural police headquarters. Typically the polygraph examiners belong to the psychological evidence section of their forensic science laboratories. The laboratory staff does not consist of police officers but of technical officers, who are also engaged in research. Most prefectural police headquarters have only one or two examiners, and they are entrusted with the responsibility for all examinations in the prefecture. Approximately 40 percent of the examiners are solely occupied with polygraph examinations. Most examiners perform other duties, such as offender profiling or document

253

examination. Although the number of female examiners is increasing in recent years, the percentage remains low at about 10 percent. Examiners have at least a bachelor's degree. About 40 percent have a master's degree, typically in psychology or behavioral science in a university or a graduate school. A few examiners have a PhD.

With the baby-boom generation retiring in recent years, many young examiners were recruited in the last decade. About 40 percent of the examiners in Japan have less than ten years' experience with the polygraph. There is a rising tendency to acquire a master's degree, with more than half of the young examiners having a master's degree. The newcomers have some research experience. They all attend domestic conferences related to psychology or psychophysiology, and 70 percent have presented their own research at those conferences. Their academic backgrounds fall in different areas of psychology: cognitive psychology, psychophysiology, social psychology or clinical psychology. About 20 percent of the newcomers have a background in psychophysiology. When recruited, most of these newcomers did not have advanced knowledge of psychophysiology, but they receive psychophysiological training after being hired.

Training system

There exists a well-elaborated polygraph training system in Japan. Japanese polygraph examiners need specialized skills and scholarship in psychology and psychophysiology because they are required to conduct the polygraph examinations as experts. Training is provided at the Training Center of Forensic Science, affiliated with the National Research Institute of Police Science (NRIPS). The center furnishes new examiners with the necessary forensic science training and gives experienced examiners useful information about new and specialized techniques in physical evidence analysis. The Training Center of Forensic Science affiliated with the NRIPS is the only official training school in Japan. There are no private training schools in Japan.

Examiners are provided with different types of training at different stages of their careers. There are five training courses: the basic course, the specialized technical course, the advanced course, the research course, and the management course. In the first year after recruitment, the examiners are obligatorily trained in the basic course. This three-month course is held annually and is taken by newcomers from all Japanese prefectural police headquarters. During the course, all newcomers stay together in a dormitory. The basic course provides fundamental knowledge in psychology, physiology, psychophysiology, and statistics in addition to knowledge that is indispensable for a member of the police, e.g., law. They also acquire specific knowledge about the CIT. In addition to learning the CIT principles, there are practical exercises on how to measure and analyze psychophysiological indices and prepare the CIT questionnaires. There is an opportunity for research and basic course attendees are required to present their research in the conference during the next year. They learn the essentials of being a researcher: how to design an experiment, how to carry it out, how to write research reports and articles and so on. An internship in near prefectures and a visit of the court is also programmed. After having finished the basic course, newcomers are given a certificate. Only newcomers with this certificate can perform polygraph examinations.

The specialized technical course lasts between seven and ten days. Examiners can voluntarily take the course whenever they want after the basic course. This course is offered every year and focuses upon different themes with regard to the newest techniques and apparatus. It also provides an opportunity to discuss pressing issues. The course enables examiners to renew and improve their CIT examinations. Attendees are provided with the newest knowledge related to psychology, psychophysiology, and physiology. At the same time, it provides an opportunity to exchange information, helping participants to improve their skills.

About three years after the basic course, the obligatory advanced course is scheduled. This course lasts twenty days, and is held every other year. The course is designed to ensure that examiners are exercising what they learned through the basic course and to deepen their knowledge. In this course, they discuss the CIT questionnaires they constructed for actual criminal investigations and how to measure all physiological indices effectively in various circumstances. They can get advice from skilled examiners who sometimes are invited as teachers.

A minimum of six years of experience is needed to join the research course. In the research course, examiners are provided with the opportunity to study in a domestic or an overseas institute. The length of the domestic course is six months and overseas is for three months. Apart from their regular work, the focus during this course is on conducting research. At the end of this course, attendees are required to present the results of their research at the NRIPS. They are recommended to present their results in conferences and to write a scientific paper.

To become a polygraph-section chief in the prefectural police headquarters, examiners must take the management course. This course takes seven days and provides the necessary knowledge for an administrator, such as how to improve their subordinates' techniques and how to educate police officers on the principles of the polygraph examination and its effectiveness. To apply the CIT successfully, it is very important to educate police officers. Attendees discuss their cases, the accuracy of their examinations and preparation for the court.

Through these five training courses, Japanese polygraph examiners become well-trained. In addition to the official trainings, polygraph examiners hold voluntary workshops, reading sessions, and case studying sessions. Many examiners participate in these workshops and present their cases and research results to brush up their techniques.

Daily use of the CIT

The Control Question Test (CQT) is no longer applied in Japan. Without exception, the CIT is currently the only method used in polygraph examinations. In this section, I will explain the common procedure in applying the CIT, from the request for the examination to the report of the result.

Request of the CIT

The CIT can be requested in criminal investigations when police investigators want to find out whether the suspect knows certain details of the criminal case, whether the suspect conceals information or to verify the suspect's denial of having crime-related information. Japanese police officers are educated by the polygraph examiners on the CIT and how it can be effectively utilized in criminal investigations. This education program is held a few times each year for almost all police officers of the Criminal Affairs Division, the Community Safety Division, and the Traffic Division. Educating such a wide range of divisions is of importance because the CIT is conducted in various crimes, including murder, theft, robbery, arson, assault, molesting, juvenile crime, and hit-and-run crimes. These educational programs focus on the following issues:

- The CIT does not reveal whether the person tells a lie or not, but whether the person has information about certain details of the criminal case.
- The CIT questions are constructed in such a way that only a person familiar with the crime can differentiate between the crime-related items and the control items. The CIT is grounded on the principle of discrimination based on recognition of crime-related details. Lying is not a necessary prerequisite.

- If the examinee knows the crime-related item through the media, town rumors, police interrogation or any other source, the question cannot be used in the CIT.
- The CIT is most effective when it is carried out at an early stage of the investigation, because examiners can only make good CIT questions when the information has not been exposed to examinees.

Taking these points into consideration, the police investigator requests a CIT by calling the polygraph examiner of the forensic science laboratory of his/her prefecture. The police investigator briefs the examiner on the case. The examiner judges whether the case is appropriate for the CIT examination through a preliminary meeting with the investigator and, if needed, through observation of the crime scene. If a CIT examination is possible, the head of the police station officially sends a written request to the head of the forensic science laboratory. The head of the forensic science laboratory instructs one of the examiners to perform the examination, and the CIT is constructed and carried out by this examiner.

Requests can be rejected for one of the following reasons. First, when people have severe health problems that prohibit them from taking the examination. Second, the CIT is not conducted on pregnant women because of consideration to the health of the mother and child. Third, people who lack basic communication skills don't take the test, because the examinee must understand the content of the CIT questions. These matters are assessed by the examiners before the formal request.

The polygraph examination can only be performed with the examinees' written consent. If the examinee refuses to take the examination, the CIT cannot be conducted. The police investigator provides the examinee with a brief explanation of the CIT before a written consent is obtained. In the pre-test interview before the actual CIT, the polygraph examiner explains the details of the examination and reconfirms the consent of the examinee. Although there are some cases in which the examinee refuses to take the CIT, their number is low. Examinees who are already in custody may consult with their lawyer as to whether to take the test. However, regardless of the lawyer's advice, examinees must make their own decisions whether to take the test. Therefore the CIT can be conducted without the lawyer's approval.

Additionally, the CIT cannot be conducted if there are no crime-related items which only the offender knows. Performing the CIT with an innocent-but-informed examinee may result in a false-positive error (see Chapter 10 of this volume). Questions regarding criminal intent and motive are also not used in the CIT examination.

The CIT can be applied in each crime case, where there are crime-related items which only the offender knows. These crimes include, but are not limited to, violations of criminal law, most frequently theft, robbery, injury case, murder, arson, and kidnapping. Violations of the Special Act such as Marijuana and Stimulant Dealing Law, Cannabis Control Law, the Swords and Firearms Control Law, and other laws can also be tested. By the same token, violation of the Road and Traffic Law, the Nuisance Law, and others are also eligible for the CIT in Japan.

Most examinees are suspects, but non-suspects can also be tested because the CIT plays an important role in the prevention of false accusations. In case of theft from a workplace, for example, the CIT may be conducted on all employees working there. Even if one employee is suspected, the CIT is usually conducted on the other employees in order to cover all possibilities. The CIT is rarely performed on the person who claims to be the victim, except when the investigator suspects that the victim's complaint is false. To assist an interrogation and in the search for further evidence, Japanese police investigators often request the CIT.

Setting up the CIT

The polygraph examiner constructs several CIT questions on the basis of the available information about the criminal case. The examiner obtains this information, in most cases, from the preliminary meeting with the investigator, but observation of the crime scene and interview with the victim are also conducted when needed.

How to generate questions

The CIT questions consist of one crime-related, critical item and several control, non-critical items. In order to conduct an effective CIT in a limited time, the most appropriate five or six questions are typically used. However, the examiner always develops more questions in order to be able to respond to specific circumstances. This is because statements from the examinee, especially during the pre-test interview, may dictate changes in the critical items.

The CIT examination is well prepared through the meeting with the investigator, inspecting the case documents, and seeing the actual crime scene or photographs of it. At first, the examiner selects several core critical items based on the following three principles:

(1) Exclude items that have been leaked to the examinee.

The examiner must first exclude items that have been leaked to the examinee. Because there are various ways in which the information could have leaked out, the examiner considers those possibilities. In the preliminary meeting, the polygraph examiner assesses leakage to the examinee from investigative activities. If the examinee was already interrogated, the items that were discussed in the interrogation are not usable in the CIT. Of course, the interrogation team, being exposed to the CIT educational programs, knows that items that leaked out to the examinee cannot be used. Therefore, the interrogation team usually tries to avoid mentioning any potential CIT items. The examiner tries to find out from the interrogation team what information has been discussed during the interrogation. If the examinee witnessed or visited the scene of the crime, the examiner notes what the examinee saw and how he/she came to know the information. It is important to confirm how the information was given to the examinee throughout the entire investigation. Furthermore, information that was reported in the mass media such as newspapers, television, or the Internet is checked, and leaked items are excluded. The statement of the examinee is also important, because the examiner needs to know how the examinee denies the charge. What items are usable varies according to this statement, because the examinee may admit some facts and deny others. The examiner excludes items which the examinee admitted to be aware of.

(2) Pick up more memorable items

Even some items that have been protected from leaking cannot be used in the CIT. The examiner selects those items which are considered to be memorable for the offender. The examiner must select items which are highly likely to be recognized by the offender during the CIT. To achieve this goal, examiners must empirically consider the following points:

• One's own actions are remembered better than merely seeing or hearing.
• Intentional and deliberate acts are encoded stronger than the accidental acts.
• Unexpected events which the offender needed to address in order to complete the crime are memorized deeply.

- Items encoded with strong emotion are most memorable.
- Minor details, such as numbers, are not likely to be memorized.
- The memory of color is obscured, especially when the crime occurred at night.

(3)   Select items that provide evidence for prosecution

Even if the item has not been leaked out and is considered memorable, it is not always significant for the investigation. For an effective CIT, the examiner must determine whether the item is suitable as a constituent element for prosecution. In the case of a robbery, for example, the examiner will formulate questions regarding the stolen objects and the offender's action against the victim. If the examiner would only test for recognition of the stolen objects but not the offender's action against the victim, the crime cannot be proven as "robbery" but only as "theft." When choosing items, it is necessary to take the entire crime into consideration.

Following the above three principles, several effective critical items are selected. Then, the examiner formulates the appropriate non-critical, control items for each CIT question (CIT questions are typically composed of one critical item and three or four non-critical items). The following points must be emphasized when formulating the non-critical items:

- To prevent false-positive test outcomes, the innocent examinee should not be able to discriminate the non-critical items from the critical item. Therefore, the critical and non-critical items should belong basically to the same category.
- However, items that are too similar or are confusing to the examinee are not appropriate.

Two CIT methods: the Known Solutions CIT and the Searching CIT

Two variants of the CIT are used in Japan, which are named the Known Solutions CIT and the Searching or Probing CIT. These methods differ with regard to whether the examiner knows which item is the critical one. In the preceding section I described how questions are generated for the Known Solutions CIT. In this case, the examiner knows which item is related to the crime and thus would be recognized by guilty examinees. The Known Solutions CIT is the most frequently conducted CIT method in Japan.

A Searching CIT can be conducted using questions about items that were not yet revealed in the investigation. In the case of a purse snatch, for example, the "location where the bag was thrown away after it was stolen" is typically tested in the Searching CIT. Similarly, the "location where the fuel was obtained" is often asked in the case of arson. The examiner formulates questions using a series of items which may reasonably be associated with the crime, in order to reveal new information. If the questions of the Searching CIT are adequately formulated, they should not differ from those used in the Known Solutions CIT, as far as the offender is concerned. The only difference is that neither the examiner, nor the investigator knows which item is the critical one. Therefore they try to develop items that cover all possibilities. The Searching CIT often helps the investigation by revealing details previously unknown to the investigators and consequently leading them to corroborating physical evidence. For example, in an arson case, if the location where the fuel was obtained is revealed, this in turn would entail investigative authorities to check CCTV footage and thus come up with evidence. Therefore the examination is sometimes performed using only the Searching CIT.

The following examples describe how the examiner sets up either the Known Solutions or Searching CIT. The CIT questions for both methods are often presented visually using a map, line drawings, photographs, or real objects to enhance understanding and recognition of the items. Usually the examiner prepares the CIT in two or three days, although the CIT is sometimes conducted urgently on the day of the request.

As mentioned above, the polygraph examiner formulates the questions. For example, in a case of a murderer who strangled the victim with a belt in a house, questions could be formulated as follows.

If the examinee says that he/she doesn't know any information, one may ask for the place where the incident took place.

> Question 1: Where did the murder take place? (the Known Solutions CIT)
> 1. A town?
> 2. B town?
> 3. C town?
> 4. D town?
> 5. E town?

There are various ways to phrase this question. For example, "Do you know if the murder took place in A town?", "Did the murder take place in A town?", "Did you commit the murder in A town?" and so on. However, the question must be formulated in a unified manner for all items within a set. In Japan, the examinee is not compelled to answer in a certain manner, although it is generally assumed that a verbal denying answer will be made. Thus, the answer is typically "No," but the examinee can answer "I don't know," "I don't remember," and so on. For example, the examinee may give the answer "I don't know" to the question "Did the murder happen in A town?" and the answer "No, I didn't" to the question "Did you commit the crime in A town?" It is, however, important that the core meaning of the questions and answers remains constant, irrespective of their specific formulation.

Using a map delimited by five circles which do not overlap one another, the examiner can ask about the place more specifically, assuming that the examinee knows the location of the incident.

1. In the area of number 1?
2. In the area of number 2?
3. In the area of number 3?
4. In the area of number 4?
5. In the area of number 5?

If the place has specific features, the question can be specified using those features. For example:

1. Near the school?
2. Near the park?
3. Near the hospital?
4. Near the post office?
5. Near the supermarket?

When the examinee says that he/she knows the area but not the house where the incident took place, the examiner can use the photograph of the house.

1. The house of number 1?
2. The house of number 2?
3. The house of number 3?
4. The house of number 4?
5. The house of number 5?

The manner in which the question is asked will depend on the situation and the examinee's level of understanding.

The question related to the modus operandi of the murder is a core question in most murder cases.

Question 2: What was the method of the murder? (the Known
            Solutions CIT)
1. By beating?
2. By stabbing?
3. By drowning?

    4. By strangling?
    5. By poisoning?

The question can also be phrased in various ways as mentioned above. For example, "Do you know the victim was murdered by beating?" or "Did you murder the victim by beating?"

Or the examiner can ask about the specific tool that was used in the murder.

    1. A bat?
    2. A knife?
    3. A tub?
    4. A belt?
    5. A poison?

If the examinee knows that the victim was strangled, the examiner can ask what object was used for the strangling.

    1. A rope?
    2. A belt?
    3. A necktie?
    4. A towel?
    5. A scarf?

If the dead body was found in an immaculately clean bed with covered blankets, the investigators could assume that the murderer made the bed for the victim after the murder. If so, the following question can be appropriate:

    Question 3: Where was the victim's body found? (the Known
                Solutions CIT)
    1. On the floor?
    2. On the sofa?
    3. In the bed?
    4. In the bathroom?
    5. In the closet?

This question can also be presented using the floorplan of the house.

From the same point of view, the following question can be used to ask about actions of the murderer with the victim's body after the murder:

    1. Put it in a garbage bag?
    2. Put it in a cardboard box?
    3. Covered it with a blanket?
    4. Covered it with a carpet?
    5. Sunk it in water?

If the belt used in the murder has not been found before the CIT, the examiner can ask for the hiding place in a Searching CIT:

> Question 4: The disposal configuration of the murder tool (the Searching CIT)
> 1. Concealed?
> 2. Handed over?
> 3. Sold?
> 4. Thrown away?
> 5. Buried?

Furthermore, the examiner can ask for the place of disposition.

> Question 5: Where was the murder tool disposed of? (the Searching CIT)
> 1. On a mountain?
> 2. In a sea?
> 3. On a road?
> 4. In a house?
> 5. In a store?

This question can be also asked using a map delimited by five circles, or using the geographical names as mentioned above. In the examination, the examiner selects the most appropriate presentation manner fitting the situation. Therefore, the above questions serve only as examples.

Conducting the CIT

After setting up the CIT, the examiners conduct the test. Almost all examinations are performed in either the examination room in the police headquarters or the appropriate room in the police station. Temperature and humidity must be kept constant and noise minimized in the examination rooms.

The examiner has a final meeting with the police investigator to update the examiner's information about the investigation and to inform the investigator about the CIT questions that will be asked.

The examiner prepares the apparatus. The CIT used in Japan is based on simultaneous measurement of several physiological indices: the respiration pattern, skin conductance response, changes in heart rate, and normalized pulse volume. Heart rate is calculated from R-R intervals based on an electrocardiogram, and normalized pulse volume is also calculated from pulse volume and intensity of transmitted light. The examiner verifies the normal functioning of the apparatus for all indices. At the same time, the examiner adjusts indoor conditions for the examination.

Pre-test interview

The pre-test interview is conducted before the CIT. Demographic information of the examinee, such as name and age, is confirmed. The examinee's physical condition is also ascertained in detail, from drug use to hours of sleep. If the medical condition of the examinee is not adequate for the examination, the CIT may be postponed. The examiner provides the examinee with detailed information about the CIT procedure, and confirms the consent of the examinee again and examines the written consent. After that, the examiner checks once again for any leakage of information. Examinees are asked to tell what they know about the crime. Furthermore, if needed, the examiner asks directly whether the examinee knows specific items, such as, "what type of weapon was used?"

The card test

After the pre-test interview, the card test is demonstrated to all examinees. The purpose of this test is to confirm the examinee's understanding of the procedure and check their physiological response pattern, as well as to check the apparatus. The examinee chooses one card from four to six alternatives, and is required to memorize the number of the chosen card. The question concerns which card has been chosen and the examinee is required to verbally deny all options. During the card test the examinee can experience the way that the questions are asked, the interval between test items, how to respond, and so on. The card test also provides the examinee with the opportunity to ask the examiner questions if in doubt.

The CIT

The examiner provides an explanation of all test items to the examinee beforehand. If the examinee does not understand an item, the examiner explains it more carefully. The examination using CIT often takes about two or three hours as a whole. For each question, each item is presented once within a set, and the set is repeated three to five times with a different order of the items in each presentation. The inter-items interval varies between 20 and 30 s. Because each question requires that much time, the examiner conducts only needed and effective questions. The examinee is assumed to make a verbal denying answer to each question, as mentioned before. If the examinee answers inappropriately, for example with a response latency that is too long or an unnaturally strong voice, the examiners may omit the requirement of giving a verbal answer.

During the actual examination, the examiner monitors the examinee carefully in order to detect countermeasures. The examiner records the various events, such as a finger or foot movement, a deep breath, a sniff, a cough, a yawn, or noise. Because there are individual differences in how these countermeasures affect physiological responses, the examiner attends to the examinee's physiological responses in each case. If the examiner thinks that the examinee intentionally applies countermeasures, he must instruct the examinee to stop doing it. Although the examiner makes various counter-countermeasure efforts, such as asking questions in different ways or timing, a judgment is rendered impossible when the examinee continues to carry out countermeasures.

After the examination, the examiner assesses whether the examinee reacted nervously to certain items. The examiner evaluates whether the elicited responses were caused by recognition of the items, or from individual reasons unrelated to the incident.

Reporting the result of the CIT

The examiner observes the changes of each index with extreme care. He/she reviews each response in each question, and briefly informs the investigator of the results. The examiner makes a judgment on the basis of visual inspection. He/she ascertains whether the examinee showed discriminative responses on the basis of the response pattern, the difference between the mean responses to critical and non-critical items and the consistency of the responses across sets. The changes of each index is covered in the next section. The examiner sometimes uses the within-examinee standardized responses to compare responses to critical vs. non-critical items within or between sets. Of course, they are also taking into account the raw values of the various responses. In case of consistent differential responding to the critical items, the examiner concludes that the examinee is aware of the critical items of the criminal case. In absence of discriminative responses, he/she judges that the examinee does not know the critical items.

In Japan, examiners currently don't use any formulated scoring system. With the new apparatus, mentioned below, examiners can know the averages and the standard deviations of the responses for each index, but they don't make judgments based just on these values. Because there are considerable individual differences in autonomic responses, the typical statistical methods are not used in Japanese CIT. For the same reason, specific decision rules with regard to the weighting of the various responses and the cutoff scores are not set. In addition, the quantification methods are not fully established yet for some indices. Therefore at this time judgments of CIT outcomes are made by visual inspection of the physiological responses, rather than by formal algorithms and statistical procedures. Of course examiners can be assisted by using scoring methods, such as the ranking method proposed by Lykken, although it is believed that this scoring method isn't going to make much difference on the quality of the final judgment relative to visual inspection. Eventually examiners responsibly evaluate the various responses in light of their knowledge based on their practical experiences and accumulated training. Currently, NRIPS is researching quantification methods and statistical procedures in order to examine whether they can improve classification decisions of examinees based on CIT questions (Matsuda *et al.*, 2006, 2009).

Judgments about whether or not an examinee knows a particular crime-related item are made for each question separately and examiners never make a decision about guilt or innocence. The CIT, as used in Japan, is designed to reveal what the examinees recognize and what they don't recognize. It is important to emphasize that the CIT cannot reveal why an examinee recognizes certain crime-related items and why he/she doesn't recognize other crime-related items. For example, suppose an examinee responded to the critical item on just one out of five questions. This may be an innocent examinee who happened to respond to one item for various reasons, or he/she may be an offender who forgot, or did not pay attention to most crime details for some reasons. CIT examiners are unable to identify the reasons why the examinee responded or didn't respond to some critical items. The examiner can tell the investigator only which items the examinee recognizes and the investigator can try to specify the reasons why the examinee recognized some items.

If the responses to the items of a certain question are ambiguous or inconsistent, no decision can be made for that question. The examiner also does not make a decision if the data includes too much noise or too many countermeasures. Note that the decision is made for each question, and not for the entire examination. Thus, the examiner may conclude that the examinee did not recognize the place of the murder but did recognize the murder weapon.

The examiner finally gives a formal written expert opinion on the basis of the results of the examination to the head of the police station as required. In some prefectures, examiners write their expert opinion for all examinations, and in the other prefectures, examiners write an abridged edition of their expert opinion for all examinations.

The investigators use the results of the CIT together with other evidence for further investigating the case. The results of the CIT are sometimes used as an explanatory data when the investigator seeks an arrest warrant and as evidence brought to public trial.

Apparatus and indices

To improve the accuracy and reliability of polygraph examinations, the NRIPS introduced in 2003 a new portable digital polygraph system for field examinations (Hirota *et al.*, 2005). This system was distributed to all the forensic science laboratories across Japan. In conjunction with the conventional polygraph indices of respiration, electrodermal responses, and finger plethysmogram, the new system is capable of measuring electroencephalogram, electrocardiogram, normalized pulse volume, and other psychophysiological responses from sixteen channels. The circuit, electrodes, and electrode paste for skin conductance measurement conform to the recommendations of the Society for Psychophysiological Research (Fowles *et al.*, 1981). This system is now widely used in Japan.

Each index has a particular pattern when the critical item is recognized, which in Japan is known as the critical pattern. The typical critical pattern is the occurrence of a skin conductance response (SCR), inhibition of respiratory amplitude, reduction of respiratory rate, deceleration of heart rate (HR), and decrease of normalized pulse volume (NPV). The NPV is a new cardiovascular index. It is a more sensitive index of the peripheral vascular tone than the traditional photoplethysmogram (Sawada *et al.*, 2001). The NPV can be measured easily by attaching the probes to the fingertips. Light transmitted through the finger is measured by a near-infrared light-emitting diode and a phototransistor. In the CIT, the NPV shows a significantly larger decrease to the critical item than to non-critical items, during the first approximately 15 s after item presentation (Hirota *et al.*, 2003).

Figures 14.1–14.4 show examples of actual CIT records with the critical patterns. The indices used to evaluate whether there is a discriminative response pattern differ between individuals. The examiners evaluate which indices are appropriate for the examinee, and their decision is mainly based upon the selected indices. The figures show examples of four examinees, in which different indices were used. Because an examinee tends to retain the same effective indices for the entire examination, different sets from different questions are shown here. The record of channels, from top to bottom, show respiratory changes, skin conductance level (SCL), SCR, pulse volume, HR, and NPV.

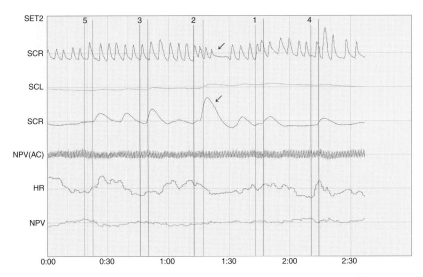

Figure 14.1a. An example of responses of Examinee A. In the question displayed in this figure, inhibition of respiration and larger SCR are shown after presentation of "2," which was the critical item.

As can be seen in Figure 14.1a, Examinee A showed enhanced physiological responses (larger SCR amplitudes and inhibition of respiration) to critical item "2," compared to the non-critical items. Similarly, Examinee A showed larger SCR and inhibition of respiration to the critical item "3" in another question (Figure 14.1b). Examinee B's responses are shown in Figures 14.2a and 14.2b. Here the discriminative responses appeared in SCR and HR, but not in the other indices. Specifically, this examinee responded to the critical item "1" (Figure 14.2a) and "4" (Figure 14.2b) with larger SCR and lower HR, compared to the non-critical items. As for Examinee C, the examiner could judge whether she recognized the critical item by SCR and NPV as shown in Figures 14.3a and 14.3b. In Figures 14.4a and 14.4b, Examinee D didn't show any SCR, but the inhibition of respiration was distinctly evident.

Values of the CIT

In Japan, the CIT is widely used as a scientific method to verify whether an examinee has information about the details of a crime or

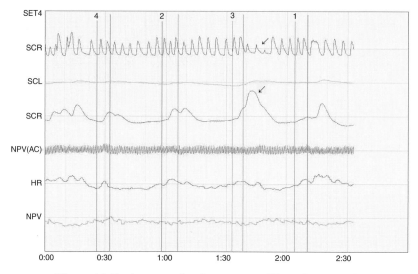

Figure 14.1b. An example of responses of Examinee A. The question displayed in this figure is different from that of Figure 14.1a, but similar responses are shown after presentation of the critical item "3."

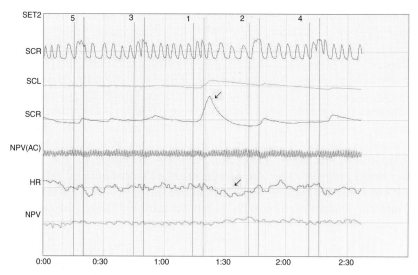

Figure 14.2a. An example of responses of Examinee B. In the question presented in this figure, larger SCR and HR deceleration are shown after presentation of the critical item "1."

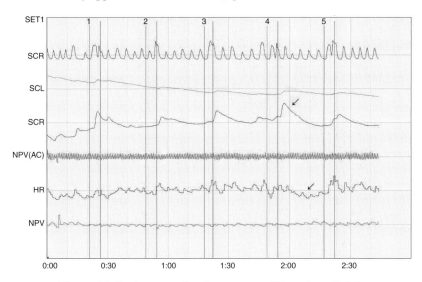

Figure 14.2b. An example of responses of Examinee B. The question presented in this figure is different from that of Figure 14.2a, but similar responses are shown after presentation of the critical item "4."

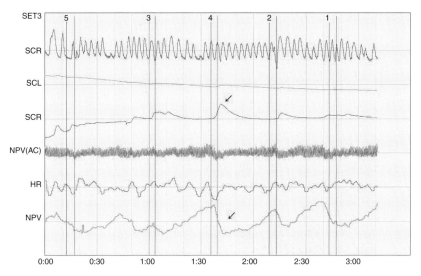

Figure 14.3a. An example of responses of Examinee C. In the question displayed in this figure, larger SCR and lower NPV are shown after presentation of the critical item "4."

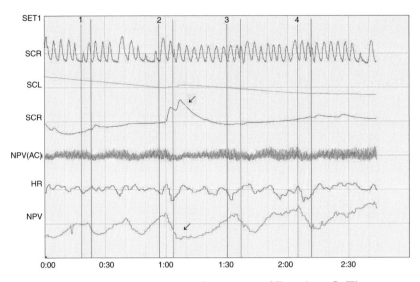

Figure 14.3b. An example of responses of Examinee C. The question presented in this figure is different from that of Figure 14.3a, but similar responses are shown after presentation of the critical item "2."

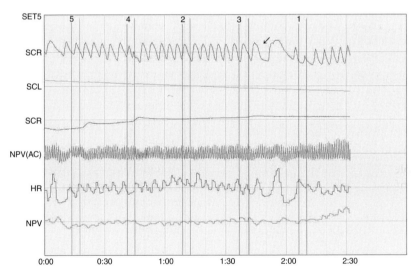

Figure 14.4a. An example of responses of Examinee D. In the question presented in this figure, inhibition of respiration is shown after presentation of the critical item "3."

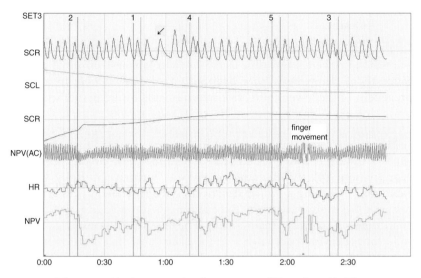

Figure 14.4b. An example of responses of Examinee D. The
question presented in this figure is different from that of Figure
14.4a, but similar responses are shown after presentation of the
critical item "1."

not. The validity and accuracy of the CIT seems to be high. However,
this conclusion is difficult to draw because in Japan judgments are
made not for the examinee but for each question. Yokoi *et al.* (2001)
computed the accuracy of the practical examinations, using 217
examinations including 1,137 questions. They calculated the sensitivity and the specificity from the data separately for each question
(i.e., the examiner's judgment on each question was compared with
the examinee's memory of that particular question). Only examinations after which the examinee confessed were included in the sample. The estimated sensitivity (i.e., the probability that the examiners
inferred "positive" when the examinee did in fact recognize the critical item) was 87.8 percent and the specificity (i.e., the probability
that the examiners inferred "negative" when the examinee did not
recognize the item) was 64.8 percent. However, as mentioned above,
this is a very selected sample that did not include examinees who were
revealed to be innocent after the CIT and consequently the estimated
specificity was relatively low. Therefore, a large-scale follow-up study
that will include examinees who were proven to be innocent is currently being planned.

Court

In 1968, the Supreme Court ruled that the results of the polygraph examinations were admissible as evidence in Japanese criminal courts. Since then, many cases have been admitted as evidence. In judicial precedent of the lower court, five requirements for admissibility of the polygraph examination were indicated: (1) the apparatus capability and its operating technique were sufficiently credible; (2) the examiner has sufficient qualification in terms of his/her experience and techniques; (3) the examinee provides informed consent prior to the polygraph examination; (4) the documentation was written faithfully by the examiner, including a proper description of the whole process and the result of the examination; (5) the examinee's physiological and mental condition was suitably maintained. The result of the examination is sometimes provided as evidence in the court, and the examiner appears as a witness for the prosecution as needed. The examiner coherently explains the results and the principles of the CIT examination. The results of the polygraph examination are utilized as one piece of evidence together with other physical evidence.

Academia

In Japan, there is a flourishing exchange of knowledge and ideas between polygraph examiners and university and other academic researchers. Polygraph examinations are recognized as an important research field by academic associations, and many polygraph examiners have participated in psychological and psychophysiological conferences during the past few decades. Moreover, almost all examiners recruited in the last decade have attended domestic conferences, and many of them have even had the experience of presenting their research in those conferences. Furthermore, as mentioned above, the examiners are required to conduct research as part of their training. The examiners and researchers sometimes forge links by undertaking joint research projects. In the annual meetings of the Japanese Psychological Association, a CIT workshop has been held every year for more than ten years. In that workshop, the examiners speak about their practical examination experiences and their research, and the researchers provide their comments based on their expert point of view. These interactions are important in maintaining the high quality of polygraph examinations in Japan.

In May 2009, the new citizen-judge system started in Japan. Under this system, ascertaining the authenticity of the suspect's statement is of great importance. In order to ensure that the statement was properly obtained in the interrogation, investigators and prosecutors are required to make the interrogation process more open. The CIT can directly and scientifically estimate whether the examinee's statement is true or false. Because the CIT provides supportive evidence, polygraph examinations are expected to play a more important role than ever before in criminal investigations. The polygraph examiners in Japan will continue conducting the scientific CIT steadily in order to live up to these expectations.

REFERENCES

Fowles, D. C., Christie, M. J., Edelberg, R., Grings, W. W., Lykken, D. T., and Venables, P. H. (1981). Committee report. Publication recommendations for electrodermal measurements. *Psychophysiology*, 18(3), 232–239.

Hirota, A., Matsuda, I., Kobayashi, K., and Takasawa, N. (2005). Development of a portable digital polygraph system. *Japanese Journal of Forensic Science and Technology*, 10(1), 37–44 (in Japanese with English abstract).

Hirota, A., Sawada, Y., Tanaka, G., Nagano, Y., Matsuda, I., and Takasawa, N. (2003). A new index for psychophysiological detection of deception: applicability of normalized pulse volume. *Japanese Journal of Physiological Psychology and Psychophysiology*, 21, 217–230 (in Japanese with English abstract).

Matsuda, I., Hirota, A., Ogawa, T., Takasawa, N., and Shigemasu, K. (2006) A new discrimination method for the Concealed Information Test using pretest data and within-individual comparisons. *Biological Psychology*, 73, 157–164.

(2009) Within-individual discrimination on the Concealed Information Test using dynamic mixture modelling. *Psychophysiology*, 46, 439–449.

Sawada, Y., Tanaka, G., and Yamakoshi, K. (2001) Normalized pulse volume (NPV) derived photo-plethysmographically as a more valid measure of the finger vascular tone. *International Journal of Psychophysiology*, 41(1), 1–10.

Yokoi, Y., Okazaki, Y., Kiriu, M., Kuramochi, T., and Ohama, T. (2001). The validity of the guilty knowledge test used in field cases. *Japanese Journal of Criminal Psychology*, 39(1), 15–27 (in Japanese with English abstract).

15 The Concealed Information Test in the courtroom: legal aspects

Gershon Ben-Shakhar and Mordechai Kremnitzer

Overview: This chapter focuses on the admissibility of evidence based on CIT outcomes in criminal trials. We adopted the criteria formulated in *Daubert* v. *Merrell Dow Pharmaceuticals Inc.* (1993) to evaluate admissibility. The literature on polygraph admissibility, which revolved only on the CQT, suggests that this technique does not meet the Daubert criteria. An examination of the CIT by these criteria reveals that although the current CIT research body suggests that it has a good potential for meeting the Daubert criteria, it is premature to recommend at this time that CIT outcomes will be used as admissible evidence in criminal trials. The main reason for this reservation is that the bulk of the CIT research is an experimental laboratory research and very little information exists today on CIT validity in the realistic forensic context. We recommend that future CIT research will examine the validity of this technique in realistic settings, or at least rely on laboratory experiments that better approximate realistic conditions.

Introduction

The question of whether polygraph tests' results should be used as admissible evidence in criminal courts is almost as ancient as polygraph testing itself. The first attempt to introduce polygraph test results into the US courtroom was made as early as 1923 (*Frye* v. *United States*). In the Frye case, the court rejected the polygraph testimony, but more importantly the ruling in this case has become a precedent for the admissibility of all scientific evidence in US courts for many years to come. Specifically, the Frye rule conditioned legal admissibility of a scientifically based technique on its acceptance by the relevant scientific community. However, polygraph technology has considerably developed since the Frye ruling, which related to a very early version of the polygraph developed by Marston (1917) on the basis of changes in systolic blood pressure. In addition, the approach of US federal courts towards expert scientific testimony has also changed since the 1923 Frye ruling. Specifically, in 1993 new guidelines were set by the US Supreme Court (see *Daubert* v. *Merrell Dow Pharmaceuticals Inc.*, 1993). The four criteria formulated in Daubert are:

(1) testability, or falsifiability (i.e., whether the theory or technique on which the testimony is based can be tested);
(2) error rate (i.e., whether the technique has a known error rate in its application);
(3) peer review and publication (i.e., whether the theory or technique in question has been subjected to peer review and publications); and
(4) general acceptance (i.e., whether the theory or technique in question has been generally accepted by the relevant scientific community).

It should be pointed out that these criteria are neither binding, nor exhaustive, but were mentioned as examples. In reality the trial judge must determine in each case whether or not the expert testimony will assist the trier of fact. However, as an expert testimony that does meet these four criteria is likely to be admissible in US courts, we decided to use them to asses whether the Concealed Information Test (CIT) may be regarded admissible in the US legal system and whether we believe it has a potential to be used in other legal systems. A similar approach was adopted by Vrij (2008) who examined various detection methods in light of the Daubert criteria. In other common-law countries, like Great Britain and Israel, the legal criteria for admissibility of scientific evidence are more flexible. However, for the sake of this article, we are following the stricter criteria laid down in Daubert.

The debate about admissibility of the CQT[1]

The debate of whether polygraph tests' results should be considered as admissible evidence in criminal courts has almost exclusively focused on the polygraph technique widely used in North America and Israel, called the Control (or Comparison) Questions Test (CQT) and mostly ignored the CIT (see Ben-Shakhar, 2002; Daniels, 2002; Gallai, 1999; Harnon, 1982; Honts *et al.*, 2002; Iacono and Lykken, 2002; Saxe and Ben-Shakhar, 1999). In particular, two studies examined the admissibility of the CQT in light of the Daubert criteria (Gallai, 1999; Saxe and

---

[1] Although the present book deals with the CIT, we included this debate about the admissibility of the CQT because the issue of polygraph admissibility was raised in courts only in relation to the CQT.

Ben-Shakhar, 1999) and reached similar conclusions. Gallai concluded that "the results of polygraph examinations as practiced today (i.e., the CQT) should not be admissible evidence in federal courts" (Gallai, 1999, p. 88). In analyzing the four Daubert criteria, Gallai (1999) demonstrated that the CQT does not satisfy these criteria, with the possible exception of peer review and publications (it should be noted that many of the publications related to the CQT are various critics of the technique). Saxe and Ben-Shakhar (1999) focused on the modern concept of scientific validity (e.g., Messick, 1995) and demonstrated that the CQT lacks several critical components of construct validity and discriminant validity. More recently, Vrij (2008) also examined whether the CQT meets the Daubert criteria and reached a similar conclusion. A different opinion was expressed by Daniels (2002) who wrote that, "The general legal rules and theories of admission of evidence, and of scientific evidence in particular, would seem to favor polygraph admission" (Daniels, 2002, p. 338). However, Daniels ignored the critical issues raised by Gallai (1999) and Saxe and Ben-Shakhar (1999) and did not demonstrate how the CQT meets any of the Daubert criteria.

Indeed, even after the Daubert precedent, polygraph tests' results have been overwhelmingly rejected by US federal courts (e.g., *Commonwealth of Massachusetts* v. *Woodward*, 1998; *United States* v. *Cordoba*, 1998; *United States* v. *Scheffer*, 1998). However, the present volume is focused on a completely different method of psychophysiological detection, namely the CIT and in this chapter we raise the question of the potential admissibility of CIT results in criminal courts.

Should CIT outcomes be admitted in criminal procedures?

This question was raised before in a single article, which concluded that, the CIT "is capable, if carefully administered, of meeting the recently set Daubert criteria" (Ben-Shakhar *et al.*, 2002, p. 527). In the present chapter we re-examine this question and the conclusion drawn by Ben-Shakhar *et al.* (2002) in light of recent progress in CIT research.

In our previous paper (Ben-Shakhar *et al.*, 2002), we wrote that the CIT has much better prospects to meet the Daubert criteria than the CQT. We still hold that this is indeed the case, mainly because unlike the CQT, the CIT has a theoretical basis in psychology and psychophysiology and this is a necessary condition for construct validity. The theoretical foundation of the CIT is covered in great detail elsewhere (see Chapter 7 of this volume), so here we shall just mention that a large research body indicates that Orienting Response (OR) theory (Sokolov,

1963) accounts for the differential response pattern to the relevant (crime-related) items vs. the control-neutral items observed in the CIT (e.g., Gati and Ben-Shakhar, 1990; Lykken 1974). For example, Lykken (1974, p. 728) argued that: "for the guilty subject only, the 'correct' alternative will have a special significance, an added 'signal value' which will tend to produce a stronger orienting reflex than that subject will show to other alternatives." Thus, the CIT can reveal whether a suspect has knowledge of critical crime-related details (e.g., modus operandi, specific items that were stolen). Such knowledge can link the suspect to the culprit if it is ascertained that these critical items were not leaked out and are known only to the culprits and the investigators. This idea can be extended to other details that link the suspect to the culprit, not necessarily through the crime, but possibly through their biography (see an example in Ben-Shakhar et al., 2002). Since the psychophysiological differentiation in the CIT is mediated through a mechanism of orientation, the enhanced responses elicited by the relevant items need not be attributed to deception, motivation, or fear of punishment. Ben-Shakhar and Furedy (1990) call this a cognitive approach to psychophysiological detection, because it relies on what one knows, rather than on one's emotions, concerns, and conditioned responses. Research demonstrates that relevant information can be detected even when no motivational instructions are given to the subjects, and even when no verbal response is required (e.g., Ben-Shakhar, 1977; Elaad and Ben-Shakhar, 1989).

An examination of the CIT vis-à-vis the Daubert criteria[2]

In the following section we shall examine whether the CIT can meet the four Doubert criteria:

(1) Testability, or falsifiability: it is quite clear that the rationale behind the CIT (OR theory) can be tested and indeed has been extensively tested. In particular the prediction that personally significant stimuli (or stimuli carrying signal value, to use Sokolov's terminology) will trigger enhanced ORs has been examined and confirmed in many studies (e.g., Ben-Shakhar, 1977, 1980; Ben-Shakhar and

---

[2] Clearly there are many other legal systems, but we focus on the United States and on the Daubert criteria because the issue of polygraph admissibility has been discussed mainly in the United States and the Daubert ruling is the only legal source providing some specific guidelines for the admissibility of scientific evidence.

Gati, 1987; Bernstein, 1979; Maltzman, 1979; Verschuere *et al.*, 2004).

(2) Error rate: the predictive validity of the CIT and the two types of classification error (false-positives and false-negatives) have been tested again and again (see Ben-Shakhar and Elaad, 2003 for a meta-analytic review). This meta-analysis relied only on a single physiological measure (changes in skin conductance) and used data of eighty studies that included 169 experimental conditions. The analysis revealed impressive criterion-validity estimates (the average effect size across all studies was 1.55, which corresponds to a correlation coefficient of 0.55). But more importantly, Ben-Shakhar and Elaad (2003) identified a subset of ten studies that best approximated optimal conditions for applying the CIT (in terms of subjects' motivation, number of questions, etc.). The validity estimates based on these studies were larger than those obtained for any known technique derived from the behavioral sciences (the average effect size computed across these ten studies was 3.12, which corresponds to a correlation of 0.79 between the differential response pattern to the critical items and the criterion of guilt vs. innocence). In terms of error rates, the outcomes of these ten studies are also impressive. In five of them no false-positive errors were observed and the average rate of false-positives, computed across all ten studies, was 6.6 percent. In three studies no false-negatives were observed and the average rate of false negatives was 12.8 percent. It is clear that additional physiological measures would increase the test's validity and further reduce both types of errors (e.g., Gamer *et al.*, 2008). However, this meta-analysis was based only on laboratory studies and it is questionable whether the results can be generalized to the realistic setting. We shall focus on the question of the external validity of CIT experiments conducted in laboratory settings in a separate section.

(3) Peer review and publication: as indicated above, the CIT has been the focus of psychophysiological research at least since the late 1950s, where the two pioneering studies introducing the concept of "Guilty Knowledge" were published (Lykken, 1959, 1960). CIT studies have been published extensively in peer-reviewed journals, such as *Psychophysiology*, *Journal of Applied Psychology* and various other journals dealing with applied psychophysiology as well as forensic psychology (for a review, see Ben-Shakhar and Elaad, 2003; Ben-Shakhar and Furedy, 1990; MacLaren, 2001). However, as indicated above, these studies were almost exclusively laboratory studies based on mock-crime procedures and artificial settings.

(4) General acceptance: whereas the CQT has been under a continuous controversy (e.g., Honts *et al.*, 2002; Iacono and Lykken, 2002) and was severely criticized by many researchers (e.g., Ben-Shakhar, 2002; Fiedler *et al.*, 2002; Furedy, 1993; Iacono and Patrick, 1988; Saxe, 1991), the CIT's rationale has been widely accepted and the only reservations raised revolved around the scope of its application and whether the assumptions underlying it (i.e., the existence of a sufficient number of salient crime details, which are concealed from the suspects and the general public) can be met in realistic settings (e.g., Podlesny, 1993). For example, a survey of psychologists and psychophysiologists conducted by Iacono and Lykken (1997) found little support for CQT polygraphy, but considerable support for the CIT.

The external validity of CIT research

We demonstrated in the previous section that the CIT has a potential of meeting the Daubert criteria (see also, Ben-Shakhar *et al.*, 2002). However, this conclusion is based on research conducted in laboratory settings, where it was always guaranteed that the assumptions underlying the CIT were met. The question of external validity of this research (the extent to which the results of laboratory CIT studies can be generalized to field settings where the CIT would be applied) depends on whether these assumptions can be met in the realistic setting. In this section we wish to examine this issue, which we believe is critical for the admissibility of CIT outcomes as evidence in criminal courts. For example, the second Daubert criterion requires that the technique will have a known error rate in its application. However, currently the error rate can be estimated only from laboratory studies. Three major factors that may differentiate controlled laboratory experiments from realistic settings where the CIT can be applied should be considered in order to examine the issue of external validity:

(1) *The availability of a sufficient number of critical items (features of the crime scene) that culprits perceive during the criminal act, process and store in memory, such that they will be remembered during the interrogation*: this is clearly critical because differential responding to the critical items depends on their recognition as significant (i.e., crime-related) by the examinee. Unfortunately, almost all CIT studies used very simple tasks, where the experimenters guaranteed that all subjects learned all the relevant items. Furthermore, the subjects are typically tested immediately after being exposed to the

critical information, thus memory does not play an important role in the experimental situation. In real life, on the other hand, the culprit is faced with a complex scene, and it is questionable whether all details are indeed noticed, processed, and stored in memory. Criminal suspects are very rarely tested immediately after committing the criminal act. Typically, they may be tested days, weeks, and sometimes months after the crime has been committed. These critical differences between the applied and the simulated settings may account for the relatively large rates of false-negative outcomes observed in the only field CIT studies reported so far (see Elaad, 1990; Elaad *et al.*, 1992). While the rates of false-positive errors obtained in these studies were as low as those reported in laboratory experiments (2 percent in the former study, which relied only on the electrodermal measure, and 5 percent in the latter study, which utilized a combination of electrodermal and respiration measures), the rates of false-negative errors were much larger (42 percent in the former study and 20 percent in the latter). Thus, the effects of perception and attention during criminal acts as well as memory for the critical details on the outcomes of the CIT should be closely examined. Ideally, this should be done by conducting well-designed field studies. However, this is extremely difficult mainly because ground truth criterion is typically unavailable in realistic cases and the use of confessions as a criterion is highly problematic (see Iacono, 1991). A different approach is to rely on experimental research that better approximates the realistic situation and to manipulate the factors differentiating between laboratory and real-life conditions and examine their impact on the outcomes of the CIT. An initial experiment designed to examine this issue was reported by Carmel *et al.* (2003). Specifically, this experiment employed a two-by-two between-subjects design, with the following two factors: type of mock crime (standard vs. realistic) and the time interval (immediate vs. a week after executing the mock crime). In the realistic condition, participants were allowed to stay at the simulated crime scene for a limited time and were neither informed about most critical details, nor were they reminded before taking the test about the critical items. In the standard condition, on the other hand, no time limit was set and participants were reminded of all the critical items before taking the CIT. Following administration of the CIT, participants in both mock-crime conditions were tested for memory of the critical items. The results of this study revealed that the realistic mock crime was associated with overall lower recall rates and weaker detection efficiency than the standard procedure. However, these effects were mediated by the type of CIT questions used, such that the decline in memory and detection efficiency was observed mainly for peripheral items that were not directly relevant to the mock crime (e.g., a picture on the wall), but not for items that were central to the event (e.g., the amount of money stolen). The results further indicated that a CIT based exclusively on the central items was unaffected by the type of mock-crime procedure. More recently, Gamer *et al.* (2010) also demonstrated that central items are recalled after a two-week period. Thus, these studies imply that a careful selection of central items (e.g., modus operandi, type of weapon used) can produce high accuracy levels, not only in the artificial laboratory conditions, but also in realistic settings. Surprisingly, Carmel *et al.* (2003) demonstrated that the time of CIT administration had no statistically significant effect on the CIT's outcomes, nor did it interact with the type of mock crime. This finding is consistent with results reported by Hira *et al.* (2001, 2002) who conducted a mock-crime CIT study and used electrophysiological brain activity (i.e., event-related potentials, or more specifically the P300 component; see Chapter 4 of this volume) as their detection measure. Nine "guilty" participants were tested both immediately and one month after committing the mock crime and all of them were correctly identified at both time points. In their second study, Hira *et al.* (2002) re-tested five of the nine original subjects a year later and once again correctly identified all of them. Thus, these studies indicate that the CIT may be effective even when administered a long time after the crime. It is however clear that this line of research should be continued and extended before the CIT can be considered as admissible evidence.

(2) *The CIT is protected against countermeasure manipulations*: countermeasures are deliberate actions taken by guilty or knowledgeable suspects to distort their physiological responses such that they appear innocent or unknowledgeable. The effects of countermeasures are described in great detail in a separate chapter in this volume (see Chapter 11), so we shall present here just the main points. Various studies demonstrated that it is possible to train knowledgeable subjects to produce or enhance their responses to the neutral-control items (either by physical or by mental activities), such that they are undifferentiated from the unknowledgeable, or innocent subjects (e.g., Ben-Shakhar and Dolev, 1996; Honts *et al.*, 1996, 1985, 1987, 1994; Kubis, 1962). The possible use of countermeasures by guilty suspects is another factor differentiating laboratory studies from realistic settings, as subjects volunteering to participate

in experiments have no motivation to apply countermeasures. The use of countermeasures may have also contributed to the relatively large false-negative outcomes observer in the two field studies reported by Elaad and his colleagues (Elaad, 1990; Elaad *et al.*, 1992). Possible means to protect the CIT against countermeasures are discussed in Chapters 6 and 11 of this volume and we refrain from repeating them, but from the legal perspective it is important to demonstrate that the CIT is a valid test, even under conditions that do not exclude the use of countermeasures.

(3) *Critical CIT items are not leaked, such that innocent suspects are unaware of them*: whereas the first factor was necessary for detecting guilty or knowledgeable individuals, this factor is crucial for protecting the innocent suspect from being falsely classified as guilty. In some cases, information leakage may not constitute a severe problem, because innocent suspects failing a CIT could explain how they became aware of the critical items (e.g., cite a newspaper which mentioned this information while describing the crime). But there are cases where innocent suspects might be unable to account for their knowledge of some critical details (e.g., suspects can be exposed to some critical items during the interrogation without being aware of the circumstances in which this occurred, and without being able to prove that the information has been leaked). The issue of information leakage is covered in separate chapter of this volume (Chapter 10), so we shall relate to it just briefly here. Several studies examined the effects of exposing the critical information to "innocent" subjects in mock-crime experiments (Ben-Shakhar *et al.*, 1999; Bradley *et al.*, 1997; Bradley and Rettinger, 1992; Bradley and Warfield, 1984; Giesen and Rollison, 1980; Stern *et al.*, 1981) and generally demonstrated that exposing innocent participants to the critical items increased the rates of false-positive outcomes to unacceptable levels (e.g., 25 percent in Bradley and Warfield, 1984, and 50 percent in Bradley and Rettinger, 1992). Several means to protect the CIT against information leakage are discussed in various other chapters of this volume (see Chapters 10, 14 and 16), so we refrain from repeating them. But, from the legal perspective, like in the case of countermeasures, it will be needed to demonstrate, either that leakage of critical information can be avoided, or that some physiological measures can be sufficiently sensitive to differentiate between individuals who were actually involved in a crime and who that were just exposed to the crime-related information. We believe that the best way to protect the CIT against information leakage would be

to make some administrative changes in police practices, such that critical features of an investigated event are identified and concealed (from the press as well as from the suspects) at the outset of the investigation. The Japanese experience (see Chapter 14 of this volume for a description of the CIT usage in Japan) suggests that such changes are possible (Fukumoto, 1980; Nakayama, 2002; Yamamura and Miyata, 1990). In addition, the two field studies based on realistic criminal investigations conducted by the Israeli police (Elaad, 1990; Elaad *et al.*, 1992) suggest that critical information did not leak to the innocent suspects, as the false-positive rates in these studies were very low.

Conclusions

The above analysis demonstrates that there are several crucial differences between the bulk of the studies conducted to validate the CIT and the forensic settings to which the CIT would be applied. These differences bring us to the conclusion that although the CIT has the potential of meeting all four Daubert criteria, it is premature at this point to rely on the CIT as an admissible evidence in criminal courts. A pre-condition for CIT admissibility should be accumulation of solid field studies demonstrating the testability and error rates criteria in field settings, or at least experimental research that approximates field setting. In this respect, our conclusion is similar to that made by Vrij (2008), but differs somewhat from the recommendation made in our earlier paper (Ben-Shakhar *et al.*, 2002). In that article, we concluded that, "the GKT, properly administered, could yield admissible evidence for criminal courts" (Ben-Shakhar *et al.*, 2002, p. 536). However, the term, "properly administered" was not precisely defined and it is unclear whether it would be feasible to create the "proper" conditions in the realistic setting. For example, if proper administration includes the condition that all CIT items were noticed by the culprit, it is unclear how one can guarantee that this condition would indeed be met in the field.

It may be encouraging to note that the CIT has been applied for several decades in Japan (see Chapter 14) and that CIT outcomes are often admitted by Japanese courts (Fukumoto, 1980; Nakayama, 2002; Yamamura and Miyata, 1990). Nakayama (2002) reviewed several field studies conducted to validate the use of the CIT. These studies, which were based on confessed suspects, produced correct detection rates of guilty suspects ranging from 75 percent to 88 percent, with very few false-positive outcomes (2 percent or less). However, these studies were published in Japanese and it is difficult to evaluate them. In particular, it is unclear whether confessions were obtained independently of the CIT outcomes (for an elaboration of this methodological issue, see Iacono, 1991). Nevertheless, the fact that the CIT is routinely used in Japan means that Japanese investigators are capable of identifying a sufficient number of critical items at the crime scene (see several examples in Nakayama, 2002) and that the Japanese police managed to create investigative environments where critical items are concealed from suspects as well as from the general public. The Japanese experience proves that contrary to claims made by Podlesny (1993) and others, the CIT can be effectively used in forensic settings.

Another possible application of the CIT is for corroborating confessions. Confessions outside of courts are a challenge to the judicial system, when they serve as a sole or main basis for conviction and are contested in court. Contrary to common intuition even without special methods of pressure, the mere situation of being in arrest and under interrogation may lead to a false confession (Horselenberg *et al.*, 2003; Kassin and Kiechel, 1996; Report of the Royal Commission on Criminal Justice, 1993). It is extremely difficult to distinguish between a true confession and a false one. Some legal systems demand an "additional something" to the confession as a condition for conviction. This "addition" is some fact in the world outside of the confession that fits the confession (even an element of the confession that is not crucial for the case against the defendant). It is easy to imagine that an innocent suspect may have picked up this fact from a publication in the media, from a question of his interrogator or from general knowledge. The seemingly easy solution is to demand that a confession be corroborated by an indepedendent incriminating piece of evidence, for example an eyewitness. Such an approach can be expensive to society since guilty people will walk free when no such corroboration can be found. It is therefore essential to establish "half way" methods that increase or reduce the reliability of the confession without putting too great a risk on society due to acquittals of the guilty. A properly constructed CIT could become such a method. In order to make the CIT a proper legal test for the reliability of a confession it will be necessary to use precautions: to ensure that it was not the CIT that was used to induce the interrogee to confess and to ensure that the knowledge of the suspect does not stem from the media or from the interrogators. This will require probably a full documentation of the interrogation – including the part performed by undercover agents and a clear order of stages – confession first and CIT afterwards.

In conclusion we would like to point out that although we believe that the CIT has the potential of being admissible in criminal courts, its actual use as admissible evidence will depend on further studies establishing its validity in criminal settings.

REFERENCES

Ben-Shakhar, G. (1977). A further study of dichotomization theory in detection of information. *Psychophysiology*, 14, 408–413.

(1980). Habituation of the orienting response to complex sequences of stimuli. *Psychophysiology*, 17, 524–534.

(2002). A critical review of the Control Questions Test (CQT). In M. Kleiner (ed.), *Handbook of Polygraph Testing* (pp. 103–126). San Diego: Academic Press.

Ben-Shakhar, G., and Dolev, K. (1996). Psychophysiological detection through the guilty knowledge technique: the effects of mental countermeasures. *Journal of Applied Psychology*, 81, 273–281.

Ben-Shakhar, G., and Elaad, E. (2003). The validity of psychophysiological detection of deception with the Guilty Knowledge Test: a meta-analytic review. *Journal of Applied Psychology*, 88, 131–151.

Ben-Shakhar, G., and Furedy, J. J. (1990). *Theories and Applications in the Detection of Deception: A Psychophysiological and International Perspective.* New York: Springer-Verlag.

Ben-Shakhar, G., and Gati, I. (1987). Common and distinctive features of verbal and pictorial stimuli as determinants of psychophysiological responsivity. *Journal of Experimental Psychology: General*, 116, 91–105.

Ben-Shakhar, G., Bar-Hillel, M., and Kremnitzer, M. (2002). Trial by polygraph: reconsidering the use of the GKT in court. *Law and Human Behavior*, 26, 527–541.

Ben-Shakhar, G., Gronau, N., and Elaad, E. (1999). Leakage of relevant information to innocent examinees in the GKT: an attempt to reduce false-positive outcomes by introducing target stimuli. *Journal of Applied Psychology*, 84, 651–660.

Bernstein, A. (1979). The orienting response as a novelty and significance detector: reply to O'Gorman. *Psychophysiology*, 16, 263–273.

Bradley, M. T., and Rettinger, J. (1992). Awareness of crime-relevant information and the guilty knowledge test. *Journal of Applied Psychology*, 77, 55–59.

Bradley, M. T., and Warfield, J. F. (1984). Innocence, information, and the guilty knowledge test in the detection of deception. *Psychophysiology*, 21, 683–689.

Bradley, M. T., MacLaren, V. V., and Carle, S. B. (1997). Deception and non-deception in guilty knowledge and guilty actions polygraph tests. *Journal of Applied Psychology*, 81, 153–160.

Carmel, D., Dayan, E., Naveh, A., Raveh, O., and Ben-Shakhar, G. (2003). Estimating the validity of the Guilty Knowledge Test from simulated experiments: the external validity of mock crime studies. *Journal of Experimental Psychology: Applied*, 9, 261–269.

Commonwealth of Massachusetts v. *Woodward* (D. Boston, 1998), SJC-07635.

Daubert v. *Merrell Dow Pharmaceuticals, Inc.*, 113 S. Ct. Supp. 2786 (1993).

Daniels, C. W. (2002). Legal aspects of polygraph admissibility in the United States. In M. Kleiner (ed.), *Handbook of Polygraph Testing* (pp. 327–338). San Diego: Academic Press.

Elaad, E. (1990). Detection of guilty knowledge in real-life criminal investigation. *Journal of Applied Psychology*, 75, 521–529.

Elaad, E., and Ben-Shakhar, G. (1989). Effects of motivation and verbal response type on psychophysiological detection of information. *Psychophysiology*, 26, 442–451.

Elaad, E., Ginton, A., and Jungman., N. (1992). Detection measures in real-life criminal guilty knowledge tests. *Journal of Applied Psychology*, 77, 757–767.

Fiedler, K., Schmid, J., and Stahl, T. (2002). What is the current truth about polygraph lie detection? *Basic and Applied Social Psychology*, 24, 313–324.

Frye v. *United States*, 293 F. Supp. 1013, 1014 (App. D.C. 1923).

Fukumoto, J. (1980). A case in which the polygraph was the sole evidence for conviction. *Polygraph*, 9, 42–44.

Furedy, J. J. (1993). The "control" question "test" (CQT) polygrapher's dilema: logico-ethical considerations for psychophysiological practitioners and researchers. *International Journal of Psychophysiology*, 15, 263–267.

Gallai, D. (1999). Polygraph evidence in federal courts: should it be admissible? *American Criminal Law Review*, 36, 87–116.

Gamer, M., Kosiol, D., and Vossel, G. (2010). Strength of memory encoding affects physiological responses in the Guilty Action Test. *Biological Psychology*, 83, 101–107.

Gamer, M., Verschuere, B., Crombez, G., and Vossel, G. (2008). Combining physiological measures in the detection of concealed information. *Physiology and Behavior*, 95, 333–340.

Gati, I., and Ben-Shakhar, G. (1990). Novelty and significance in orientation and habituation: a feature-matching approach. *Journal of Experimental Psychology: General*, 119, 251–263.

Giesen, M. and Rollison, M. A. (1980). Guilty knowledge versus innocent associations: effects of trait anxiety and stimulus context on skin conductance. *Journal of Research in Personality*, 14, 1–11

Harnon, E. (1982). Evidence obtained by polygraph: an Israeli perspective. *The Criminal Law Review*, 329–348.

Hira, S., Sasaki, M., Matsuda, T., Furumitsu, I., and Furedy, J. J. (2001). Pz-recorded P300 is highly accurate and sensitive to a memorial manipulation in an objective laboratory guilty knowledge test. *Psychophysiology*, 38, S50.

(2002). A year after the commission of a mock crime, the P300 amplitudes, but not reaction time, are sensitive guilty knowledge test indicators. *Psychophysiology*, 39, S42.

Honts, C. R., Hodes, R. L., and Raskin, D. C. (1985). Effects of physical counter-measures on the physiological detection of deception. *Journal of Applied Psychology*, 70, 177–187.

Honts, C. R., Raskin, D. C., and Kircher, J. C. (1987). Effects of physical countermeasures and their electromyographic detection during polygraph tests for deception. *Journal of Psychophysiology*, 1, 241–247.

(1994). Mental and physical countermeasures reduce the accuracy of polygraph tests. *Journal of Applied Psychology*, 79, 252–259.

(2002). The scientific status of research on polygraph techniques: the case for polygraph tests. In D. L. Faigman, D. H. Kaye, M. J. Saks, and J. Sanders (eds.), *Modern Scientific Evidence: The Law and Science of Expert Testimony*, Volume 2 (pp. 446–483). St. Paul, MN: West Publishing.

Honts, C. R., Devitt, M. K, Winbush, M., and Kircher, J. C. (1996). Mental and physical countermeasures reduce the accuracy of the concealed knowledge test. *Psychophysiology*, 33, 84–92.

Horselenberg, R., Merckelbach, H., and Josephs, S. (2003). Individual differences and false confessions: a conceptual replication of Kassin and Kiechel (1996). *Psychology, Crime & Law*, 9, 1–8.

Iacono, W. G. (1991). Can we determine the accuracy of polygraph tests? In J. R. Jennings, P. K. Ackles, and M. G. H. Coles (eds.), *Advances in Psychophysiology*, 4 (pp. 1–101). London: Jessica Kingsley.

Iacono, W. G., and Lykken, D. T. (1997). The validity of the lie detector: two surveys of scientific opinion. *Journal of Applied Psychology*, 82, 426–433.

(2002). The scientific status of research on polygraph techniques: the case against polygraph tests. In D. L. Faigman, D. H. Kaye, M. J. Saks, and J. Sanders (eds.), *Modern Scientific Evidence: The Law and Science of Expert Testimony*, Volume 2 (pp. 483–538). St. Paul, MN: West Publishing.

Iacono, W. G., and Patrick, C. J. (1988). Assessing deception: polygraph tecchniques. In R. Rogers (ed.), *Clinical Assessment of Malingering and Deception* (pp. 205–233). New York: Guilford Press.

Kassin, S. M., and Kiechel, K. L. (1996). The social psychology of false confessions: compliance, internalization and confabulation. *Psychological Science*, 7, 125–128.

Kubis, J. F. (1962). *Studies in Lie Detection: Computer Feasibility Considerations*. Technical Report #62–205, prepared for the Air Force Systems Command. Contract No. AF 30 (602) -2270, project No. 5534, Fordham University.

Lykken, D. T. (1959). The GSR in the detection of guilt. *Journal of Applied Psychology*, 43, 385–388.

(1960). The validity of the guilty knowledge technique: the effects of faking. *Journal of Applied Psychology*, 44, 258–262.

(1974). Psychology and the lie detection industry. *American Psychologist*, 29, 725–739.

MacLaren, V. V. (2001). A quantitative review of the Guilty Knowledge Test. *Journal of Applied Psychology*, 86, 674–683.

Maltzman, I. (1979). Orienting reflexes and significance: a reply to O'Gorman. *Psychophysiology*, 16, 274–281.

Marston, W. M. (1917). Systolic blood pressure symptoms of deception. *Journal of Experimental Psychology*, 2, 117–163.

Messick, S. (1995). Validity of psychological assessment: validation of inferences from persons' responses and performances as scientific inquiry into score meaning. *American Psychologist*, 50, 741–749.

Nakayama, M. (2002). Practical use of the concealed information test for criminal investigation in Japan. In M. Kleiner (ed.), *Handbook of Polygraph Testing* (pp. 49–86). San Diego: Academic Press.

Podlesny, J. A. (1993). Is the guilty knowledge polygraph technique applicable in criminal investigations? A review of FBI case records. *Crime Laboratory Digest*, 20, 57–61.

Report of the Royal Commission on Criminal Justice (1993; Cm 2263; Chair: Lord Runciman).

Saxe, L. (1991). Lying: thoughts of an applied social psychologist. *American Psychologist*, 46, 409–415.

Saxe, L., and Ben-Shakhar, G. (1999). Admissibility of polygraph tests: the application of scientific standards post-Daubert. *Psychology, Public Policy and Law*, 5, 203–223.

Sokolov, E. N. (1963). *Perception and the Conditioned Reflex*. New York: Macmillan.

Stern, R. M., Breen, J. P., Watanabe, T., and Perry, B. S. (1981). Effects of feedback of physiological information on responses to innocent associations and guilty knowledge. *Journal of Applied Psychology*, 66, 677–681.

United States v. *Cordoba*, 158 (D. California, 1998), aff'd, SA CR 95–39-GLT[SF].

United States v. *Scheffer*, 118 S. Ct. Supp. 1261 (D. Washington, 1998), aff'd, USCA Dkt. No. 95–0521/AF (US Court of Appeals for the Armed Forces).

Verschuere, B., Crombez, G., De Clercq, A., and Koster, E. (2004). Autonomic and behavioral responding to concealed information: differentiating defensive and orienting responses. *Psychophysiology*, 41, 461–466.

Vrij, A. (2008). *Detecting Lies and Deceit. Pitfalls and Opportunities*, 2nd edn. West Sussex: John Wiley and Sons.

Yamamura, T., and Miyata, Y. (1990). Development of the polygraph technique in Japan for detection of deception. *Forensic Science International*, 44, 257–271.

Part IV

Conclusions

16 Practical guidelines for developing a CIT

Ewout Meijer, Bruno Verschuere, and
Gershon Ben-Shakhar

Overview: In this chapter, we will formulate guidelines on how to develop a good CIT. These guidelines are based upon empirical data from CIT research as well as on theory on memory and orienting. We will outline how best to formulate questions and answer alternatives, how to conduct, score, and report the outcomes of the test. If these guidelines are followed, we are confident that the CIT can make an important contribution to police investigations.

The present book reviewed and summarized a large database of research on the Concealed Information Test (CIT), and a compelling case for its widespread adoption by law enforcement agencies was made (see Chapter 1). Clearly, designing adequate test questions is crucial for successful implementation and, as outlined in Chapter 8, good CIT questions need to fulfil two criteria. First, they need to refer to crime-relevant details that are present in the perpetrator's memory. Second, this information does not need to be known to an innocent suspect. The latter criterion primarily poses practical challenges to the police investigation process. Details of the crime should, for example, not be released through the media, nor be disclosed to a suspect in any interrogation preceding a CIT. The former criterion – what information is present in a suspect's memory – on the other hand, is not under the control of the investigative authorities.

In this chapter, we will formulate guidelines on how to develop a good CIT, thereby maximizing detection efficiency and ensuring proper reporting. These guidelines are based upon two main sources. First and foremost, they are based on empirical data from CIT research or related fields. Second, they are based on predictions that follow from theory underlying the CIT. Given that the majority of CIT research is based on measurements of the autonomic nervous system (see Chapter 2 of this volume), we limit our recommendations to this type of test.[1]

---

[1] Nevertheless, some of the recommendations, particularly those related to the choice of salient critical items would be valid for any type of CIT.

Memory

In order to be present in a guilty suspect's memory, information must have been encoded at the time of the crime, and stored until the CIT is conducted. Encoding refers to how one transforms sensory input into a representation that can be placed into memory, and storage refers to how this encoded information is retained in memory (Sternberg, 1999). Even though offenders' memory for crimes is a relatively understudied area, research from related fields provide important insights into which crime-scene details are most likely to be encoded and stored in memory.

Eyewitness research has shown that increased emotional arousal causes an attentional narrowing (Christianson, 1992). This attentional narrowing results in superior encoding of central details, while undermining the encoding of peripheral details. A classic example of this attentional narrowing can be seen in an armed theft victim who remembers the weapon that was pointed at him or her, but cannot remember nor identify the perpetrator. For this reason, the attentional narrowing phenomenon is also referred to as the "weapon focus" effect (Loftus *et al.*, 1987). Given that the perpetrator of a crime may well experience enhanced stress levels, central details are likely to be better encoded at the cost of peripheral details. Test questions should therefore best address central details of the crime.

Several CIT studies have confirmed that central details (i.e., information reflecting the essence of a scene or event) are better encoded than peripheral details (i.e., thematically irrelevant information). Carmel *et al.* (2003), for example, instructed participants to steal a CD-ROM from an office. Next, they compared the recall of the central details directly related to this theft such as the color of the CD-ROM and its location in the office, with peripheral items referring to items which happened to be in the office (the soft drink and newspaper found on the desk and the picture on the wall). Indeed, 90.2 percent of the central items were recalled, compared to only 65.9 percent of the peripheral items. Similar findings were reported recently by Gamer *et al.* (2010).

Also of interest here is the literature on the "enactment effect." Research has shown that memory for action phrases (e.g., "open the door") that are actually performed is superior to memory for the same phrases when they have only been listened to (Engelkamp, 1998). Although this "enactment effect" has not yet been replicated in the context of the CIT, we recommend the use of deliberate actions that were performed by the perpetrator rather than items that were merely seen or heard during the crime.

Recommendation 1: CIT questions should address salient, central details of the crime as well as actions performed by the perpetrator

Besides successful encoding, storage of information is also essential for a successful CIT. In other words, once encoded, information must not be forgotten. The prevailing theory on forgetting is interference theory (Underwood, 1957). This theory states that forgetting mainly occurs due to the processing of other, competing information. There are at least two ways this mechanism can threaten the validity of a CIT. First, the amount of potentially interfering information regarding crime details is especially high with serial perpetrators. Information from other crimes committed by the same perpetrator may interfere with that for the crime under investigation. Caution should therefore be taken when the suspect is likely to be a serial perpetrator. Second, the amount of inferring information increases with time. It is therefore recommended to administer the CIT as soon as possible after the crime has been committed.

Recommendation 2: the CIT should be administered as soon as possible after the crime has been committed

Orienting

As outlined in Chapter 7 of this volume, the CIT finds its theoretical foundation in research on orienting theory. The critical items differ between guilty and innocent examinees in stimulus significance. Because all items are equivalent in stimulus significance for innocent examinees, they will elicit orienting responses of similar magnitude that will gradually habituate. For the guilty examinee, however, the critical items will elicit enhanced orienting responses that will habituate more slowly. In the next section we describe guidelines that are derived from this theoretical framework, including guidelines on the number of questions, the type of items to be presented with each question, and the physiological measures that should be recorded.

Number of questions

The false-positive rate of a CIT is, among others, determined by the number of questions and the number of items presented with each question. Given that enough central details are available, more questions will result in higher accuracy. In their meta-analysis, Ben-Shakhar and Elaad (2003) found a positive correlation ($r = 0.26$) between the number of questions and CIT detection efficiency. Studies with CITs consisting of at least five questions reached the highest accuracy levels. As explained above, however, it is important that these questions refer to material that is encoded and maintained in the perpetrator's memory.

If less than five questions are available, a solution is repeating one or more questions. Elaad and Ben-Shakhar (1997) and Ben-Shakhar and Elaad (2002) demonstrated that detection efficiency increases with the number of repetitions of the CIT questions. Given that detection efficiency decreases with the addition of questions referring to peripheral or non-salient items (Carmel *et al.*, 2003; Jokinen *et al.*, 2006), it seems preferable to identify a small number of salient items and repeat the questions related to these items, rather than trying to enhance the test by including questions referring to non-salient items. Ben-Shakhar and Elaad (2002) found that significant detection can be achieved even with a single question, but it is important to realize that the risk of a false positive (e.g., through leakage) is greater when using a single question compared to multiple questions. As a loose rule of thumb we recommend a minimum of three questions that should be repeated.

Recommendation 3: a CIT should consist of as many salient questions as possible. If less than five salient items can be identified, a smaller number of questions (at least three) referring to salient items can be used with repetitions of each question

Items

After identifying the critical items that will be addressed in the CIT, the control items need to be selected. The following three factors should be taken into account in this context: first, orienting theory states that any salient item will evoke a response. Thus, using a highly salient critical item may evoke an orienting response even in innocent suspects, increasing the risk of a false-positive outcome. Thus, the critical items should not be more salient or more plausible than the control items. It is advisable to test a priori whether all items are equally plausible by means of a Doob Kirshenbaum procedure (Doob and Kirshenbaum, 1973). With this procedure, all items are presented to a panel of naïve volunteers, with the question to pick the item they find most plausible. If, in such a procedure, the critical item is chosen more often than any of the others, the items must be changed, or the test question needs to be discarded. It is also possible to administer the CIT to known innocents and check whether the critical items elicit larger autonomic responses than the neutral ones (see Lykken, 1998). An additional solution is to preview the test items with the examinee prior to conducting the test. All questions and items can be shown to the suspect before the test is actually conducted. This gives the suspect the opportunity to admit knowledge of any correct item beforehand, and explain how s/he became aware of it, or point out any items that are salient for different reasons. This procedure not only familiarizes the suspect with the test items, but allows for adjustment, and if necessary exclusion of bad test items. In a recent study, Verschuere and Crombez (2008) showed that such a previewing procedure does not diminish detection efficiency.

Second, in order to maximize detection efficiency, it is advisable to select items that can be easily differentiated. Research has shown that the orienting response generalizes to stimuli that share common features with the significant stimulus (Ben-Shakhar et al., 1996). A string of murder weapons, for example, can therefore better consist of easily differentiated items (knife, gun, rope, axe, poison), rather than several different types of knives.

Finally, orienting theory predicts that the first item that is presented always elicits a novelty response. The critical item should therefore never be presented first, and the item that is presented first (typically called the "buffer item") should be excluded from the analysis.

Recommendation 4: items need to be maximally distinct, but equally plausible

The effects of overt deception and motivation to avoid detection may exert their influence by increasing the significance of the critical items, augmenting the orienting response. Verbally answering the presentation of each item with "no," for example, has been shown to increase detection efficiency in laboratory settings (Ben-Shakhar and Elaad, 2003). Although not all studies could replicate this effect, there is no evidence that verbal denial would be detrimental for CIT detection efficiency. Furthermore, requiring a verbal "no" answer provides the examiner with important information on whether the examinee is engaged in the test.

Physiological measures

The CIT originally described by Lykken (1959) used Skin Conductance Response (SCR) as the sole dependent measure. Still, the orienting response is also characterized by changes in a range of other physiological measures, including heart rate deceleration (Graham and

Clifton, 1966) and respiratory suppression (Lynn, 1966). Consequently, a number of other measures have been shown to increase CIT detection efficiency. In Chapter 2, Gamer reviews the combination of different indices of the autonomic nervous system for their incremental validity (Sechrest, 1963). He points out that laboratory studies have shown that combining skin conductance with respiratory and cardiac measures enhanced the validity of the CIT, but also that this increase is relatively small. Given its high validity, the amount of research conducted, and the relative ease and low costs of measurement, SCR is the default measure for the detection of concealed information.

In addition to SCR, respiration and heart rate can be monitored. It is important to realize, however, that registering multiple signals also introduces several obstacles. Most importantly it requires more sophisticated decision-making. What conclusion would one draw, for example, when only the respiration measure, but neither SCR nor heart rate indicates the presence of concealed information? Because not all measures discriminate equally well, a decision rule incorporating different weights is crucial here. And even though information for these weights can be derived from laboratory studies (Gamer *et al.*, 2008), it is unknown whether they would generalize to the field.

We are also somewhat reluctant to currently recommend the use of reaction-times (see Chapter 3), event-related potentials (see Chapter 4), and fMRI (see Chapter 5) for applied purposes. All these measures show great promise for the CIT and may reach high detection efficiency. However, the empirical database for these measures is smaller than for SCR and their validity remains to be established under different circumstances. For example, only very few mock crime studies have applied these measures so far and they have never been examined in field studies.

Recommendation 5: during a CIT, at minimum, skin conductance should be measured. Additionally, heart rate and respiration can be monitored

Response scoring

Besides the number of questions and the number of items, a third factor determining false-positive rate is the threshold that is chosen for a guilty outcome. The traditional method for scoring the CIT is the Lykken scoring procedure. This procedure assigns a score of 2 to each CIT question if the largest response was elicited by the critical item, a score of 1 if the second largest response was elicited by that item, and a score of 0 otherwise (Lykken, 1959). With n questions, the

Lykken-score varies between 0 and $2n$, and the threshold for a guilty outcome is typically set at n, meaning that a score of at least n indicates recognition. The Lykken scoring procedure has several advantages: it is widely used in research and has been reported in many publications. More importantly, the conditional distribution of the Lykken scores for unknowledgeable examinees is known and consequently the probability of a false-positive outcome can be easily calculated (Timm, 1989).

One shortcoming associated with the Lykken scoring procedure, however, is that it does not take into account the relative difference between the critical and control items. When the response to the critical item is three times as large as the next largest response, the Lykken score will be the same as when it is only slightly larger. An alternative approach for calculating a detection score is to standardize the response to the critical item relative to the mean and standard deviation of all responses of a given examinee within one question or a block of several questions and then average across questions and physiological measures (Ben-Shakhar, 1985). Like the Lykken scoring procedure, the use of average z-scores also allows for the computation of the probability of a false positive outcome, and z-scores are also commonly used in research.

Recommendation 6: CIT responses should be scored using the Lykken-scoring procedure and/or the within-individual standardization procedure

Response scoring can be done in a qualitative, semi-quantitative or quantitative manner. Computerized scoring is advisable to enhance standardization and reliability (Kircher and Raskin, 2002). Research that compared human with computerized scoring has shown that "the formula is better than the head" (Szucko and Kleinmuntz, 1981, p. 495). Moreover, there is no reason to avoid the use of a computerized quantitative scoring procedure nowadays. Such a procedure provides the best way to obtain objectivity and high reliability. Thus, we recommend the computerized scoring procedure because it is most objective and reliable.

Recommendation 7: physiological responses should be quantified using computerized algorithms, rather than qualitative or semi-quantitative procedures

Reporting

In case of an incriminating outcome, the probability of a false-positive result should be calculated and presented in the report, as it allows for proper weighing by the court. In case of an exculpatory outcome, it is important to mention that, besides innocence, there are a variety of reasons that can account for false-negative outcomes such as forgetting or impaired memory formation by alcohol and/or drugs intoxication at the time of the crime (Kopelman, 2002; White *et al.*, 2000), or the use of countermeasure techniques (for a detailed discussion see Chapter 11 of this volume). Finally, it is important to realize that the low probability of a false-positive outcome is lost if one makes a decision (regarding knowledge of the concealed details) on the basis of individual questions. The outcome of a CIT should therefore be always based on the test as a whole, rather than on individual details of the crime. A reliable decision on a single question can only be made if this question has been repeated several times.

Clever Hans

Clever Hans was a horse that allegedly was able to solve mathematical problems. When given additions, subtractions, or multiplications by its trainer, Hans would correctly tap out the answers with its hoof. Initially, this performance puzzled everyone. A formal investigation by German psychologist and biologist Oskar Pfungst in 1907, however, revealed that it was not its arithmetical capabilities that were special, but rather it was Hans' capability of observing behavior that was extraordinary. Pfungst showed that Hans could only tap out the correct answer when the questioner knew the correct answer, and the horse could see the questioner. Further examinations revealed that involuntary head movements by the questioner would give away the correct answer, and based on this observation, Hans would stop tapping when the correct answer was reached. When the questioner did not know the answer himself, or presented the problem outside Hans' visual field, Hans lost his ability to tap out the correct answer (Stanovich, 2008).

The case of Clever Hans illustrates what is now known as the observer-expectancy effect: expectations and biases of an experimenter can be communicated to experimental subjects in subtle, unintentional ways, and these cues can significantly affect the outcome of the experiment (Rosenthal and Fode, 1961). Needless to say, a CIT is not immune to these experimenter effects and precautions should be taken to minimize their effects. Ideally, this can be done by making sure the experimenter is blind to the correct alternative. If an experimenter-blind protocol is not feasible, the test can be automated, using a computer to present the questions and the items.

Recommendation 8: the CIT should be administered blind or computerized but preferably blind and computerized

Global guidelines for the successful development of a CIT were outlined above, based on research on memory and orienting. From these guidelines, it may be clear that a proper application of the CIT requires some background in psychology, statistics, and psychophysiology on the side of the examiner. We therefore recommend a science-practitioners model, as is common in many other fields of applied psychology: researchers are also practitioners and vice versa (Shapiro, 2002). Fields like clinical psychology and neuropsychology have generally adopted such a model where psychologists conduct scientific research, but also test and treat patients. We are confident that if these guidelines are followed, the CIT can make an important contribution to police investigations.

REFERENCES

Ben-Shakhar, G. (1985). Standardization within individuals: a simple method to neutralize individual differences in skin conductance. *Psychophysiology*, 22, 292–299.

Ben-Shakhar, G., and Elaad, E. (2002). Effects of questions' repetition and variation on the efficiency of the guilty knowledge test: a reexamination. *Journal of Applied Psychology*, 87, 972–977.

(2003). The validity of psychophysiological detection of information with the Guilty Knowledge Test: a meta-analytic review. *Journal of Applied Psychology*, 88, 131–151.

Ben-Shakhar, G., Frost, R., Gati, I., and Kresh, Y. (1996). Is an apple a fruit? Semantic relatedness as reflected by psychophysiological responsivity. *Psychophysiology*, 33, 671–679.

Carmel, D., Dayan, E., Naveh, A., Raveh, O., and Ben-Shakhar, G. (2003). Estimating the validity of the guilty knowledge test from simulated experiments: the external validity of mock crime studies. *Journal of Experimental Psychology: Applied*, 9, 261–269.

Christianson, S. A. (1992). Emotional stress and eyewitness memory: a critical review. *Psychological Bulletin*, 112, 284–309.

Doob, A. N., and Kirshenbaum, H. M. (1973). Bias in police lineups – partial remembering. *Journal of Police Science and Administration*, 1, 187–293.

Elaad, E., and Ben-Shakhar, G. (1997). Effects of item repetitions and variations on the efficiency of the guilty knowledge test. *Psychophysiology*, 34, 587–596.

Engelkamp, J. (1998). *Memory for Actions*. Hove: Psychology Press.

Gamer, M., Kosiol, D., and Vossel, G. (2010). Strength of memory encoding affects physiological responses in the Guilty Actions Test. *Biological Psychology*, 83, 101–107.

Gamer, M., Verschuere, B., Crombez, G., and Vossel, G. (2008). Combining physiological measures in the detection of concealed information. *Physiology and Behavior*, 95, 333–340.

Graham, F. K., and Clifton, R. K. (1966). Heart-rate change as a component of the orienting response. *Psychological Bulletin*, 65, 305–320.

Jokinen, A., Santtila, P., Ravaja, N., and Puttonen, S. (2006). Salience of guilty knowledge test items affects accuracy in realistic mock crimes. *International Journal of Psychophysiology*, 62, 174–184.

Kircher, J. C., and Raskin, D. C. (2002). Computer methods for the psycho-physiological detection of deception. In M. Kleiner (ed.), *Handbook of Polygraph Testing* (pp. 287–326). San Diego: Academic Press.

Kopelman, M. D. (2002). Psychogenic amnesia. In A. D. Baddeley, M. D. Kopelman, and B. A. Wilson (eds.), *Handbook of Memory Disorders*, 2nd edn. (pp. 451–471). Chichester: John Wiley & Sons.

Loftus, E. F., Loftus, G. R., and Messo, J. (1987). Some facts about weapon focus. *Law and Human Behavior*, 11, 55–62.

Lykken, D. T. (1959). The GSR in the detection of guilt. *Journal of Applied Psychology*, 43, 385–388.

(1998). *A Tremor in the Blood*. New York: Plenum Press.

Lynn, R. (1966). *Attention, Arousal and the Orienting Reaction*. New York: Pergamon.

Rosenthal, R., and Fode, K. L. (1961). The problem of experimenter outcome-bias. In D. P. Ray (ed.), *Series Research in Social Psychology*. Washington, DC: National Institute of Social and Behavioral Science.

Sechrest, L. (1963). Incremental validity: a recommendation. *Educational and Psychological Measurement*, 23, 153–158.

Shapiro, D. (2002). Renewing the scientist-practitioner model. *The Psychologist*, 15, 232–234.

Stanovich, K. E. (2008). Getting things under control. The case of clever Hans. In *How to Think Straight about Psychology* (pp. 85–102). Boston: Allen and Bacon.

Sternberg, R. J. (1999). *Cognitive Psychology*. Orlando: Harcourt Brace College Publishers.

Szucko, J. J., and Kleinmuntz, B. (1981). Statistical versus clinical lie detection. *American Psychologist*, 36, 488–496.

Timm, H. W. (1989). Methodological considerations affecting the utility of incorporating innocent subjects into the design of guilty knowledge polygraph experiments. *Polygraph*, 18, 143–157.

Underwood, B. J. (1957). Interference and forgetting. *Psychological Review*, 64, 49–60.

Verschuere, B., and Crombez, G. (2008). Deja vu! The effect of previewing test items on the validity of the Concealed Information polygraph Test. *Psychology, Crime & Law*, 14, 287–297.

White, A. M., Matthews, D. B., and Best, P. J. (2000). Ethanol, memory, and hippocampal function: a review of recent findings. *Hippocampus*, 10, 88–93.

Epilogue: current status and future developments in CIT research and practice

Gershon Ben-Shakhar, Bruno Verschuere, and Ewout Meijer

This volume, focusing on memory detection, provides a comprehensive and updated review of the Concealed Information Test (CIT) from almost all aspects: the measures used for detecting concealed knowledge (behavioral, autonomic, and brain-related measures); the underlying theories that may account for the effects observed in the CIT; its usage in forensic and clinical settings; its legal aspects and also the weaknesses of the test such as its vulnerability to countermeasures and to information leakage as well as its practical limitations. In this final chapter, we wish to briefly summarize the current status of the CIT and discuss several possible future developments.

Current status

Five decades of extensive research that has been conducted since the pioneering studies reported by David Lykken (1959, 1960) revealed that at least under controlled laboratory conditions, the CIT emerges as one of the most valid and accurate tools originating from psychology and behavioral sciences. For example, the meta-analytic study reported by Ben-Shakhar and Elaad (2003) showed that the average effect size (standardized mean difference between responses to concealed items of knowledgeable and unknowledgeable subjects) computed across all mock-crime experiments was 2.09, which is equivalent to a correlation coefficient of 0.65. Furthermore, when considering only mock-crime experiments that applied the CIT under optimal conditions (at least five CIT questions, motivational instructions, and a deceptive verbal response), the average effect size increased to 3.12, which is equivalent to a correlation coefficient of 0.79. It should be noted that this result reflects the validity of a single measure (SCR) and recent studies indicate that this can be enhanced by additional autonomic measures (see Chapter 2 of this book by Matthias Gamer). Moreover, it is now becoming clear that concealed information can be validly assessed not only by autonomic nervous system measures, but also by response latencies (see Chapter 3 by Bruno Verschuere), event-related brain potentials (see Chapter 4 by Peter Rosenfeld) and brain imaging methods such as fMRI (see Chapter 5 by Matthias Gamer). Response latencies have practical potential as they are very cost-effective and easy to apply. The central nervous system measures are less likely to be applied on a broad scale in the near future, but they can lead to important theoretical advancements. These tools provide researchers with new and powerful means to examine what happens in the brain when someone is concealing certain information. A positive side-effect of the brain imaging research on concealed information is that it brought a renewed interest in the Concealed Information Test.

Pitfalls and solutions

Throughout fifty years of research the CIT has proven to be a reliable and valid way to assess concealed information. However, the CIT is not flawless and several chapters covered various threats to its validity.

First, leakage of information to unaware subjects may lead to enhanced responses to crime-related items and eventually to a misclassification of the informed innocent suspects as guilty. Michael Bradley, a pioneer researcher of this issue, reviewed the current knowledge about information leakage and its possible damaging consequences (see Chapter 10 of this volume by Bradley *et al.*). Interestingly, Bradley noticed that one may also take advantage of information leakage. In certain situations, innocent subjects may be aware of critical information but hesitant to reveal that information. Innocent civilians, for instance, may know the secret hiding place of criminals or terrorists. Out of fear of being punished, they may not be willing to share that information with investigative authorities. In such circumstances, the CIT may be used to extract information, although this, of course, raises severe ethical issues. Still, the idea of using the CIT in groups of either innocent (Chapter 10) or guilty subjects (Meijer *et al.*, 2010) is an exciting new application of the CIT.

Second, the CIT is not resistant to faking. The use of various countermeasure manipulations by guilty suspects may increase their responses to the neutral-control items, thereby minimizing differential responses to the critical items. This may lead to a misclassification of guilty or knowledgeable suspects as innocent and thereby increasing the false-negative outcomes. This issue was reviewed by Gershon Ben-Shakhar (Chapter 11), along with possible solutions to this problem. One promising approach was offered by Elaad and Ben-Shakhar, who proposed to use covert measures (see Chapter 6). The idea is elegant and simple. If suspects are not connected to electrodes and are unaware of being tested by a polygraph, they are unlikely to engage in faking. Clearly, there are enormous legal and ethical concerns about this approach and the challenge is for researchers to come up with new ways to use covert measures in an ethically acceptable way.

Third, there are concerns about the artificial nature and questionable external and ecological validity of CIT research. Almost all CIT studies were conducted in laboratory settings, where participants (typically undergraduate students) are requested to commit a mock crime (e.g., steal an envelope, containing some money and jewelry), learn a list of code words, or write down a list of biographical details. In all these procedures the critical CIT items are a-priori defined and it is generally guaranteed that participants learn all items to perfection. Typically, participants take the test soon after they learned the items. Clearly, as highlighted by both Don Krapohl (Chapter 8) and Eitan Elaad (Chapter 9), in the realistic forensic setting, things are very different. Specifically, there are many differences between the average undergraduate student and the average criminal suspect. Also, the investigators can never ascertain that the culprits actually noticed the various items they wish to include in the CIT. Nor can they guarantee that culprits will remember those items when they take the test, weeks and sometimes months after the crime. Furthermore memory of crime details may be distorted by post-event information (e.g., Loftus, 2003).

There are two possible ways to examine these issues. For example, a systematic examination of each of these factors can be conducted under controlled laboratory conditions. Researchers have begun to undertake this enterprise, for example by examining the detection efficiency of a laboratory CIT with a sample of actual criminals (Verschuere et al., 2005, 2007). Carmel et al. (2003), Gamer et al. (2010) and Seymour and Fraynt (2009) used more realistic versions of the mock-crime paradigm, where the critical items were not explicitly specified and memorized by the subjects and the administration of the CIT was delayed by a week or two. The results of these studies revealed that memory and differential responding to the critical CIT items may depend on the type of the items used. Specifically, central items, that are directly related to the mock crime (e.g., the stolen articles), are much less affected by memory loss and produce differential response pattern after a week or two. On the other hand, peripheral items (e.g., a picture hanging on the wall) are poorly recalled and produce weak differential responses when the test is delayed. These results may have important practical implications for item selection and for constructing an optimal CIT (see Chapter 16). The long experience of Japanese polygraph examiners who routinely use the CIT has brought them to similar conclusions (see Chapter 14 by

Akemi Osugi). This initial research should be continued and extended. For example, mock-crime experiments differ from real crimes in various other features. Most notably, the stress and anxiety involved in realistic crimes are completely absent from the typical mock-crime experiment. As there is ample evidence that emotional arousal during encoding may affect memory in various ways (e.g., Adolphs *et al.*, 2005; Kensinger, 2007), it is important to manipulate the level of emotional arousal while executing the mock crime.

Another solution is to conduct field studies, were the validity of the CIT can be assessed with real suspects tested under realistic settings. The few field studies conducted so far (Elaad, 1990; Elaad *et al.*, 1992; Hira and Furumitsu, 2002) suffer from methodological problems. The studies by Elaad and his colleagues (Elaad, 1990; Elaad *et al.*, 1992) relied on non-optimal usage of the CIT, as the average number of CIT questions used in these tests did not exceed two and the CITs were always administered following a Control Questions (CQT) polygraph test. Moreover, all these studies relied upon confessions as a ground truth criterion, but this is a problematic criterion as confessions are not independent of polygraph tests outcomes (see Iacono, 1991). Future field studies need to examine the validity of a properly designed CIT. Importantly, ground truth should be established completely independently of the CIT, or other polygraph tests' outcomes and the CIT should be administered as early as possible and separately from any other test. We hope to welcome such research from Japan, where the CIT is applied on a large scale.

Fourth, when applying the typically conducted ANS-based CIT, there is no way to verify that the examinee was paying attention to the test stimuli. Most often, CIT stimuli are either read by an examiner or presented visually on screen. Guilty examinees that do not fully process the stimuli, intentionally (by using countermeasures) or unintentionally (as a result of fatigue, laps of attention, etc.), may not respond to the CIT items. In contrast to the ANS-based test, the CIT format that has been typically used in ERP, RT, and fMRI research does include a means to assess attention. This test format includes target items to which participants are required to give a unique response. Thus, participants are required to press one button for critical and control items, and another for target items. This assures that attention is being paid to the stimuli. Importantly, target items allow the examiner to set a criterion for valid data (e.g., a minimum percent of correctly classified targets, a target P300 of a certain μV, an increase in target RTs as compared to irrelevant RTs). As far as we know, it has never been empirically examined whether the use of such a criterion actually increases

CIT validity. This should be examined not only for the ERP/RT/fMRI, but also for the ANS-based test (for an early investigation of this issue see Ben-Shakhar et al., 1999).

One practical point that has been largely neglected by CIT researchers is the incremental validity of the CIT itself. Positioning the CIT at the early stage of a criminal investigation forces the investigative authorities to disclose much potential evidence to the suspect at this early stage. As a consequence, this evidence can no longer be used strategically as an interrogation procedure, although it has been shown to increase deception detection skills of interrogators (Hartwig et al., 2005). An interesting avenue for future research could be comparing the CIT to such interrogation procedures.

Future usage of the CIT

In spite of the great potential of the CIT, it has been rarely implemented by law-enforcement agencies and it has been used extensively only in Japan (see Chapter 14 of this volume by Akemi Osugi). It is difficult to understand why the CIT has been rarely applied in the West. Several possible reasons for this are discussed by Don Krapohl (see Chapter 8 of this volume). However, we believe that the main reason is the strong belief of Western polygraph investigators that they have an alternative method (the CQT), which is highly accurate and much easier to implement than the CIT. Unfortunately this belief of many practitioners has no scientific foundations, as the CQT has neither theoretical justification nor solid empirical research supporting its validity (see, for example, Ben-Shakhar, 2002). More extensive application of the CIT requires that polygraph examiners and law-enforcement authorities fully realize and acknowledge the problems related to the CQT. However, these problems have been identified over and over again in the literature without any serious impact on field practice. Moreover, discussions about applicability of the CIT seem to be dictated by the issue of whether the CIT can fully replace the CQT (e.g., Podlesney, 1993, 2003) whereas, as explained in the epilogue, it was never the intention of the CIT. The primary question that should be answered here is whether a CIT can be applied in a substantial proportion of the cases. Still it is more likely that investigative authorities of countries without a history of CQT usage will implement the CIT.

An additional factor that may play a role in the limited field use of the CIT is a lack of communication between researchers and practitioners. In many fields of applied psychology common practice dictates that the so-called science-practitioners model (Shapiro, 2002) will be adopted (i.e., meaning that researchers are also practitioners and vice versa). Fields like clinical psychology and neuropsychology have generally adopted this model where psychologists conduct scientific research, but also test and or treat patients. In the case of the CIT, it would be considered a rarity that those people conducting and publishing research on the CIT also conduct tests of criminal suspects. Such an approach, however, might be needed in order to implement the CIT, as police investigators are unlikely to successfully implement the method on their own. Adopting a science-practitioner model may set off the use of the CIT in the field.

Clearly, a more extensive application of the CIT for forensic purposes will depend also on future research of this method. We believe that with advances in research along the lines suggested above, as well as further basic research on the neuronal mechanisms responsible for the CIT effect, this technique can emerge as an effective scientifically based method for the detection of concealed knowledge and thus make important contributions to law enforcement and the prevention of terrorism.

REFERENCES

Adolphs, R., Tranel, D., and Buchanan, T. W. (2005). Amygdala damage impairs emotional memory for gist but not details of complex stimuli. *Nature Neuroscience*, 8, 512–518.

Ben-Shakhar, G. (2002). A critical review of the Control Questions Test (CQT). In M. Kleiner (ed.), *Handbook of Polygraph Testing* (pp. 103–126). San Diego: Academic Press.

Ben-Shakhar, G., and Elaad, E. (2003). The validity of psychophysiological detection of deception with the Guilty Knowledge Test: a meta-analytic review. *Journal of Applied Psychology*, 88, 131–151.

Ben-Shakhar, G., Gronau, N., and Elaad, E. (1999). Leakage of relevant information to innocent examinees in the GKT: an attempt to reduce false-positive outcomes by introducing target stimuli. *Journal of Applied Psychology*, 84(5), 651–660.

Carmel, D., Dayan, E., Naveh, A., Raveh, O., and Ben-Shakhar, G. (2003). Estimating the validity of the guilty knowledge test from simulated experiments: the external validity of mock crime studies. *Journal of Experimental Psychology: Applied*, 9(4), 261–269.

Elaad, E. (1990). Detection of guilty knowledge in real-life criminal investigations. *Journal of Applied Psychology*, 75, 521–529.

Elaad, E., Ginton, A., and Jungman N. (1992). Detection measures in real-life criminal guilty knowledge tests. *Journal of Applied Psychology*, 77, 757–767.

Gamer, M., Kosiol, D., and Vossel, G. (2010). Strength of memory encoding affects physiological responses in the Guilty Action Test. *Biological Psychology*, 83, 101–107.

Hartwig, M., Granhag, P. A., Stromwall, L. A., and Vrij, A. (2005). Detecting deception via strategic disclosure of evidence. *Law and Human Behavior*, 29, 469–484.

Hira, S., and Furumitsu, I. (2002). Polygraphic examinations in Japan: application of the guilty knowledge test in forensic investigations. *International Journal of Police Science and Management*, 4(1), 16–27.

Iacono, W. G. (1991). Can we determine the accuracy of polygraph tests? In J. R. Jennings, P. K. Ackles, and M. G. H. Coles (eds.), *Advances in Psychophysiology*, 4 (pp. 1–101). London: Jessica Kingsley

Kensinger, E. A. (2007). Negative emotion enhances memory accuracy. *Current Directions in Psychological Science*, 16, 213–218.

Loftus, E. F. (2003). Make-believe memories. *American Psychologist*, 58, 867–873.

Lykken, D. T. (1959). The GSR in the detection of guilt. *Journal of Applied Psychology*, 43, 385–388.

(1960). The validity of the guilty knowledge technique: the effects of faking. *Journal of Applied Psychology*, 44, 258–262.

Meijer, E., Smulders, F., and Merckelbach, H. (2010). Extracting concealed information from groups. *Journal of Forensic Sciences*.

Podlesny, J. A. (1993). Is the guilty knowledge polygraph technique applicable in criminal investigations? A review of FBI case records. *Crime Laboratory Digest*, 20, 57–61.

Podlesney, J. A. (2003). A paucity of operable case facts restricts applicability of the guilty knowledge technique in FBI criminal polygraph examinations. *Forensic Science Communications*, 5, Retrieved June 21, 2010 from www.fbi.gov/hq/lab/fsc/backissu/july2003/podlesny.htm.

Seymour, T. L., and Fraynt, B. R. (2009). Time and encoding effects in the concealed knowledge test. *Applied Psychophysiology and Biofeedback*, 34, 177–187.

Shapiro, D. (2002). Renewing the scientist-practitioner model. *The Psychologist*, 15, 232–234.

Verschuere, B., Crombez, G., De Clercq, A., and Koster, E. H. W. (2005). Psychopathic traits and autonomic responding to concealed information in a prison sample. *Psychophysiology*, 42, 239–245.

Verschuere, B., Crombez, G., Koster, E. H. W., and De Clercq, A. (2007). Antisociality, underarousal and the validity of the concealed information polygraph test. *Biological Psychology*, 74, 309–318.

Index

9/11, 116

Aaron, 142
Abe, 95, 107
Abootalebi, 72, 74
activation likelihood estimates (ALE),
    97–103, *see also* neuroimaging
    methods
Adler, 33
admissibility, 274, 276–287
Agosta, 54
Aine, 236
Ainsworth, 31, 33–34
alcohol, 8
Aldridge-Morris, 237
Algom, 52
Allen, 49–50, 63, 69, 72–76, 84, 180, 208,
    236–238, 241–244, 247
Alzheimer's disease, 247
Amato-Henderson, 180
Ambach, 33, 35, 38
American Polygraph Association, 153
American Psychiatric Association, 236
American Psychological Association, 19
amnesia, 231, 245
Anderson, 152
anterior cingulate cortex, 102–104
anxiety, 8, 121, 124–125, *see also* defensive
    reflex (DR)
apnea, 143
Ardon, 236
area under ROC curve
    signal detection theory, 72, 84
Aron, 102
arousal, *see* autonomic nervous system
    (ANS)
Association Reaction Method, 48
attention, 34, 52
automated scoring, 161
autonomic nervous system (ANS), 27–28,
    35–37, 40, 90–91, 96, 107–108,
    129

Ax, 13

Baddeley, 180
Baker, 152
Balloun, 33, 136
Bar-Hillel, 19, 278
Barland, 151
Barlow, 121
Barnhardt, 8
Barry, 30, 32, 143
Bass, 121
Bauer, 233–235, 243
Bauermann, 40, 49, 56, 96, 98
Bayesian analysis, 72–73
Bechara, 246
behavioral measures, 40, 46–62
Beijk, 106
Bell, 233
Bendfeldt, 236
Ben-Shakhar, 15, 19–20, 28, 30–33, 35,
    37, 40, 46, 51, 57, 63, 70, 75, 95–96,
    107, 115, 118, 130–131, 134–136,
    138–140, 158, 160–161, 171, 173–
    174, 176, 178–179, 181, 190, 191,
    194, 197, 200, 208, 210–212, 277–
    285, 294–297, 299
Bergman, 6
Bernstein, 280
Berntson, 35, 37
Berti, 40
Bertrand, 237
Best, 300
Bhatt, 245
Biroschak, 72
Bles, 108
blood pressure, 123, *see also* cardiovascular
    measures
Boehm, 247
Bond, 187
Bonferroni correction, 94
bootstrapping, 8, 67–70, 72–74, 76, 81,
    84–85

Bosh, 49
Bovenschen, 236
Bowers, 243
Bradley, 31, 33–34, 36, 137, 153, 159–160, 190–192, 194–197, 284
Brand, 153
Brandsma, 236
Braun, 236
Breen, 284
Brenner, 116
Brook, 106
Brubaker, 91
Brunia, 74
Buckley, 38
buffer item, 172, 297
Burgoon, 133

Cacioppo, 35
Canada, 7
Cantwell, 65
card test, 5, 18, 55, 265
cardiac blood pressure, 143
    see also cardiovascular measures
cardiovascular measures, 8, 32–35, 37, 39–41, 121, 143, 175
Carle, 284
Carmel, 57, 138, 158, 177, 282–283, 294, 296
Castiello, 54
central details, 283, 294
Cephos Corp, 91
cerebral blood oxygenation, 46
Cestaro, 116
Chajut, 52
Chedid, 56
Christ, 91, 102–103
Christianson, 294
Chuang, 245
CIA, 70
citizen-judge system, 274
Clever Hans, 300
Clifton, 298
clinical application, 231
cognitive control, 107
cognitive impairments, 232
Cohen's d, 30, 48, 51, see also effect size
Coles, 68
Commonwealth of Massachusetts v. Woodward, 278
Comparison Question Technique (CQT), 33, 129, 151, 153, 175, 181, 200
Complex Trial Protocol (CTP), 56, 63, 77, 79, 82–86, 209, 212
conditional response, 130, 141
confessions, 5, 7, 70, 162, 176, 183, 286

Connolly, 39, 74
Consemulder, 236
construct validity, 278, see also validity
control items, 260, 296
Control Question Technique,
    see Comparison Question Technique (CQT)
Cook, 28
Corbetta, 103
correlation 68–69
countermeasure, 4, 9, 15, 22, 58, 63, 74–82, 86, 114–115, 119–120, 160, 179, 200–201, 205–209, 200–214, 266, 283
covert measures, 36, 114–127, 210, 212
Crane, 152
Crawley, 103
criminal courts, 274
Cristie, 121
critical items, 260
Crombez, 31, 33, 35, 37, 46, 51–53, 57, 103, 107, 280, 297–298
cross correlation, 72–73, 76
Curran, 247

D'Esposito, 102
Damasio, 233, 235, 246
Daniels, 277–278
Danielson, 49, 69
Dattilio, 108
Daubert criteria, 277–278, 281
Davatzikos, 104
Davidson, 6, 28, 134
Davis, 91, 103
Dawson, 202, 205
Dayan, 57, 282, 294, 296
De Clercq, 31, 33, 35, 37, 53, 103, 280
De Houwer, 52, 54–55
deception, 8, 13, 102, 106–108, 130, 133, 155, 164
Deese-Roedeger-McDermott, 244
defensive reflex (DR), 131
Degner, 59
Degrootte, 51
DePaulo, 47–48, 133
Devilly, 236
Devitt, 32, 283
dichotomization, 138–139, 141
Dick-Barnes, 236
differentiation of deception (DoD), 90–91, 95–98, 102–107, 133
Dihle, 236
discriminant analysis, 38, 106
discriminant validity, 278
dishabituation, 30, 136, see also orienting response (OR)

dissociation, 201, 207, 235–242
dissociative Identity Disorder (DID), 232, 235–242
distraction, 207
Dolan, 95
Dolev, 32, 37, 283
Donchin, 8, 20, 46, 48–50, 56, 58, 65–69, 72, 75–77, 97
Doob Kirschbaum procedure, 296
dorsolateral prefrontal cortex, 102–103, 106
dot probe task, 53
Downar, 103
drugs, 8
Drummond, 36
Duncan, 102
Duty, 103

Eberhardt, 36
ecological validity, 67, 142
Eddy, 47
Edelberg, 268
Eden, 97
Eder, 56
Edwards, 233
effect size, 30, 47, 51, 55
Effting, 236
Efron, 68
Eich, 236
Eickhoff, 98, 100
Elaad, 6, 8, 15, 20, 29–33, 35, 37, 40, 46, 57, 75, 96, 107, 115, 117–118, 121, 133–134, 137, 143, 152, 157–158, 171–172, 174–175, 177–179, 190, 192, 201, 207, 210–212, 279–280, 282, 284–285, 295–297
electrodermal response (EDR), 27, 30–32, 35–40, see also skin conductance response (SCR)
electroencephalogram (EEG), 64, 90, 152, see also event related potential (ERP)
electromyographic recordings (EMG), 212
Ellis, 233
Ellwanger, 245
Elzinga, 236
emotional conflict, 132–133, 141
emotion, 13, 32
Employee Polygraph Protection Act, 160
employee screening, 70
enactment effect, 36,
encoding, 294
Engelhardt, 52
Engelkamp, 294
error rate, 94
Escrig, 36

ethical, 124
event-related potential (ERP), 8, 20, 22, 40, 49–50, 63–89, 178, 208
Eves, 39
evidence, 274
examiners, 253
explicit memory, 241, 244, 246–247
external validity, 69, 166, 281
extraversion, 8
Extrinsic Affective Simon Task (EAST), 54
eye blinks, 125, 153
eye-tracking, 125
eyewitness, 155, 180

Fabiani, 65, 68
facial temperature, 36, 46
Fahy, 237
false confessions, 161, 176,
    see also confessions
false negative, 15, 119, 159, 166, 174, 177–179, 183, 205–206, 280
false positive, 12, 14, 21–22, 58, 72, 74, 81, 161, 163, 191, 194, 196, 280
Farrow, 95
Farwell, 8, 20, 46, 48–50, 56, 58, 66–69, 72, 75–76, 97, 152, 208
FBI, 155–156, 164, 182
fear, 130–131, see also anxiety
feature-matching approach, 140–141
Federal Employee Polygraph Protection Act, 70
feedback, 134
Fein, 36
Ferrara, 54
Fiedler, 281
field studies, 174–177, 179, 183, 269, 285
finger pulse, 34–35, 117, 141, 193, 211,
    see also cardiovascular measures
fingerprint evidence, 12, 16, 21
functional magnetic resonance imaging (fMRI), 20, 40, 49, 56, 90–113, 129, 142, 153, see also neuroimaging methods
Fode, 300
Foerster, 39
forensic psychophysiology, 103
Forensic Science Laboratory, 253
forgetting, 295
Forster, 103, 247
Foster, 74, 108, 244
Fowles, 235, 268
Fox, 246
Fraynt, 57
Friedman, 244
Friston, 92

Frith, 108
Fritz, 48
Frost, 297
Frye v. United States, 276
Fukuda, 153
Fukumoto, 8, 285
Fullam, 95, 97
functional brain response, 9
Furedy, 19, 31–32, 37, 72, 91, 95, 106, 133–134, 190, 279–281, 283
Furumitsu, 20, 86, 283

Gallai, 277–278
galvanic skin responses, *see* skin conductance response (SCR)
Gamer, 31–33, 35, 38–41, 46, 49, 56, 96, 98, 103, 107, 129, 132, 142, 193, 280, 283, 294, 298
gang members, 196
Ganis, 91, 95
guilty action test (GAT), 191–194, 197
Gati, 140, 279–280, 297
Geddes, 33
Geldreich, 5
generalization, 136, 139, *see also* orienting response (OR)
Genovese, 94, 100
George, 91, 95, 104
Giesen, 121, 189–190, 284
Gigliotti, 95
Gilovich, 184
Ginton, 29, 57, 176, 282
Glisky, 236
Gödert, 31, 33, 35, 39, 41, 95
Golden, 74
Gora, 245
Graf, 243
Graham, 132, 297
Granhag, 181, 184
Gratton, 68
Greely, 108
Greenwald, 54
Greneśko, 105
Grier, 72
Grings, 268
Gronau, 31, 51–52, 58, 284
Grossman, 121
group CIT, 196
Grueter, 233
Gruzelier, 39
Gudjonsson, 121, 242
guidelines, 293
Gurevich, 91
Gustafson, 6, 133–134

habituation, 30, 35, 39–40, 46, 50, 68, 135–136, 138, 141, 179, *see also* orienting response (OR)
Halligan, 233
Hamaker, 236
Hamamoto, 86
Hare, 33
Harnon, 277
Harnsberger, 116
Harrison, 48
Haynes, 108
heart rate, 33, 35, 38, 40, 46, 143, *see also* cardiovascular measures
Henke, 47
Hermans, 236
hidden measures, *see* covert measures
Hikita, 161
Hira, 20, 86, 156–157, 161, 175, 178, 180–182, 283
Hirota, 55, 267–268
Hirsch, 39
hit rates, 29, 76, 80–81, 104
Ho, 233
Hodes, 283
Hollien, 116
Holmes, 33
Honts, 32, 105, 115, 118, 153, 160, 179, 195, 205–208, 212, 277, 281, 283
Horneman, 28, 133, 190
Horowitz, 105
Horselenberg, 286
Horst, 233
Horvath, 28, 33, 116
Houston, 83
Hughes, 95, 106
Huntjens, 236
Hwalek, 48
hyperventilation, 121, 132

Iacono, 7, 9, 14, 21–22, 49, 69, 72, 74, 76, 108, 121, 136, 153, 160, 176, 201, 237–238, 277, 281–282, 286
Iidaka, 103
Illes, 108
illusion of transparency, 184
Imamura, 161
Implicit Association Test (IAT), 54–55
implicit memory, 234, 241, 244, 246–247, *see also* memory
inconclusive zone, 195
incremental validity, 40, *see also* validity
inferior frontal gyrus, 102–104
informed innocent, 189, 194
inhibition, 200
Innocence Project, 162

innocent informed, 192, *see also* leakage
inter-stimulus interval (ISI), 50
interference theory, 295
inter-identity amnesia, 236–237
Israel, 6
Ivanov, 65

Jackson, 30
Jameson, 236
Janisse, 33, 36
Japan, 6, 8–9, 12, 17, 20, 22, 32, 97, 151,
    156, 163, 171, 181, 253–275
John Reid, 5
Johnson, 8, 69, 71, 95, 98, 105,
    107, 244
Johnston, 40
Jokinen, 138, 296
Jones, 97
Josephs, 286
Jungman, 29, 57, 282

Kahneman, 136
Kalbfleisch, 115
Karim, 107
Karis, 65
Kassin, 182, 286
Kaszniak, 247
Katkin, 246
Kaylor, 95, 106
Keeler, 5, 159–161
Kennerknecht, 233
Kerlin, 50
Keth, 31
Khalilzadeh, 72
Kiechel, 286
Kiehl, 103
Kindt, 237
Kircher, 32–33, 38, 105, 277, 283, 299
Kiriu, 273
Kirsch, 246
Kirschenbaum, 296
Kleinmuntz, 299
Klimecki, 40, 56, 98
Knepp, 121
known solution CIT, 260–264
Kobayashi, 268
Kong, 236, 241
Konieczny, 159
Kopelman, 300
Kosiol, 283, 294
Kosslyn, 91
Koster, 31, 33, 37, 52–53, 103, 280
Kozel, 91, 95, 98, 104–105, 107
Kramer, 77
Kremnitzer, 19, 278
Kresh, 297

Krug, 36
Kubis, 6, 201, 206–207, 283
Kubo, 49
Kugelmass, 29–30, 131, 133–134
Kuramochi, 273

Labkovsky, 49, 56, 79–81, 86
Laken, 95, 98, 107
Lance, 36
Lang, 36, 132
Langleben, 46, 91, 96–97, 102, 104, 108,
    153
Lankappa, 106
laser doppler vibrometry, 125
Laurens, 103
law enforcement agencies, 9
Layered Voice Analysis, 116, *see also* voice
    stress
Lazar, 94
Le Febvre, 74
leakage, 155, 183, 187–199, 284
Lee, 98
LeFebvre, 86
legal issues, 9
Leo, 183
Leonarde Keeler, 5
Levine, 36
lexical decision task, 53
Liddle, 103
lie detection, *see* deception
Lieblich, 6, 29–30, 134, 138
Locker, 53
Loewenstein, 236
Loftus, 180
logistic regression, 38, 40, 104
Logothetis, 92
Lorig, 32
Lozano, 35
Lubow, 36, 153
Ludwig, 236
Lui, 56, 70–71, 80, 85
lying. *see* deception
Lykken, 3–7, 9, 14, 27–28, 31, 66, 75,
    90–91, 96, 103, 106, 114, 135–137,
    151–152, 154, 157–158, 160, 171,
    179, 181, 188, 190–191, 197, 206,
    208, 231, 267–268, 277, 279–281,
    297–298
Lykken-score, 299
Lynn, 135, 298

Macaulay, 236
Mackenzie, 236
MacLaren, 29–30, 196, 280, 284
malingering, 231, 243, 245
Maltzman, 280

Mandler, 243
manual scoring, 161
Marchand, 74
Marcuse, 5
Marston, 47, 276
Martin, 236
match to sample , 234, 245
Matsuda, 55–56, 267–268, 283
Matsumoto, 103
Matthews, 300
Matusuda, 268
Mazzeri, 65
McDermott, 91, 244
McGhee, 54
McGregor, 108
McGuire, 189
McKie, 95
McKoon, 82
mechanism, 128, 143
medications, 232
Meijer, 40, 49, 56, 72, 74, 85
Meissner, 182
Meixner, 20, 70, 79, 81–83
memory, 9, 15, 74, 102–103, 106, 190
mental imagery, 205
Merckelbach, 40, 49, 52, 72, 74, 85, 236, 286
Merikangas, 108
Merskey, 236–237
Mertens, 72–73, 75–76, 209, 238, 244
Messick, 129, 278
meta-analysis, 99
meta memory, 237
Miccoli, 36
middle frontal gyrus, 102
Mikulis, 103
Miretzky, 152
misinformation, 180
Miyake, 9, 153
Miyata, 8, 285
Mizutani, 9
mock crime, 28, 52, 58, 63, 67, 74, 76, 82, 95, 105, 158, 174, 177
modified Stroop, see Stroop task
Mohamed, 98
Moore, 33
Moradi, 72
Mosmann, 46, 50
motivation, 107, 133–134, 139, 141, 206
Movius, 49–50, 236–237, 241–242
Mullen, 242
multiple personality disorder (MPD), see Dissociative Identity Disorder (DID)
multiple probe protocol, 75

Munro, 152
Murai, 97

N1, 68, see also event related potential (ERP)
N2, 68, see also event related potential (ERP)
Nagano, 268
Nakayama, 8, 20, 32, 156, 159, 180, 197, 285–286
Nasman, 65
National Academies of Sciences, 19, see also National Research Council (NRC)
National Research Council, 19, 57, 116, 123, 129, 179
National Research Institute of Police Science (NRIPS), 254
Naveh, 57, 282, 294, 296
Nelson, 236
neuroimaging methods, 8, 40, 90–91, 94, 96–97, 104, 106–108
Newcombe, 246
Nichols, 94
Niendam, 74
Nijenhuis, 236
Nissen, 236
Nittono, 49, 55
Nogawa, 103
nonverbal cues, 133
normalized pulse volume (NPV), 268
North America, 6, 70
Nose, 97, 106
Noteworthiness, 137, see also significance
novelty, 139–141
NSA, 70
Nuñez, 102–103

O.J. Simpson, 154
O'Gorman, 28, 30
O'Toole, 160
observer-expectancy effect, 300
oddball task, 46, 48, 51, 53–58, 129
Office of Technology Assessment (OTA), 7
Ogawa, 55, 267
Ohama, 273
Öhman, 136, 246
Okazaki, 273
old-new effect, 244, 247
orienting response (OR), 27, 30–32, 35, 39–40, 103, 128, 135, 188
Orne, 28, 31, 133
Osugi, 181
overt denial, 194, see also verbal responding
Owen, 102

P300, 8–9, 48–49, 58, 63–71, 73–84, 86, 129, 136, 209–210, *see also* event related potentials (ERP)
P900, 63, 86, *see also* event related potential (ERP)
Padgett, 91, 95, 104
Paller, 247
Parasympathetic, 32, *see also* autonomic nervous system (ANS)
pathological lying, 242
Patrick, 7, 14, 281
Pavlidis, 36, 123, 152
Pavlov, 130, 135
peak of tension test, 5, 159–161
Peper, 33
peripheral details, 177, 283, 294
peripheral physiological measures, *see* autonomic nervous system (ANS)
Perry, 284
Peters, 236
Pfungst, 300
Phaf, 236
physiological measures, 4, 8–9, 14, 28, 37–38, 40, 46, 50–51, 57, 96, 103, 105
Piper, 237
Plethysmography, *see* finger pulse cardiovascular measures, 153
Plumpe, 233
Podlesny, 28, 31, 33–34, 155–157, 182, 281
Poldrack, 102
police lineup, 74
Polich, 68
Pollina, 36, 123
polygraph, 3, 5–7, 17–20, 51, 57, 70, 91, 107, 160, 165
Posey, 33
positron emission tomography (PET)., 92
Post, 236
Postma, 236
Powell, 242
practice, 211
Pratarelli, 53
Prati, 55, 59
predictive validity, 280
Prefectural Police Headquarters, 253
prefrontal cortex, 97, 102, 106
pre-test interview, 257, 265
previewing, 297
principal component analysis (PCA), 71
Priori, 107
probable lie test, *see* Comparison Question Technique (CQT)

Probing CIT, *see* Searching CIT
prosopagnosia, 231, 233–235, 246
Pseudologia Fantastica, 242, *see also* pathological lying
Psychopathy, 9, 215–230
psychophysiology, 21, *see also* autonomic nervous system (ANS); neuroimaging; and event-related potentials (ERPs); pulse volume *see* finger pulse
punishment, 131, 133, 141
pupil, 36, 125, 136, 153
Putnam, 236
Puttonen, 296

Quigley, 35

Raman, 233
Raney, 48
Rashba, 37
Raskin, 28, 31, 33–34, 38, 105, 151, 179, 201, 205, 277, 283, 299
Rassin, 236
Ratcliff, 82
Ravaja, 296
Raveh, 57, 282, 294, 296
reaction time (RT), 152, 210
real-life, 171–186
recall, 136
receiver operating characteristic (ROC) curve, 30, 173, *see also* signal detection theory
recognition, 153, 155, 166, 193
recommendations, *see* guidelines
Rees, 108
refreshing memory, 195
Reid, 179
Reinhart, 245
relevant question, *see* Comparison Question Technique (CQT)
reliability, 39
Report of the Royal Commission on Criminal Justice, 286
report, 266
respiration, 8, 31–32, 37–41, 46, 117, 174, 208, 211–212
respiration line length, *see* respiration
response inhibition, 128–129, 142
response latency, *see* reaction time (RT)
response scoring, 299
Rettinger, 31, 284
Revell, 104
Richards, 142
right frontal cortex, 102, 104, 106
Rill, 31, 33, 95
Robbins, 102

ROC, *see* receiver operating characteristic (ROC) curve
Roediger, 244
Roepstorff, 108
Rollison, 284
Rosenfeld, 8, 20, 46, 49, 56, 58, 64–65, 67–77, 79–86, 97, 136, 152, 208–210, 212, 245
Rosenthal, 300
Ross, 236
Rosseel, 51
Rothenberg, 82
Rothermund, 56
Rovner, 205, 211
Ruckmick, 5
Rugg, 247
Ryan, 49

Sadato, 103
Santtila, 296
Sargeant, 74, 244
Sartori, 54–55
Sasaki, 208, 283
Sato, 187
Sawada, 268
Saxe, 277–278, 281
Schachter, 13
Schacter, 236
Schmand, 74, 244
Schmid, 281
Schnyer, 247
Schwartz, 54
science–practitioners model, 301
scoring system, 206, 266
searching CIT, 5, 81, 196, 260–264
Sechrest, 298
Seifert, 46, 50, 82
Sekera, 245
sensitivity, 104–105, 273, *see also* hit rates, specificity, false negative, and false positive
serial murder, 154
serial perpetrators, 295
Seymour, 46, 50, 57–59, 82, 137, 152
Shafto, 50, 82
Shafto, 46
Shapiro, 301
Shigemasu, 267
Shlomo, 52
Shue, 49, 76
Shulman, 103
Siddle, 30, 136
signal detection theory, 30, 81
signal value, *see* significance

significance, 133, 136–137, 140, 142, 181
Silberman, 236
Simpson, 108
simulators, 244
Singer, 49, 76
Sip, 108
skin conductance response (SCR), 27–28, 30, 35–36, 38–40, 46, 50–51, 96, 211, *see also* electrodermal response (EDR)
Slowik, 38
Smith, 49, 74
Smolders, 34
Smulders, 40, 49, 72, 74, 85
Soares, 246
Society for Psychophysiological Research (SPR), 19, 66
Sokolov, 30, 103, 131, 135, 138, 140, 278
Sokolovsky, 82, 86
Sol Kugelmass, 6
Sommers, 116
Song, 245
Soskins, 49, 74
Spanos, 237
specificity, 104–105, 273, *see also* hit rates, sensitivity, false negative, and false positive
Spence, 8, 91, 95, 97, 106–107, 133
Sperling, 233
spiration, 27
Squire, 243
Stahl, 281
standardization, 8, *see also* z-scores
Stanovich, 300
Stark, 33, 246
startle reflex, 132, 142
state anxiety, *see* anxiety
State v. Badger, 33
Stekelenburg, 32
Stern, 190, 284
Sternberg, 294
Stoeter, 40, 49, 56, 96, 98
storage, 245
Stormark, 246
Stose, 91
stress, 115, 121, 123, 176
Stroop task, 52, 54
Supreme Court, 274
Suzuki, 32, 40, 143
Sweet, 245
sympathetic nervous system 33, 35–36, *see also* autonomic nervous system (ANS)
Szucko, 299

Tabbert, 246
Taira, 97
Takasawa, 55, 267–268
Tanaka, 268
target, 191, 194, 209
task-switching, 102
temporoparietal junction, 102–103
Thackray, 6, 28, 31
theory, 128–150, 152
thermal imaging, 36, 123, 152
Thompson, 91
Thoneey, 153
threat, 131, see also anxiety
three stimulus protocol, 63, 73–75,
    77, 84
time of CIT administration, 283
Timm, 31, 132, 136, 152, 299
Todd, 91
tone detection task, 53
training, 200
Training Center of Forensic Science,
    254
training courses, 254
trait anxiety, see anxiety
Tranel, 235, 246
TrusterPro
    voice stress analysis, 116
Turkeltaub, 97
Tversky, 140
T-wave amplitude

United States (U.S), 6, 20, 70, 83, 91, 108
Underwood, 295
United States v. Cordoba, 278
United States v. Scheffer, 278
unobtrusive, see covert measures
Uruno, 161
Uyterlinde, 236

vagal nervous system, 35
Vaitl, 33, 246
validity, 9, 27, 29–30, 32–33, 35, 37–38,
    40–41, 46, 50, 57, 59, 90, 106–108
Van Baelen, 52
Van Bockstaele, 31
van Boxtel, 32
Van Buskirk, 5
van den Hout, 52, 237
van der Hart, 236
Van Diest, 132
van Dyck, 236
Van Essen, 91
Van Hoesen, 233
van Honk, 236
van Hooff, 74, 244

Vandenbosch, 35
Vasoconstriction, 141,
    see also cardiovascular measures
Velden, 36
Venables, 268
verbal responding, 132–133, 190
Verfaellie, 234–235, 243, 246
Verschuere, 31, 33–35, 37–39, 46, 49,
    51–53, 55–57, 59, 103, 107, 132–133,
    136–137, 142–143, 153, 188, 195,
    280, 297–298
Victor Hugo, 9
Vincent, 133
virtual reality, 209
voice stress analysis, 116
Voss, 247
Vossel, 31, 33, 35, 40, 46, 49, 56,
    95–96, 98, 107, 280, 283, 294,
    298
Vrij, 133, 277–278, 285

Wagner, 136
Waid, 28, 136
Wallin, 30
Warfield, 284
Warner, 164
Watanabe, 284
Watson, 91
wavelet classifier method, 72
weapon focus effect, 294
Weekes, 237
Weingartner, 236
Welling, 233
Wentzek, 233
Whalen, 65
White, 300
Wickens, 77
Wiens, 246
Wiersema, 49
Wilbur, 236
Wilkinson, 95, 106
Williams, 33
Willingham, 236
Willrich, 33
Wilson, 28, 152
Winbush, 32, 283
Winograd, 49, 56, 78, 82
Winslow, 163
Woertman, 236
Wojdak, 65
Wolf, 49, 72, 74
Wölk, 36
Wolpe, 108
Wong, 233
Wood, 30

working memory, 102–103, 107
Worsley, 94

Yamahura, 9
Yamamoto, 103
Yamamura, 8, 161, 285
Yoga, 207
Yokoi, 273

Yonelinas, 53
Yurgelun, 91

Zeffiro, 97
Zhu, 8
Zimmermann, 36
Zogmaister, 54
z-scores, 173, 299